Communication and Media Studies

An introductory coursebook

Geoff Gration
John Reilly
John Titford

South-East Derbyshire College

M
MACMILLAN

First published 1988
Reprinted 1990

Published by
MACMILLAN EDUCATION LTD
Houndmills, Basingstoke, Hampshire RG21 2XS
and London
Companies and representatives
throughout the world

Designed by Jim Weaver

Illustrations by Gecko Ltd

Cartoons by Brian Walker

Printed in Hong Kong

British Library Cataloguing in Publication Data
Gration, Geoff
Communication and media studies: an
introductory coursebook.
1.Mass media
I. Title   II.Reilly, John   III.Titford,
John
302.2'34   P90
ISBN 0–333–43623–7

Acknowledgements

Much of the material used in this book has been based upon work we have done over a number of years with the help of colleagues and students at South-East Derbyshire College, all of whom we should like to thank for their support and encouragement.

Special mention should be made of the following friends and colleagues for their freely-given assistance and contributions: Ian Baird; Heather Bridge; Michael Doyle; Sue Harrison; Philip Holmes; Linda Morey; Malcolm Mortimer; Dave Newman; David and Sheila Popple; Richard Scollins; Roy Slater.

The authors and publishers wish to thank the following who have kindly given permission for the use of copyright material: The Advertising Association for statistics; The Advertising Standards Authority for sample adjudications; Alexander Colbear Advertising Agency for a sample media advertising schedule; The Associated Examining Board for past examinations questions; BLA Business Publications Ltd for *Viewpoint Number 22 — Marketing Case Studies (Turtle Wax)* (conceived, written and published by BLA Business Publications Ltd, 2 Duncan Terrace, London N1 8BZ on behalf of the ITV companies); British Union for the Abolition of Vivisection for a poster; Brookside Productions Ltd for a photo; Campaign for Nuclear Disarmament for a handbill; Central Independent Television for photos and advertising rate details; Channel 4 for photos; Conservative Research Dept for a poster; Elida Gibbs Ltd for an advert; Freemans Ltd for an advert; Granada Television Ltd for a photo; Graphic Communication Centre Ltd for extracts from *Instant Art — Book 2*, 1981; Guardian Newspapers Ltd for an extract; Health Education Authority for leaflets and statistics; Heathrow Ltd for extracts from its Heathrow guides; HMSO for statistics; The Independent Broadcasting Authority for an extract from its guidelines on portrayal of guidance; LIFE for a poster; London Transport; McGraw-Hill Book Company for adapted material from *The Dynamics of Human Communication* by Myers and Myers, 4th edition, 1985; Michael Joseph Ltd for an extract from *Kes* by Barry Hines; National Union of Journalists for an extract from its Code of Conduct; Nottingham Playhouse for a press release and extracts from the programme for *Buster's Last Stand*; Pan Combine Ltd for an advert; Perpetual Group for an advert; *Punch* for a cartoon; Radio Trent, Ilkeston Co-op Travel, The Swinging Sporran and Midlands Promotions for radio advertising scripts, a client brief and advertising rate details; Regional Newspaper Advertising Bureau for a Medicheck target area map; Roffey Park Institute Ltd for extracts from its 1986–1987 prospectus; Secretary of State, Massachusetts for extracts from the adults' and children's guide to The Massachusetts State House; Syndication International for articles; Times Newspapers Limited for articles, for a facsimile of the first issue of *The Times* and for other material.

Other photographs were taken by Geoff Gration, Phil Holmes and John Titford.

Every effort has been made to trace all the copyright holders but if any have been inadvertently overlooked the publishers will be pleased to make the necessary arrangement at the first opportunity.

Contents

How to use this book

This book is intended to be used by students following a course in Communication Studies or Media Studies at GCSE or 'A' Level, as well as those who have to complete a Communications module within a broader course such as one offered by B/TEC or SCOTVEC.

The existence of a Communication Studies component in a large number of recent curriculum initiatives is ample evidence of an increasing awareness of the need to improve students' overall social and communication skills.

It is our intention that teachers and pupils should regard this book as a kind of 'menu', to be used in any way that seems appropriate. Part 1 of the book begins with a number of basic concepts and skills which are then developed and consolidated. Part 2 consists of case studies, each of which may be used whenever it would be most useful or relevant. Part 3 consists of a number of free-standing practical assignments, each of which is complete in itself. Some practical advice on how to tackle the kind of project work required by a number of examining boards concludes this section.

The flexibility of this book enables the pupil to pick and mix in such a way as to experience Communication Studies as an integrated whole. Practical work is a vital component in any Communications course, and so Part 1 contains its own built-in practical tasks to be used in addition to the material available in Parts 2 and 3.

This book is the result of several years of experience in the teaching of Communication and Media Studies; it takes as its starting point the belief that effective communication is a skill which can be learned and taught like any other skill. We hope that users of the book will find that their practical skills and their understanding of the communication process will grow and develop as time goes by; we have tried as far as possible to adopt a non-partisan approach to the subject, outlining different views that may be held about the exact nature of communication, but leaving the reader to choose between various approaches and make his or her own decisions on more contentious issues.

We have assumed for much of the time that this book will be used by a teacher together with pupils in a group, but it would be perfectly appropriate for an individual to use it on his or her own as a tailor-made course book or revision aid.

PART 1 Communication Theory: the Background

CHAPTER 1 *You the receiver*

This chapter contains the following sections:

- Introduction to communication and media studies
- Receiving messages
- Dealing with messages
- Filtering, distorting and blocking messages
- Self-assessment
- Further work
- Further reading

Introduction to communication and media studies

It is often said that some conflict or disaster in human relationships has come about because of a 'breakdown in communication', or that one of the key skills needed by people who want to play a full part in society is an ability to 'communicate'.

Yet only in recent years has the study of communication in all its aspects been widely practised and accepted as a key element in the education of students of all ages, be they at school, at college, in work or out of work.

We all spend our waking lives involved in a complex web of communication, as senders or receivers of messages of varying degrees of complexity. We talk, listen, write, read, watch the television, listen to the radio, signal our thoughts and feelings to others for whole hours at a time, yet seldom pause to reflect upon what we are doing or how effectively we are doing it.

Good and effective communication can be learned; we can develop the skills necessary to send messages which are coherent and appropriate to others — and, just as important, we can learn to be sensitive receivers of messages of various kinds relayed to us by others.

Effective communication is not just a matter of possessing a range of skills. Skills have to be used appropriately according to the situation in which we find ourselves, and having regard to the people with whom we hope to communicate. A complex and sophisticated piece of written English which might be appropriate as an essay for a University Professor would hardly help us communicate with a five year old child, and your skill — if you possessed it — in using sign language would be of no value to the deaf if the person you were with did not have the skill or knowledge to interpret such language.

Effective communication demands both skill and sensitivity to others. Some people seem blessed with an apparently easy and relaxed ability to communicate which is the envy of those who know them — but everyone can improve his or her ability to do so. In this book we will be examining and practising those skills which lead to successful communication.

Receiving messages

You could say that communication takes place when messages of various kinds are sent and received, so the communication process involves **senders** and

receivers of messages. In order to illustrate your own continuous involvement in the communication process, we are going to focus on you as a receiver of messages in this chapter. Over the past 24 hours you will have received probably hundreds of different messages. For example, you may have received a letter from a friend, you may have watched the news on breakfast-time television, or perhaps you have read the newspaper.

TASK *1*   Individually produce a list of every message you have received over the past 24 hours.

Now get together in one large group and produce one list which covers all of the different messages received over the past 24 hours.

If you look at the total group list, you will see that many different types of message can be conveyed in a number of different ways. To make sense of your final group list it will help to classify the items in it in some way. There are several ways of doing this. One way would be to classify your items in terms of the relationship between the sender and the receiver, e.g. messages from family, messages from friends, messages from people in authority, etc. Another way might be to classify the list in terms of the methods, or senses used to receive the messages, e.g. messages which were heard, messages which were seen or read, etc.

TASK *2*   Individually classify your list under those headings which make most sense to you. Write these headings down.

Now compare your headings with those of other members of your group. What are the similarities and differences between the various sets of headings? Is it possible to say that one system of classification is better or more logical than others?

A simple model of classification

A **model** is a means of structuring and presenting an idea, a relationship or a process. The purpose of a model is to present a complex idea in a simple way, and for this reason most models have a visual or diagrammatic form. In this book you will find several models which attempt to help you to understand the processes of communication. You will also be encouraged to devise your own models to explain and express your ideas.

In Fig. 1.1 there are two simple models, both of which put **you, the receiver** at the centre of things and then attempt to classify incoming messages in terms of the means or methods by which they were sent.

These two models are presented here not because they are the only classification systems available (you may have come up with some very different systems in TASK 2), but simply because in communication studies, messages are conventionally classified under the heading of **means** of communication. Let's look at some basic terminology.

Means of communication

Means is a term which is used loosely and generally to refer to the way or method by which messages are sent and received. Sometimes the term is used to refer to the human senses which are involved; for example, we may talk about 'tactile means of communication', that is communicating by touch. Alternatively, the term may refer to a technical system of communication; for example, we may talk about television as a means of communication.

Under the general heading of **means** are two additional terms which are a little more precise. These are **forms** and **media** of communication. Fig. 1.1 illustrates both of these classification systems.

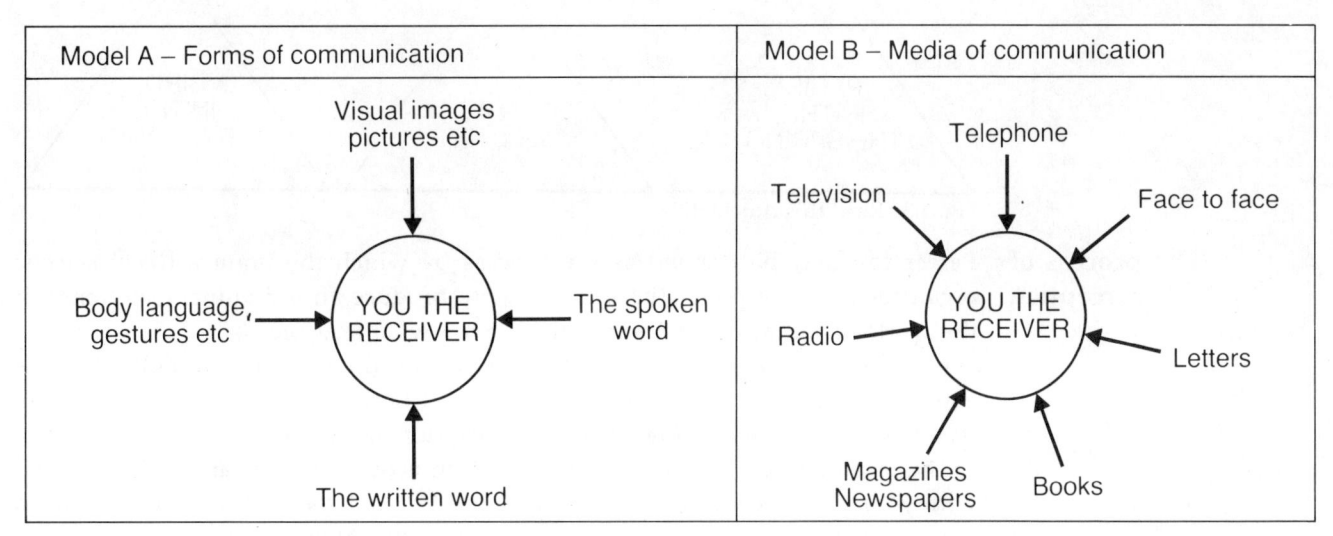

Fig. 1.1 Means of communication

Forms of communication. A **form** refers to the system or code by which a particular message has been organised. For example, in language we may talk about the 'spoken form' or the 'written form' of words. 'Body Language' is yet another form, in that messages are organised in a different way, often using a special set of rules, for example the 'V sign' gesture. Model A classifies messages in terms of **forms** of communication.

Media of communication. A **medium** (plural: **media**) refers to a means of communication which often combines several forms of communication and which often involves the use of a particular technology. For example, television is a complex medium which combines the forms of the spoken and written word, and a variety of pictorial forms. Model B classifies messages in terms of **media** of communication.

Dealing with messages

So far we have emphasised the fact that each day we receive many different messages, and many different types of message. However, we have not said anything about how we deal with all of this information. Fig. 1.2 shows a simple model which suggests what we may do with the messages we receive. It is a very simple model which only tells us that we can deal with incoming information in three broad ways; we can ignore it, act upon it immediately, or think about it and respond later. As a model it doesn't tell us very much about the psychological processes involved in these three options. In any study of communication it is important to have some understanding of the psychological process known as **perception.**

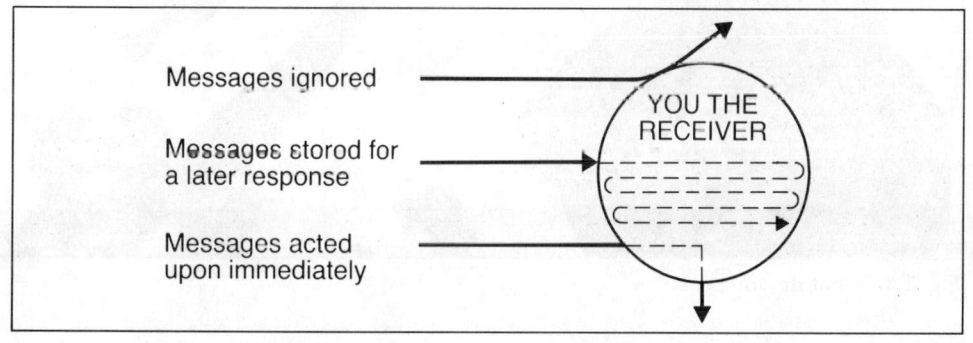

Fig. 1.2 Dealing with messages

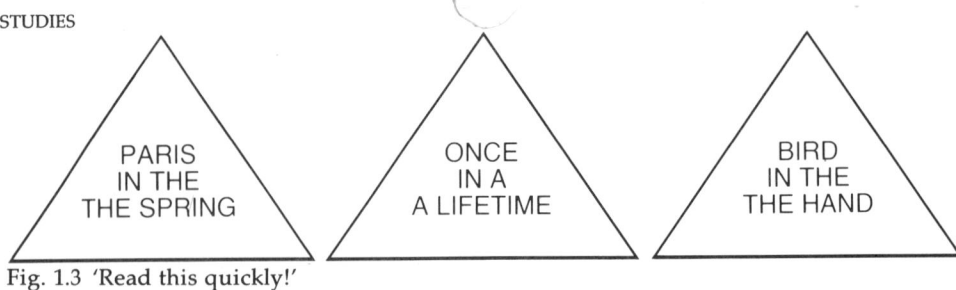

Fig. 1.3 'Read this quickly!'

The process of perception

Perception may be defined as the process by which the brain actively selects, organises and interprets stimuli in order to produce an individual experience of the world. Look at Fig. 1.3 and quickly read what you see.

Most people when they read these captions for the first time do not notice the extra 'the's' and 'a's'. Perhaps you still haven't noticed them? Why do you think it is that most people do not read these captions accurately?

The important point here is that perception is an automatic and active process with your brain deciding what you will and will not see. In this case your brain has decided that since the 'the' is grammatically unlikely, it is not prepared to allow you to see it. This example shows us that perception is an active process in the sense that you do not simply open your eyes and ears and allow the world to come flooding in, unaltered. The brain filters, selects and interprets. The example in TASK 3 below illustrates this same point.

TASK *3* Look briefly at Fig. 1.4. Write down your first impressions of what you see. It may help to draw a simple sketch of your impressions. Now discuss and compare your findings with those of other members of your group.

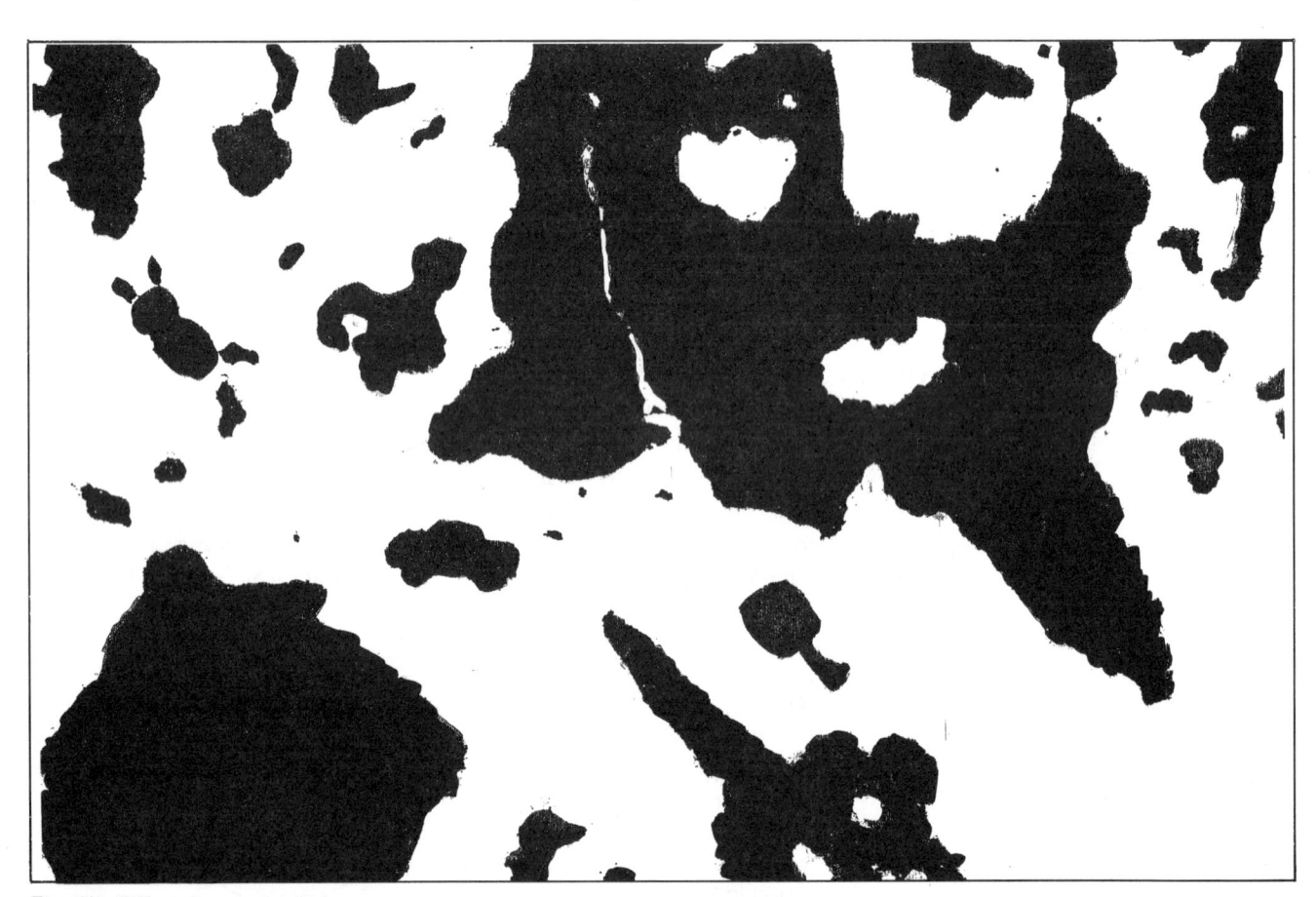

Fig. 1.4 'What do you see?'

It would be wrong to think of perception as some kind of trick which the brain occasionally plays upon us in the form of clever visual illusions. The important point about perception is that there is nothing which we know, see, hear, taste or feel which hasn't first been filtered and organised by the brain. Even as you are reading this, your senses are being bombarded with stimuli from the outside world. Your eyes are focusing on these marks on the page and relaying an understanding of them to your brain. Other people may be talking around you, in which case your ears will be receiving the sounds of their voices. The pressure of your shoe against your foot may be sending a variety of sensations to your brain. Depending on what you last ate, and when, there may be a particular taste in your mouth. Of course, you are not fully conscious of all of the stimuli which are happening around you. Perhaps you were not conscious of the pressure of your shoe until it was pointed out to you. Perhaps you were concentrating hard on reading this page, in which case the background noise in the room, or outside, may have faded into an indistinct blurr. Are you conscious of other noises, other voices now?

Psychological factors in perception

All of the time then, even though you may not be aware of it, your brain is working hard to concentrate on certain stimuli whilst ignoring certain others. Some stimuli you may never be aware of, and some you may experience differently to the way in which others experience them.

What exactly are the factors involved which explain why one individual's perception of a particular situation may differ from that of another individual? An obvious factor might be a variation in the accuracy and reliability of the eyesight and hearing of different people. This is an example of a **physical factor** influencing perception. However, perhaps more important than this are the **psychological factors** which can affect, often subtly, our perception of the world. Some of these factors are summarised below.

Expectation. As we saw with the example in Fig. 1.3, we often see and hear what we expect to see and hear. Similarly, you may have noticed in TASK 3 how a particular image in the figure was not apparent until it had been pointed out by someone. This illustrates how the brain often needs a *hunch*, or an *idea*, to enable it to sort out confusing information.

This process of expectation can apply when meeting someone for the first time. Suppose you are about to meet someone who has been described to you as 'untrustworthy' and 'devious'. Could it be that you now have an expectation of this individual which may *colour* your perception of them?

Motivation. If we have a strong need or desire for something we may find that our perception is influenced or even dominated by this. The expression 'a one-track mind' is often used to describe an example of where someone's perception may be dominated by a particular set of needs. Another familiar example might be where hunger, or thirst, focuses our attention on matters connected with food and drink.

Fig. 1.5 attempts to illustrate a rather different example of motivation affecting perception. This figure shows how a busy shopping centre might look to someone who is anxious about getting to the railway station in time for an important journey. The individual focuses on those aspects of the environment which are relevant to the particular goal which he or she is trying to achieve. In this case the individual's attention is focused on a clock and on a bus about to leave for the railway station.

Fig. 1.5 One individual's perception of a shopping centre

Occupation and special interests. An individual's job, hobby, or special interest may help to shape and influence perception. For example, an architect and bricklayer may look at the same house but see different things. The architect may be impressed by the 'majestic rise and fall' of the roof of an old Victorian house, but be annoyed that the owners have replaced the original window frames with aluminium units. On the other hand, the bricklayer's attention may be drawn to the condition of the brickwork and the craftsmanship of the Victorian builders.

Values and attitudes. Put simply, **values** and **attitudes** refer to our likes and dislikes which are formed by influences on us throughout our lives, especially in childhood. For example, a strong dislike of smoking may be related to the influence of our parents. A fuller discussion of values and attitudes is given in Chapter 10.

An example of how values and attitudes may influence perception comes from the world of politics. For instance, if we are committed to a particular political party or persuasion, we may find it difficult to listen to an opposing argument. In effect, we may either switch off completely from what is being said to us, or we may only hear those parts of the argument which confirm our dislike of our opponents.

Filtering, distorting and blocking messages

We have looked at perception and some of the psychological factors involved in influencing perception. From the examples given so far it should be clear that in communication the messages we receive are influenced and coloured by our own thoughts and emotions. Often this process of perception runs smoothly; for example, a lot of the time people agree over what they see and hear. However, there are other times when the process of perception does not run smoothly. There are times when thoughts and emotions colour our impressions to the point that they become distorted and lead to a blocking or a breakdown of communication. Many disagreements and arguments between people can be traced back to differences caused by problems in perception. What are these problems in perception?

It is very easy to understand how a physical disability such as being hard of hearing or having very poor eyesight might create problems in perception and therefore in communication. It is equally clear that trying to understand someone speaking in a foreign language would create difficulties for most of us. Physical disability and foreign languages are clear and familiar instances of what we might call **physical barriers** to communication.

However, it is less obvious that there are many **psychological barriers** to communication which can affect all of us without our being aware of it. As we have seen in the previous section, perception is a powerful influence with the brain continually filtering and shaping our experience of incoming information. If we are to become effective communicators we must first be aware of some of the barriers which might cloud our judgement and prevent us from becoming clear receivers of messages.

TASK 4 Read the extract below which comes from an AEB A-level Communication Studies Case Study paper. What problems do you think the character depicted in this passage might face in communicating with young people?

You'd never believe there were four million unemployed in this country! I have enough trouble getting youngsters to apply for trainee posts, let alone sorting out the ones who are worth interviewing. If anyone asks me why British industry's going up the Swanee, I'll tell them − it's the uneducated rubbish these comprehensive schools keep turning out these days. In the old days when there were still some good grammar school boys around, you could reckon on picking up a dozen good lads each year and their O levels meant something − you could rely on them. Nowadays you just wouldn't believe it − they all come festooned with fancy certificates − CSEs, GCEs, RSAs and half of them aren't worth the paper they're written on. These teachers have a lot to answer for!

When you try interviewing them, it's amazing: there seems to be no relationship between the academic results, the school reports and the youths I see in front of me. Some of them don't even wear a tie, let alone a suit, and they positively flaunt their earrings at me. Some of them don't seem to have an opinion of their own − it's all 'y'know' and 'all right' − and the only interests they profess are in the most powerful noisy motorbikes they can find and the latest skiffle groups I've never heard of. The rest of them are all question, question − and no appreciation of the need to make profits to keep the company going. One of them, the other week, lit up a cigarette in the middle of the interview − at least he had the politeness to ask if he could and I was so taken aback I'd said yes before I could think of anything else. Then he goes on to challenge me as to whether we do anything socially useful as a company and next thing he's asking me why we had to make 200 workers redundant last year! And his school report said he was a mature young man intellectually capable of grasping a complex argument!

The funny thing is that some of them seem to settle down once they get here, once they begin to find out what the real world's about, but I begin to think that there's almost nothing I can do to predict which ones are going to be any good. They all fail the written arithmetic test − it's that Modern Maths again − so I've not much to go on that looks any good. Sometimes I think we might as well put all the names into a hat and pull the first five out. Maybe we ought to stop looking at teenagers at all and only interview the 25-year olds.

Arthur Dewhurst, Manager of Training.

(Source: AEB A-level Communication Studies, Paper 2, 1984).

(a)

(b)

(c)

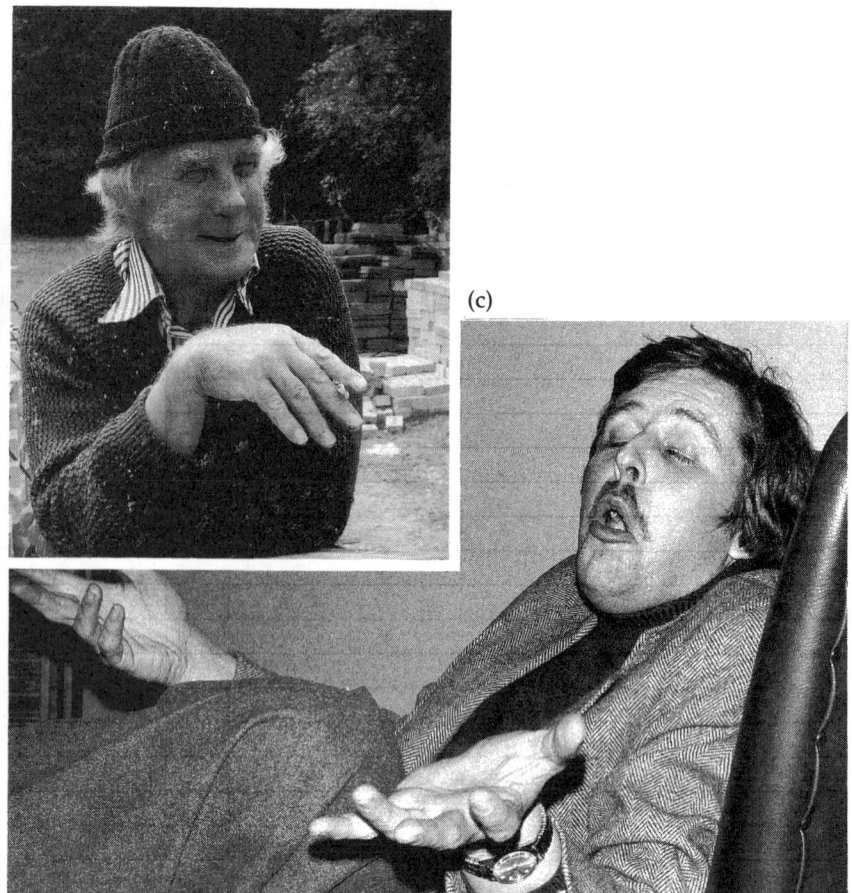

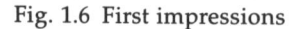
Fig. 1.6 First impressions

There are several psychological processes which can act as barriers, colouring, distorting or even blocking communication. Let's look more closely at just four: **stereotyping, prejudice, projection** and **poor listening skills.**

Stereotyping   How good are you at making judgements about people on the basis of first impressions?

TASK 5   Look at the people shown in Fig. 1.6. Try and estimate their age, occupation and basic personality. (Some factual information about each of these people is given towards the end of this chapter.)

One of the problems in making judgements on the basis of first impressions is that we tend to pigeon-hole people and put them into categories called **stereotypes**. Most stereotypes are based upon simple characteristics such as accent, dress and general appearance. A typical example would be that of the conventionally-dressed businessman. The problem with stereotyping is that once we have categorised someone, we may then go on to assume other things about them. For example, we may say: 'Ah businessman, married, two children, detached house, company car, conventional etc . . .'

TASK 6   Here are some possible stereotypes. Do stereotypes exist for each of these, and if so can you agree on what the appropriate qualities for each are?
—A librarian   —A 'heavy metal' fan   —A male model
—A second-hand car dealer   —A school teacher   —A lorry driver

'I'm not Irish, I only took the name of O'Toole because I thought it would help my career!'

Fig. 1.7 A familiar stereotype

Prejudice   The word **prejudice** literally means to pre-judge, to make a judgement about someone or something before we have seen or heard the detailed evidence. It is possible to be prejudiced against or in favour of someone. For example when asked to pass an opinion on their own child a parent might say that they are prejudiced and bound to say something favourable. However, it is more usual to think of prejudice as something negative, something which biases us against an individual or group of individuals. In this case, stereotypes and prejudice often go together, hand in hand. We can laugh at the cartoon in Fig. 1.7 because we recognise the stereotype of the Irishman which is often presented to us through the medium of jokes. However, if we were actually to believe the nuances of this particular stereotype and allow it to bias our judgement of real Irishmen, then we could be said to be prejudiced.

An interesting point to consider here is how influential stereotyping in the media, like newspapers and television, could be in maintaining and fostering prejudice. In television, for example, there is no doubt that stereotypes are frequently featured in many comedy series and soap operas. Most people would say that this is quite harmless, and that television is simply reflecting the attitudes and images which already exist in the minds of the audience. However, others would argue that the issue is not as simple as this, and that television and newspapers have a way of making stereotypes appear 'believable', as though they were accurate descriptions of real groups of people. In this way, they would argue, stereotyping in the media could reinforce or even help create prejudice. What do you think? Could stereotyping in the media have undesirable social effects?

Projection   **Projection** is the tendency for us to interpret the behaviour of other people by projecting our own feelings and views onto what they do and say. For example, a cousin has started making regular visits to your elderly grandmother who now lives on her own. Do you assume that the cousin is after something, an inheritance perhaps? Or do you simply assume that she is genuinely concerned with the old lady's welfare? Obviously, what you know, or rather what you think you know, about your cousin may influence your judgement here. However, equally relevant may be the process of projection. For example, perhaps *you* are preoccupied with the notion of your grandmother dying and leaving you some money. Perhaps *you* are anxious about exactly what is written in her will. For these reasons, you may project your own motives onto your cousin and assume that *she* is equally preoccupied with what she can get from the old lady. In this example, you may have been so busy projecting your own feelings onto your cousin that you are unable to perceive what her true motives may have been.

Poor listening skills

Stereotyping, prejudice and projection are all psychological barriers which may interfere with our ability to view a situation fairly and clearly. However, even if our mind is open and free from such preoccupations, we may still have problems in receiving messages accurately, simply because we are unskilled as a listener.

In unfamiliar situations, such as meeting new people for the first time, a lack of confidence may cause problems. For example, if we are conducting an interview for a project, we may be so preoccupied in working out what questions to ask that we do not pay full attention to the answers. In such a case, a skilled communicator would go armed with a tape recorder and a list of written questions.

In other situations tiredness or even carelessness may interfere with our capacity to listen. There are many factors involved which prevent us from being skilled listeners. Perhaps the biggest problem of all is that listening appears to be so natural, unlike reading and writing which we consciously have to learn. Perhaps we take listening for granted and assume that, like breathing, it requires no effort at all. The biggest problem in trying to encourage people to improve their ability to listen is to get them to recognise that listening is a skill which one can do well or badly.

TASK 7

Read the following extract on **listening** and produce a checklist of guidelines for improving listening skills

But we can help listening whenever we want to. We can tune out any speaker, any time, at will. We can listen and still have some spare time for our own thinking. The use or misuse of this spare time holds the key to how well a person can listen to the spoken word.

Most of us misuse the spare time by going on private sidetracks. We daydream while we are 'listening' to a friend or to a lecture. At first, this presents no problem, for we are able to catch every word the friend or the professor is saying, and still think of what we are going to say next, or what we are going to do tonight, etc., and there is plenty of time to do all this extra thinking. Actually, we can hardly avoid doing this since it has become a strong habit over the years. So we go back and forth between what the speaker is saying and our private world. But sooner or later we stay a little too long on one of these mental sidetracks, and when we focus our attention back, the speaker is ahead of us. We lost something that was said. If it is something important we may not understand the rest of the conversation, and therefore we find it easier and easier to slide off on our sidetracks for longer periods of time. When the speaker is finished, it is not surprising that we actually heard only half of what was told us.

When we do not agree with a speaker, we have a great tendency to prepare a rebuttal while the other person is still talking. We hear the first few words or sentences, get an idea of what the speaker is saying, decide we don't agree, and here we go preparing our answer and waiting impatiently for our turn to speak. Sometimes, we don't even wait, and we interrupt the speaker who never gets a chance to finish his thought. Unfortunately, when we do not hear a speaker out completely, we really do not know for sure what is being said. People we do not agree with are often the most difficult people to listen to. Usually we have little difficulty listening to someone telling us how great we are or how smart we are, but listening to a professor who tells you your paper certainly did not deserve any better than a 'D' is a lot more difficult.

We often get distracted by a speaker's accent, mannerisms, the way he or she is dressed, the language used, delivery, etc. Some people simply won't listen to a person because he wears long hair, or she is dressed too flashily. Or if they are willing to listen, their listening will be affected by the preconceived ideas they have because of the speaker's dress or appearance. This of course is hardly conducive to effective listening. It is difficult to fight off these distractions. Yet as we become aware of all the little things that can get in the way of good listening, we might be in a better position to train ourselves to overcome them. In addition to the physical distractions created by the appearance of the speaker, the use of language may turn us off. Most of us react very strongly to certain emotionally loaded words, trigger words. Whenever these words are pronounced by someone, it's as though a red flag had been waved in front of our nose, and we react, usually emotionally and strongly. These words, of course, are different to each of us. If we can try to identify these words, they somehow lose some of their impact on us when we hear them, and at least we may not block out what a speaker has to say simply because one of our own loaded words was uttered.

(Adapted from *The Dynamics of Human Communication*, Myers & Myers)

Self-assessment

1. Distinguish between the following terms:
   - means of communication
   - forms of communication
   - media of communication
2. Explain what is meant by the 'process of perception'.
3. List the main factors involved in influencing the process of perception. Illustrate each factor with an example of your own.
4. Distinguish between stereotyping and prejudice.
5. List the main barriers to communication using an example to illustrate each one.
6. In communication studies what do we mean by a 'model', and what is its purpose?

Further work

1. Consider a British soap opera like *Coronation Street*, or *EastEnders*, and write down any stereotypes which you can identify.
2. In addition to soap operas there are other influences in society which help create and maintain stereotypes. Produce a list of such influences and write brief notes about each.
3. Write an essay with the following title: Discuss the importance of perception in face to face communication between individuals.
4. Discuss with friends, or family, their pet hates. Can you identify any examples of prejudice?

Information for Fig. 1.6

Person in a): English; 22 years of age; secretary to a sales/marketing director of a printing company.

Person in b): English; 58 years of age; retired Economics and Business Studies lecturer.

Person in c): English; 31 years of age; teacher of English in a secondary school.

Further reading

Abercrombie M.L.J, *The Anatomy of Judgement* (Hutchinson, 1968)
Gregory R.L, *Eye and Brain* (Weidenfeld and Nicolson, 1977)
Thouless R, *Straight and Crooked Thinking* (Pan, 1974)

2 *You the sender*

This chapter contains the following sections:

- **Sending messages**
- **Senders and receivers together**
- **Communication as a skilled performance**
- **Self-assessment**
- **Further work**
- **Further reading**

Sending messages

We began Chapter 1 by suggesting that the communication process involves both the sending and receiving of messages. So far we have concentrated on **you the receiver**. In this chapter we will focus upon **you the sender**. As well as being a receiver, you will also have sent hundreds of different messages over the past 24 hours. For example, you may have telephoned a friend, sent a letter, or had an argument with someone. The use of the words 'sender' and 'sent', implies that all of these messages were communicated by you quite deliberately and intentionally. In fact, this may not be the case. Often we send messages to people without being fully aware that we are doing so. As we shall see in the next chapter this is particularly the case with body language i.e. gesture, facial expression, etc. For example, when we talk to people we don't particularly like, we often try and disguise our true feelings out of politeness although we don't always succeed.

TASK 1

Make a list of all of the messages which you have sent during the past 24 hours. Try to include messages which you think you may have sent without actually having intended to do so.

Now get together in one large group and compare and contrast your lists.

In the previous chapter we looked at possible ways of classifying messages received. Now let's consider the same thing for the messages sent. For example, it may be possible to classify these messages into those which were consciously and deliberately sent, and those which were not. Alternatively, they may be classified in terms of the means of communication used.

TASK 2

Think of all the possible ways of classifying your list from the previous task.

Now get together as one group and compare and contrast your classification systems. Is there one which is better or more logical than another?

Purposes of communication

One way of classifying messages is by **purpose** i.e. why a message was sent. For example, the purpose of a DHSS leaflet on Family Income Supplement is mainly to **inform** people of the benefits to which they are entitled and to help **explain** how to go about getting them. However, the communication purpose of a poster advertising a students' union disco might be to **persuade** people to attend, whilst at the same time **informing** them of the details.

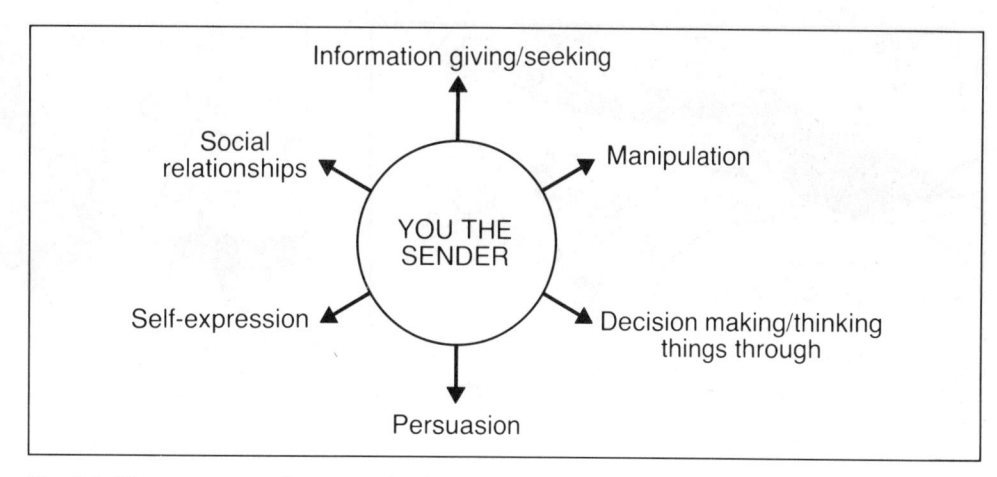

Fig. 2.1 The purposes of communication

In Fig. 2.1 there is a simple model which attempts to classify messages in terms of the purpose for which they were sent. As we know already this is only one possible classification system, but it is sufficiently important to require a closer look. Before doing so there are two general things worth stressing. The first is that all communication has some purpose or other. Even so called 'idle chit-chat', which on the surface may appear pointless, serves to maintain social relationships. The second is that much communication fulfils several purposes at the same time. For example, the purpose of explaining to a French tourist where the station is may be to give information, but it might also serve to show off your excellent knowledge of the French language!

Let's now have a look at a series of cartoons which illustrate those purposes of communication shown in Fig. 2.1.

Of all the purposes to which communication can be put, perhaps **information seeking** and **information giving** are the most common.

Fig. 2.2 Information seeking/information giving

Fig. 2.3 Persuasion

Much communication involves **persuasion**. A discussion between friends about a future holiday may be designed to persuade them that Spain is a better option than France. Advertising has the main purpose of persuading people to buy a particular product or use a particular service.

Fig. 2.4 Manipulation

Fig. 2.5 Social relationships

There is an obvious overlap between being persuaded that someone's opinion is the correct one, and being **manipulated** by someone to do something for them. Both persuasion and manipulation involve influencing opinion and behaviour. However, one difference is the extent to which we may be willing to be influenced. Persuasion implies a preparedness to accept an alternative point of view or willingness to change an original course of action. However, with manipulation we may be forced into a course of action against our will. Blackmail is a classic example of this. Alternatively, we may be manipulated by being deceived of the manipulator's true motives and intentions. For example, a politician may attempt to win votes by deliberately distorting the presentation of an issue in so subtle a way as to conceal what is happening. In examples like this one the dividing line between persuasion and manipulation becomes increasingly thin.

The category of **social relationships** is a broad one. It can include communicating with people because of feelings of loneliness and the need for comfort. It can also include communicating with people to preserve and maintain a particular relationship. A lot of polite conversation falls into this category; for example, exchanging comments about the weather with the next-door neighbour.

A lot of face to face communication involves **self-expression**. This can range from wanting to state a personal point of view on a topical issue, to just plain showing off! A great deal of body language, and of dress and hair styles serve this particular purpose.

Fig. 2.6 Self-expression

One effective way to make a personal decision is to talk things over with a friend. They may not actually come up with the right advice, but the simple process of talking it through may help in finding a solution. This **decision-making** purpose of communication can often be fulfilled by talking a problem over in one's head. This is an example of **intrapersonal communication.**

Fig. 2.7 Decision making/thinking things through

TASK 3

The model, Fig. 2.1 p.15, suggested that there are six broad purposes to which communication can be put. However, there are weaknesses with any system of classification. With some of the headings used above there are areas of overlap; with others the categories may be too broad and in need of sub-division.

Produce an alternative list for classifying messages in terms of purpose. Write down one example to illustrate each of your headings.

Individual needs and obligations

Individual needs and obligations and communication purpose are two sides of the same coin. The main reason why we communicate for a particular purpose is that we have a **need** or feel an **obligation**. For example, one reason why someone may spend an extremely long time discussing an apparently trivial problem with a friend is perhaps because they feel a great need for personal contact. Similarly, whether or not we spend time exchanging pleasantries with an elderly aunt may be related to our sense of obligation.

The important point to appreciate here is that the needs and obligations felt by individuals may vary considerably from personality to personality. For example, some people are more anxious and dependent upon friends than others, and so a great deal of their time may be spent building and maintaining social relationships. Extroverts may feel a greater need for self-expression than introverts and may earn themselves the label of show off. Some individuals may feel a great need to use people to further their own self-interest and so may become known as manipulators.

The kind of personality we are, and the profile of our various needs, may result in our having a particular **communication style.** Of course, communication style is only partly determined by personality. The situation we are in also determines the way we behave. For example, even the most ebullient of extroverts will behave in a sober and sombre manner at a funeral! Nevertheless, the idea of communication style related to personal needs and personality is an interesting one which is worth exploring more fully.

TASK 4

Below are a number of possible communication styles presented in a light-hearted and deliberately exaggerated form. Discuss how accurate you think these descriptions could be in summing up certain individuals which you may know. (In your discussion you may like to consider the tendency to explain someone's behaviour in terms of stereotypes, rather than in terms of specific factors such as the situation and the individual's actual personality.)

The over-talker. This is the individual who talks excessively to the point that the listener either switches off, or is simply unable to follow what is being said. The reasons why individuals may over-talk can vary; some may over-talk by habit; others may only talk excessively when in situations of anxiety or stress.

The under-talker. Of this individual it may often be said that it's difficult to get anything out of them. Some under-talkers may appear to be unresponsive, bored, or just plain rude. Others may appear to be shy and socially awkward with people. As in over-talking, the reasons why someone may under-talk will vary from individual to individual.

The barker. This is the individual who answers questions abruptly and asks questions as if giving orders. Some barkers may appear to be aggressive and impatient. Others may appear simply to lack the skill, or the confidence, to respond in softer, more socially acceptable ways. Whatever the underlying causes of this style might be, communicating with a barker often feels like being verbally punched or stabbed.

The acutely concerned. The acutely concerned individual spends a great deal of his or her time listening intently and sympathetically to other people. A mildly worried frown, an intent gaze, and an occasional nodding of the head are common features of this individual in action. Often the acutely concerned person may be genuinely interested in hearing about other people's needs and worries. However, occasionally an acutely concerned individual may be more interested in projecting an image of his or herself as a caring, listening person.

Oh really? So what? The 'Oh really? So what?' individual can come in a variety of forms. For example, some may appear to be bored and uninterested in almost everything people have to say to them. Others may appear to be less laid-back, and may actively counter what is said to them with comments like: 'Oh really? That's nothing; you ought to see our ...' or, 'Well actually, *my* mother is ...'.

Senders and receivers together

Feedback So far we have talked separately about the receiving and sending of messages as though they were two isolated activities. In face to face communication, what we may now call **interpersonal communication,** this is not the case. In a typical conversation involving two people each participant is both a sender and a receiver at the same time. Fig. 2.8 shows an informal interview in which the interviewer, the woman, listens carefully to the interviewee. The interviewer is obviously a receiver of what is being said to her, but at the same time she is also a sender, giving information back to the interviewee. Can you determine what she is conveying to the man?

In Fig. 2.8 this sending of unspoken information to the interviewee is just one possible example of **feedback**. Feedback can be defined as the response to a previous message. In conversation it can take the form of a spoken comment, made when the other person has stopped speaking; for example, 'I'm sorry but I didn't quite catch that'. Alternatively, feedback can take the form of a facial expression sent at the same time as the spoken message is being received.

An important feature of feedback is that it tells us, as communicators, whether our message is being understood or appreciated. In this sense feedback provides us with an opportunity to adjust our style and our message to suit different individuals and different situations. However, whether we take up the opportunity

Fig. 2.8 An example of interpersonal communication

available to us and use this feedback is a different matter. As we shall see in the following section, an ability and a willingness to be sensitive to feedback is a characteristic of an effective communicator.

Encoding and decoding

We have just said that in much interpersonal communication the participants are busy both receiving and sending messages, sometimes simultaneously, sometimes in close succession. We also know that the process of perception is continually taking place acting as a filter, and sometimes as a barrier, between the receiving and sending of messages. There is another way of saying this, using two key communication terms. We may say that in much interpersonal communication, each participant is busy both **decoding** messages received and **encoding** other messages which may then be sent. Decoding can be defined as the process of understanding and interpreting messages. In a sense this is what we have previously described as a part of perception. Encoding can be defined as the process of translating ideas, opinions and feelings into messages in a form which is likely to be understood when sent.

A sender-receiver model

One way of summing up this process of encoding and decoding is to use what is known as a simple **sender-receiver model** of interpersonal communication. The model in Fig. 2.9 attempts to bring together some of the ideas covered so far.

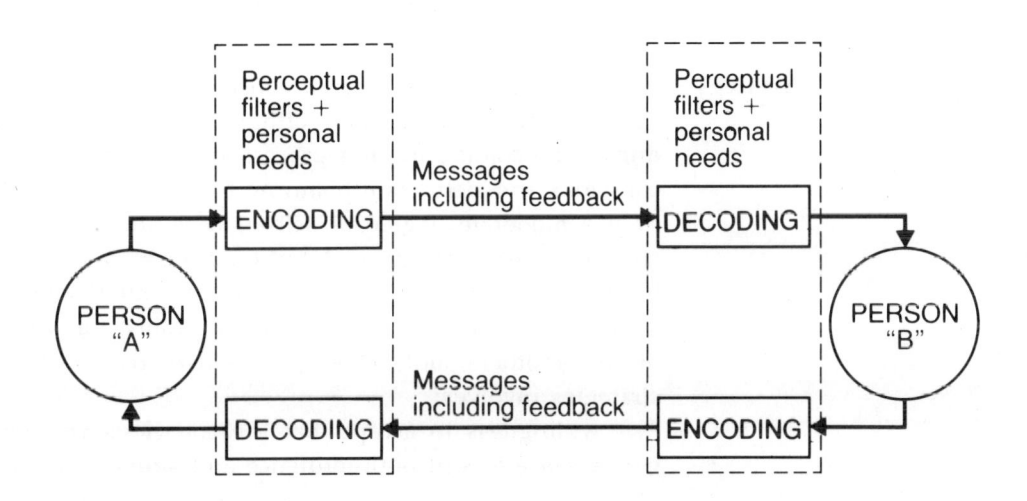

Fig. 2.9 A sender/receiver model of interpersonal communication

Communication as a skilled performance

The underlying assumption of this book is that interpersonal communication is a skill which can be analysed, practised and improved. One of the problems involved in communicating is that many people simply do not recognise the need to improve their communication skills. They regard communicating as something which is done quite naturally and therefore assume that no problems can exist. Others may want to improve their effectiveness, but feel that short of a major personality change there is nothing which can actually be done.

In this section we shall present a model of communication which attempts to identify the key components of a skilled and sensitive performance. These components are listed below.

Flexibility This is a general openness of mind which is an essential prerequisite for change. Without a genuine willingness to learn, it is doubtful that much learning will actually take place. Specifically flexibility involves:
— a recognition of the importance of open, effective communication;
— a willingness to admit to personal weaknesses and communication difficulties.

Self-knowledge This involves an ability to analyse behaviour and motives, 'warts 'n' all', and also an ability to see oneself as others do. Specifically self-knowledge involves:
— an awareness of any personal prejudices, stereotypes, a tendency to project, etc.;
— an awareness of our characteristic style of communicating, e.g. do we have a tendency to manipulate, to dominate, to talk too much, too little, etc.?

Empathy with an audience All of us have a tendency sometimes just to talk, oblivious of the needs of the people who may be listening. We are used to the notion of a comedian preparing his or her jokes to suit an audience. We know that if the comedian doesn't pitch the jokes at the right level they are likely to be booed off stage. But how often do we look upon the participants in a discussion or a conversation as an **audience**? How often do we bother to think about whether what we are saying or doing is being appreciated by our audience? **Empathy** means the ability to try and understand the needs of our audience, literally to try and put ourselves momentarily into their shoes. Specifically empathy involves:
— an ability to appreciate that our audience may have different values, needs and levels of background knowledge to ourselves;
— a willingness when communicating to adjust our behaviour to suit the needs of our audience rather than simply satisfying our own egos.

Strategy **Strategy** refers to the idea of consciously trying to adjust or modify our own communication performance, either before in the form of deliberate planning, or during the communication process itself. Some people may find this notion of conscious and deliberate planning offensive, as somehow unnatural. However, even a moderate degree of self-analysis should tell us that we use deliberate strategies and techniques a lot of the time already. For example, what individual has never used flattery and charm to 'get round' somebody? What we are talking about here is the use of strategies to adjust our own performance to suit the needs of others, not selfishly to satisfy our own. Specifically the notion of strategies involves:
— a willingness to accept that the conscious and deliberate adjusting of our performance to suit both audience and situation is neither artificial nor selfish.

— an ability and a willingness to experiment and to try alternative ways and styles of communicating, e.g. listening more instead of impatiently trying to butt in.

Sensitivity to feedback

As we have already discussed, sensitivity to feedback from others is a key ingredient of good, effective communication. A good illustration of this is to consider what happens when we are unable or unwilling to respond appropriately to feedback. If we are rather talkative by nature and fail to recognise certain danger signs in the facial expressions of others we may soon earn ourselves a reputation for being boring. It we are rather quiet and seem unable to respond to the encouragement of others we may convince people that we are cold and unapproachable.

As skilled communicators we should not only be sensitive to the feedback given to us by our audience, but occasionally we might actually *invite* feedback e.g. 'I'm sorry, am I explaining this too quickly?'

Specifically, sensitivity to feedback involves:
— an ability to recognise the language of feedback, facial expressions, gestures, position of body etc.;
— a willingness and an ability to respond appropriately to feedback.

 *5* Produce a visual model which presents interpersonal communication as a skilled performance which is open to analysis, practice and improvement. You may wish to base your model on the headings and notes given above, in which case you should feel free to amend these notes in any way you think appropriate.

Self-assessment

1. List the main purposes of communication and give an example of each.
2. Distinguish between communication purpose on the one hand, and individual need and obligation on the other.
3. What is meant by 'communication style'? Illustrate your answer with examples.
4. Distinguish between intrapersonal communication and interpersonal communication.
5. Write detailed notes on the nature and role of feedback.

Further work

1. Make a list of the purposes of communication which you think are illustrated in the following story.

The cuffs of Derek's faded Levi jacket were pulled well back to expose the freshly engraved tattoos on his wrists. With thumbs hooked on his belt, and with shoulders back, he pushed open the lounge bar door and strolled in.

Slowly he made his way to the bar, nodding to a friend who sat near the jukebox

'Pint of bitter, mate,' drawled Derek.

'Coming right up,' answered the barman.

'Nice day, isn't it?' he added.

'Yeah, suppose so,' Derek replied.

Derek lifted his pint and moved to the jukebox. A pair of legs barred his path.

'Shift,' he snarled and they did.

Derek worked for the new unisex boutique which had just opened in town. He was the bouncer there but he sometimes stood in for the fitting lad. Today was pay day. He felt like a million bucks. He reached into his pocket and gently squeezed the £36 which was in there. He let out a wild scream of delight.

'Yippee!'

Derek shoved 10 pence into the jukebox and selected 'Somebody's gonna get their head kicked in tonight'.

Derek fancied himself with the women, and let's face it, they fancied him. He positioned himself next to Dolores, an overlocker from the local knitting factory.

'You goin' down Rockers later?' he asked Dolores, drooling devastatingly over his pint as he did so.

Dolores resisted a bit, blushed, swooned and finally, softly, said:

'Yeah; go on then!'

Suddenly, before Derek had time to respond, the door was flung open. The Kirk Hallam Killers burst in! They were looking for aggro. Dolores clung onto Derek and chatted nervously: 'Derek, ooh Derek, what do they want, what are they goin' to do ...?'

'Never mind Dolores,' said Derek, 'I'll handle this ...'

2. Take a copy of the *Sun* and *The Times* and discuss the contents of these newspapers in terms of the communication purposes which they serve.

3. Try and analyse your own strengths and weaknesses as a communicator using the model you produced earlier. Produce a set of notes to summarise your results. Be sure to include comments about your attitudes, as well as your skills.

Further reading

Fiske J, *Introduction to Communication Studies* (Methuen, 1982)
Open University, *Making Sense of Society* (Block 3, Unit 7) (Open University Press, 1979)
Berne E, *Games People Play* (Penguin, 1970)

3 *Non-verbal communication*

This chapter contains the following sections:

- **What is non-verbal communication?**
- **Body language**
- **Other ways in which non-verbal communication takes place**

- **Self-assessment**
- **Further work**
- **Further reading**

What is non-verbal communication?

We now know something about the reasons people have for communicating messages to each other, and the ways in which those messages are sent and received. In this chapter we will begin to consider in more detail the process of communication between people and the means available to us if we wish to communicate.

We can start with a means of communication which is often both very simple and yet amazingly powerful called **non-verbal communication.**

TASK 1

Look at Fig. 3.1. Each person you see is busy communicating a message of some kind, although none is actually speaking. Try to establish what message is being communicated in each case, and try to describe and analyse the means being used by the sender.

(a)

(b)

(c)
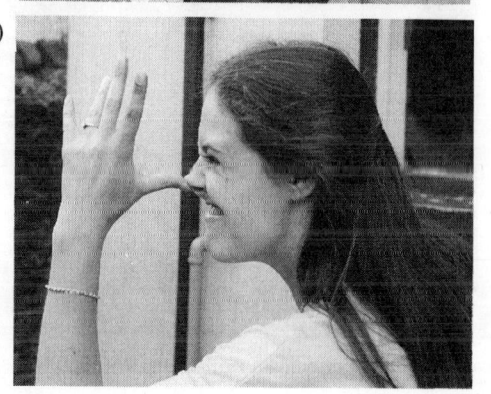

Fig. 3.1 Non-verbal communication in action

The sending of messages by using the head, face, arms, legs and other parts of the body is a very basic and primitive human activity. Distant ancestors of thousands of years ago would signal to each other in this way before the full development of human speech, and young babies still relay messages to their parents in this way before they have learned to use words. Deaf and dumb people use a highly developed form of non-verbal communication in their sign language, and dealers in the American Stock Exchange or bookmakers at a race course still use hand signals in situations where the spoken word might not be heard because of noise or distance.

We can use non-verbal communication (N.V.C.) instead of the spoken word — as the bookmaker does — or we can use it at the same time as we are speaking, to reinforce our message; a dynamic public speaker who bangs the table or waves his or her fists in the air is doing precisely this.

N.V.C. is a more powerful means of communication than is sometimes given credit for, and yet messages are often sent or received unconsciously. A person being interviewed may be nervously tapping his or her fingers on the table; if the interviewer notices this fact and interprets it as a sign of anxiety, he/she will have received and understood a message that was never consciously being sent. In other words, there are messages which are deliberately sent and received, but sometimes unconscious messages are sent which are only picked up by the receiver.

TASK *2* Look at the photos in Fig. 3.2. In each case there is an individual who is sending a message of a non-verbal nature of which he or she is possibly unaware. Try to give your own interpretation of each non-verbal message shown.

(a)
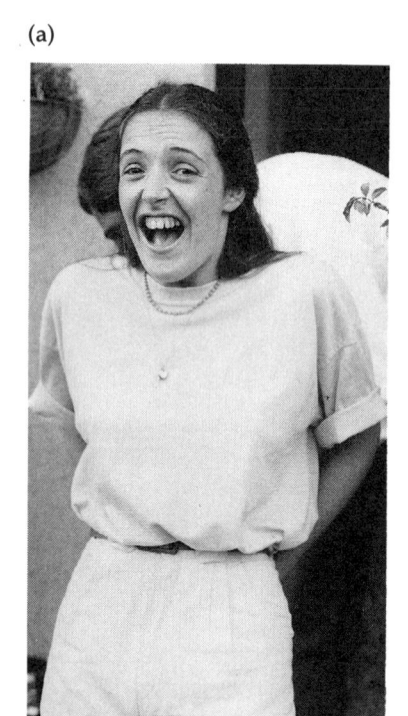

(b)

(c)

(d)

Fig. 3.2 Unconscious non-verbal messages

So what exactly is non-verbal communication? In simple terms we could say that N.V.C. is the communication which passes between individuals to replace or reinforce the use of words. This is deliberately a very broad definition, and would include the following:

— The use of visual forms of communication like drawing, painting, architecture, sculpture, decorative art. Many graphs or charts and diagrams rely more upon non-verbal than verbal means to put their message across, and archaeologists rely very heavily upon artefacts like weapons, pots and vases to provide 'communication messages' from civilisations long since disappeared.

— Movement and dance. Ballet and mime are forms of non-verbal communication, and so is instrumental music.

— The use of time. You might well decide that a company who replied to a letter promptly was better organised and managed than one which delayed for days or even weeks. If you asked someone face-to-face to write a reference for you for a job you dearly wanted and that person took several minutes to reply, you might be slightly perturbed: were they giving it deep thought and consideration, or were they thinking about a tactful way to say no?

Precisely because this subject is such a broad one, this chapter is restricted to the more basic forms of N.V.C. which involve the use of our bodies and parts of our bodies to send messages — consciously or unconsciously, as we have seen — to other people. This will include a final section on physical appearance and the use of objects.

Body language

If you were to take a good look at any group of human beings in a social situation — at a party, in a meeting or at a sporting event, for example — you would find that communication was taking place between people nearly all the time and in a variety of different ways. Not all that communication would be by word of mouth; messages are sent to others through the use we make of our bodies — that is, we are all senders and receivers of **body language**.

Before we examine body language in some detail, let us consider why this particular form of non-verbal communication is so vital to us in our everyday lives.

Body language is ubiquitous — that is, you find it all around you wherever you look. It has been said that 'You cannot *not* communicate'; we give out signals to other people through body language whether we like it or not. Two people may decide to ignore each other and therefore choose not to speak to each other. But that does not mean that there is no communication passing between them — every time one of the two people turns his or her back on the other, or scowls or frowns, communication is happening even though no words are being spoken.

We are often unaware of the body language messages which we are sending. If we speak or write, we have a fairly clear idea of the exact message which we are relaying; but something about the way we stand or a particular facial expression of which we are unaware may be interpreted by others in a surprising way. Perhaps you know a person who looks rather snooty and supercilious, looking down his or her nose at everyone, and yet is really a very nice and modest individual who would be upset at the thought that a certain unconscious facial expression was being misinterpreted. We often have less control over the messages we are sending through our body language than we would like. As receivers, we must be careful to examine our own perceptions of other people based upon their body language. Are we prejudiced against people for no good reason? Are we stereotyping individuals in an unjustifiable way?

Body language can be enormously powerful. Something about a person we meet may put us on our guard against them — perhaps they look moody or stand-offish, perhaps they smile too little or too often, perhaps they stare at us or never look us in the eye. First impressions based upon such body language messages may stay with us for a long while because of the power they have over us, and nothing that a person might say or do might ever change our initial unease and mistrust. If a person spoke pleasant words to you but did so with a sneer or a scowl, which message would you trust — the words spoken, or the look given?

The picture of a human figure shown in Fig. 3.3 reinforces the point that we continually send body language signals whether we are aware of it or not.

Body language can be classified in the following way: **bodily contact; physical proximity; orientation; posture; gesture; facial expression; eye contact.** Let us look at each of these in more detail.

Fig. 3.3 An 'anatomy' of body language — 'We cannot not communicate'

Bodily contact   Physical contact between people is one of the most basic kinds of social act available to us. Such contact is found in all animal behaviour, but some people would argue that only human beings use **bodily contact** — a handshake, for example — in a fully symbolic way.

Who we touch, and when, and in what way, is determined by:

— Age. It seems natural to us to see adults cuddling children — their own or other people's — and we generally find that more touching takes place between adults and children and between children and children than happens between adults.

— Sex. Our feelings about touching between adults is partly determined by the sex of the individuals involved. It might strike us as unusual to see two married couples greeting each other by the women shaking hands and the men kissing each other. Our reaction, would be affected by our own social and cultural expectations. Casual or light touching on permitted parts of the body between adults of the same sex or different sexes is usually intended and interpreted as a friendly gesture, falling short of the intimate touching which we think of as specifically sexual.

— Relationships. Individuals will touch members of their own family or close friends in a way that might be misunderstood or misinterpreted if a stranger was involved. Families differ in their attitude towards touching; do you know some families who touch when they meet other families, and others who don't?

— Culture. British people tend to be fairly reserved about touching as a public act; other cultures readily accept hugging or kissing on the cheek between adults of the same sex, and Eskimos rub noses as a sign of intimacy and friendship. Why do you think that embracing between footballers of the same sex after a goal has been scored is a generally acceptable cultural act?

Touch is an especially important factor in the following situations or relationships:

— Care of children, old people or invalids. Touch can be used to bring comfort to someone we care for. A child who is often touched by his or her parents will gain some sense of security from that touching, while a child who is never touched risks feeling isolated. Touch can be therapeutic if we are comforting the sick or the aged, and is used in so-called Encounter Groups to help those who are unable to express affection or hostility.

— Helping to establish friendly relationships. A limited amount of touching — a hand on another person's arm or shoulder, for example — can help to build a relationship.

— Aggression. Most touch between people is of a fairly soft and delicate nature, except for a very strong hug or embrace. Touch used to show aggression, by contrast, is frequently strong and much more powerful, possibly involving grasping, hitting or kicking.

We frequently make use of touch and the power of touch in social situations, such as:

— Greetings and farewells. This might involve a handshake, an embrace or a kiss.

— Congratulations. This could vary from a pat on the back to the footballers' embrace.

— Gaining attention. A child might grab hold of an adult when it wants attention; an adult may lay a hand on the arm of someone involved in a conversation in order to break into that conversation.

— Ceremonies. Ritual and symbolic acts frequently involve touching — so a boxing referee will hold aloft the hand of the winner in a fight, or a priest will lay his hand on the head of a communicant.

The whole subject of touching is imbued with social and cultural taboos — that is, notions of what kind of touching is acceptable between various individuals in various situations, public and private. People will often go to extraordinary lengths *not* to touch strangers — watch people as they walk along a crowded street, doing their best not to touch anyone, and apologising if any physical contact happens by accident.

Physical proximity Cultural expectations and taboos are also at work when it comes to **physical proximity**; the distance we feel necessary to keep between ourselves and others.

We spend much of our life, especially in the public domain, with a kind of invisible 'bubble' around us, expecting no-one to invade our space except by accident or unless the situation dictates it.

How much space we expect to have around us can be determined by:

— The occasion. We would hardly expect a dentist or a doctor to keep his/her distance from us during treatment, nor would we expect to retain our personal space uninvaded if we were on a crowded bus or train or at a football match.

— Status/relationship. A judge in court keeps a significant distance between himself/herself and the accused, as does a headteacher who is reprimanding a pupil. Friends and relations, on the other hand, will happily stand or sit closer to us than strangers would.

— Culture. Our expectations about personal space are determined in part by our nationality and culture. It is sometimes said that Arabs and Latin Americans tend to stand very close to each other and that Swedes and Scots keep the greatest distance between one individual and the next.

— Personality. Experiments have shown that introverts (private people who relate more to themselves as individuals than to others), prefer more personal space around them than more outgoing extroverts.

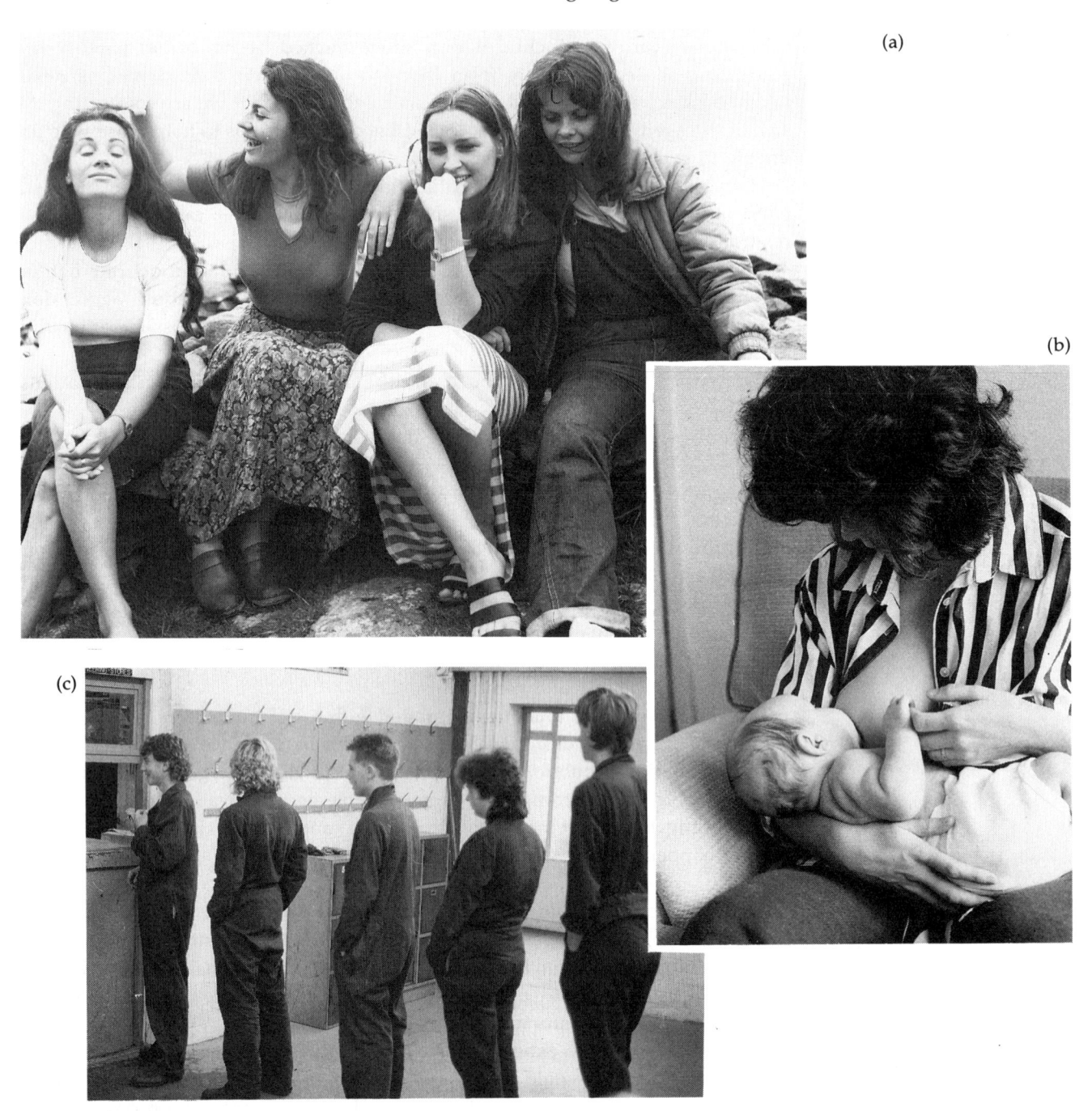

(a)

(b)

(c)

Fig. 3.4 Bodily contact and physical proximity

Changes in proximity between people are often used to signal a desire to begin or to end an encounter; you would move towards someone with whom you hoped to have a conversation, and then move away again once that conversation was nearing its end.

One classification of personal space is given below; does it seem to agree with your own experience?
- Intimate = Up to 1½ feet
- Casual personal = 1½—5 feet
- Social consultative = 5—12 feet
- Public = Over 12 feet

Can you decide how much personal space you need or are happy with? Can you think of occasions on which this space was invaded? What was your response?

TASK 3   Look at Fig. 3.4. What can you deduce about the relationship between the people in each photo from the bodily contact or degree of physical proximity observable in each case?

Orientation   Whether involved in the act of communication ourselves, or watching others communicate (what Desmond Morris refers to in a book title as *Manwatching*), there is much to be learned from the physical closeness or lack of closeness which exists between the participants in that act. But we also need to be aware of where people place themselves in relation to each other — a phenomenon we will call **orientation**: during a wedding service the bride and bridegroom stand next to each other, facing forwards, during much of the ceremony, but before the service is over they usually turn to face each other — a position which we expect from two people with an intimate relationship.

Try to visit a Court of Law. In a Magistrates' Court the positioning of people in relation to each other is highly significant and symbolic. Although taller people might often seem to dominate their shorter counterparts, it is often the case that individuals of a superior status remain seated while a person in a subservient role is standing. This is the case in a Magistrates' Court: frequently the three magistrates are seated, but placed on a raised platform, while the accused is asked to stand at key stages in the proceedings. The magistrates sit facing the accused, since what is happening is a kind of ritualised confrontation. Those whose role in the case is more neutral or advisory — the probation officers, members of the social service team, the press and witnesses — normally sit on both sides of the courtroom, facing into the centre at a 90° angle to the magistrates and the accused.

If you visited a school where the teacher stood at the front of the class and the pupils were sitting in rows, and then went to a different school where the teacher was seated and the desks were arranged in a circle, what conclusions might you draw from each of the two classroom arrangements? Do you think that classroom seating arrangements reflect the personality and style of the teacher, or the subject being taught?

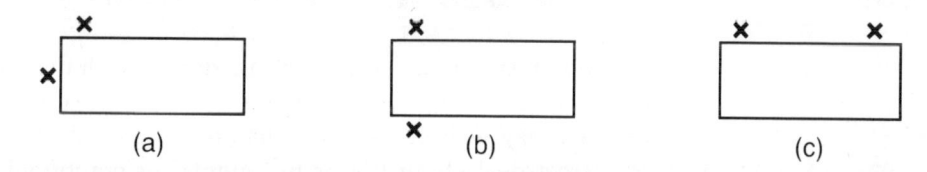

Fig. 3.5 Orientation

TASK 4   Imagine that you entered a room where two people were sitting around a table; what might be the relationship between these two people if their placing in relation to each other, their orientation, was as is shown in Fig. 3.5?

Posture   So far we have been looking at non-verbal communication specifically as it exists between pairs or groups of people — whether individuals make physical contact with each other, how close they place themselves to others, and where they stand or sit in relation to those around them.

   Now we shift our focus to look at the individual; how he or she sends messages — consciously or unconsciously — by non-verbal means.

TASK 5   Look at Fig. 3.6. What is being communicated in each case by the posture of the person in question?

(a)

(b)

Fig. 3.6 Posture

(c)

   Whether standing, sitting, lying down, walking or running, there is often something about our body **posture** which relays a message to those around us — and this may well be unconscious on our part. A person who slouches may tell us a great deal about his or her mental or emotional state; a soldier on guard duty with a stiff and formal posture is relaying a message on behalf of himself and the organisation to which he belongs.

If you were interviewing a candidate for a job, you would pick up a number of signals or messages about an individual by the way he or she entered the room and by the way the candidate stood, walked and sat down. There are dominant and submissive postures, friendly and aggressive postures, confident and nervous postures. Posture is very much a matter of how we use and move the whole body, rather than individual parts of it.

The following three factors may influence a person's posture:

— Cultural convention. Posture, like much non-verbal communication, is affected by cultural norms and expectations. A Muslim would believe that it was appropriate to prostrate one's body on the ground in the presence of Allah, while a Christian might feel that a slight bow as you approached the altar would be all the change in posture required to show respect.

— Attitude to others present. In an animated conversation between friends, each might lean towards the other, while sworn enemies might stand aloof from each other, or even adopt a hunched-up, aggressive posture.

— Emotional state. A person feeling happy and content with the world might quite literally 'walk tall' with an upright posture, while a depressed or anxious person would be likely to slouch whilst walking or sitting.

Can you think of any other factors which affect posture?

One distinctive feature of human interaction is the tendency people have to adopt the posture of those with whom they are talking. Look out for this yourself. If one person stands with folded arms, does anyone else unconsciously copy the posture? This phenomenon is known as **postural echo**.

Gesture

TASK 6

Look at the hand gestures below; what message do you think is being communicated in each case?

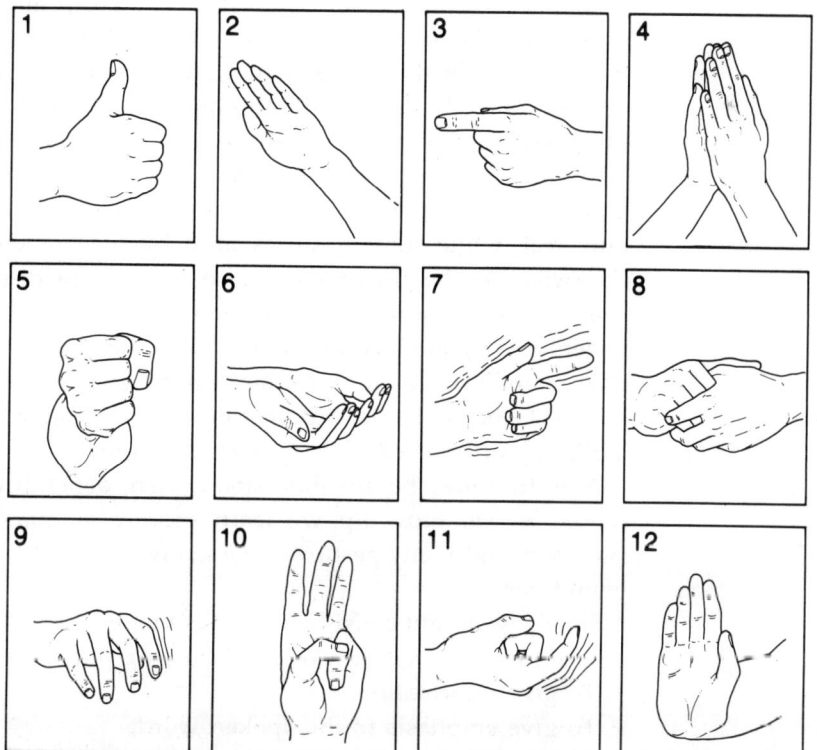

Fig. 3.7 Gestures

Posture describes the way in which we use and move our whole body; **gesture** refers to the use of part of the body to communicate with others. Like posture, gesture may be conscious or unconscious; a wave to a friend is a deliberate signal of greeting, while a person nervously playing with a watch strap or shirt button is probably quite unaware of the message which others are receiving.

Some gestures — a handshake, for example — are complementary, needing two people to make them complete, but most of the time we choose our own gesture and leave others free to respond with gestures or words of their choice.

All moving parts of our bodies are available to us if we wish to make use of a gesture:

— The head. Holding the head to one side while listening to someone speak shows an involved interest, while in many cultures a simple nod of the head signals 'yes'.

— The arms. Both arms held above the head might signal 'Victory!', while arms folded tightly across the chest might indicate anger or a sulk.

— The hands. Hands forced down into trouser pockets is a gesture indicating boredom or defiance, while hands formed into a fist shows aggression. Have you ever found yourself using hand gestures while speaking on the telephone? If the other person isn't there to see the gesture, what function does it perform?

— Legs and feet. Making a kicking motion with the leg might signal 'Get out of here!', while crossing the legs and bouncing one leg up and down might show impatience.

Gesture is a form of language: we can use gestures in combination with each other or while we are speaking, and using modifications based upon 20 or so key gesture signs we can signal a wide range of messages. A 'V' sign made with the palm outwards, for instance, signals victory, while the same sign with the palm facing the sender is a well-known obscene gesture.

Some gestures have become stylised over the years — so a military salute is a symbolic remnant of the removal of one's cap and is a way of presenting an unclenched fist to another person. Other gestures have changed or vanished over the years — so the obscene 'fig' sign so familiar to Shakespeare in the 16th century (made by forcing the thumb between the first and second fingers of the same hand) has now all but disappeared from British culture.

Cultural differences are very much in evidence when it comes to gesture. Some gestures — the tapping of the nose to indicate complicity for example — are fairly universal, while some gestures used by the French (such as moving your fist clockwise on the tip of your nose to indicate drunkenness) are unknown in Britain. Other gestures have different meanings for different nationalities: crossed fingers mean good luck in Britain, but would signal the end of an affair if used in Greece or Turkey; the circle sign made with the forefinger and thumb which means 'Good, O.K.' in Britain can refer to money in some countries, or mean 'nothing', or be used as an obscene gesture.

A gesture may be misunderstood, then, depending upon where we find ourselves; as we grow up we learn gesture language just as we learn spoken language, and many gestures, like many words, do not cross cultural or national boundaries.

Finally we might consider why it is that gestures are used; try to find examples of gestures used for each of the following purposes:

— To give information;
— To give emphasis to the spoken word;
— To communicate an emotional state;
— To express a relationship.

Facial expression   Few other parts of the body can begin to compete with the face when it comes to non-verbal communication. A complex variety of different facial muscles allows transmission of an enormous range of messages, and facial gestures, like all other gestures, may be made unconsciously − all the more so because, unless we choose to look in a mirror, we often have no idea about the exact **facial expressions** we are making. We may believe that our face is signalling openness and friendliness, only to find that other people have interpreted our expression differently.

How do you respond to a person who smiles a lot, to a person who scowls and frowns and to a clown in the circus with a painted smiling face? Have you ever misinterpreted someone else's facial signals?

Consider the parts of the face over which our muscles have control, and which we can use to send non-verbal signals using a wide range of combinations: forehead; eyebrows; eyelids; eye; nose; cheeks; lips; tongue; chin.

TASK 7   Compile a list of facial expressions and describe each as carefully as you can giving a meaning or meanings for each expression. Cut out examples from newspapers or magazines if you wish.

Much of the time our facial expressions are made unconsciously; a sorrowful person doesn't deliberately set out to compose a sorrowful expression any more than we would make a conscious effort to screw up our faces and grimace at the sight of something grotesque or unpleasant, or blush if embarrassed.

There are times, though, when we consciously use the face to send signals: we might open our eyes wide when listening to someone talking as a deliberate attempt to show interest, or we might smile at a person we find amusing in order to give positive feedback and encouragement.

Eye contact   Most facial expressions are dominated by what the eyes are doing; a smile accompanied by dull expressionless eyes is hardly a real smile at all − or at best a half-hearted attempt at a smile. Whether we are aware of it or not, we pay great attention to other people's eyes during interpersonal communication.

When two people meet they look each other in the eye to show a willingness to interact. Such early glances usually last from one to ten seconds in duration, while during a normal conversation **eye contact** is intermittent, with each person looking at the other from 30% to 60% of the time. Eye contact can be rewarding and satisfying, but too much may be embarrassing, since it might give a person the idea that he or she was being assessed in some way. In tense social situations too much eye contact can cause self-conscious people to feel great stress.

It is said that the eyes are the mirror of the soul, so we can tell a great deal about a person just by looking into their eyes. If you see something, or somebody that interests you a great deal the pupils in the centre of the eyes dilate and grow bigger, enabling you to get 'a better look'; not only that, but while the pupils are dilated in this way the eyes can appear more attractive.

TASK 8   Answer the questions below on the eyes and eye contact:
− Phil sees Jane at a party. He looks at her as a signal of interest. What are Jane's possible reactions? Interpret the meaning of each.
− Mark is being interviewed by Mr. Smith. He does not look at Mr. Smith (a) when he, Mark, is speaking, and (b) when Mr. Smith is speaking. How might Mr. Smith interpret both (a) and (b)?

— A has just met B in a bar, and during conversation he looks at B for longer than usual. How might B interpret this if (a) both are male (b) B is female?

Your answers might help you complete the following statement: Interpretation of eye contact depends upon . . .

TASK 9

Now that we have considered the subject of body language in some detail, you should be in a position to carry out a simple practical exercise. Sit or stand opposite one other person and try to convey each of the following messages by non-verbal means:
— 'Don't say a word!'
— 'Come forward slowly.'
— 'What an unpleasant smell!'
— 'I'm fed up.'

Now write down five messages of your own; don't show these to your partner, but try to send each in a non-verbal way. Was every message understood in the way you intended? Now the sender and receiver can change roles and repeat the exercise.

Other ways in which non-verbal communication takes place

Physical appearance

Non-verbal communication is perhaps at its most obvious when we smile at a friend or wave someone goodbye; body movement used for the purpose of N.V.C. is referred to as **kinesic behaviour.** But we can communicate a good deal about ourselves without ever moving any body parts at all:
— Our clothes will often relay a strong message to others around us.
— Our use of cosmetics on face, hands and even toes may tell others what kind of people we are, or would like to be.
— Our hair may be styled in a particular way which satisfies us but may incidentally lead to others making judgements about us.
— Even our physique may communicate to others something about our own self-image, especially if we have spent some time doing body-building exercises.

We may have set out quite deliberately to create an image for ourselves — one that either follows or ignores current trends in fashion. In doing this, we may have been influenced by:
— Social norms in the form of fashion. Are skirts long or short? Are trousers tight or baggy? Is hair artificially coloured or natural?
— Group membership. Uniforms abound in society — the uniform of the police or the armed forces, the uniform of the punk, the uniform of nuns, nurses, footballers, traffic wardens . . . Would you describe the blue pin-stripe suit worn by many members of the House of Commons as a uniform?
— Social status. Judges in certain law courts wear a gown and wig as symbols of status; countless modifications and additions to military uniforms reflect quite subtle variations in status.
— The desire to be sexually attractive. Make-up, tight clothing or flesh-revealing clothing may signal our desire to be thought sexually attractive.

TASK 10

Look at Fig. 3.8. For each photo try to say what message is relayed by each person's clothing and general physical appearance.

Fig. 3.8 Physical appearance

Use of objects   The possession or use of an object or objects by an individual may also communicate a message to those nearby by non-verbal means. The word 'Fascist' comes from the Latin 'Fasces', a bundle of rods carried by an officer in Roman times as a symbol of status and power, and in the novel by William Golding, *Lord of the Flies*, any boy who wished to speak to the others was supposed to be holding the conch shell as proof that it was his turn to be listened to. A Bishop carries a crosier or crook as a symbol of office, and a soldier may carry a 'swagger stick' to reinforce his status.

Do you know people for whom a car is more than just a vehicle for moving around in, but has a symbolic meaning? Is a car for some drivers just an extension of the old medieval suit of armour — a symbol of power and status? Try to list a range of different cars and say what you might guess about their occupants.

TASK // Extend the following table by listing a number of objects and describing how each might be used as an agency of non-verbal communication, by whom and in what circumstances.

OBJECT	USE OF OBJECT AS AN AGENCY OF N.V.C.
Cigarette holder	May be used by men or women as a symbol of elegance and social status.
Porsche sports car	May be used by men or women as a symbol of wealth and social status.

Conclusion Never underestimate the power of non-verbal communication. Experiments have shown that where two conflicting messages are sent, one by the verbal channel (speech) and one by the non-verbal channel, the non-verbal message is dominant. In other words, if a person smiles at you and says 'I am really very angry with you', the message you are likely to receive is that the person is not really angry at all.

This dominance of N.V.C. over verbal communication is referred to as the **primacy** of N.V.C.

In a sense, the term 'non-verbal communication' is a misleading one, because we very often use N.V.C. at the same time as we are speaking — in which case N.V.C. serves to reinforce the verbal utterance. We will have more to say about this under the heading of **paralanguage** in Chapter 4.

Individuals vary in terms of their skills at using and interpreting N.V.C.; some people are very sensitive to non-verbal signals, others less so. Have you ever wanted someone to go away and leave you because you had something else to do? What signals did you send? How were they received and responded to? If your non-verbal signals were ignored, it may be because they weren't clear (the sender's fault) or because they weren't properly decoded and understood (the receiver's fault). Some non-verbal signals can be ambiguous, just as words can be i.e. they might be interpreted in more than one way.

We can close this chapter by summarising N.V.C. in terms of its *uses* and *meaning*.

The *uses* of N.V.C.:
— to communicate interpersonal attitudes and emotions;
— to support verbal communication;
— to replace speech.
The *meaning* of N.V.C.:
— it is a kind of language, and as such it needs to be encoded and decoded by people who follow shared rules and understanding.

Meaning in N.V.C. can depend upon:
— cultural and national differences; one person's friendly gesture might be another's obscene insult;
— historical differences — N.V.C. signals have changed over centuries of history. Touching one's forelock as a sign of respect to the local squire is now almost a thing of the past;
— context. A wave of the hand may be a greeting or a desperate attempt to catch someone's attention in an emergency;
— the sensitivity of the sender and the receiver; a person may smile to show friendliness, only to have the smile misinterpreted as a gloat.

Self-assessment

1. Give your own definition of Non-Verbal Communication.
2. List and describe *four* factors which affect our use of bodily contact.
3. List and describe *four* factors which affect the amount of space we expect to have between us and other people.
4. Explain the difference between posture and gesture.
5. Describe *four* gestures and give the usual meaning of each.
6. Describe how (a) the eyes and (b) clothing may be used in non-verbal communication.

Further work

1. Compile your own scrap book or file containing sketches or pictures cut out from newspapers or magazines which illustrate non-verbal communication in action.
2. Write an essay with the following title: Discuss the importance and use of non-verbal communication in interpersonal communication.
3. Read the following extract from *Kes* by Barry Hines. Billy Casper is involved in a confrontation at school with a boy called MacDowall. Write down the examples of non-verbal communication which appear in the extract and discuss the meaning and significance of each.

Billy walked round to the back of the school and crossed the strip of asphalt to the cycle shed. Look-outs were posted at either end of the shed, and in one corner a gang of boys was assembled; some smoking, some hanging around in the hope of a smoke. The three smokers were hanging around. So was MacDowall.

'Got owt, Casper?'

Billy shook his head.

'Tha never has, thee. Tha just cadges all thine. Casper the cadger, that's what they ought to call thee.'

'I wouldn't gi' thee owt if I had, MacDowall.'

'I'll gi' thee summat in a minute.'

Billy crossed in front of the row of bicycles parked with their front wheels slotted into concrete blocks. One machine was mounted, the rider backpedalling vacantly, as though waiting to be snapped by a seaside photographer. Billy leaned on the corrugated tin wall at the other end of the shed and looked out across the asphalt. Directly opposite was the door of the boiler house. At one side of the door were eight dustbins in a line, and at the other side, a heap of coke. The door was painted green.

'What's tha gone over there for, Casper, frightened?'

Billy ignored him and continued to stare out. MacDowall, pinching a tab between his middle finger and thumb nails, twitched his head in Billy's direction.

'Come on, lads, let's go and keep him company.'

Grinning, he led the line of smokers across the shed, and they took up position in the corner, behind Billy. Billy half turned, so that his back was against the tin, and the gang were down one side of him.

'What's up, Casper, don't tha like company?'

He winked at the boys around him.

'They say thi mother does.'

The gang began to snigger and snuggle into each other. Billy turned his back on them again.

'I've heard tha's got more uncles than any kid in this city.'

The shout of laughter seemed to jerk Billy round as though it had pulled him by the shoulder.

'Shut thi mouth! Shut it can't tha!'

'Come and make me.'

'Tha can only pick on little kids. Tha daren't pick on anybody thi own size!'

'Who daren't?'

'Thee! Tha wouldn't say what tha's just said to our Jud. He'd murder thi.'

'I'm not frightened of him.'

'Tha would be if he wa' here.'

'Would I heck, he's nowt, your Jud.'

'Tha what! He's cock o' t'estate, that's all.'

'Who says? I bet I know somebody who can fight him.'

'Who? . . . thi father?'

The gang laughed and began to fan out behind MacDowall.

MacDowall was furious.

'Your Jud wouldn't stick up for thee, anyroad. He isn't even thi brother.'

'What is he then, my sister?'

'He's not thi right brother, my mother says. They don't even call him Casper for a start.'

'Course he's my brother! We live in t'same house, don't we?'

'An' he don't look a bit like thee, he's twice as big for a start. You're nowt like brothers.'

'I'm tellin' him! I'm tellin' him what tha says, MacDowall!'

Billy ran at him. The gang scattered. MacDowall took a step back, lifted one knee, and pushed Billy off with his foot. Billy came back at him. MacDowall delivered a straight right, which caught Billy smack in the chest and bounced him back on to his arse.

'Get away, you little squirt, before I spit on thi an' drown thi.'

Billy got up, coughing and crying and rubbing his chest. He stood at a distance glancing round, his fingers clenching and unclenching. Then he turned and ran out of the shed, across the asphalt to the pile of coke. He scooped up two handfuls, then, cupping this stock to his chest with his left hand, he began to throw it lump by lump into the shed. MacDowall turned his back and hunched his shoulders. The others scattered, knocking bicycles off balance and sending them toppling against other bicycles, which leaned over and swayed under the weight. The coke clattered against the tin with such rapidity that the vibrations produced by each clatter were linked together into a continual ring. One lump hit MacDowall in the back, another on the leg. He cursed Billy and began to back out, peeping over his raised left arm. Then, as Billy stooped for fresh ammunition, panting and pausing for a moment's rest, MacDowall straightened up and ran at him. Billy turned at the footsteps, threw and missed, then tried to escape up the coke, his pumps sinking out of sight at every step. MacDowall reached the bottom of the heap at full speed, and with his feet pushing off firm ground, dived and landed full length on Billy's back. The coke scrunched, and the lumps were ground together and moulded into shifting waves under the weight.

'Fight! Fight!'

(From *Kes* by Barry Hines, Penguin paperback edition)

Further reading

Argyle M, *Bodily Communication* (Methuen, 1975)

Argyle M, *Person to Person* (Harper & Row, 1979)

Berne E, *Games People Play* (Penguin, 1970)

Morris D, *Gestures* (Jonathan Cape, 1979)

Morris D, *Manwatching* (Jonathan Cape, 1977)

4 *Language and meaning*

This chapter contains the following sections:

- **What is language?**
- **The acquisition of language**
- **Language and meaning**
- **Meaning going astray**
- **Self-assessment**
- **Further work**

What is language?

We all use language in our daily lives, and we all know people who are effective communicators when it comes to using spoken or written words. It is very satisfying to be able to use stylish, elegant language with a sophisticated 'turn of phrase' when the occasion demands it. But there is more to being an effective speaker or writer than the ability to use complex and ornate language; we need to be mindful of our audience when we use language and we need to be sensitive to the particular situation in which we find ourselves. Above all, we need to have the *will* to communicate effectively and to develop an empathy with our listeners or readers to the point that we really care about them and wish to be fully understood. There are times when we need to be sophisticated and times when we need to be simple, but it is fundamentally true that good language is language which is expressed in such a way that it communicates effectively to an audience, while bad language is language which fails to communicate its meaning. With this in mind, we must now try to decide what exactly we mean by the word **language.**

Non-verbal communication can be thought of as a kind of language, whether we think of a simple gesture like 'thumbs up' or a more complex system of signalling like deaf-and-dumb sign language made with the hands and arms. Gestures are usually a symbolic way of sending a message, and the use of symbols to stand for or represent things, thoughts or ideas is one of the hallmarks of what we choose to call language.

Fig. 4.1 '... there is more to being an effective speaker or writer than the ability to use complex and ornate language'

It would be difficult to find one single definition of the word with which everyone would agree; consider the following three statements — what does the word language mean to you in each one?

— Watch your *language*!

— Flowers are the *language* of love.

— Non-verbal communication has its own *language*.

This chapter focuses upon that particular kind of language which we use nearly every day of our lives, and which most commonly springs to mind when we think of what the word means. Our own working definition to suit our present purposes can be: 'Language is a set of sounds made with the voice and the written symbols which represent those sounds.'

Notice that we mention the spoken word first in this definition; just as non-verbal communication pre-dates the spoken word, so the spoken word itself has an infinitely longer history than the written word. People could speak for thousands of years before they could write, and even today there are many people the world over who can speak but not write their own language.

Is it important to study language and the use we make of it? You must decide for yourself, but consider these two points first:

— Language is the most complex and sophisticated means of communication available to an individual. It may not always be the most powerful — we have already said that N.V.C. often has more primitive force than the use of words — but the range of meaning available to us through language is enormous. If you have just read and understood this last sentence, you have been decoding what is after all a very complex message expressed in words. We might take the use of language for granted, but to speak it or to write it is evidence of a very clever and complicated mental activity happening inside our head.

Most of us spend much of our waking life sending or receiving spoken or written messages; an adult speaks on average 30 000 words a day, and a total of 600 million words in an average lifetime. Whether we like it or not, language has a profound effect on our lives which we can hardly ignore. But do only human beings use language?

Many animals communicate with each other using language of a kind. A bird-call can act as a warning to another bird, and a bee returning to a hive with information about the location of a rich source of honey does an elaborate dance to share its knowledge with other bees. Chimpanzees in captivity can learn to push labelled buttons or levers in a certain sequence in order to obtain food. The chimpanzee may signal the following message in this way: 'Please — Mr. Keeper — can — I — have — some — bread — PLEASE!' This, surely, is language of a kind? But chimpanzees have less complex brains than we do, they don't have the same vocal equipment that we have, and they don't have the means that we have available for transmitting language and knowledge from one place to another or from distant generations to the present generation. Above all, the chimpanzee's use of language lacks the full force and range of human language in which a series of spoken sounds or written letters can symbolise so much of human experience in an abstract way.

Language as a system of symbols

'Of all forms of symbolism, language is the most highly developed, most subtle, and most complicated.' (S.I.Hayakawa)

What do we mean when we talk about human language being 'symbolic'? A **symbol** is a sign which stands for or represents something else; that something else which is being symbolised is known as the **object**. Sometimes a sign will actually look like that which it represents — so a cross drawn on a piece of paper

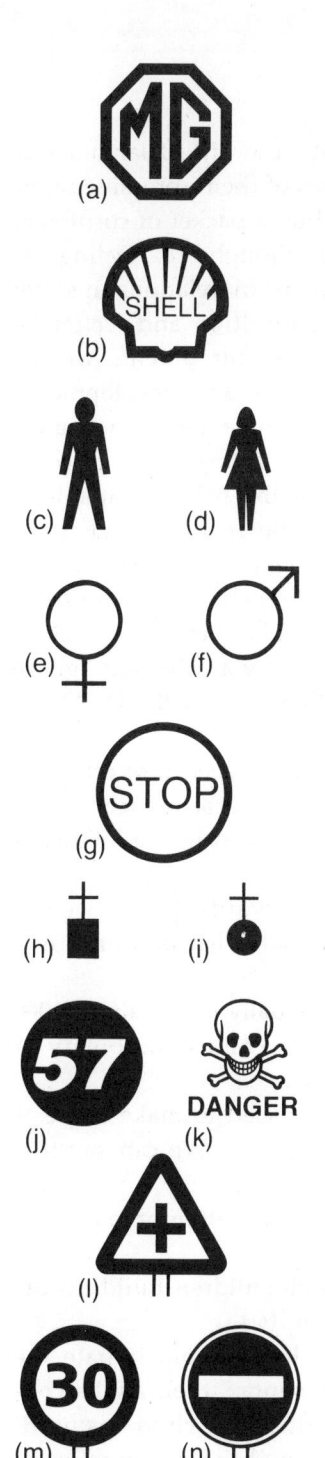

Fig. 4.2

to represent Christianity bears a physical resemblance to the cross on which Jesus was crucified, and the road sign representing a T junction resembles the roads as they appear at such a junction. Signs which resemble their object are known as **icons**.

Now consider a set of traffic lights: in Britain a red light symbolises 'Stop'; a green light symbolises 'Go'; an amber light symbolises 'Prepare to stop' and red and amber together symbolise 'Prepare to go.' Traffic lights employ a symbolic language – each light symbolising a certain message, and the red and amber lights together signalling a different message from red alone or amber alone. But traffic lights are not icons; a red light doesn't physically resemble the action of stopping in the way that a cross on a piece of paper represents a wooden cross used in a crucifixion. What has happened with traffic lights is that we have *agreed* as a society that the red light symbol shall represent 'Stop'; we might be surprised to find that in some states of the U.S.A., for example, a red light has a slightly different meaning, as follows: 'Stop – unless you wish to make a right turn and the road is clear, in which case you may go ...' The meaning conveyed by traffic lights, then, is a matter of convention – we all need to agree what the symbols shall mean.

What does all this have to do with language? Language, like traffic lights, is symbolic but does not consist of icons. There is no physical resemblance between a word and that which it symbolises – so a long word like 'micro-organism' symbolises something very small, while quite a small word like 'whale' relates to a very large creature. Language, like traffic lights, relies for its meaning upon a convention or agreement between the sender and the receiver that a certain symbol shall represent a certain object. Most of the time this works quite well – we agree that the word 'ship' means one thing, while the word 'donkey' means something very different. But if you listen to people involved in a heated argument, you may well find that the root cause of their disagreement centres upon their different interpretations of certain key words. 'Peace' might mean one thing to a member of CND, and something quite different to a supporter of a NATO nuclear policy; 'quality' in education might mean one thing to a person concerned with sexual and racial equality in the classroom, but quite another to a supporter of traditional educational institutions.

Disagreements over the meaning of words are most likely to occur when we are talking about abstract concepts rather than physical objects, and it is a strange but true fact that language and the meaning of words are most likely to let us down precisely when we are talking about the most powerful elements in human experience: love, hate, anger, jealousy, faithfulness, forgiveness ...

We can now build upon our original definition of language, saying that language is a series of symbols, consisting of words which have no physical similarity to that which they are symbolising, but have a meaning agreed upon – in theory, at least – by both sender and receiver.

TASK 1

1. Look at Fig. 4.2. For each sign say what it represents, and then decide whether it is an example of an **icon** or a **symbol**.
2. Write down your own definition of the following words, then compare your interpretation with that of those around you:
   - Fascist
   - Socialist
   - Love
   - Freedom
   - Justice

The acquisition of language

Acquisition in childhood

Of all the gifts ever given to children by their parents, the gift of language is perhaps the most valuable. We need to remind ourselves of the impressive range and versatility of language — how it can enable us to buy a packet of cornflakes in a shop but also allow us to transfer very complex thoughts or feelings to another person. It has its limitations — some problems in relationships, for example, can only be partly solved by words, leaving intuition and feeling to play a major part — but when we learn language from our parents we are receiving as a gift the result of thousands of years of human language development.

We begin to learn in childhood, then, languages which have taken thousands of years to evolve. Learning a language when we are very young seems to come very easily to us: in the first two months of life, any healthy baby is capable of making all the sounds necessary to speak every language in the world. Even sounds which we find difficult and have to re-learn later in life if we study a foreign language — like a pure 'u' sound in French, or a French 'r' pronounced at the back of the throat — are natural to a young baby. What happens, of course, is that parents respond to and reinforce certain sounds made by a baby, and ignore others. Why do you think the first word spoken by a baby is usually 'Da-Da' — even said when the baby is looking at his or her mother?

A child learns to make individual sounds by imitating the speech of others — but these sounds need to be put together in an acceptable sequence if true language is to be the result. Language can be usefully classified in the following way:

— **Lexis**. This refers to the vocabulary of a language — the words it uses; we can talk about the **lexical** features of a language, and say that a list of words is a **lexicon.**

By the time a child is three years old, he or she can usually speak about 1000 words, and understand a total of 2000. At that stage, the child's vocabulary or lexical store of material is growing by leaps and bounds.

— **Syntax**. This refers to the order in which words are placed to make sense — that is, the **grammar** and **grammatical structure** of a language. We can say that language has **syntactical** features.

We shall return to these terms later in this chapter when we attempt to analyse dialect varieties of language.

Not all linguists agree on the precise manner in which children build up the ability to construct syntactically-accurate sentences or units.

The **behaviourist** school of thought claims that children simply imitate the syntax of people around them; if a child uses 'correct' syntax, then adults congratulate him or her and thus reinforce the linguistic pattern the child has used.

If you had a young child who had been saying 'I caught' for a number of months, but then suddenly said 'I catched', would you be glad or disappointed? Why? What rules of language might the child be learning or applying?

Other linguists, like Naom Chomsky, believe that every child in the world is born with a deep-seated, intuitive knowledge from birth of a **deep structure** or blueprint for language which makes the learning of its own particular language an easy matter. Chomsky believes that all languages throughout the world may be different on the surface, but that they all share this fundamental deep structure.

In other words, those who belong to the behaviourist school of thought believe that a child begins life with a blank mind, a *tabula rasa*, upon which language is imprinted over time as the child experiments and copies others; the deep structure

Fig. 4.3 By the time a child is three years old, he/she can usually speak about 1000 words

school of thought believes that a programme for language already exists in the child's mind, waiting to be activated by contact with the language of others.

Try to tape-record a very young child speaking. What range of vocabulary does it have? What use does it make of word order? Do you get the feeling listening to the child that it is simply imitating other people, or is it slowly developing an understanding of language based upon an already-existing 'deep structure'?

As we grow older, we do develop an understanding of the rules of grammar which exist within our own language and apply them without conscious effort. We know almost by instinct, it seems, that we should say '*I* saw *him*' and '*He* saw *me*', and we change 'I' to 'me' and 'he' to 'him' according to a pattern we have learned over the years, but might find it hard to explain to anyone else.

In English, word order is more vital than it is in Latin. Our hidden rules tell us that the following conversation has no real meaning because the word order is wrong:

'Hill climbed up the I.'

'Really, Oh? English strange what speak you!'

To learn a foreign language, of course, involves understanding a new set of rules about word order. If we were to translate literally from French, we would talk of 'a boat red' ('un bateau rouge'), while the German phrase 'Ich habe den Mann gesehen' would translate as: 'I have the man seen'.

Many languages used today do in fact come from one common root language of thousands of years ago — English and a wide variety of other languages are said to have developed from an original Indo-European language or group of languages. What this means is that, despite the surface differences, many languages do share a good deal in common in terms of structure.

Structure in language

When we talk about 'structure' in language, we are referring to those rules which must be applied when linking words together to form sentences. We have seen how important word order is when making statements that convey meaning to someone else, but even within the accepted rules of word order, the possibilities open to us are enormous. If you were to speak aloud all the 20 word sentences theoretically available to you in the English language, it would take ten million, million years to do so! That gives everyone— not just linguistic geniuses like Shakespeare — the chance to make a number of totally original statements in a lifetime if he or she feels so inclined. Of course it is possible to construct a sentence which follows the rules of grammar, but which still fails to have any meaning: 'Bright woolly jungles sleep peacefully in otherwise truthful bungalows'. Does this sentence follow the rules of grammar? Can you construct another one like it which makes as little real sense?

TASK 2

The following extract is part of a poem from *Through the Looking-Glass* by Lewis Carroll, and is an example of a nonsense language he calls 'Jabberwocky'.

Although most of the words used in the poem are nonsense, the general structure of the language, and all the linking words like 'and' and 'the' are perfectly standard and normal.

1. Read through the extract and substitute a 'normal' word for each of the words in italics e.g. 'Twas *Easter* and the . . .'

Twas *brilling*, and the *slithy toves*
Did *gyre* and *gimble* in the *wabe*;
All *mimsy* were the *borogoves*,
And the *mome raths outgrabe*.

2. Now compile a list of all the alternatives used by the class and decide whether each alternative is:

— A noun, i.e. the name of an object, person or place e.g. brick, Peter, Edinburgh.

— An adjective, i.e. a word which desribes a noun e.g. red, large, funny.

— A verb, i.e. a word that indicates an action taking place e.g. I throw, he coughed, she pondered.

What you will almost certainly find is that everyone, whatever word they have substituted, will have chosen a word from the same group, i.e. noun, adjective, verb. Has everyone in your class chosen a verb as a substitute for 'gimble', for example?

This exercise indicates just how deep-seated our sense of structure in language really is. As we speak, read or listen, we are constantly expecting and anticipating what will come next — we expect to find a verb of some sort in the poem after the word 'did', and would be happy with nothing else.

Are you so familiar with language that you can predict what somebody is about to say while they are speaking? Do your conversations with friends consist of someone interrupting someone else once it is clear what the speaker means? Look at the following example of a conversation; Sarah knows what Jane is about to say, and can interrupt her unfinished sentence without being thought rude:

Jane: 'I nearly had a nasty accident yesterday. I walked over to Paul's school and I'd almost reached the gates, but you know what it was like — it snowed all morning and when I came to that icy patch near the . . .'

Sarah: 'I know — I nearly injured myself on that same patch outside the shops . . .'

What Sarah is doing here is using her knowledge of the structure of language to predict what she has not yet heard.

Do you know anyone who refuses to be interrupted and insists on finishing every sentence? Do you find conversation with such a person difficult?

TASK 3 A good example of an exercise which focuses upon the structure of language and is often used in schools to test a pupil's ability in comprehension is the *cloze* exercise. Complete the following example by writing down the words you think are missing from the story:

'A few years ago in Kabul a man appeared, looking _____ his brother. He asked all _____ merchants of the market place if they _____ seen his brother and told them where he _____ staying in case _____ brother arrived and wanted _____ find him.'
(*Answers at the end of this chapter*)

How many did you get right? This should have been an easy exercise, as all the words omitted carry very little of the vital meaning of the passage. Now try the next paragraph in the story:

'The next year he was back and repeated the _____. By this time one of the members of the American _____ had heard about his _____ and asked if he had found his brother. The man answered that he and his brother had _____ to meet in Kabul, but neither of them had said what year.'
(*Answers at the end of this chapter*)

This should have proved more difficult — the words omitted are harder to predict, and there are more choices.

As we read words on a page or listen to words spoken, our minds are active, not passive; we are busy sorting the language received into a number of categories: words which are vital to the meaning, words which are less vital to the meaning. We tend, therefore, to skip over words like 'and' and 'the' much of the time, reserving our main energies and attention for those vital words which convey the heart of the message. Our perception of each word is rather different according to its function as a carrier of essential meaning.

A skilled eavesdropper could probably reconstruct an overheard conversation between two people quite successfully if only a handful of key words were picked up clearly. But as we read the written or printed word we may have a range of options open to us: you may skim-read a newspaper article or a light novel, whereas you would pay close attention to every word of a complex poem which didn't yield its meaning immediately. A proof reader employed by a publishing company whose job it was to check the printed accuracy of a text would need to read each word in a very mechanical way, paying as much attention to the correctness of spelling and printing as to the meaning. It is even rumoured that some proof readers read their texts backwards! Why might this be an appropriate technique in the circumstances?

Language and meaning

Fig. 4.4 Words don't mean; people mean

The general study of the relationship between language and meaning is usually referred to as **semantics**. It can be a fascinating but also a complicated subject, and reference to a book entitled *Language in Thought and Action* by S.I. Hayakawa for an intelligent but entertaining introduction to this field of study is recommended.

The meaning of a word depends upon all sorts of factors, not the least of which is the **intention** of the speaker or writer who uses that word. One person may use the word 'Socialist' in a favourable way, while someone else might use the same word as an insult. It is sometimes said that 'Words don't mean; people mean'.

The context within which a word is used affects its meaning. The word 'nature' carries a different meaning in each of the following sentences:
– He has a very nice *nature*;
– We went on a *nature* walk.

Meaning also depends upon **geographical factors.** To call someone 'homely' in England would mean that they were down-to-earth, unpretentious, or even cosy – while to an American the same word would refer to someone plain or even ugly in appearance. A road sign at a level crossing which read 'Do not cross while the lights are flashing' might be very clear to someone from the South of England but might well be interpreted differently in the North, with the meaning: 'Do not cross *until* the lights are flashing'.

We examine geographical differences of this sort later in the next chapter when we have a closer look at dialect. For the time being, we must remember that meaning in language is not always as fixed and precise as we might believe. A further complication is that words have a habit of changing their meaning with time e.g. the word 'gay' has acquired a quite new meaning in the last few decades, and reading literature written a few hundred years ago in English might send us running for a dictionary. A dictionary, however, cannot be relied upon to tell us exactly what a word means but rather what a word *almost* means. The words given in a definition do not have a completely different meaning from the key word but rather they have a slightly different shade or **nuance** of meaning.

Encoding and decoding

We have already seen in Chapter 2 that when we turn a message which exists inside our heads into language – either spoken or written – then we are engaged in the activity of **encoding**. The listener or reader, hearing or reading and then understanding our message, is engaged in the activity of **decoding**. We can encode and decode messages using a number of different media – we might choose to draw a picture, for example – but here we are concerned specifically with spoken and written language. Sometimes our message is received and understood in the way in which we intended it to be; at other times we may be misunderstood — there may be a **communication breakdown.**

In practice, this explanation of encoding and decoding may be too simple. Do we think first and then speak afterwards, or do we think aloud in words? Have you ever found that you can clarify your thoughts by putting them into words? Have you ever found yourself saying something that you hardly knew that you knew before you said it? Do you ever think aloud by talking to yourself?

In fact the distinction between a thought and the words which express that thought is in many ways a false one — the thought and the words are often mixed up together.

Can people with no experience of language think? How? To some extent the thoughts available to us are limited by the language available to us. Do people with a wide vocabulary have more complex thoughts?

Some people would claim that the language available to us also affects our perception of the world around us — they say that because there are 13 different words for 'snow' in the Eskimo languages, then Eskimos perceive 13 different kinds of snow in a way that those of us living in warmer climes would not. Does that seem to you to be a reasonable argument?

We have deliberately posed a number of questions in this section, just touching upon some of the main problems faced by linguists studying the large and complex area of meaning in language.

Denotation and connotation

The meaning which any given word has for us may be composed of a number of different levels or layers. The word 'pig' is in many ways a simple and precise word referring to an animal we might see in a farmyard. This simple and straightforward meaning is called the word's **denotation** — the word 'denotes' or refers, to the animal itself. But 'pig' may mean something else, depending upon the situation or context. Someone may wish to brand a man a 'Male Chauvinist Pig', or a New York policeman may be called a 'pig' as an insulting term. Now we are dealing with a different layer of meaning which has to do with the associations the word has for us, and the ideas or feelings it triggers off in our mind or emotions. This is what we speak of as the **connotations** of the word — the extra meanings a word has because of what we associate with it.

Some connotations are shared by many people — so few individuals would fail to have some unpleasant feelings when the word 'rat' is mentioned. Other words have differing connotations depending upon the culture in which they are used, or even upon the individual — so the word 'tomato' has special connotations if

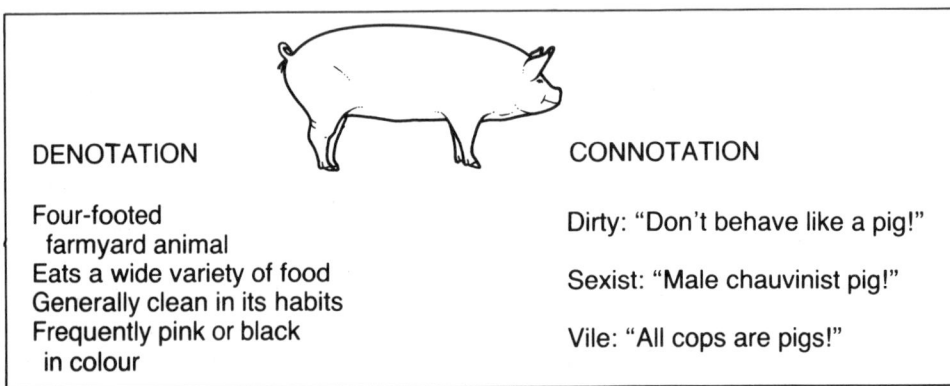

DENOTATION

Four-footed
 farmyard animal
Eats a wide variety of food
Generally clean in its habits
Frequently pink or black
 in colour

CONNOTATION

Dirty: "Don't behave like a pig!"

Sexist: "Male chauvinist pig!"

Vile: "All cops are pigs!"

Fig. 4.5 Do you think the connotations listed here are unfair to the poor hapless farmyard animal?

eating tomatoes makes you sick, and the name Mandy might be special if you were once very fond of a girl with that name.

There is a well-known phrase in *Romeo and Juliet* by Shakespeare: 'That which we call a rose by any other name would smell as sweet.' Is this true? Would a rose smell as sweet if you called it 'dung'? Is the word 'dung' itself a dirty word, or does it just have certain special connotations for you?

Emotive language   People frequently use words or phrases which have very strong connotations for the listener or reader; they may do so unconsciously, or they may — like some advertisers, journalists, politicians and others — use words with strong connotations quite deliberately, to shock or manipulate the feelings of others.

Language with powerful connotations which affects our feelings and emotions is called **emotive language**. So: 'Soap is *cheap* this week.' Here the word 'cheap' has its usual and non-emotive meaning of 'not expensive'. 'He played a *cheap* trick.' Here the word 'cheap' has an effect upon our emotions through the connotations it has of deceit and underhand trickery.

We tend to use emotive language to suit our own purposes. A person who works while colleagues are on strike might be greeted with the taunt of 'blackleg' or 'scab' — both strongly emotive words — while some employers might prefer to think of such a person as an 'independent worker'. A 'terrorist' to one person might be a 'freedom fighter' to another, and a 'yob' to one person might simply be a 'youngster' to another.

 *4*

1. Look at the sentences below, and then (a) define what the word 'common' means in each case and (b) say whether the word is being used emotively or not:
   - The lowest *common* factor;
   - They played football on the *common*;
   - He was a *common* lout;
   - He lacks *common* decency.
2. Look at the following list of words and decide whether each usually (a) has favourable connotations (b) has unfavourable connotations or (c) is more or less neutral:
   Slovenly; dapper; uncouth; merry; puny; juvenile; infant; infantile.
3. Pick out the emotive words from the following extract from Adolf Hitler's *Mein Kampf* (from a translation by James Murphy):

   'It must not be forgotten that the present rulers of Russia are blood-stained criminals, that here we have the dregs of humanity which, favoured by circumstance of a tragic moment, overran a great state, degraded and destroyed millions of educated people out of sheer blood-lust, and now for nearly ten years they have ruled with such savage tyranny as was never known before.'

We can summarise the difference between denotation and connotation in the following table:

DENOTATION	CONNOTATION
is:	*is*:
Factual	Emotive
Objective	Subjective
is used to:	*is used to*:
Inform	Persuade
Explain	Insult or praise
Report	Sell
Describe	Motivate

Levels of meaning Some linguists argue that the connotations that certain words have can account for up to 60% of their meaning — and we must expect many words to have at least two levels or layers of meaning, consisting of denotation and connotation.

But human beings have a habit of making life even more complicated when they communicate through language. There would be fewer problems if everyone said what they meant all the time but they don't always do so, or not in a direct and straightforward way. Imagine a blazing row between a husband and wife sparked off by the husband asking the question: 'Have you mowed the lawn yet?' The question might sound innocent enough, but depending upon the timing and the precise tone of voice used, the wife may or may not be justified in believing that the true meaning behind the words was something like: 'I've been working ever since breakfast time, while you appear to have been lazing around — look — you haven't even mowed the lawn!' Similarly, an encounter between two neighbours in which one said: 'Nice day, isn't it?' will probably not really be a conversation about the weather, but just a way of one person saying to another: 'I'm a pleasant person who would like to communicate with you — let's strike up a conversation talking about something neutral, until we can find some other topic of mutual interest.' This kind of verbal interchange — usually referred to as 'small talk' — is known as **phatic** communication; its main function being to oil the wheels of interpersonal communication.

There are therefore more layers of meaning in language than we might imagine. Supposing you read an advertisement in a newspaper which says: 'Great men drive Jaguars', beneath the surface of this direct statement is a further message being hinted at or suggested, something like: 'If you drive a Jaguar, then you become a great man'. Such a suggested further message underlying the simple meaning of the words is known as **implication**. The sender of such a message **implies** more than is obvious on the surface; if the receiver picks up the implication and understands it, then the sender **infers**, or makes an **inference**. Very similar to the use of implication is what is referred to as **innuendo** (from the Latin, meaning 'by nodding'); to make an innuendo is to make a hint to your listener without being completely frank and open. To turn to a back-seat driver and say: 'I do love a bit of peace and quiet when I'm driving, don't you?', would be an indirect way of hinting that the person should stop talking.

To fully understand human language in use involves an awareness of such different layers of meaning; we seem to enjoy from a fairly early age the game of saying one thing but meaning another. Nowhere is this more obvious than in the use of **irony** or **sarcasm.** Supposing you were at a party, and a friend approached you and said 'Great party, isn't it?' These words could be accompanied by a smile or a laugh, and an excitement in the voice — in which case the words could be taken quite literally and you would know that your friend was having a wonderful time. But supposing the same person said the same words but using different non-verbal signals: her arms hung loosely at her side, her eyes turned towards the ceiling, a bored tone in her voice and a scowl on her face? Suddenly the message would be completely different: your friend was bored to tears, thoroughly fed up. You would know that she was being **ironical**. There are two interesting points to note about this example of irony:

— Irony consists in saying precisely the opposite of what you really mean — a device which must make us think about layers of meaning very carefully indeed!

— You will not understand the true message being sent by a person using irony unless you pay very careful attention to the non-verbal signals. The words themselves are of no help to you — they are not a true statement of fact at all — and you must put all your trust in your ability to decode non-verbal messages.

There is a very fine dividing line between irony and **sarcasm**; you might consider that a person who said 'Great party, isn't it?' accompanied by a scowl was being not just ironical, but also sarcastic. We usually use the word 'sarcasm' when we wish to talk about irony which is used in a hurtful way, or as a means of insulting someone or putting them down — it would be the technique you were using if you shouted out 'Great shot!' sarcastically at a footballer who had just sliced the ball and missed the goal by a wide margin. Pupils in schools and students in colleges often accuse their teachers of being sarcastic. Would you agree? What are your own feelings about the use of sarcasm in interpersonal communication?

Meaning going astray

The fact that there are sometimes several layers of meaning in operation when people communicate through language means that a very close rapport or understanding needs to exist between a sender and a receiver if messages are to be transmitted and understood with accuracy. People who share a similar culture and values and already have a strong rapport will usually communicate with ease, often knowing what the other person is about to say even before words are uttered. But if there is any significant cultural discrepancy between individuals, then every message will need to be encoded and decoded very carefully and fully. We even say of some people: 'They don't speak my language' — meaning that they view life in a very different way from ourselves, have different thoughts and different values, making communication rather difficult.

In any communication which uses language, there are responsibilities carried by both the sender and the receiver:
— The **sender** must be as clear and precise as possible, being particularly careful to bear in mind the special needs of the receiver. So it would be important to speak quite loudly to a person with hearing difficulties; to speak fairly slowly and simply to a person who did not speak the same language very fluently; to use simple language when talking to, or writing for, a child. This need to be sensitive to those who listen to you or who read what you have written is a vital element in effective communication; you must have an awareness of your **audience**.
— The **receiver** needs to pay close attention to the message being sent. If the message is a written one, it will need to be read with care; if a message is spoken, then the receiver will have to listen carefully — not just to the words being said, but also to other clues to the meaning such as tone of voice and non-verbal signals. Just as a sender must bear in mind any particular problems encountered by the receiver, so the receiver might have to make due allowances for a sender's difficulties in transmitting spoken or written messages. Another of the receiver's responsibilities is to provide the sender with **feedback** whenever a message isn't clear — so you might say: 'I'm sorry — would you mind saying that again?' or 'What exactly do you mean by "light gauge" guitar strings?'

Let's consider an example of language in action. Supposing you worked in the despatch department of a large company and you received a note headed: 'This order is very urgent.' What would it mean to you? Has the sender made his or her message clear? How urgent is 'urgent'? Does it mean within the week or within the day? You might provide feedback by telephoning the person who had sent the note and asking for clarification, in which case a more precise message may be provided: 'This order needs to be completed by 3 p.m. on Friday, 21st August, 1987.'

TASK 5 Here are four examples of statements that might be misunderstood or poorly understood. Expand each one so that its message becomes clear. You are free to invent details of your own in order to provide a model of a clear memo in each case.

1. Let me have the caravan towing bars as soon as you can.
2. We must reduce costs this year.
3. We must increase our profits this year.
4. All orders must be dealt with as soon as possible.

It is worth remembering that the sender of a message will often assume that it is the receiver's fault if a message isn't understood — especially in a company or institution where the sender enjoys a higher status than the receiver. Many communication problems could be avoided by the sender simply inviting feedback wherever appropriate: 'Is that clear?' 'Would you like me to go over that again?'

Very often the difference between successful and unsuccessful communication in language is a matter of small and subtle differences in the way in which a message is expressed. Supposing a husband and wife sat down to dinner one evening to eat a meal cooked by the husband, and the wife said: 'Where did you get this meat?' Would the husband feel complimented or insulted? How might the question have been re-phrased to alter its meaning if it *was* intended as a compliment?

We have already noted the fact that the English language depends very heavily upon correct word order if a message is to be clear and precise in its meaning. One misplaced word can cause real problems. What is wrong with the sentence: 'My coat needs cleaning badly.'?

If we take a simple enough word like 'only' we can demonstrate the problems and pitfalls. You might read a notice on a park gate which said: '*Only* dogs on a lead allowed in this park.' There is a problem in communication here: are the owners of these dogs excluded from the park? Try to decide what the sender really meant, and re-phrase the sentence accordingly.

Now try putting the word 'only' in as many different places as possible in the following sentence: 'In Wales the red tulips grow on the green hills'. (For example: 'Only in Wales ...', 'In Wales only ...' etc.) How and when does the meaning change?

Ambiguity Sometimes we may speak or write a message using language which could be interpreted in more than one way. We know exactly what we mean, but the receiver may have real problems deciding which of two or more possible meanings is the intended one. This ability of language to carry more than one meaning is known as **ambiguity**, and we might describe a message as being **ambiguous**. It would be wrong to pretend that ambiguity puts communication at peril every minute of every day, but a study of ambiguity can be vital in reminding us of the need for precision and accuracy in our use of language.

Often the sender is unaware that he or she has been ambiguous until the fact is pointed out by the receiver. How might each of the following be misunderstood?
— Moments later she was laughing again as she wiped the dishes with her daughter.
— Why kill yourself with your weekly wash? Use electricity instead!
— All the teachers in our school are certified.

TASK 6 Each of the following statements is ambiguous in some way. For each try to write down as clearly as you can what you think each writer *intended* to mean, and then what the statement *apparently* means. (For example: 'Wanted: Plumber to put in cold water tank.' *Intended* meaning: 'A plumber is required to install a cold water tank'. *Apparent* meaning: 'A plumber is required to be dropped into a cold water tank'. *Be careful*: your own explanations must not be as ambiguous as the original statements!)

— H.C. Parr of Glasgow was second in the class for dairy shorthorn cows.
— Meat shortage: MPs attack minister.
— Balloon race: six drop out.
— Bikini schoolgirl is suspended by head.
— General MacArthur flies back to front.

— Super train talks.
— Indian women make beautiful carpets.
— Injury forces Connors to scratch.
— Reagan picks his spot.
— Vietnamese families settle in well.

You might like to make your own collection of examples of language which fails to achieve what it sets out to do because of unfortunate phrasing, misspelling or printing errors. Newspapers can be a good hunting ground, as can holidays abroad. Your collection might include items like the following:

— Take your pick for our pastries;
— If you are satisfactory, tell your friends; if you are unsatisfactory, warn the waitress;
— Please don't lay any stranger bodies in the W.C.;
— Colonel Jones was a battle-scared veteran;
— Colonel Jones was a bottle-scarred veteran;
— Four miles away Officer Tippitt was shot by his patrol car;
— I got lost in the dessert;
— The acting was bad; the scenery was poor; the play was a flob.

We examine language and language use in more detail in Chapter 5. To round off this chapter, here is a simplified model on the subject of 'language and meaning' which incorporates much of what we have been looking at so far. You might like to use it for revision purposes, or to bring together your own ideas on language and meaning based upon the topics we have covered so far.

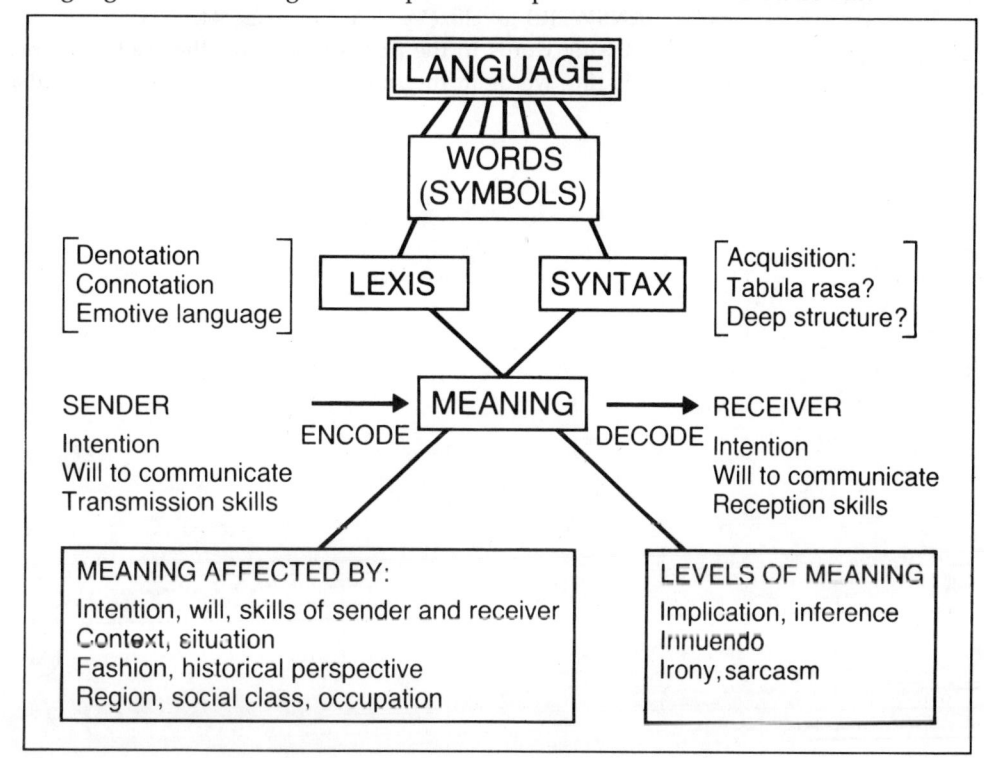

Fig. 4.6 Language and meaning: a simplified model

Self-assessment

1. Write down your own definition of 'language'.
2. Define: symbol; icon.
3. How does a child acquire language?
4. Define: encoding; decoding.
5. Define: denotation; connotation.
6. What is 'emotive language' and what does it attempt to do?
7. What is the difference between 'implication' and 'inference'?
8. What is ambiguity?

Further work

1. Find *two* advertisements from newspapers or magazines which use emotive language. Cut these out and stick them on a piece of paper or photocopy them. Write a brief account beneath each advertisement, pointing out its use of emotive language and its attempts to persuade the reader.
2. Form a small group of people. The group's task is to invent an imaginary product. First, write a factual, denotative description of your product; secondly, write an advertisement for your product using emotive language which might persuade someone to buy it. Use your second account as a 'radio advert' to be tape-recorded. Play back each recorded advert. What techniques were used? Would people have been persuaded to buy your product?
3. Write an essay with the following title: Discuss the proposition that 'human language is a unique and complex means of communication'.

A Further reading list on the subject of 'language' can be found on p.70.

ANSWERS to 'cloze' exercise on page 44.
Missing words in the first passage: for; the; had; was; his; to.
Missing words in the second passage: performance; Embassy; inquiries; agreed.

5 *Language in use*

This chapter contains the following sections:
- **Spoken and written language**
- **Dialect and accent**
- **Appropriate language**
- **Self-assessment**
- **Further work**
- **Further reading**

Spoken and written language

We have already noted the fact that human beings could speak before they could write, and even in our own print-dominated world, no matter how much at home we may feel when writing or reading the written word, much of our daily experience is still dominated by the activities of speaking and listening.

Speech is usually used in face-to-face situations and may be reinforced or complemented by non-verbal signals and by the use of the voice to put across special shades of meaning. Writing tends to be rather more formal, except in the case of relaxed and informal letter writing, for example, and when we use the written word we can think at greater length about exactly what we wish to say and even revise what we have written if necessary.

When we listen to someone else speaking, the speed of delivery of the message or messages is determined by the sender; when we read the written word, however, we can more or less adopt a reading speed which suits us, and can return to re-read parts of the message if we wish.

Whether it is more appropriate to use speech or writing for any given message depends very much upon the situation in which we find ourselves.

TASK 1

1. Give *three* examples of situations in which speech would be a more appropriate medium than writing.
2. Give *three* examples of situations in which writing would be a more appropriate medium than speech.
3. Give *three* examples of situations in which you would wish to reinforce the written word with the spoken word, or vice-versa.

British education and its public examinations have tended to undervalue the spoken word until fairly recently; you will find no shortage of text books dealing with written formats like the Report, the Memo, the Essay or the Letter, but it is only in the last few years that a significant number of course books have appeared for use in schools and colleges which recognise the fact that speaking and listening are skills which need to be learned and practised if effective communication is to take place.

This chapter places particular emphasis upon the spoken word, but also looks at ways in which speech and writing differ as means of communication.

Spoken English   Many languages used throughout the world, French or Italian for example, are **phonetic** languages — that is, any given letter is usually pronounced in the same way every time we read it, and once we have learned the sound represented by each letter, we should be able to pronounce any word whether we have seen it before or not. English is not like this; it is a mongrel language of mixed ancestry, and we can never be sure that any given letter will be pronounced in the same way every time we come across it, nor that the same sound will always be represented by the same letter or letters.

TASK 2

1. Write down *two* words each containing the letter 'c', where the way in which we pronounce the 'c' is different in each word.
2. Do the same for the letter 'g'.
3. It is possible to talk of a hard 'c' and a soft 'c' and of a hard 'g' and a soft 'g'. Can you decide which is which from your answers to questions 1 and 2?
4. Write down as many words as you can which contain the letters 'ough', with the 'ough' part being pronounced differently in each word.
5. Consider the sound 'or' in the word 'cork'. Write down all the ways you can think of in which this particular sound may be represented in writing, e.g. t*augh*t, etc.
6. Consider the words 'tr*ough*', 'w*o*men' and 'na*ti*on'. Can you see how the imaginary word 'ghoti' might be pronounced if you were feeling in a frivolous mood?
7. Give *two* different pronunciations for each of the following words, and indicate in each case how the *two* change the meaning of the word: tear; read; bow.

Pronouncing English correctly, then, is no easy matter — not even for a native speaker of English, never mind for a person who has to learn it as a second or third language.

The root of the problem is this: there are 45 different sound units we use when we are speaking, but in writing we only have the 26 letters of the alphabet to help us. Sometimes two or more letters in combination give us a special sound, e.g. *ch*urch; tro*ph*y; rou*gh*; *th*ink. Can you think of other letter combinations which give a special sound? Is the 'th' combination pronounced in the same way in the words '*th*ese' and '*th*ink'? If there is a difference, can you describe it?

The commonest single sound in English is the short 'er' sound in the word 'father'; yet this sound can be spelt in so many different ways, e.g. *a*live, p*o*lite, etc.

Think of words which you find difficulty in spelling — does the word 'separate' give you problems, for example? How many of your problems are caused by the need to represent this 'er' sound we are talking about?

During the late 19th century a special alphabet was agreed upon which could be used to represent sounds exactly; it is known as the International Phonetic Alphabet (IPA) and would be used, for example, by students of dialect.

In IPA one sound is represented by one letter or symbol only; so whenever the short 'er' sound is pronounced, it is represented by this symbol ə. So the word 'father' would be written as ƒa:ǂə.

Would you approve of the idea of English spelling being completely altered — of using a phonetic alphabet like the IPA, for instance, instead of the complicated spelling we now use? Could you foresee any complications? Wouldn't it mean that a person from the North of England would then spell a word like 'grass' differently to a person from the South?

Spoken English in   Imagine you are listening to a conversation between two close friends, Jill and
action   Paul, in which words are flowing freely and both speakers are feeling relaxed.

What *exactly* is being said by each speaker? The answer may surprise you. As you listen to a person speaking, your brain is busy decoding the key elements in the message being transmitted, and to do this it filters out a great deal of material which it finds irrelevant or redundant, and may even fill in gaps left by the speaker.

A typical conversation between two reasonably fluent people would appear like this if you wrote down every word being said and every sound being made:

> Jill: 'So he thought it'd be nice to to go on this ... what'd'you call it Pennine Way Walk last week it's erm it's across country as far as well it starts just north of the border and it's ...'
>
> Paul: 'Didn't he didn't he do that last year with his father or ...'
>
> Jill: 'Yeh and this time his father he's about oo er sixty or somethin' says he wants to go again and his father (chuckle...) his father gets upset 'cos his car gets stuck at er Yet ... Yetholm or some place and ...'
>
> Paul: 'Ha I bet he was really mad he's ...'
>
> Jill: 'Mad you're not kiddin' he thinks that car's well it cost him about ten thousand you know ...'

What we have here is called a **transcription** of the spoken word — that is, every word or sound has been faithfully recorded and written down or transcribed. Notice that the transcription is not punctuated in the way that normal written English would be. Do you think it should have been? Notice also that to leave a space between each word is only something you do when you are writing English; a speaker will run words together with no such gaps. We would write 'Are you all right?', but a speaker would say: 'Areyouallright?'

Try to do some transcription work of your own; tape record a conversation and then make a written transcript of what is said, or use a ready-made tape recording of conversation such as *Advanced Conversational English* by David Crystal and Derek Davy (Longman Group, 1975).

 **TASK 3**

1. Look back at the conversation between Jill and Paul; make a list of all the features of spoken English which appear there, i.e. every feature which tells you that this is a transcription of a real conversation, not a piece of written English as such.
2. Now compare your list with the following list — and write down one example from the transcription of each feature mentioned:
   (a) Repetition;
   (b) Contractions, i.e. words being shortened in some way;
   (c) Words omitted;
   (d) Pauses or gaps;
   (e) 'Fillers' i.e. words or sounds which are used to keep the flow of language going, without having much of a part to play in the message itself;
   (f) False starts to a word, or false starts to a sentence.
3. Translate this same conversation into a piece of flowing written English of the sort you would use if you were writing direct speech in an essay or a short story. You might begin like this:
   > 'So he thought it would be nice to go on the Pennine Way Walk last week — it involves walking across country ...'
   Note carefully what changes you have to make from the original.
4. Try to decide whether each of the following examples is a piece of written English or a transcription from a real conversation. Give your reasons in each case:
   (a) 'Listen — these two blokes I know that are stewards have been flying exactly six years — and they've been all over the place — and they — Paris, Lisbon, Cairo — every

place — on their passes you know — and this one guy met this girl in — eh — Paris and . . .'

(b) 'Two men that I know have been working as stewards for the airlines, and have been flying exactly six years. They have travelled extensively and visited a number of large cities. One man worked on the Paris route and met a girl who was to become his wife.'

(c) 'It's built up all the way so for goodness sake watch your speed. Then you'll see a big park with green railings on the left — oh, I forget — they're digging up that bit of road . . .'

(d) 'You see that bit there. Well, if you pull it over this way you'll see the switch, Right? There we go. Watch your fingers underneath. There — see what I mean?'

When speaking you can add variety to language by the use of a number of devices listed below. We call these **paralinguistic** features of language — that is, features that have to do less with *what* you say than *how* you say it.

— **Volume**. You vary your volume when you are speaking, consciously or unconsciously, according to the situation in which you find yourself. Try to say what would be the appropriate volume to use in each of the following examples, giving your reasons in each case:

1. Making an announcement in front of a class of school pupils.
   'The arrangements we have made are as follows . . .'
2. Telling a child a story at bedtime: 'Once upon a time there were three little pigs . . .'
3. Stopping a passer-by to ask directions: 'Excuse me, but could you tell me . . .'

— **Stress**. You can stress certain words you are saying in order to emphasise them. Sometimes by choosing to stress a particular word you can affect the meaning: *John* ran to the railway station. (Here you are emphasising the fact that it was John, not someone else, who ran to the station.) John *ran* to the railway station. (Here you want to stress the fact that he ran, and didn't just walk.)

Consider the following sentence: 'The man in the showroom told me the video game was £20.' Try speaking this sentence aloud a number of times, giving one word or a number of words extra stress so as to bring out each of the meanings emphasised in the following:

1. It wasn't the *woman* in the showroom who told me.
2. It wasn't the man in the *accounts department* who told me.
3. The man in the showroom made a point of *telling* me the price, not just handing me a price list.
4. The man didn't tell me the *mechanical football* game was £20.
5. The man told me that £20 was the *old price* — and that the game now costs £25.

— **Tone**. Some people are said to have *monotonous* voices — that is, they speak in what is called a *monotone*, never raising or lowering the pitch as they speak. Generally speaking, the more variety of tone put into your voice, the better — you hold the attention of your listener much more easily and are a more effective communicator.

Read aloud each of the three sentences which follow as if you were (a) amazed (b) curious (c) angry (d) sympathetic:

1. 'Hello — when did you get back?'
2. 'I've just heard.'
3. 'What did you say?'

What did you notice about the tone of your voice in each case?

— **Pace**. Spoken English varies in pace and rhythm — unlike the written word, which comes at you in a steady and unchanging flow. Speakers also pause from time to time; how are pauses indicated in written English?

Read aloud each of the following at an appropriate pace and with suitable pauses:

1. Talking to a large audience in a big, echoing hall: 'Ladies and gentlemen I would like to explain the various parts of this building to you first there is the reception area ...'
2. Reading from an exciting story full of action: 'Suddenly he grasped Bond by the throat almost choking him to death until suddenly 007 answered back with a "thud" in the man's chest he sent him reeling ...'

If you want to hear paralinguistic features of language used to brilliant effect, listen to actors or comedians who speak in public for a living. Note carefully how they use volume, stress, tone, pace and pause to devastating effect, creating comedy and manipulating their audience in the process.

Dialect and accent

Dialect Everyone has a **dialect**. It may be that when speaking you use a standard form of the English language — 'B.B.C.' or 'Oxford' English as it is sometimes known, which is a dialect in its own right — or you may use a non-standard dialect because of the area in which you live, your occupation or the social class to which you belong.

English and Russian are sufficiently different to be thought of as different **languages**, but Geordie and Cockney are different English **dialects**. A dialect is a variety which exists within a language and has its own vocabulary and grammar which makes it distinct from other varieties.

When you were a child playing games in the playground and you wanted a moment or two's pause from the game, did you use a special 'truce term' which you said aloud to indicate that you weren't playing for a while? You might have said 'Kings' or 'Crosses', 'Barley', 'Fainites', 'Skinch', 'Cree' or 'Keys'? Which word you used would be related to the area in which you lived, each being a dialect term dependent upon geographical area.

Look at Fig. 5.1; your own particular 'truce term' should appear; is the map accurate as far as your region is concerned?

Have you ever heard, or do you ever use, the word Mardy, referring to a spoilt child, a soft person or a cry-baby? If the word is familiar to you, you probably live in Derbyshire, Nottinghamshire, Leicestershire or areas nearby — this is the 'Mardy' area in which the word is commonly used. People from other parts of the country would find 'Mardy' an unfamiliar dialect term, and wonder what on earth you meant by it.

Dialect, then, is a matter of the words and grammatical structures used when speaking a language (and sometimes when writing it, too ...). **Accent** refers to the way in which words are pronounced. Before looking at this in more detail, we need to think about the history of the English language — where it has come from, and how it has changed over the years. Only then can we make any real sense of the subject of dialect and accent in English.

English is the most widely-used language in the world. People living in what is now England were originally known as 'British', and spoke a variety of Celtic languages which still survive today in Welsh or Gaelic speaking parts of Britain. During the 5th and 6th centuries AD, the British people suffered a series of invasions from various tribes who came from what is now North Germany and Denmark — and these invaders brought their own language with them, known by scholars as Old English or Anglo-Saxon. The language we know as 'English',

Fig. 5.1 Truce terms in Great Britain

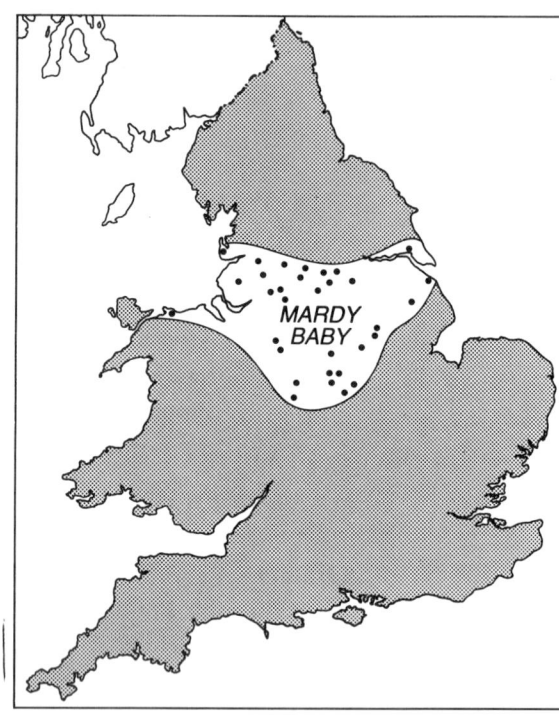

Fig. 5.2 The 'Mardy' area of Derbyshire, Nottinghamshire, Leicestershire and surrounding region

therefore, was originally a Germanic language; in the 9th and 10th centuries further invasions by Vikings changed this Old English language in a number of ways, until, in 1066, the Norman invasion was to result in thousands of words of French (and ultimately Latin) origin finding their way into the English language.

If we could go back in time to the 14th century, we would find that everyone in England spoke with a regional dialect; people spoke and wrote their own variety of the language according to their own locality, and it was only in the 14th century that one regional dialect based upon London began to emerge as a standard against which others were eventually measured.

Britain's role as a colonial power resulted in the borrowing of a number of words and expressions from many other world languages, so that the English language in the 20th century is a rich mixture with a vocabulary and a grammar drawn from many different sources.

Use a dictionary to find out which language or languages gave us the following words now used in English: bungalow; democracy; century; bread; lieutenant; television; caravan.

Where do English dialects come form? The answer is that they have always been there — individual communities have developed their own special use of language over the centuries, and while the standard form of English centred on London and the South-East has changed over the years, local dialect has tended to remain more traditional. Dialect is *not* 'sloppy speech', but has a pedigree as old as Standard English, if not older in some cases.

Does it surprise you to know that dialect is a traditional way of speaking with an excellent pedigree? If it does, you may have fallen victim to the 'propaganda' that Standard English has practised over the years, suggesting that only Standard English speakers speak 'proper' English.

TASK 4

1. Read the following example of local dialect carefully; it is taken word-for-word from the speech of a Derbyshire collier called Jack Hill, a man in his 80s who speaks with quite a broad local dialect.

   Try to make a list of all the words or expressions in this story which seem to you to be different from Standard English usage.

   When I were younger there were about six or seven miners — and all t'miners' wives were sick to bloody death — there were a ghost kept appearing in Heanor churchyard. And they all decided, like, about twelve on 'em, decided to take four on 'em in turns every night to catch this ghost. Well there were one got at each corner, like, and this bloody ghost . . . no ghost came one night, no ghost came another night — but about third night this ghost come appearing — come from somewhere — and he starts coming towards them and shouting — and he frit all the women to death in Heanor, this man did — he'd got a sheet ower him, you know. And he sees these colliers and they were all armed with pickshafts, hammers, shovels . . . Anyroad, this here ghost sees these colliers and they went for him, and he dobbed down onto a grave and he keeps scrattin' and scrattin' and he says: 'I can't get in! I can't get in!' and one chap hits him on t'back of t'head and says: 'You've no bloody business out!'

   We can classify your list of non-standard features in the following way:

   — **Accent**. Little attempt has been made here to represent Jack Hill's accent, but notice that he pronounces 'the' as 't', and 'over' as 'ower'.

   — **Lexical** features. This means words which are not used in Standard English and would probably not appear in a dictionary. Words like 'frit' and 'dobbed down' come in this category; what do you think they mean? Do you use lexical features of dialect in your own speech, words which you probably wouldn't hear from a London-based television or radio announcer, for example?

   — **Syntactical** features. This means the way in which a speaker handles the grammar or structure of the language. In Standard English you would say 'When I *was* younger' — but Jack Hill says 'When I *were* younger'. Now the word 'were' does appear in Standard English, but it is used in the plural ('We were', 'They were'); here Jack Hill uses it in the singular, after the word 'I'. Can you find any other examples of non-standard syntactical features in the passage? Do you use non-standard grammar when you speak? Supposing that more people in England say 'I *were* going' rather than the standard 'I *was* going' (and this is probably true) then who is wrong? Can a native speaker of English ever make a mistake?

2. Make your own tape recording of a dialect speaker and then make a written transcription of what you have recorded and try to isolate the lexical and syntactical features. You could use a pre-recorded tape for this purpose, such as *English Accents and Dialects* by Arthur Hughes and Peter Trudgill (Edward Arnold).

So far we have looked at regional dialect, now we turn to two other kinds of dialect: occupational dialect and class dialect.

— **Occupational dialect.** If a lawyer refers to a 'decree nisi' in a divorce case, or a builder looks at the roof of a house and admires the 'barge boards', they are using a specialised dialect drawn not from the area in which they live, but from their occupation. They are employing an occupational dialect.

Much occupational dialect comes under the heading of what we call **jargon**. People often differ in their definition of this term — some use it to refer to the use of long and unnecessary words in a clumsy way, or to the use of efficient and straightforward technical terms by people involved in a number of specialist activities.

People's motives for using jargon may differ; one person might use a jargon term for the sake of simplicity and exactitude, while someone else might launch into jargon in order to impress those around and even to put them down. Jargon is perhaps as often abused as it is used.

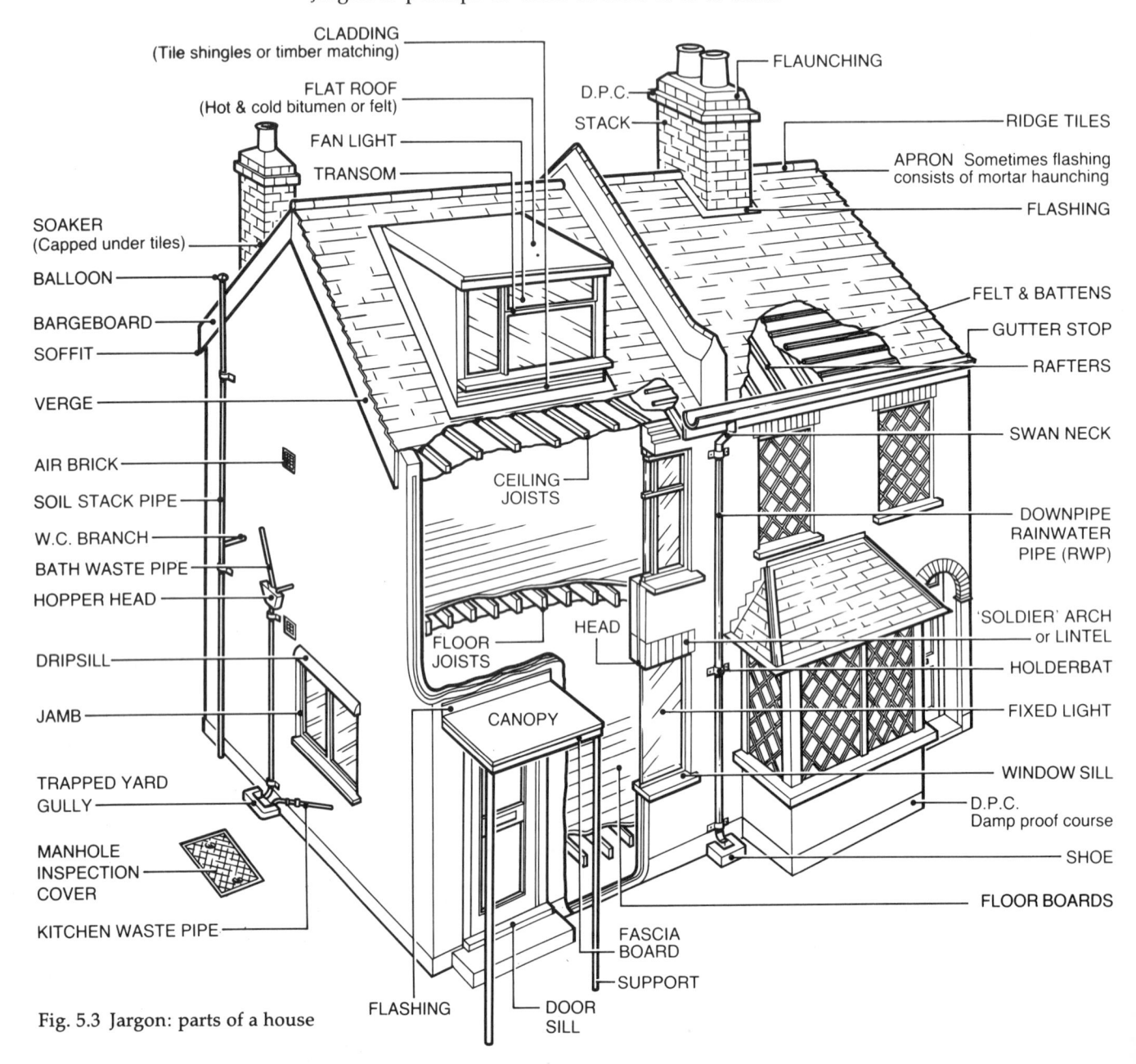

Fig. 5.3 Jargon: parts of a house

TASK *5*   Look at Fig. 5.3. It is labelled to show the technical terms used in the construction trade to describe the various features of such a house.

Choose *four* or *five* labelled items and describe each *without* using the technical term with which it is labelled.

Now say whether you think the use of technical terms or jargon in the construction trade is justified.

3. The following table lists a number of occupations or activities, and for each gives one example of a jargon word or expression used by people working within the occupation or activity named.

Define the jargon words listed, and then collect *five* or *six* more jargon words or phrases used within each occupation:

OCCUPATION/ACTIVITY	JARGON
Police Force	GBH
Legal Profession	Affidavit
Cricket	Night watchman
Football	Sweeper
Snooker	Plant
Darts	Double Top
Education	The Rising Fives
Medicine	Prolapsed intervertebral disc
Travel Agents	Standby flight
Estate Agents	Des. Res.
CB Radio	Smokey Bear
Drug abuse	Cold Turkey
Restaurants	Sauté
The Stock Exchange	Gilts
Knitting	One pearl, one plain
Card playing	Misère
The Church	Atonement
Biology	Photosynthesis
Chemistry	Titration
Physics	Refraction
Carpentry	Ratchet brace
Plumbing	Scribing gauge
Fabrication	Podger spanner
Engineering	Jaw tap wrench
Electrical	Pipe vice
Motor engineering	Torque wrench

4. Find *six* examples of your own of jargon from the press, pamphlets, hand-books, etc. Write these down, together with their source and see if other people can identify and define each example you've found. You might find useful material in the rule-books of games, the highway code, specialist magazines, cookery books and so on.

— **Class dialect** Although dialects may be determined by region or occupation they may also be affected by the social class to which you belong — or to which you would *like* to belong. The study of the relationship between language and social class is known as **sociolinguistics**.

It was 600 years ago that one particular dialect of English, centred around the cultural centres of London, Oxford and Cambridge, began to be thought of as a form of **Standard English.** This particular dialect has grown in influence over the years, and to many people there is a special prestige in speaking and writing it. It is the kind of language which we hear most often during the fairly formal broadcasts on the TV and radio, and is often referred to as 'BBC English' or even 'Oxford English'. The influence of the public schools in the past and the media during this century have helped give the impression that Standard English is correct, while regional dialects are incorrect. A great proportion of people concerned with parliament, the law and many other prestigious professions, conduct their everyday business using Standard English.

Because of its prestige, Standard English is thought of as the educated way of speaking all over the country, and the question of the relationship between social class and language then arises. By and large the higher up the social scale you go, the greater the number of people you find speaking Standard English, no matter where they live in the country. So a barrister from London, for example, may sound very similar to a barrister from Newcastle-Upon-Tyne, whereas a manual worker from the East End of London sounds very different to a manual worker from Newcastle — both probably have strong regional dialects.

Whatever dialect we may use in speech, however, all schools teach Standard English when children learn to read and write, and nearly all printed material produced in Britain is written in Standard English.

Do you think that Standard English performs any useful service? Would it matter if everyone spoke and wrote their own local variety of the language? Does Standard English have a power and influence out of all proportion to the number of people who use it? Do you know anyone who has deliberately tried to lose a local dialect and learned to speak Standard English? Did they succeed in making the change?

It has been calculated that only 12% of the English population speak Standard English, even though most people are able to write it. Regional dialects are measured against this Standard and often looked down upon when they fail to conform. Does this seem reasonable?

We often use our own awareness of dialect to 'place' people in a particular locality or social class. An extreme example of this came to light in 1954, when a man called Professor Alan C. Ross published an article on the social implications of how people use language. His ideas were taken up in a semi-humorous way by Nancy Mitford in a book called *Noblesse Oblige*. Here she refers to 'U' and 'Non-U' use of language, i.e. upper class and non-upper class. This wasn't intended to be a very serious approach to language, but it does point out the fact that many upper class speakers of the language can very easily spot others of their own class and upbringing by listening closely to the words being spoken.

TASK 6

1. Below are two lists of words — on the left is the commonly-used 'Non-U' word, and on the right is the 'U' equivalent used by a variety of speakers from Sloane Rangers to Aristocrats as a kind of 'tribal dialect' which may be used on occasions to build group solidarity and deter outsiders.

   The last *five* spaces in the right-hand column are blank. Decide which 'U' word would be used in each case?

NON-U	U
Lounge	Drawing-room
Toilet	Lavatory/loo
Teacher	School Master or Mistress
Pleased to meet you	How do you do?
Greens	Vegetables
Notepaper Dinner (for the midday meal) Mirror Serviettes A jack (when playing cards)	

Why do you think that 'U' speakers use the more down-to-earth word 'Lavatory' than the rather more polite-sounding 'Toilet'?

2. All Americans are 'Non-U' by definition. Pick out the words or expressions in the passage below that reveal it to be American English, and explain the meaning of the Americanisms:

'You want to get to the gas station from here? All right, leave the apartment, take the elevator down to the lobby, keep on the sidewalk two blocks, past the drug store and the diner and you're there. Tell the guy with the suspenders that you've got a problem. He'll fix you up real good.'

3. It would be hard to imagine anything less 'U' than Cockney Rhyming slang, in which a word or phrase is replaced by other words which rhyme with the original. Try to decipher each of the examples of rhyming slang used in the passage which follows:

'I was taking the *cherry'og* for a *ball o'chalk* down the *frog and toad* when a *jam jar* pulled up — it was the *Sweeney Todd*! I stepped into the nearest *rub-a-dub* and met me old *China*, Bill Smith, with his *trouble and strife*. He wasn't feeling too good — had a *Conan Doyle* on his *fife and drum* and a bit of trouble with his *raspberry tart*. Felt a bit hungry, so I had a *Jack the Ripper* off some old fellow who's a bit *Lakes of Killarney* and *Mutt and Jeff,* and went home to enjoy it in front of the *Aunt Mariah* with a cup of *Rosie Lee*. Then up the *apples and pears* for a bit of *bo-peep* . . .'

Accent We now have a good working knowledge of what dialect is and how it may be used by a variety of people.

But what is **accent**? While dialect is a matter of the words used when speaking, accent is to do with how these words are pronounced.

We know that accents differ in various parts of the English-speaking world, but the pronunciation of English has also changed over the centuries since the days when Anglo-Saxon was spoken by most people in England. The English language, like most languages, hasn't stood still over the centuries; new vocabulary has come into it, while some words have dropped completely out of use (some of these are still used by local dialect speakers). The grammar of English has become simplified so that English verbs are infinitely easier to learn than French verbs, for example, and English has none of the varied word-endings used in German.

At the same time, English pronunciation has undergone dramatic changes; have you ever wondered why a word like 'knight' is spelt in the way it is, when its modern pronunciation is more like 'nite'? The fact is that the current spelling of the word did originally reflect its pronunciation — in the 14th century, for example, in the days of the English poet Geoffrey Chaucer, the pronunciation would have been 'kernicht'.

This historical development of the language may have significance for the way that you pronounce words today. Do you sound the letter 'r' when you say 'barn', as West Country speakers and Americans do? How do you pronounce the word 'grass'? Do you use a short 'a', or a long 'a' which sounds like 'ah'? How do you pronounce the word 'summer'? Do you use a full 'u' with your lips fairly close together, or are your lips fairly far apart? If you use a short 'a' in 'grass' and a full 'u' in 'summer', the chances are that you live, or were born, in the Midlands or the North of England. But scholars believe that up to the 16th century everybody in England would probably have used a short 'a' and a full 'u' in these words. What has happened since is that Southerners have tended to change the language, leaving those in the Midlands and the North with the more traditional pronunciation. Neither way of pronouncing these words is right or wrong — we are just looking here at accent differences determined by historical and geographical factors.

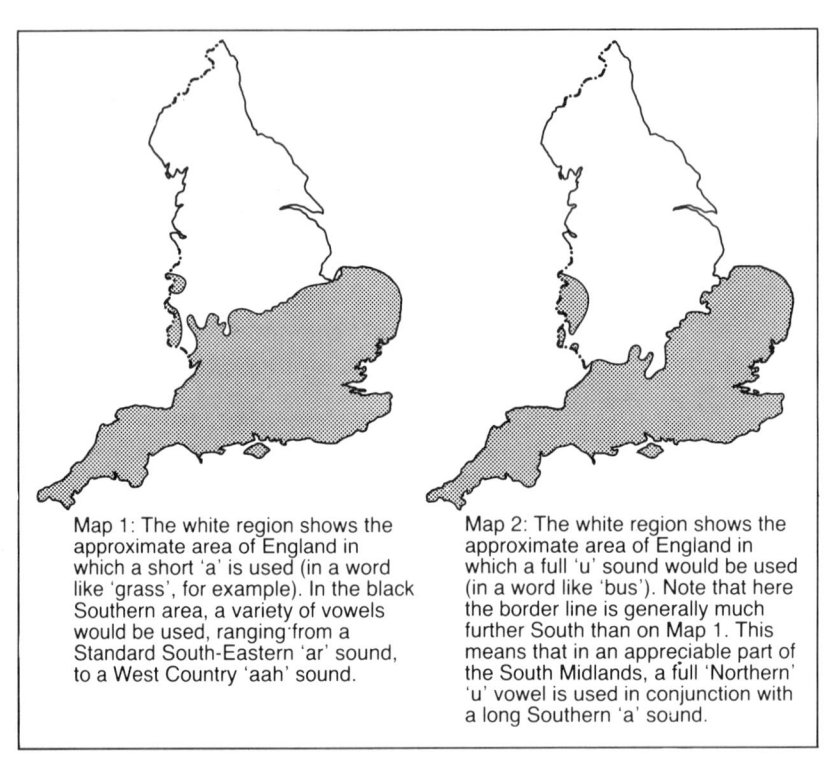

Map 1: The white region shows the approximate area of England in which a short 'a' is used (in a word like 'grass', for example). In the black Southern area, a variety of vowels would be used, ranging from a Standard South-Eastern 'ar' sound, to a West Country 'aah' sound.

Map 2: The white region shows the approximate area of England in which a full 'u' sound would be used (in a word like 'bus'). Note that here the border line is generally much further South than on Map 1. This means that in an appreciable part of the South Midlands, a full 'Northern' 'u' vowel is used in conjunction with a long Southern 'a' sound.

Source: 'Ey Up Mi Duck!', Part One, by Richard Scollins and John Titford
Fig. 5.4 Accent: the short 'a' and full 'u'

Has anyone ever made fun of the way you speak? Has anyone ever said that they can't understand a word you say? Is that the sender's fault or the receiver's fault? Do you make judgements about people because of their accent? Would you ever try to modify your accent if you went to live somewhere else, or went for an interview for a job where you thought the employer might have some fixed idea about acceptable accents?

Some accents seem to be more widely acceptable than others. People who might say they don't like the sound of a Birmingham accent, a Glasgow accent or a Liverpool accent might nevertheless be very fond of a Welsh accent, a Devon accent or an Edinburgh accent. Can you account for this? Does social class have anything to do with such judgements?

Just as one particular dialect — Standard English — has special prestige in Britain, so one particular accent is sometimes taken as a model of good

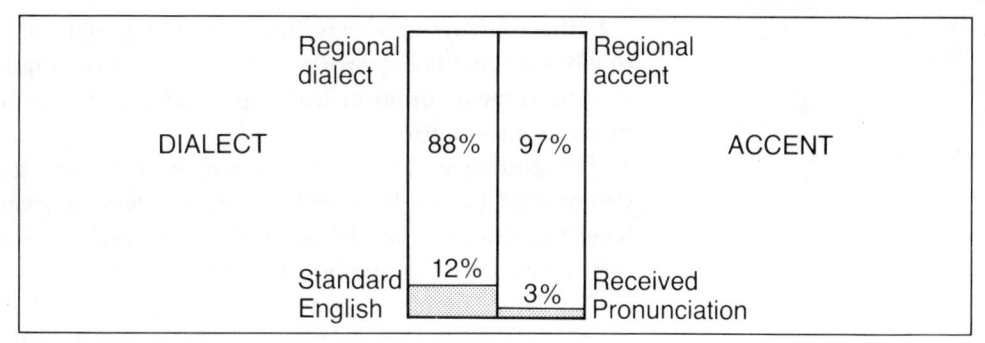

Fig. 5.5 % of the population of England who use
(a) Standard English
(b) Received pronunciation

pronunciation. This is known as **Received Pronunciation,** or RP for short. It is spoken mainly by well-educated Londoners and a certain number of people from the rest of the country. But no speaker, no matter how well-educated or high up the social scale who uses a short 'a' in 'grass' is speaking Received Pronunciation.

Even fewer people use RP than use Standard English. We said that 12% of speakers in England use Standard English — but only 3% use Received Pronunciation.

Look at Fig. 5.5. We can see that 12% of the population of England speak Standard English, where 88% do not. Of the 12% who speak Standard English, only a quarter (3% of all English speakers) use Received Pronunciation; that leaves 9% of the population who speak Standard English, but with some regional form of accent.

Accent, unlike local dialect, rarely finds its way into print; some novelists and some poets try to use the 26-letter alphabet to reflect an accent by using unusual spelling, but the result can be messy and unclear unless it is handled carefully. Only the International Phonetic Alphabet can get anywhere near the representation of a particular accent accurately.

Before leaving the subject of dialect and accent, remember:
− Everyone speaks in one dialect and with one accent. It is impossible to speak without a dialect or without an accent;
− Standard English is in itself a dialect, not an absence of dialect;
− Received Pronunciation is in itself an accent, not an absence of accent.

Appropriate language

No matter how much you know about language, and no matter how wide your vocabulary and your general ability to express yourself in words may be, you will not be an effective communicator unless you use language which is appropriate to your audience and appropriate to any given situation. Above all, it is essential to have the *will* and the *desire* to communicate in a comprehensible way.

Most people find that as they move through a typical day, they are required to play a number of roles, each of which requires a slightly different use of language. The same person might find that he or she will play the role of parent, friend, workmate, boss or employee as the day goes on; they are a parent to their own children one minute, but the child of their own mother or father the next; they take orders from one person at work, and then have to pass on their own orders to someone who is responsible to them. A clergyman uses one form of language for his wife, another for his children, and another from the pulpit for his congregation.

In these circumstances we use a kind of 'situational dialect' or **register** according to what we feel is appropriate. The varieties of language we use in speech and in writing depend upon at least three factors: 1. the audience   2. our role   3. the occasion or situation.

— **The audience.** The language we use with any given audience will be partly determined by the level of language we feel they can comprehend. The age and level of education of the audience may make a difference, as might our own relationship with a person or group of people.

— **Our role.** The language we use with people will be determined by the role we are playing at any given moment — it might be teacher, pupil, boss, employee, adviser, patient, parent, son or daughter, friend, colleague and so on.

— **The occasion or situation.** A husband and wife on their wedding day will find themselves speaking to each other in different ways as the day goes on. There is the language expected of them during the wedding ceremony, at the reception, with friends afterwards, and intimately with each other when they are alone. It will be the occasion or situation which determines the register they use at any one moment.

Very often our use of appropriate register depends upon the degree of formality required by any situation. The range of language available to us to suit the formality of the occasion may be very great. Consider the following questions arranged in descending order of formality:

— 'Would you care for a cigarette?'
— 'Would you like a cigarette?'
— 'Do you want a cigarette?'
— 'Do you want a fag?'
— 'Wanna fag?'
— 'Fag?'

Write out a similar range of sentences from the most formal to the least formal beginning with: 'Would you care for a cup of tea?'

Spoken English often appears to us to be less formal than written English but this is not always the case, and both written and spoken language have their own formal and less formal varieties.

One of the results of our borrowing vocabulary from other world languages is that we have available to us a number of words which mean almost the same thing, but are used according to the degree of formality felt appropriate in any given situation.

The table below shows a typical range of vocabulary based upon a scale of formality:

VERY INFORMAL (SLANG)	INFORMAL (COLLOQUIAL)	FORMAL	VERY FORMAL
puke	throw up	be sick	vomit
put the boot in	beat someone up	attack	assault
boozer	pub	public house	licensed premises
goggle box	telly	T.V. set	television receiver
bookies	betting shop	bookmaker	turf accountant
pissed off	fed up	miserable	dejected
tickling the ivories	playing the joanna	playing the piano	playing the pianoforte

There are not always four varieties of a word available to choose from — in many cases the choice is narrower, although it could sometimes be wider.

Colloquial language is fairly informal, more often used in speech than in writing; **slang** is very informal language, not usually found in written form, and may be very short-lived and affected by changing fashion. The slang expressions of earlier generations, e.g. bounder, cad, etc. have long since passed out of common use. Standard English has its colloquial and slang expressions, as does local dialect — but we should not confuse slang (which may well be used throughout the entire country and be of fairly recent origin) with local dialect (which is only used in one locality and probably has much older origins).

TASK 7

1. Using a large piece of paper turned sideways, make *four* columns headed: SLANG; COLLOQUIAL; FORMAL; VERY FORMAL.

   Now work across the columns, writing in the more formal and less formal varieties of any given word as we have done in the table above.

   Start by putting each of the following in your VERY FORMAL column, and working across the page for each one: exhausted; to deceive someone; automobile; obese; spectacles.

2. Here are *five* examples of different language registers; in what situation might each be appropriate?

   — Having a great time, folks — wish you were here;

   — I observed Vehicle B proceeding in an easterly direction towards the Bristol inter-section . . . ;

   — I hope you're being a good girl for mummy . . . ;

   — I must protest in the strongest possible terms about the disgraceful level of courtesy I received from your staff;

   — I am speaking to you from the Cabinet Room at 10, Downing Street. This morning the British Ambassador in Berlin handed the German Government a final note stating that, unless we heard from them by 11 o'clock that they were prepared at once to withdraw their troops from Poland, a state of war would exist between us. I have to tell you now that no such undertaking has been received, and that consequently this country is at war with Germany.

3. If we wanted to analyse any given language register, we could do so much in the same way as we examined local dialect — that is, by considering *lexical* and *syntactical* features separately. Look again at the examples of register above; what can you say about the use of vocabulary and grammar in each? Don't fall into the trap of thinking that 'long words' and 'long sentences' are necessarily difficult and complex. The word 'Hippopotamus' is a long word but not a difficult one, and you could easily speak a long sentence which was not a very complicated statement grammatically.

The idea of **register** was first developed by a man called Basil Bernstein. He chose to refer to the more complex and sophisticated forms of register (spoken or written) as the **Elaborated Code**. The language used in the Elaborated Code would contain a fair number of 'difficult' words, and would employ complex syntax or grammar.

For Bernstein the idea of register had implications for the social and class structure of a country. Socially, the Elaborated Code would be available to middle class, articulate people who might meet a great variety of other people at work and at play, and would feel happy discussing quite complex ideas and concepts. There is no suggestion here that middle class speakers use the Elaborated Code all day long in every social situation — it is just that it is a register to which they have access when the occasion demands.

Bernstein called a less sophisticated and complicated form of register the **Restricted Code**, which is simpler in its use of vocabulary and grammatical construction.

Socially, the Restricted Code is used by a significant number of working class people, who perhaps travel less often, meet fewer people in their everyday lives, and talk much of the time to family and friends who understand their meaning easily because of shared assumptions and shared experiences. Some working class speakers only have access to this Restricted Code; the Elaborated Code might be a closed book to them.

Bernstein and others maintained that problems can arise for, say, a child from a working class home who is educated in a school where teachers use the Elaborated Code. Middle class children might find this no problem, but the working class child from a background where only the Restricted Code was ever used might be disadvantaged. A relationship between a middle class child and his or her parents might be one of reasoned argument: 'You shouldn't do that because . . .', whereas children from a different social background may simply be given an order with no explanation: 'Don't do that!'

There are a lot of generalisations at work here. You might like to disagree with Bernstein — many people have! Is it true that 'working class language' (if there is such a thing) is a simpler form of language than that used by the middle class? Are those from working class backgrounds less able to converse with a wide range of people than those from the middle class are? Do you know anyone from a middle class, well-educated background who cannot converse freely with individuals who do not share his or her background?

TASK 8

1. Take a large sheet of paper and turn it so that the long edge is at the top; draw headed columns on the sheet as follows:

No.	Written or Spoken	Audience	Formal or Informal	Example

Read each of the ten EXAMPLES of language use given below and fill in the columns as follows:

Column 1. Number each item.

Column 2. Decide whether each example would be in a *written* or *spoken* form.

Column 3. What would the likely *audience* for each message be?

Column 4. Is each message generally *formal* or *informal* in style?

Column 5. Using your own experience and any other material you can find, use the Example column to write the first few sentences of your own for each Example 1–10. You will need to get into the role, e.g. imagine you are a solicitor in court, etc. and make an attempt at using the appropriate lexical and syntactical features of the register required. Try to keep a keen sense of audience as you write.

EXAMPLES:

1. A solicitor addresses magistrates in court.
2. A clergyman delivers a sermon.
3. One stranger gives directions to another.
4. A radio announcer interrupts a programme to give a news-flash.
5. A father tells his young daughter she'll go to the zoo if she's good.
6. A sex-scandal story on the front page of the *Sun* (complete with headline).
7. A report on proceedings in parliament from a quality daily newspaper.
8. A dentist talks to a six-year old patient.
9. A school-leaver phones a company to enquire about an advertised job vacancy.
10. A letter of complaint about a faulty washing machine.

Fig. 5.6 is a simplified model which attempts to summarise much of what we have been discussing in this chapter. Make use of it for revision or to consolidate your own ideas and what you have learned.

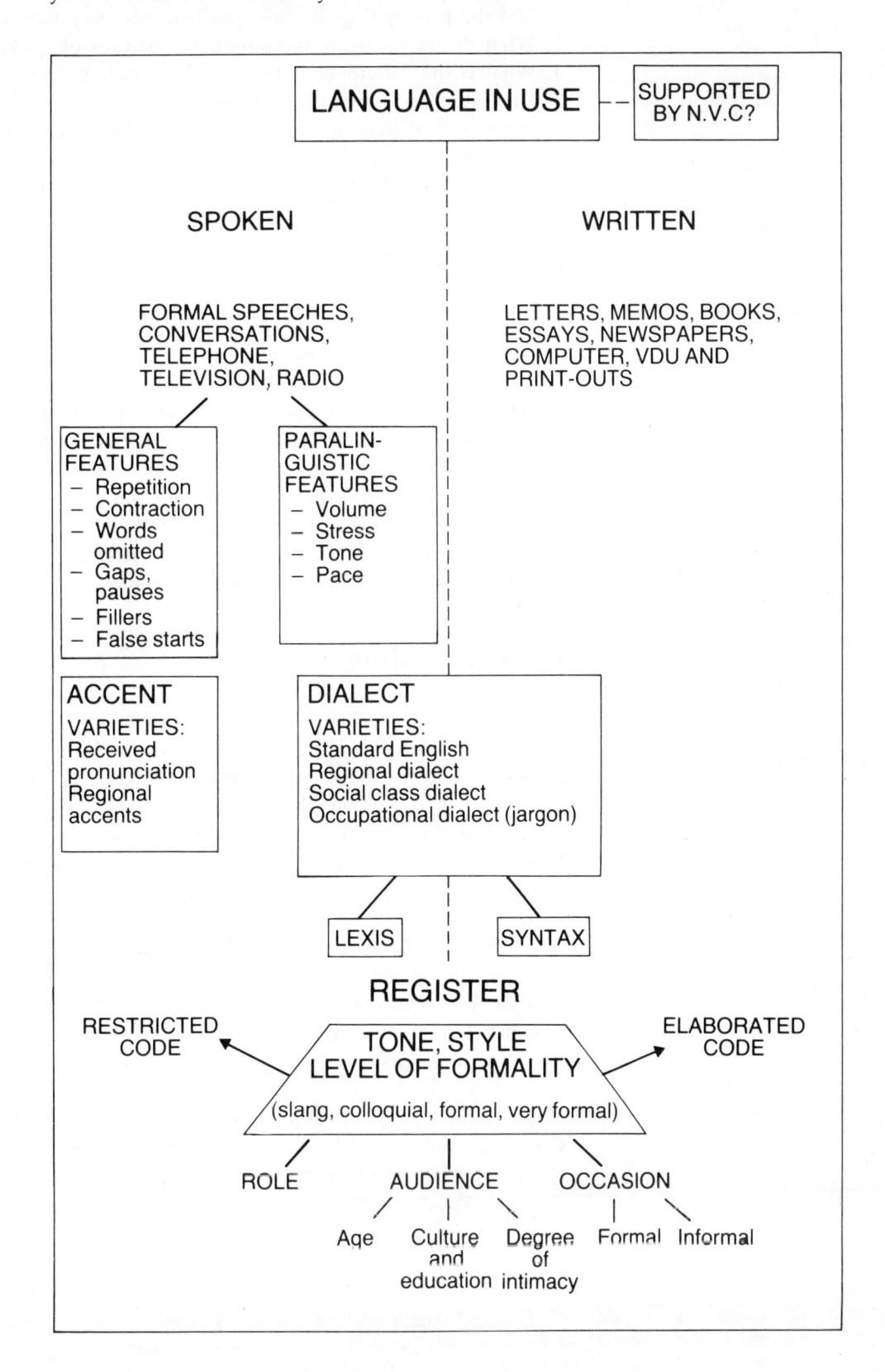

Fig. 5.6 Language in use: a simplified model

Self-assessment

1. What is the International Phonetic Alphabet?
2. List the principal distinguishing features of spoken English.
3. What do we mean by paralinguistic features of spoken language?
4. What is the difference between lexical and syntactical features of language?
5. Give your own definition of jargon.
6. What is the difference between Standard English and Received Pronunciation?
7. What is 'register'? What is its relationship to social class?
8. What is the difference between the Restricted Code and the Elaborated Code?

Further work

1. Find an example of an Estate Agent's description of a house for sale. Read it out loud. Can other people pick out the jargon words or expressions used? Can people guess the likely price of the house from the description alone?
2. Write an essay with the following title: 'Spoken and written English are more like two separate languages than two varieties of the same language.' Discuss, using examples of both written and spoken language.
3. Write an essay with the following title: 'Jargon may be used or abused. At its best it can facilitate communication between individuals and groups; at its worst it can act as a barrier to communication.' Discuss, using examples of jargon as evidence of any points you make.

Further reading

Brook G.L, *English Dialects* (Andre Deutsch, 1963)
Burgess A, *Language Made Plain* (Collins, 1984)
Burton S.H, *Using English* (Longmans, 1976)
Fromkin V and Rodman R, *An Introduction to Language* (Holt-Saunders, 1983)
Gregory M and Carroll S, *Language and situation* (Routledge & Kegan Paul, 1978)
Hayakawa S.I, *Language in Thought and Action* (Harcourt Brace, 1978)
Hughes and Trudgill P, *English Accents and Dialects* (Edward Arnold, 1979)
Potter S, *Our Language* (Penguin, 1969)
Quirk R, *The Use of English* (Longmans, 1968)
Stringer D, *Language Variation and English* (Open University)
Trudgill P, *Sociolinguistics: An Introduction* (Penguin, 1974)
Wakelin M, *Discovering English Dialects* (Shire, 1979)
Wakelin M, *English Dialects: an Introduction* (Athlone Press, 1977)

(Tape recordings of spoken English which may be of interest include:
Crystal D and Davey D, *Advanced Conversational English* (Longmans)
Hughes A and Trudgill P, *English Accents and Dialects* (Edward Arnold, 1979)

6 *Groups and meetings*

This chapter contains the following sections:
- **Groups**
- **Meetings**
- **Self-assessment**

- **Further work**
- **Further reading**

Groups

What are groups?   One of the reasons why human beings have become such a successful and dominant species is because of a deep-seated human willingness to co-operate with others; we are basically a tribal species, keen to be gregarious and quick to seek the companionship of others.

It is natural for human beings to form groups. What is a group? Essentially, a group is a collection of people with enough in common to have a shared identity. Not all groups stay together as a group for a long period of time; for example you may form part of a group of people with a common interest while on holiday but disperse and never meet the group again once the holiday is over. Not all groups need be formal; look at the table below:

Formal	*Informal*
Committees	Peer groups
Tribunals	Discussion groups
Commissions	Leisure groups

Can you think of other formal and informal groups? We have made a very rigid distinction here between the formal and the informal; can you think of groups which might fit somewhere in the middle, being neither very formal nor very informal, but fairly formal or fairly informal?

The characteristics of formal and informal groups could be thought of as follows:

Characteristics of formal groups	*Characteristics of informal groups*
Conform to set rules, written or unwritten, and may have a formal constitution	May have no set rules, or rules which evolve and change
Have fixed roles played by individuals, a division of labour	May have no fixed roles or division of labour, or these may evolve and change
Have formal hierarchies	May have no formal hierarchies, or hierarchies which evolve and change

Notice that informal groups, being generally more relaxed and *ad hoc* in the way they operate, have a lot of flexibility when it comes to changing their composition or working practices to suit the group's changing need or mood. An informal group may have no written rules or constitution, but might still have an accepted code of behaviour which its members are required to follow, i.e. the group might impose norms of behaviour upon its members.

TASK 1

Make a list of the formal and informal groups to which you belong. Do they share the characteristics which we have just mentioned? What norms of behaviour does each group expect from its members?

Why do groups form?

Groups form because people have communal needs:
— The need to *communicate* with others;
— The need to make *social contact* with others;
— The need for *mutual support*;
— The need for *solidarity* with others;
— The need for *group identification*;
— The need for *social status*;
— The need to be with people who share a common *purpose* or *interest*.

TASK 2

For each of the following groups, say which of the needs listed above might have led to the group's formation and continued existence:
— A trade union;
— A singles club;
— An old age pensioners' club;
— A youth club;
— A women's group.

Group conflict and conformity

If a group is to continue to exist, and to succeed and prosper, it needs to maintain a balance between the individuals within it, even where there are differences of opinion or personality clashes which make life difficult. Some people would argue that it is one function of communication to restore balance or equilibrium in interpersonal relationships; they would say that a group that is already well-balanced will resist any form of change, while any threat to that balance will be dealt with in such a way that equilibrium can be restored.

People in groups tend to act alike much of the time, strengthening group solidarity — they tend to adopt a kind of herd instinct and follow the crowd. There is also a great deal of evidence to show that there is strong pressure on individuals to conform in a group, which means that people tend to adapt themselves to the values, attitudes and communication styles of those around them.

Fig. 6.1 Group conflict: conflict within a group may be the result of tensions existing between individuals with incompatible personalities

No matter how strong group cohesion may be, it can be threatened from time to time by disagreements between individuals; the conflict within a group which results may have a number of root causes:

— **Personality clashes.** Conflict within a group may be the result of tensions existing between individuals with incompatible personalities.

— **Differing interests**. A group may run into difficulties if individual interests within the group begin to move in different directions.

— **Differing values.** Group cohesion will be under threat if some individuals hold fundamentally different values from others, or have a very different sense of priorities.

Each group will develop its own methods of dealing with conflicts which threaten to weaken or destroy it; someone may have to give way, a compromise may have to be reached, or one or more people may actually leave the group altogether.

Hierarchies in groups and organisations

Many groups are organised on a **hierarchical** basis, whereby people have a higher or lower status according to who they are or what responsibilities they carry. This may be true even of quite small informal groups, but it is often much more rigid and complex in those formal and large groups which we refer to as **organisations.** Whatever type of organisation we analyse, whether it be industrial, commercial, financial or educational, we will usually find a pecking order of status, with people placed on specific levels or grades according to the work they do and the role they perform. It is usually the case that a small minority (or élite) of individuals give orders and directives which the majority then have to carry out. In this state of affairs, everyone apart from those at the very top and bottom of the organisational 'pyramid' has both 'superiors' and 'inferiors' to communicate with.

The hierarchical system of organisation can be represented in the form of a pyramid, with each person or groups of people placed within it according to their grade. In a commercial organisation, people on different grades usually earn different salaries or wages.

In a hierarchy, **accountability** is very important. When decisions are made, the person responsible has to account for his or her actions and the consequences of those actions to those above him or her in the hierarchy, and also — to a lesser extent — to those below.

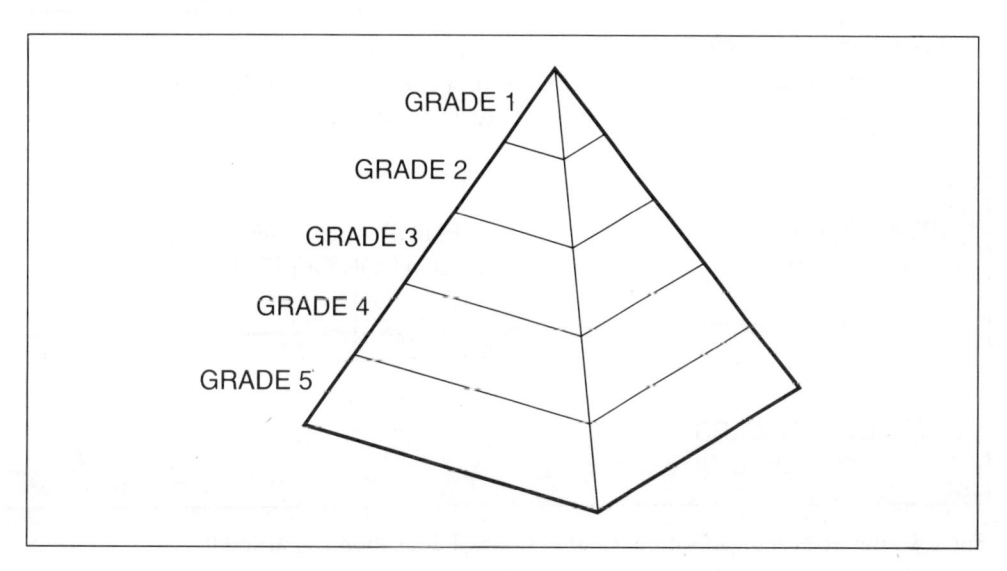

Fig. 6.2 A pyramid of hierarchy within an organisation

Figs. 6.3 and 6.4 are two simplified examples of hierarchical organisations, shown in diagrammatic form. Fig. 6.3 is based upon a printing company. Each person in the hierarchy is responsible to the person above him or her; three of the directors (finance, production and sales/marketing) are of equal status, while the chairperson is responsible to the shareholders for the efficient running of the company.

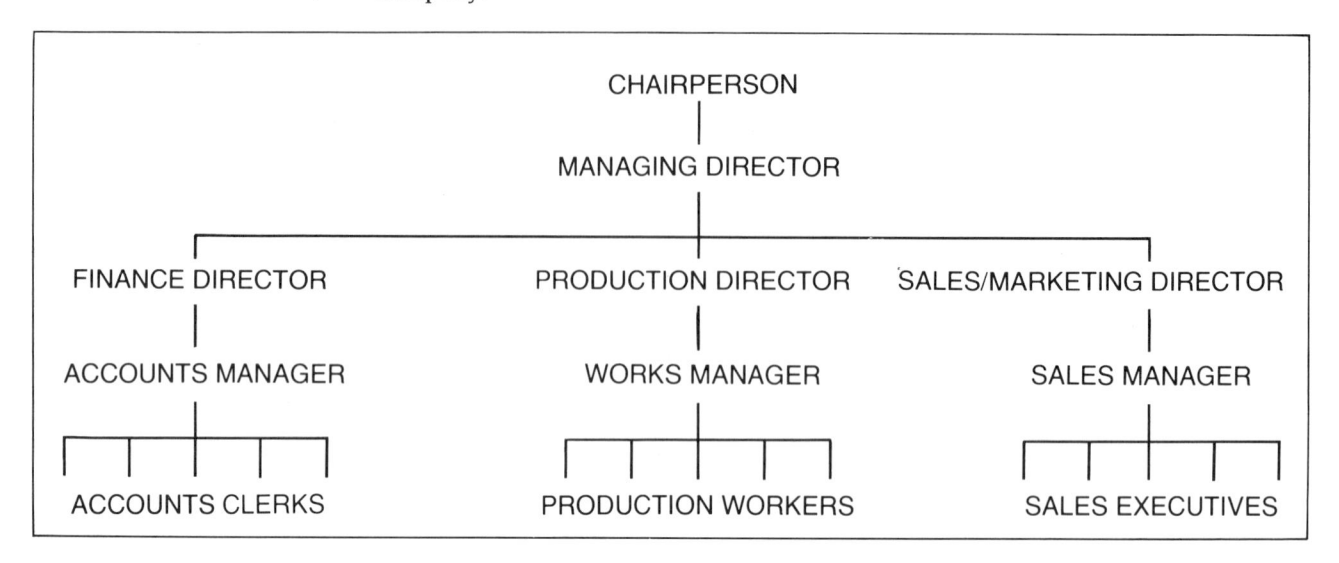

Fig. 6.3 Hierarchical organisation: a printing company

Fig. 6.4 shows the kind of hierarchical structure you might find within a County Council Education Department. Note in this case that the Chief Education Officer and his or her staff (who are all *officers* of the authority) are ultimately responsible to the County Education Committee (which consists of *elected members* of the authority).

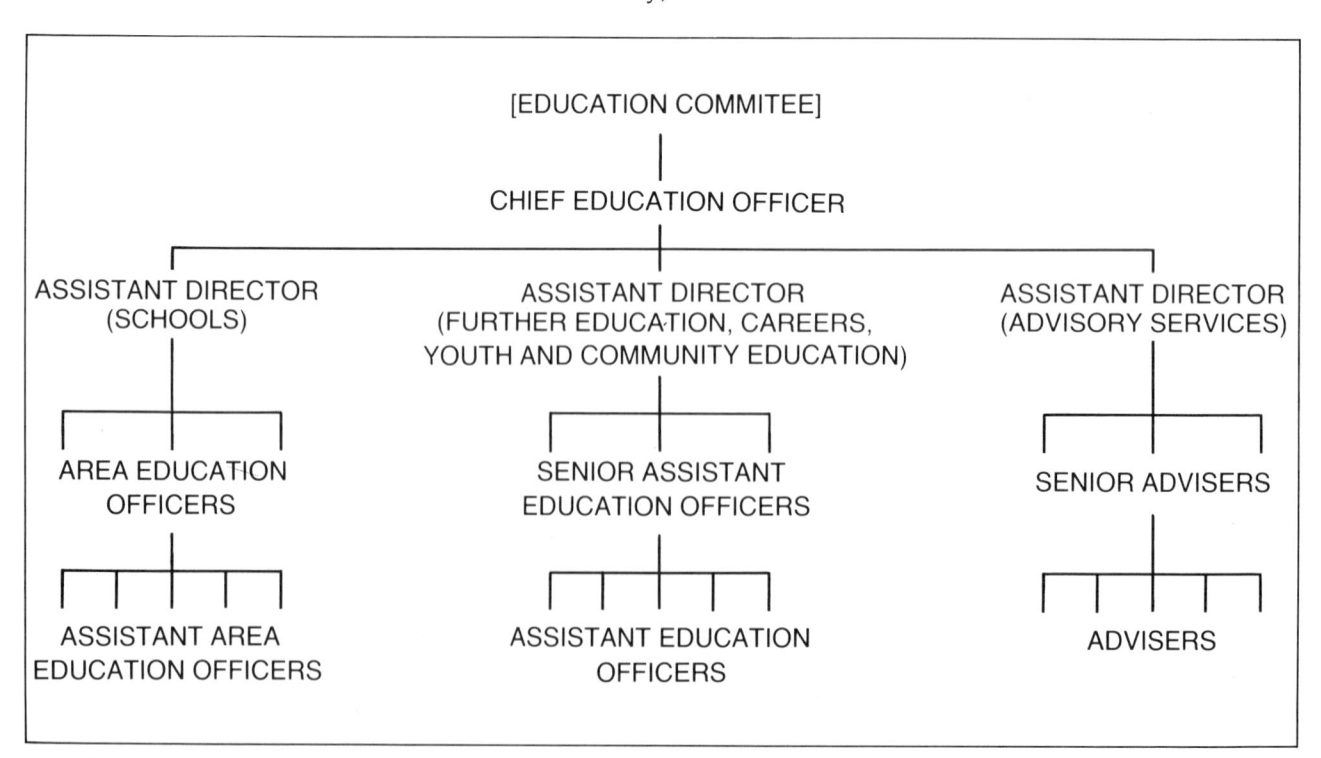

Fig. 6.4 Hierarchical organisation: County Council Education Department

 **3**

1. Draw a diagram to illustrate a hierarchical organisation or group with which you are familiar.
2. Draw a simple diagrammatic family tree to show the relationship between yourself, your brothers or sisters, your parents, grandparents, aunts, uncles and your cousins. Does your tree represent a hierarchy?

Channels of communication within organisations

Look again at Fig. 6.3. Think about the ways in which communication may travel within such an organisation; the **channels** or **routes** which communication takes might fall into one of three categories:

— **Vertical.** This refers to communication from a 'superior' to an 'inferior' (or vice-versa). In our example, this would be the route taken by written or verbal communication between the finance director and the accounts manager.

— **Lateral** or **horizontal**. A lateral or horizontal channel of communication runs between people who are on the same grade or level in the hierarchy — between the production director and the sales/marketing director or the finance director in our example.

— **Diagonal**. This type of route is a combination of the lateral and the vertical, and refers to communication which travels from one department in an organisation to another (lateral) and from a superior to an inferior or vice-versa (vertical). In the printing company, an example of diagonal communication would be a message passing between the production director and the sales manager.

A hierarchical system within an organisation can have a significant impact on the way in which people communicate with each other — on how formal or informal each person can be with those above or below him or her in the structure. A person who works in an accounts department of a large company may be friendly and relaxed with those in the same office, deferential to the Accounts Manager, and slightly sharp and bossy with the office junior. In many companies that same office junior may never communicate with people at a certain level in the hierarchy at all.

Meetings

What is a meeting?

A **meeting** may mean many different things to different people. There are formal and informal meetings, just as there are formal and informal groups, and a meeting can be anything from the Annual General Meeting of a large company through to an informal meeting of friends and peers in a relaxed social setting.

 **4**

Look at the table below, showing how meetings may take place in a number of varied social and work settings. We have left the last *five* entries blank. Write down examples of meetings which might take place within these five settings.

SETTING	EXAMPLES OF MEETINGS
Commercial company	Committee meeting
Amateur football club	Players' meeting
Education	Governors' meeting
Local political party	
Church members	
Students' union	
Armed forces	
Neighbourhood group	

Just as meetings vary in their settings, so they may also vary in their purpose. Here are four examples:

TYPE OF MEETING	PURPOSE
Labour Party Conference	To formulate policy and agree a manifesto
Annual General Meeting of a voluntary group	To review the past year and elect officers for the coming year
Social Services Case Conference	To review the progress made by a client and to decide upon future action
Protest meeting	To decide upon ways of making an effective protest

Not everyone feels happy communicating in a meeting, no matter how small or informal it may be. Do you know people who turn to you during a meeting and want to begin a person-to-person dialogue with you, ignoring the larger group?

At least three factors affect the amount and style of communication which happens in a meeting:

— The **size** of the group. Many people feel uneasy in a large meeting, and make no verbal contribution at all to its discussions.

— The **formality** of the procedure. A very formal meeting may intimidate some individuals, while those who do make a contribution probably do so in a formal and structured way.

— The **personality** and **confidence** of individuals and of the group as a whole. Some people use a meeting in order to show off their knowledge or eloquence; others help things along with a touch of well-timed humour, while less confident speakers present may well sit in silence. Very often a meeting develops a personality of its own — a combination of the individual styles of people present, with an extra dimension drawn partly from the interaction between individuals. Some meetings are a pleasure to participate in, while others can be a strain, a bore, or a waste of time.

Fig. 6.5 Not everyone feels happy communicating in a meeting . . .

Roles within meetings   In an informal meeting, people contribute to discussion and communicate with others in a fairly unstructured way, but in order that formal meetings may operate with maximum efficiency, set roles are given to certain individuals. The identity of the people who are to perform each of these set roles may be agreed by those present at the meeting in an informal fashion, but many committees which meet regularly and have important business to transact go through a process of electing key officers with specialised roles.

Focusing upon formal meetings or committees and the roles played by individuals within them, we find three crucial jobs which need to be done: those of chairman, secretary and treasurer.

— The role of **chairman**. A number of words can be used: chairman, chairwoman, chairperson or simply chair. This person's duties are as follows:
— To ensure that the committee carries out the task in hand, that the meetings proceed smoothly, and that everyone has a chance to speak.
— To suggest initiatives to the committee when appropriate, but also to urge caution if necessary.
— To make sure the committee follows its own written or unwritten rules of procedure, including the voting procedure on motions which have been proposed or amended.
— To keep discussion relevant to the task in hand, and not to favour any individual or group within the committee.

The chairman's key role as the focal point of all committee work is reinforced by the practice of all members addressing their remarks to the chairman. Even a person wishing to argue a point with a person sitting next to him or her will need to speak 'through the chair'.

— The role of the **secretary**. The role of the secretary is crucial to the efficient running of any committee; this person's workload before, during and after the committee meetings themselves is often very considerable. The secretary's duties are usually as follows:
— To establish a venue for the committee and make any appropriate booking arrangements.
— To carry out the routine day-to-day work associated with the committee, including the handling of all correspondence.
— To circulate appropriate papers to committee members in good time for committee meetings.
— To support the chairman during meetings, and to take minutes which will be circulated to members.
— To compile an agenda for each meeting in consultation with the chairman.
— To collect any apologies for absence and relay these to the committee.

The secretary sits on the right-hand side of the chairman during meetings, and needs to communicate fully with him or her at all times.

— The role of the **treasurer**. Not all committees need a treasurer as such, but most social or charitable clubs and societies have funds which need to be properly administered, and this job falls to the treasurer. His or her responsibilities are as follows:
— To manage and control all funds.
— To keep a careful account of monies received and monies spent.
— To present the committee with a financial statement whenever it needs one, and especially to present an annual treasurer's report and balance sheet, properly audited, at the Annual General Meeting.
— To advise the committee on financial matters generally.

Written documentation in meetings

The meetings of a formal committee need to be well documented, i.e. a written record of all relevant information needs to be made and kept for future reference.

The three most important records of a formal meeting are:

— **Notice**. This is a formal statement notifying members officially that a meeting is to take place, or is to be convened:

> ## THE ANNUAL GENERAL MEETING
> ### of the
> ## MENDIP ARCHAEOLOGICAL SOCIETY
>
> will take place
> ### at The George Hotel, Frome on
> ### Tuesday, 25th July, 1987 at 3.00 p.m.
> Your attendance is requested.

— **Agenda**. This is a formal notice of the 'running order' of the next meeting, and is sent out to all members prior to the committee meeting so that they may come suitably prepared. A typical agenda for an Annual General Meeting looks like this:

> MENDIP ARCHAEOLOGICAL SOCIETY
> ANNUAL GENERAL MEETING
>
> 1. Apologies for absence.
> 2. Minutes of the last meeting.
> 3. Matters arising.
> 4. Chairman's report.
> 5. Treasurer's report
> 6. Election of officers for the following year.
> 7. Any other business.

— **Minutes**. The minutes are a basic record of what was said and decided at a meeting. They are written up by the secretary from notes taken during the meeting, and are sent to all members in good time for the following meeting. Minutes allow decisions to be placed 'on record', and make people accountable for what they have said or decided, and for carrying out tasks agreed by the meeting.

Typical minutes covering part of 'Any other business' might look like this:

Mr. Dilks asked whether any progress had been made on getting permission for an archaeological dig to take place in the vicinity of the coalmine workings in Radstock. The secretary replied that a request had been forwarded to British Coal for permission to dig on their land, but that no reply had been received. He promised to look into the matter further and report back at the next committee meeting.

Committee procedure   Committees often develop their own special procedures and ways of working, but in simple terms an Annual General Meeting of the sort outlined above proceeds as follows:

— The committee meets at the place and time appointed.

— The notice, agenda, minutes of the previous meeting and any other relevant papers would already have been distributed to members. They would be expected to bring these with them.

— The chairman begins the meeting and takes the members through the agenda, item by item.

– Apologies for absence are given and recorded.

– The minutes of the last meeting are read by the secretary and agreed or amended by members as being a true record.

– Matters arising from these minutes are discussed and decisions taken if necessary.

– The chairman and treasurer give their reports and these are formally accepted by the meeting.

– Officers for the following year are appointed by whatever method has been agreed.

– Any items of other business are raised by any member, followed by discussion and decisions if appropriate.

– The chairman declares the meeting closed. If this were not an Annual General Meeting, the date and time of the next meeting would need to be agreed upon before the members disperse.

There is usually a formal procedure for making decisions at a meeting of this sort. The minutes of the previous meeting and other items on an agenda need to be officially approved by the meeting, and the procedure would usually be as follows:

A member proposes that the minutes be accepted as a true record. Someone else then 'seconds' or supports the first proposer, and the members then vote on the proposal. If you were present at such a committee, you would hear something like this:

Chairman: 'Do I have a proposal that the minutes be accepted as a true record?'
    (A member raises his or her hand)
Chairman: 'Do I have a seconder for the proposal?'
    (Another member raises his or her hand)
Chairman: 'All in favour please show.'
    (People vote by raising their hands)

Some decisions a committee has to make are not so straightforward. There may be differences of opinion, and if the meeting cannot agree or reach a consensus after some discussion, then the matter has to be 'put to the vote'. A proposer again 'proposes' or 'moves' a course of action called the 'motion', and a seconder has to be found. The meeting is then able to vote for or against, and the numbers doing so are duly recorded. Sometimes a person does not want to vote against a motion, but simply to change or amend it. In this case he or she proposes an 'amendment' which is voted on *before* the main motion. If the amendment is agreed or carried then the original motion is abandoned; if the amendment is lost the meeting votes again on the original motion.

You will find that most formal meetings make decisions in this way, though chairmen sometimes use their discretion to alter procedure slightly according to circumstance.

 **TASK 5** Carry out this group role-playing exercise which involves organising and taking part in a formal meeting.

You are to form a group which will play the role of the executive committee, i.e. a committee which has the power to take decisions and implement them, of a nationally-known 'pressure group'. Pressure groups are organisations which exist to promote a certain policy or idea, making use of persuasive communication to put across their message to the general public.

Proceed as follows:

— Choose a pressure group. There are many you can choose from, including:

RSPCA (The Royal Society for the Prevention of Cruelty to Animals);

NSPCC (The National Society for the Prevention of Cruelty to Children);

CND (The Campaign for Nuclear Disarmament);

LIFE (An anti-abortion group);

BUAV (The British Union for the Abolition of Vivisection);

ASH (Action on Smoking and Health);

GREENPEACE (A group for the protection of the environment).

— Allocate the roles of chairman, secretary and treasurer.

— Write out a notice and an agreed agenda and give each member a copy.

— Conduct the meeting according to the agenda, discussing any issues which you think would be relevant to the aims of the organisation you have chosen.

— Make decisions where appropriate.

— Have the minutes written up and distributed.

— Discuss the meeting between yourselves once it is over; what contribution did each person make? Was the meeting a success?

Fig. 6.6 summarises many of the main points covered in this chapter by means of a simplified model. Use it for revision or to consolidate your own ideas and what you have learned.

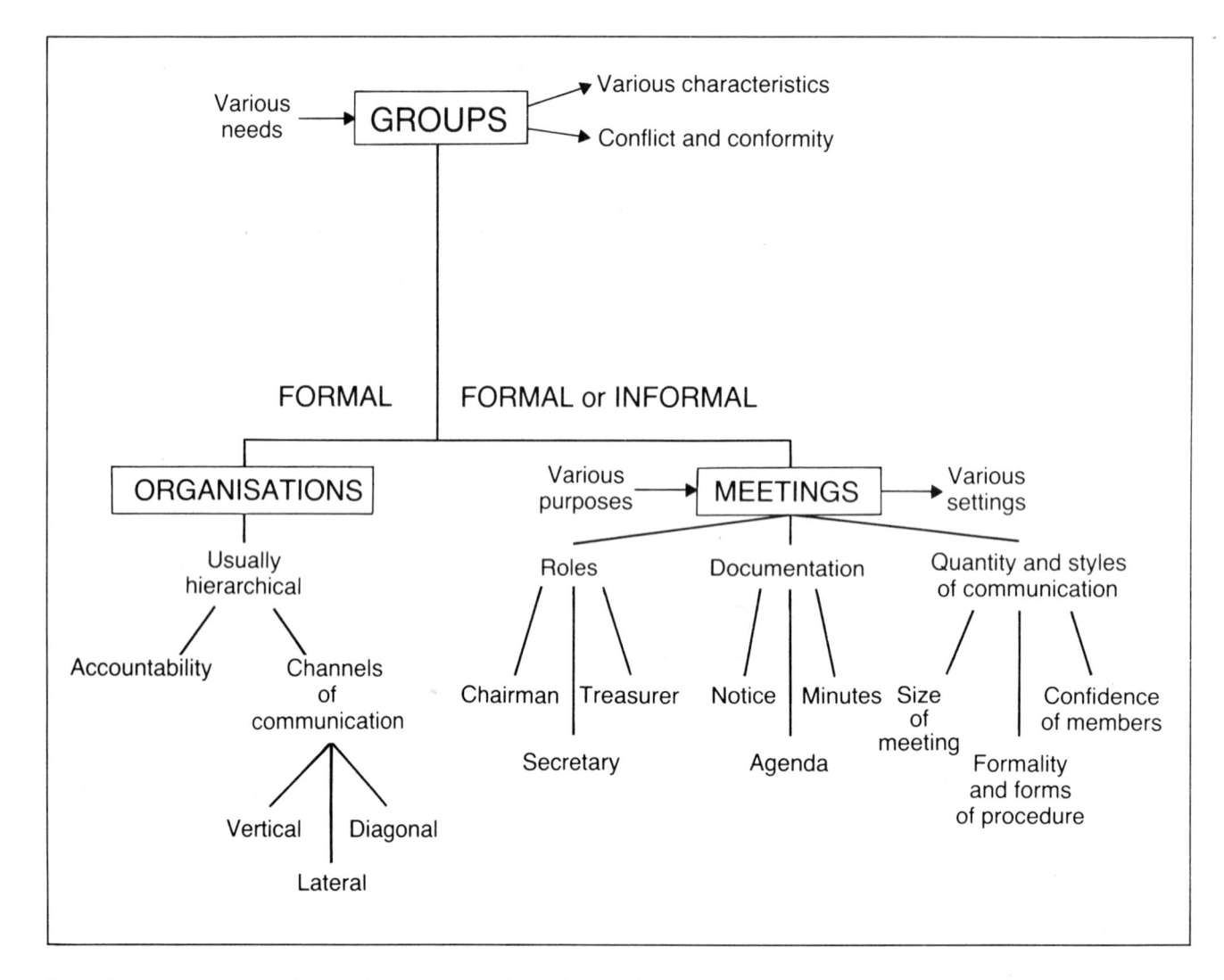

Fig. 6.6 Groups, organisations and meetings: a simplified model

Self-assessment

1. Give your own definition of a 'group'.
2. Give *three* characteristics of formal groups and *three* characteristics of informal groups.
3. Give *three* possible causes of conflict within groups.
4. Explain what is meant by saying that an organisation has a 'hierarchical' structure of management.
5. Define what is meant by a 'diagonal' channel of communication within an organisation.
6. Give *six* duties usually performed by the secretary of a meeting or committee.
7. Briefly define each of the following: notice; agenda; minutes.

Further work

1. Attend a formal committee meeting of your local council. Try to establish by observation what rules of procedure such a meeting follows and what written or unwritten rules of conduct the members are obeying.
2. Write an essay with the following title: 'The fixed rules of procedure adopted by formal groups help such groups conduct their business with a maximum of efficiency'. Discuss this proposition with examples based upon your own experience.
3. Make a list of various types of group. Complete the following table, listing your groups in the left-hand column. One example is given here to start you off.

Group	Formal or Informal	Reason for the group's existence/ Purpose of the group
Mothers' group	Informal	To act as a mutual-support group to mothers with young children who welcome help from others and feel the need to re-build their confidence in mixing with adults.

Further reading

Argyle M, *The Psychology of Interpersonal Behaviour* (Penguin, 1970)
Evans D, *People and Communication* (Pitman, 1978)
Foss B, *New Horizons in Psychology (No. 1)* (Penguin, 1966)
Sprott W.J.H, *Human Groups* (Penguin, 1970)

7 An introduction to mass communication

This chapter contains the following sections:

- **What is mass communication?**
- **Functions of mass communication in society**
- **The mass media**
- **Self-assessment**
- **Further work**
- **Further reading**

What is mass communication?

Mass communication is the sending of messages through the mass media of television, radio, newspapers, the cinema, etc.

Communication theorists have pointed to a number of characteristics which all mass communication has in common:

— It involves large, complex, formal organisations like the BBC and Twentieth Century Fox.

— It is aimed at massive audiences (unlike interpersonal communication) for example, up to hundreds of millions for an event like the World Cup Final.

— It is *public* in that anyone who has the technical means of reception, e.g. a transistor radio, can receive the message.

— It involves complex technology such as printing presses, transmitters and satellites.

— There is very little audience feedback. As D. McQuail has argued in *Communication*, 'the audience lacks representation'.

— Mass communication is *purposeful*. For example the BBC is obliged to transmit a range of informative, educational and entertaining programmes. Likewise, the *Daily Express* aims to put over a conservative view of how society should be ordered.

— It takes place through the **mass media**.

TASK *1* Re-read the characteristics of mass communication listed above and then make a list of the ways in which mass communication is different to interpersonal communication.

How has mass communication developed? Mass communication is a product of the 19th and 20th centuries. The Industrial Revolution of the 18th and early 19th centuries led to the urbanisation of Britain as millions of people began to concentrate in new towns and cities like Liverpool and Glasgow, looking for work in the new factory-based industries. These new urban centres expanded rapidly in the 19th century, some growing into massive conurbations. The populations of these cities became a mass audience with a growing need for information and entertainment. This provided an important stimulus, firstly to the development of the press and, later, to the growth of the cinema and broadcasting industries.

Newspapers, of course, could not flourish if people could not read them. This is where State intervention was important in the development of mass communication. Various governments passed legislation to improve educational provision for the new industrial working class, the Education Act of 1870 usually being credited as a major landmark in the drive towards mass literacy in Britain.

A mass literate market may have been developing but we still have to remember that the development of the mass media was still dependent on the technological advances made, in the case of cinema and broadcasting, in the late 19th and early 20th centuries.

To summarise, we can say that mass communication is the result of the trend towards a mass industrialised society in which the population has a relatively high level of literacy, allied to key developments in the world of technology.

Functions of mass communication in society

What role does mass communication play in a modern industrial society? The list below attempts to explain some of the more important functions of mass communication, although you might like to add others.

Information It is through newspapers, radio and television that the majority of the population obtains most of its knowledge about national and international affairs. Who, in Britain, would have known about the famine in East Africa if it were not for the reporting of Michael Buerk for the BBC?

Media organisations first have to collect information. In the case of **news**, the information will come from a variety of sources (staff journalists, freelance journalists, news agencies, the general public). The important point to make is that the organisation has to *select*, from the thousands of events and occurrences happening each day, the small minority which it can include in its newspaper or television programme. The *constraints* of the particular medium make this process inevitable. This process of selecting information, according to the particular **news values** of the organisation, is known as **gatekeeping**. To take a newspaper as an example, the most important gatekeeper is known as the **copytaster**. His or her job is to act as the point of contact for incoming 'raw news' and to decide whether the item should be included in the next edition, or followed up further by one of the paper's journalists. So, for every news item included in your morning newspaper, there will have been many others that were 'spiked' by the copytaster.

Fig. 7.1 The information function

CHANNEL FOUR NEWS

Entertainment The popular film industry has always been primarily a medium of mass entertainment rather than an 'art form', such has been the dominance of Hollywood and the commercial philosophy which it is based on. Similarly, light entertainment programmes are easily the most popular on television, whilst the radio stations based around pop and rock music (Radios 1 and 2 and all the Independent Radio stations) are way ahead, in terms of audience figures, of the more 'highbrow' stations like Radios 3 and 4. The fact is that most people prefer soap operas to documentaries and popular music to classical! However, as we shall see in Chapter 9 there has always been a prevailing ethos in British broadcasting that has argued that listeners and viewers should be fed on a more balanced diet than a continuous supply of soap operas, quiz shows and pop music.

Fig. 7.2 Mass communication as entertainment − *Spitting Image* (Central TV)

TASK *2* List *10* radio/TV programmes or films that are mainly entertainment-based.

Campaigning All media organisations have a particular view about how the world should be structured and how people ought to behave within it. Sometimes, the values are explicit or overt − for example, the *Morning Star* openly believes that we should adopt a social system similar to that existing in the Soviet Union. At other times, however, they are implicit or covert. These values are often expressed in the form of campaigns in favour of or against a particular social trend or government policy. A newspaper might wage a campaign in its pages against the EEC or the BBC might respond to the growing drugs problem in society through its *Drugwatch* programmes. In all these campaigns, the organisation is prepared to offer a corporate point of view to its audience, with the aim of changing either the attitudes or behaviour of that audience.

Socialisation Socialisation is the lifelong process through which an individual acquires the **culture** of his/her society. It encompasses both the acquisition of society's **core values**, e.g. individualism and competition in the USA, as well as shared **norms** of behaviour. Although the family is still the most important agency of socialisation, the mass media − especially television − have become increasingly influential in the transmission of a nation's culture from one generation to the next. It is also through the mass media that we learn many of the **norms** of behaviour in our society.

TASK 3 Re-read the above sections on Campaigning and Socialisation. Now discuss the various ways in which the mass media either lay down guidelines for the way we ought to behave in social situations, or offer us models for such behaviour. For example, are magazines entitled *Jackie* and *My Guy* likely to tell young teenage girls how they ought to live their lives if they want to be accepted by their peers? Make specific references to actual publications and programmes.

The mass media

We have already made brief references to the 'mass media' in this chapter. Let us now look at these media in greater detail. A simple definition from Blake and Haroldsen (see Further reading) might be: 'the technical devices through which mass communication takes place'.

The chart below includes a checklist of the most important and influential of the mass media, as well as homegrown and foreign examples of each.

MEDIUM	BRITAIN	FOREIGN
NEWSPAPERS	*Daily Mirror* *Today* *Yorkshire Post*	*Le Monde* (France) *Pravda* (Soviet Union) *Il Giorno* (Italy)
MAGAZINES	*Womans Own* *New Statesman* *TV Times*	*National Enquirer* (USA) *Der Spiegel* (W. Germany) *Femme* (France)
BOOKS	Publishers: Macmillan Virago Longmans	Flammarion (France) Wylie (USA) Harcourt Brace Jovanovich (USA)
RADIO	BBC Radio Four Capital Radio Radio Jackie	Radio Luxemburg Voice of America (USA) (broadcasting to Eastern Europe)
TELEVISION	BBC ITV Mersey Television	CBS (USA) Radio Telefis Eirrean (Eire)
CINEMA	Production: Goldcrest Handmade	United Artists (USA) Warner Brothers (USA)
SOUND RECORDING	Virgin Island EMI	Deutsche Grammophon (W. Germany) RCA (USA)

Fig. 7.3 The mass media

At this stage, we can point to three important trends in the development of the mass media:
— At various times over the past 150 years some media have declined in importance whilst others have become increasingly central to the workings of our society. For example, since the 1950s, television has replaced the press as the key agency of 'news telling' in society at the same time as taking over from the cinema as the population's main source of cheap entertainment.
— The technology used in mass communication has become increasingly more sophisticated over the years (for example fibre optic cables and satellites).

— Audiences have been steadily expanding in size as a result of these new technological advances. Modern satellites made possible an audience of 2.5 *billion* for the 1984 Los Angeles Olympic Games.

In this part of the book dealing with mass communication, we will look in most detail at newspapers, radio and, of course, television. As a prelude to these chapters, let us now take a broad look at these three key mass media shown in Figs. 7.4 and 7.5.

MEDIUM	MAJOR EVENTS	IMPORTANT THEMES
THE PRESS	* 1702 — First daily paper (*Daily Courant*) * 1785 — *The Times* first published * 1855 — STAMP DUTIES finally abolished * 1896 — First mass circulation, *Daily Mail* * 1912 — First million selling daily, *Daily Mirror* * 1963 — Press Council set up * 1977 — Report of Royal Commission on the Press * 1986 — *Today* and the *Independent* launched * 1987 — *News on Sunday* launched	* Development of a mass circulation daily press centred in London during the 19th and early 20th centuries * Increasing commercialisation of the press and reliance on advertising * Development of professional journalistic ethics * Concentration of ownership in 20th century and trend towards corporate, rather than individual ownership

Fig. 7.4 The development of the press

MEDIUM	MAJOR EVENTS	IMPORTANT THEMES
RADIO AND TELEVISION	* 1890s — First wireless transmissions * 1926 — British Broadcasting Corporation formed * 1926 — BBC backs Government during General Strike by TUC * 1936 — First scheduled TV service by BBC from Alexandra Palace * 1955 — ITV (Independent Television) set up * 1956 — First demonstration of video tape recording * 1962 — BBC2 established * 1962 — Pilkington Report * 1967 — Major reorganisation of BBC Radio * 1967 — First BBC local radio station * 1972 — First Independent local radio station * 1977 — Annan Report * 1982 — Channel Four came on air * 1983 — Breakfast Television * 1983 — Hunt Report on Cable * 1985 — Cable Authority established * 1986 — Contract awarded to DSB for Satellite TV channels * 1986 — Peacock Report * 1987 — BBC begins daytime service	* Regulation by the State from the outset (limited airwaves) * First of the mass media to offer supply (the technology) before the demand * Dominant ethos of PUBLIC SERVICE BROADCASTING * Change has been evolutionary * DEREGULATION likely in the 1990s and 21st century, if recommendations of PEACOCK COMMITTEE are followed

Fig. 7.5 The development of broadcasting

Self-assessment

1. List five characteristics of mass communication.
2. Briefly discuss the importance of the Information function in mass communication.
3. Define the term gatekeeping.
4. Define the term mass media and give five examples.
5. List three trends in the development of the mass media.

Further work

1. Read the following (i)–(v) and write an essay on (a) and (b) below.
   E.Katz, an American sociologist, lists five 'needs' to be fulfilled by the mass media:
   (i) Cognitive needs: the acquiring of information, knowledge and understanding.
   (ii) Affective needs: the need for emotional and aesthetic experience, love and friendship; the desire to see beautiful things.
   (iii) Personal integrative needs: the need for self-confidence, stability, status, reassurance.
   (iv) Social integrative needs: the need for strengthening contacts with family, friends and others.
   (v) Tension release needs: the need for escape and diversion.

   (a) How far do you regard this list as an accurate and adequate summary of the functions of the mass media?
   (b) Give examples of how mass media might fulfil three of these needs in Britain in the 1980s.
   (AEB A Level Communication Studies, Paper 1, 1983.)
2. Discuss a recent *Media Campaign* (for example anti-drugs) in terms of:
   – Its aims and objectives;
   – The techniques of persuasion used in the campaign;
   – Its target audience;
   – Its success or failure.

Further reading

Blake R.H and Haroldsen E.O, *A Taxonomy of Concepts in Communication* (Hastings House, 1975)

Fiske J, *Introduction to Communication Studies* (Methuen, 1982)

McQuail D, *Communication* (Longman, 1980)

McQuail D, *Towards a Sociology of Mass Communication* (Longman, 1969)

McQuail D, *Mass Communication Theory: An Introduction* (Sage, 1983)

This chapter contains the following sections:
- A brief history of the press in Britain
- The newspaper market
- Ownership and control
- Who pays for the press?
- The press and politics
- The future of the press
- Self-assessment
- Further work
- Further reading

A brief history of the press in Britain

Historically, the **press** was the first of the mass media to develop, followed by radio, cinema and television in the late 19th and early 20th centuries. The origins of the press in Britain are to be found in the early 17th century, and during its formative years the newspaper industry was subject to a great degree of governmental control and corruption. However, historians have noted how, during the next 200 years, newspapers were able to gain a much greater degree of independence from the State and establish a national commercial press based in London.

Most of the newspapers we read today were first published in the 19th century (for example, the *News of the World* in 1843 and the *Daily Telegraph* in 1855). This has been called the 'golden age' of the press, especially since the Stamp Duty (the so-called 'tax on knowledge') was finally abolished in the 1850s. An important time for the development of the press was the turn of the century, a period during which a number of today's newspapers like the *Daily Mail* (1896), the *Daily Express* (1900) and the *Daily Mirror* (1903) were first published. The *Mail*, devised by Alfred Harmsworth (later, Lord Northcliffe), is usually seen as the first of the modern mass circulation popular daily newspapers. It is also credited with helping to develop a **new journalism**, with an emphasis on entertainment as well as news-telling, a trend which has reached its logical conclusion with the styles of presentation associated with the 'pop tabloids' of the 1980s like the *Sun* and *Star*.

The first half of this century saw the newspaper industry reach its peak influence in terms of circulations and readership. The records show that the circulations of the national dailies rose by over 500% between 1918 and 1947. However, this rise in circulations was also accompanied by a significant decline in the number of titles published, giving the consumer less choice as a result. Another important trend was a concentration of press ownership in the hands of a small number of corporations.

Since the 1950s, the circulations of most types of newspaper have declined steadily, despite a rising population. Of course, television has provided an alternative source of information and entertainment; one might see 'breakfast television' as broadcast versions of popular newspapers. According to Graham Murdock and Peter Golding two other factors have also contributed to the relative decline of the newspaper:
- A decline in advertising revenue and,
- The rising cost of skilled labour.

THE DAILY Universal Register,

Printed Logographically — DIEU ET MON DROIT — By His Majesty's Patent.

NUMB. 1.] SATURDAY, JANUARY 1, 1785. [Price Two-pence Halfpenny.

The SIXTH NIGHT.
By His MAJESTY's Company
AT the THEATRE ROYAL in DRURY-LANE, this present SATURDAY, will be performed
A New COMEDY, called
The NATURAL SON.
The characters by Mr. King, Mr. Parsons, Mr. Bensley, Mr. Moody, Mr. Baddeley, Mr. Wrighten, and Mr. Palmer. Miss Pope, Miss Tidswell, and Miss Farren.
With new Scenes and Dresses.
The Prologue to be spoken by Mr. Bannister, jun.
And the Epilogue by Miss Farren.
After which will be performed the last New Pantomime Entertainment, in two Parts, called
HARLEQUIN JUNIOR;
Or, The MAGIC CESTUS.
The Characters of the Pantomime, by
Mr. Wright, Mr. Williamson, Mr. Burton, Mr. Staunton, Mr. Williames, Mr. Palmer, Mr. Waldron, Mr. Fawcett, Mr. Chaplin, Mr. Phillimore, Mr. Wilson, Mr. Alfred, Mr. Spencer, Mr. Chapman, and Mr. Grimaldi. Mrs. Burnet, Miss Burnett, Miss Tidiwell, Miss Barnes, Miss Cransford, and Miss Stageldoir.
To conclude with the Repulse of the Spaniards before
The ROCK of GIBRALTAR.

To-morrow, by particular desire, (for the 4th time) the revived Comedy of the DOUBLE DEALER, with the favorite Masque of ARTHUR and EMMELINE.
On Tuesday the Tragedy of VENICE PRESERVED; Jaffier by Mr. Brereton, Pierre by Mr. Bensley, and Belvidera, by Mrs. Siddons; And on Friday the Carmelite. Massinger's Play of the MAID of HONOUR, (with alterations and Additions) is in Rehearsal and will soon be produced.

NINTH NIGHT. FOR THE AUTHOR.
AT the THEATRE-ROYAL, COVENT-GARDEN, this present SATURDAY, January 1, 1785, will be performed, a New Comedy, called
The FOLLIES of a DAY,
Or, The Marriage of Figaro.
With new Dresses, Decorations, &c.
The principal characters by Mr. Lewis, Mr. Quick, Mr. Edwin, Mr. Wilson, Mr. Wewitzer, Mr. Bonnor, Mr. Thompson, and Mrs. Martyr; Mrs. Bates, Mrs. Webb, Miss Wewitzer, and Miss Younge.
With a new Prologue, to be spoken by Mr. Davies.
To which will be added, for the the sixth time,
A new Pantomime, called,
The MAGIC CAVERN,
Or, VIRTUE's TRIUMPH.
With new Scenery, Machinery, Music, Dresses, and Decorations.
The Scenes chiefly designed by Mr. Richards, and executed by him, Mr. Carver, Mr. Hodgins, and Assistants.
The Overture, Songs, Chorusses, and the Music of the new Pantomime, and composed by Mr. Shield.
Nothing under full Price will be taken.
The Words of the Songs, &c. to be had at the Theatre.

MR. WALTER returns his thanks to his Friends and the Public for the great encouragement and generous support he has already received from them to his new improvement in Printing, by the readiness with which they have subscribed to his intended publication of the works of some eminent Authors; and whilst he solicits a continuance of their favours, begs leave to acquaint them that by
The middle of January will be published,
In One Volume 12mo,
MISCELLANIES IN VERSE AND PROSE,
Intended as a Specimen of his Printing Types at the Logographic Office, Printing-House Square, Blackfriars.— And by the beginning of February, his first volume, containing Watts's Improvement of the Mind, with an Introduction written on the occasion, will be ready to be delivered to the subscribers.

This Day is published, Price 6d.
PLAN of the CHAMBER of COMMERCE, King's-Arms Buildings, Cornhill, London; which is open every day, for Consultation, Opinion, and Advice (verbal or in Writing) Mediation, Assistance, Arbitration, &c. in all *Commercial, Maritime,* and *Insurance* Affairs, and matters of *Trade* in general; and the *Laws* and *Usages* relating thereto.——The Address is, To the Director of the Chamber of Commerce, as above.
To be had of Richardson and Urquhart, Royal Exchange; J. Sewell, Cornhill; T. Whieldon, Fleet-street; W. Flexney, Holborn; and at the aforesaid Chamber.
Where may also be had, in one Volume Folio,
Mr. Weskett's COMPLETE DIGEST of the THEORY, LAWS and PRACTICE of INSURANCE; an entire new and comprehensive work, including all the adjudged Cases extant, with several never before printed; Extracts from the Statutes, foreign Ordinances, and marine Treaties; accounts of all the Insurance Companies the Maritime Courts, the commercial and maritime Laws, the Law of Nations, &c. the whole forming (alphabetically) a new *Lex Mercatoria.*
☞ "This Work has been compiled with great Care and Industry, by one who is evidently a Master of the Subject. It abounds with Proofs of extensive Reading, as well as mature Reflection, and judicious Remarks; and if the completest System of Insurance that has hitherto been composed be entitled to Praise, the present useful Digest must meet with the Approbation of the commercial World." Crit. Rev. Vol. 52, p. 443.—All the other Literary Journals speak in similar Terms of this Book; which had already been translated abroad.

This Day is published, in 3 Vols. Price 9s. sewed.
By the LITERARY SOCIETY,
MODERN TIMES: or The ADVENTURES of GABRIEL OUTCAST. A Novel, In Imitation of Gil Blas.
"Qui capit ille facit."
Printed for the Author, and sold by J. Walter, Printing-house Square, Black-friars; where may be had, gratis, the Plan of this Society, associated for the Encouragement of Literature, who propose to print and publish at their own Risk and Expence such original Works as they may approve of, and give their Authors all Profits arising from the same.

MRS. KING begs leave to acquaint her Friends she opens her SCHOOL at CHIGWELL in ESSEX, on Monday, the 10th of January, for the EDUCATION of YOUNG LADIES: as she has always been accustomed to watch and improve the opening mind, hopes to give satisfaction to those who trust her with so important a charge.
Till the 10th of January Mrs. King may be spoke with at Mr. Kerr's, Bitt-maker to his Majesty, in the Mews, Charing-cross.
N. B. Wanted an Apprentice and Half-boarder.

SHIP-PING ADVER-TISEMENTS

For NICE, GENOA, and LEGHORN,
(With Liberty to touch at One Port in the Channel,)
The NANCY.
THOMAS WHITE, Commander,
BURTHEN 160 Tons; Guns and Men answerable. Lying off the Tower, and will absolutely depart on Saturday the 8th instant.
The said Commander to be spoken with every morning at Sam's Coffee-house, near the Custom-house; at Will's Coffee-house, in Cornhill; and at Exchange hours on the French and Italian Walk, or
WILLIAM ELYARD, for the said Commander,
No. 16, Savage-Gardens.

Direct for LISBON,
The NANCY.
JOHN RACKHAM, Commander,
BURTHEN 300 Tons, Men answerable. Lying off Horslydown Chain; Seven-eighths of her Cargo absolutely engaged, and is obliged by Charter-party to depart on Saturday the 8th instant.
The said Commander to be spoken with every morning at Sam's Coffee-house, near the Custom-house; at Will's Coffee-house, in Cornhill; and in Exchange hours in the French and Italian Walk; or
WILLIAM ELYARD, for the said Commander,
No. 16, Savage-Gardens.

For NICE, GENOA, and LEGHORN.
(With Liberty to Touch at One Port in the Channel.)
The LIVELY,
ROBERT BRINE, Commander,
BURTHEN 209 Tons, Guns and Men answerable. Lying off Iron Gate.
The said Commander to be spoke with every Morning at Sam's Coffee-house, near the Custom-house; at Will's Coffee-house in Cornhill; and in Exchange Hours in the French and Italian Walk; or
WILLIAM ELYARD, for the said Commander,
No. 16, Savage-Gardens.

For CONSTANTINOPLE and SMYRNA, or SMYRNA and CONSTANTINOPLE,
(With Liberty to Touch at One Port in the Channel,)
The BETSEY,
ROBERT LANCASTER, Commander,
BURTHEN 200 Tons, Men answerable. Lying at Iron-Gate. Two-thirds of her Cargo engaged, and is obliged to depart by Charterparty, in all the present Month of January.
The said Commander to be spoke with every Morning at Sam's Coffee-house, near the Custom-house; at Will's Coffee-house in Cornhill; and in Exchange Hours in the French and Italian Walk; or
WILLIAM ELYARD, for the said Commender,
No. 16, Savage-Gardens.
N. B. No Goods to be taken on Board the Vessel without an Order from the Broker.

NEW NOVELS.
This Day are published, (in two Volumes, price 5s. sewed,)
THE YOUNG WIDOW; or, the HISTORY of Mrs. LEDWICH.
The HISTORY of Lord BELFORD and Miss SOPHIA WOODLEY, 3 vol. 9s. bound.
Printed for the Editor, and sold by F. Noble, in Holborn;
Where may be had lately published,
St. Ruthin's Abbey, a Novel, 3 vols. 9s. bound.
The Woman of Letters; or, History of Fanny Belton, 2 vol. 7s. bound.
A Lesson for Lovers; or, History of Col. Melville and Lady Richly, 2 vols. 7s. bound.
Literary Amusements; or, Evening Entertainer, 2 vol. 7s. bound.
Adventures of a Cavalier, by Daniel Defoe, 3 vols. 9s bound.

T. RICKABY, PRINTER,
No. 15, Duke's Court, Drury Lane;
RESpectfully informs his Friends and the Public in general, that the Partnership between him and Mr. Moore being entirely dissolved, he now intends to carry on every branch of the PRINTING BUSINESS upon his own account;—and having purchased a complete assortment of the neatest and best materials, is determined to pursue a Mode of Printing which he hopes will meet with the approbation of his employers.
N.B. Cards, Hand-Bills, Circular Letters, and all articles of the kind, accurately printed at a few hours notice. in a manner particularly neat, and at the lowest prices.
⁂ An Apprentice wanted.

To the Readers of the London Medical Journal.
This day is first published, price 1s.
SYMPATHY DEFENDED; or, the State MEDICAL CRITICISM in London; written to improve the Principles and Manners of the Editor of the London Medical Journal: To which are added the Contents of the Treatise on Medical Sympathy, and a Postscript, on account of a premature Review in a late Number of the London Medical Journal.
By a Society of Faculties;
Friends to the Public and Enemies to Imposition.
"Cum tua non edas, carpis mea carmina, Laeli,
"Carp re vel noli nostra, ede tua."
MART. Epig.
This pamphlet has been hitherto distributed gratuitously. The repeated applications for them, particularly from the country, have become so numerous, that the Society feel themselves under the necessity of putting them into the hands of a publisher.
Sold by J. Murray, Bookseller, Fleet-street.

Nondum lingua silet dextra, peregit opus.
MART.
SHORT-HAND, on the latest and most approved Principles taught by J. LARKHAM, No 11, Rose Alley, Bishopsgate Street.
It would exceed the limits of an advertisement merely to mention the various errors either in the *plan* or the number of the different schemes of Short hand hitherto made public, or to point out the peculiarities and excellencies of the present: Mr. L. therefore only begs leave to observe, that the approbation of many gentlemen well known in the literary world, and well versed in the *Theory* and *Practice* of Short-hand, expressed in stronger terms than delicacy will permit him to repeat, warrants him in saying *his* will be found a system of short and swift writing; more *easy* to acquire and retain, more *expeditiously*, more *legible* and more *regular* than any ever yet offered to the Public.
The terms of teaching *one* Guinea, the *usual* time of learning *seven* lessons.

To the Public.

TO bring out a New Paper at the present day; when so many others are already established and confirmed in the public opinion, is certainly an arduous undertaking; and no one can be more fully aware of its difficulties than I am: I, nevertheless, entertain very sanguine hopes, that the nature of the plan on which this paper will be conducted, will ensure it a moderate share at least of public favour; but my pretensions to encouragement, however strong they may appear in my own eyes, must be tried before a tribunal not liable to be blinded by *self-opinion*: to that tribunal I shall now, as I am bound to do, submit these pretensions with deference, and the public will judge whether they are well or ill founded.

It is very far from my intention to detract from the acknowledged merit of the Daily Papers now in existence; it is sufficient that they please the class of readers whose approbation their conductors are ambitious to deserve; nevertheless it is certain some of the best, some of the most respectable, and some of the most useful members of the community, have frequently complained (and the causes of their complaints still exist) that by radical defects in the plans of the present established papers, they were deprived of many advantages, which ought naturally to result from daily publications. Of these some build their fame on the length and accuracy of parliamentary reports, which unquestionably are given with great ability, and with a laudable zeal to please those, who can spare time to read ten or twelve columns of debates. Others are principally attentive to the politics of the day, and make it their study to give satisfaction to the numerous class of politicians, who, blessed with easy circumstances, have nothing better to do, than to amuse themselves with watching the motions of ministers both at home and abroad; and endeavouring to find out the secret springs that set in motion the great machine of government in every state and empire in the world. There is one paper which in no degree interferes with the pursuits of its cotemporaries; it looks upon parliamentary debates as sacred mysteries, that cannot be submitted to vulgar eyes without profanation; political investigations it apprehends to be little short of treason, and therefore *loyally* abstains from them; it deals almost solely in advertisements; and consequently, though a very useful, it is by no means an entertaining paper. Thus it would seem that every News-Paper published in London is calculated for a particular set of readers only; so that if each set were to change its favourite publication for another, the commutation would produce disgust, and dissatisfaction to all; the politician would then find nothing to amuse him but long accounts of petty squabbles about trifles in Parliament, or panegyrics on the men and measures that he most disliked; or libels on those whom he most revered. The person to whom parliamentary debates afford unspeakable delight, would find himself bored with political speculations about the measures that the different courts in Europe might probably adopt; or disgusted with whole pages of advertisements, in which he felt no concern;—whilst the plain shop-keeper who wanted to find a convenient house for his business, and the servant who purchased his paper in hopes of seeing in it an advertisement directing where he might find a place to suit him, would have their labour for their pains, in perusing publications, filled with senatorial debates, or political essays and remarks, which would direct them to nothing less than the house or place they wanted.—A News-Paper, conducted on the true and natural principles of such a publication, ought to be the Register of the times, and faithful recorder of every species of intelligence; it ought not to be engrossed by any particular object; but, like a well-covered table, it should contain something suited to every palate: observations on the dispositions of our own and of foreign courts should be provided for the political reader; debates should be reported for the amusement or information of those who may be particularly fond of them; and a due attention should be paid to the interests of trade, which are so greatly promoted by advertisements.—A paper that should blend all these advantages, and by steering clear of extremes, hit the happy medium, has long been expected by the public.—Such, it is intended, shall be the UNIVERSAL REGISTER, the great objects of which will be to facilitate the *commercial* intercourse between the different parts of the community, through the channel of *Advertisements*; to record the principal occurrences of the times; and to abridge the account of debates during the sitting of Parliament.

It is no less the interest of the proprietors of News-Papers, than of the public, that every encouragement should be given to advertising correspondents; yet this private interest of the proprietors is frequently sacrificed to the rage for parliamentary debates, to the great injury of trade; for the extreme length of these debates so greatly retards the publication of the New-Papers which are noted for detailed accounts of them, that the advantages arising from this species of intelligence, though highly acceptable in itself, are frequently over-balanced by the inconvienences occasioned to people in business by the delay. These inconveniences are great and many; it generally happens, that when either House of Parliament has been engaged in the discussion of an important question till after midnight, the papers in which the speeches of the Members are reported at large, cannot be published before noon; nay, they sometimes are not even sent to press so soon; consequently parties interested in *sales* are essentially injured, as the advertisements, inviting the public to attend them at *ten* or *twelve* o'clock, do not appear, on account of a late publication, till some hours after.—From the same source flows another inconvenience; it is sometimes found necessary to *defer* sales, after they have been advertised for a particular day; but the notice of putting them off not appearing early enough, on account of the late hour at which the papers containing it are published, numbers of people, acting under the impression of former advertisements, are unnecessarily put to the trouble of attending.—It will be the object of the *Universal Register* to guard against these great inconveniences, without depriving its readers of the pleasure of learning what passes in Parliament.—It is intended, then, that the debates shall be regularly reported in it; but on the other hand, that the publication may not be delayed to the prejudice of people in trade, the speeches will not be given on a large scale; the *substance* shall be faithfully preserved; but all the uninteresting parts will be omitted. I shall thus be enabled to publish this paper at an early hour; and I propose to bring it out *regularly* every morning at *six* o'clock. The *Universal Register* will therefore have this advantage over the *Daily Advertiser*, that, though published as early, it will contain a substantial account of the proceedings in Parliament the preceding night, which is never to be found in that paper; and compared with the other morning papers it will be found to have the merit of containing in substance, what they give in long detail (which men in business cannot well spare time to read) and, nevertheless, of being published much sooner. These circumstances, it is hoped, will give the *Universal Register* at least an *equal* claim to public favour with the parliamentary papers, and the *trading* part of the metropolis, it is presumed, will find it their advantage to give it the preference.

An essential part of the plan of this new paper is, that, for the convenience of advertising correspondents, their favours shall, *to a certainty*, be inserted on the very day that they shall direct; provided they deliver them at the office in due time. For the *strict* observance of this rule, the credit of the paper shall stand pledged; and its pretensions to public countenance will be renounced, if this fundamental principle in its institution shall ever be violated, except in cases of absolute necessity, which human prudence cannot prevent.—And here I beg it may be understood that I do not make use of the word *necessity* as a reserve, under colour of which, I may, whenever I think fit, be released from my engagements; I mean by that word a necessity arising from accidents that sometimes happen in the printing business, and from which, the most careful man cannot, at all times, be secure. But so far from wishing to shrink from my engagements, I intend, whenever the length of the Gazette, Parliamentary Debates, &c. shall render it impossible for me to insert all the advertisements promised for the day, in *one* sheet, to print an additional half sheet, and publish it with the ordinary paper without any additional charge to my customers.—From the difficulty that people experience in procuring the insertion of their advertisements even in the *Daily Advertiser*; and particularly from the impossibility of obtaining an *early* insertion at some periods of the year, it may be presumed that this regulation will greatly recommend the UNIVERSAL REGISTER to public notice, and procure it support.

These, though in my opinion good, are not the *only* grounds on which I build my hopes of success. I flatter myself, I have some claim to public encouragement, on account of a great improvement which I have made in the art of printing. The inconveniences attending the old and tedious mode of composing with letters taken up *singly*, first suggested the idea of devising some more expeditious method. The cementing of several letters together, so as that the type of a *whole word* might be taken up in as short a time as that of a *single letter*, was the result of much reflection on that subject. But the bare idea of cementing was merely the opening, not the accomplishment or perfection of the improvement. The fount consisting of types of words, and not of letters, was to be so arranged, as that a compositor should be able to find the former with as much facility as he can the latter. This was a work of inconceivable difficulty. I undertook it however, and was fortunate enough, after an infinite number of experiments, and great labour, to bring it to a happy conclusion. The whole English language is now methodically and systematically arranged at my fount: so that printing can now be performed with greater dispatch, and at less expence, than according to the mode hitherto in use.

In bringing this work to perfection, I had not my own advantage solely in view; I wished to be useful to the community; and it is with pleasure I see that the public will derive considerable benefit from my industry; for I have resolved to sell the REGISTER *One halfpenny* UNDER the price paid for seven out of eight of the morning

Fig. 8.1 The first issue of *The Times*

However, this decline is far from absolute since the past few years have shown that it is still possible to launch new titles successfully whether they are from existing publishers (the *Daily Star* in 1979 and the *Mail on Sunday* in 1982) or competely new ventures like *Today* and the *Independent* in 1986. In addition, it is likely that one of the main results of the 1986 'Wapping' dispute between Rupert Murdoch and the print unions will be a decline in the relative labour costs in newspaper production.

In the rest of this chapter we will look at the state of the newspaper market today, who owns and controls the press, how it obtains its revenue, political bias in the press and what the future might hold for newspapers in Britain.

The newspaper market

In Britain a variety of types of newspaper are published each day or week. Here is a checklist:
— National Dailies (e.g. *Sun, Star, The Times*);
— National Sundays (*Observer, People, Sunday Express*);
— Provincial Mornings (*Yorkshire Post, Western Daily Press*);
— Local Evenings (*Manchester Evening News, Nottingham Evening Post*);
— Local Weeklies (*Hereford Times, Ilkeston Advertiser*);
— Freesheets (*Trader Group, Midlands; Messenger Group, Lancashire*);
— Political Press (*Socialist Worker, Newsline*);
— Community Press (published by community groups and local organisations, e.g. *New Manchester Review* in Manchester, and *Leeds' Other Paper*, in Leeds).

 **TASK /**

Conduct a survey of all the local newspapers published in your local area. For each of the titles, find out:
— When it was first published.
— How often it is published.
— Its average circulation and its circulation area.
— Who owns it.
Present your findings in the form of a short profile, with diagrams where appropriate.

TITLE	ESTABLISHED	CIRCULATION (JULY−DEC 86)
SUN	1964	4 049 991
DAILY MIRROR	1903	3 139 179
DAILY STAR	1979	1 278 058
DAILY MAIL	1896	1 732 413
DAILY EXPRESS	1900	1 726 504
TODAY	1986	307 150
DAILY TELEGRAPH	1855	1 131 597
GUARDIAN	1821	506 886
THE TIMES	1785	467 216
FINANCIAL TIMES	1888	254 236
INDEPENDENT	1986	302 502

Source: Audit Bureau of Circulations and Benn's Media Directory

Fig. 8.2 The daily newspaper market

This section will mainly be concerned with the national daily and Sunday newspaper market. As you can see in Fig. 8.2, the most popular papers are the tabloids like the *Sun* and *Mirror* whilst the 'quality' press like the *Daily Telegraph* and *Guardian* have relatively small circulations.

TASK *2*   Present the information contained in Fig. 8.2 in an appropriate *visual* format, in a way that would be easily understood by a communication studies student.

We must, of course, remember that the readership of a newspaper is always higher than its circulation since more than one person in a family will read the paper each day. For example, the *News of the World's* readership is estimated to be over 11 million with a circulation of 5 million.

Popular and quality newspapers   As we have seen, the popular tabloids are easily the most widely read of our newspapers. Let us now look at some of the differences in style, presentation and content between the popular and quality press as shown in Figs. 8.3 and 8.4.

POPULAR NEWSPAPERS	QUALITY NEWSPAPERS
1. *Sun, Mirror, Express, Mail, Star, Today, News of the World, Sunday Mirror, Sunday Express, Mail on Sunday, Sunday People, News on Sunday.*	1. *Telegraph, Independent, Guardian, The Times, Financial Times, The Sunday Times, Sunday Telegraph, Observer.*
2. They are all tabloid in size, i.e. 16" by 23".	2. The qualities are 'broadsheets' i.e. exactly double the size of a tabloid.
3. The tabloids contain a higher proportion of photographs, illustrations and other visual material.	3. The qualities are 'wordier' in content, with much less emphasis on visual support.
4. Their style is often sensationalist in tone, with banner style headlines across the page e.g. 'Thrilled to Blitz', *Sun* 16.4.86.	4. Papers like the *Guardian* and *The Times* adopt a more sober, less emotive style of presentation, e.g. 'World Angered by Revenge Attack', *Guardian* 16.4.86.
5. In recent years the pop tabloids appear to have evolved into organs of mass entertainment as much as 'news', with their emphasis on TV soap-operas, Hollywood Stars and Page 3.	5. The main communication purpose of the quality press is to inform its (relatively educated) readership about national and international affairs.
6. The language used is simple and easy to understand, the vocabulary is narrower and the syntax is simpler.	6. Quality papers are characterised by a more complex language code, a wider vocabulary and a more complicated syntax.
7. These newspapers are read mainly by working and lower-middle class people.	7. The qualities are read, by and large, by middle class professional people.

Fig. 8.3 Popular and quality newspapers

Newspapers and social class   It is worth looking in greater detail at the relationship between **social class** and newspaper readership. A simplified way of pigeon-holing a person's social class is the ABC1C2DE classification system used by sociologists. Depending on their occupation, people are placed on a scale ranging from As, e.g. Managing directors and university lecturers to Es, e.g. unemployed, casual workers. (See Fig. 8.5.)

The sobering truth behind a staggering bender

BRITAIN ON THE BOTTLE

BOOZE-UP Britain is on a mammoth bender. Hitting the bottle has become a national pastime with drinkers splashing out a staggering £43 million EVERY DAY on their tipple.

The problem has become so widespread that the Government has been forced to set up a special "task force" to combat alcohol misuse.

A nationwide survey carried out by the organisation—Action on Alcohol Abuse—revealed yesterday that children as young as eleven are taking their homework into pubs in Devon and Cornwall.

A report on the survey also disclosed that boys aged 14 are drinking up to ten pints of beer a week in the same area.

Others of the same age are knocking back up to 20 glasses of wine or spirits.

The survey has found that 3,000 people die every year from liver diseases caused by boozing.

Signs that Britain is heading for a colossal hangover as revealed in the detailed study include:

SPECIAL education courses have been set up to encourage "sensible drinking" among ex-prisoners on probation in Somerset.

UNIVERSITY dons and

By ALAN LAW

managers of new high-tech companies in East Anglia are among those at the highest risk of alcoholism in the region.

DRINK is "very much part of the social fabric of Cambridge university and college life"...where "there is a heavy drinking culture" among students and senior staff.

Idle

ALL-DAY drinking sessions by old winos and idle youngsters in Coventry city centre are frightening away tourists.

A GROWING number of

"fun pubs" are being set up in job-starved Merseyside. They have been slammed by Margot Kenyon, director of the Merseyside, Lancashire and Cheshire Council on Alcoholism, as being "places designed more like discos for people aged about 14 or 15."

THE North West Regional Health Authority has launched a £165,000 "drink wisely" campaign after figures showed the region has the highest level of alcohol consumption in Britain—25 per cent above the national average.

The region also reporte-

● We spend £43m a day on booze
● 3,000 a year die of liver disease
● 11-year-olds do homework in pubs
● A schoolboy of 14 is an alcoholic

£2bn cost of drink problems sparks Government action

By David Cross

Action to combat the £2 billion a year problem of alchoholism will be on the agenda of a new ministerial group due to meet soon for the first time.

The group, set up last month by Mr Douglas Hurd, the Home Secretary, along the lines of the ministerial group on drug abuse, is headed by Mr John Wakeham, Leader of the House of Commons.

It will be working out a co-ordinated strategy to tackle a problem which is now the country's third biggest health hazard, after heart disease and cancer and claims up to 40,000 lives a year.

A regional survey carried out by the Press Association discloses that despite the countless accidents and personal misery caused by overdrinking, the health service could barely cope with the rising demand for treatment at the few available detoxification centres; laws against under-age drinking and drinking and driving were not enforced; only 13 per cent of drivers involved in accidents were breathalyzed; and most companies had not yet formulated an alcoholism policy to help staff with a drinking problem.

Sales of alcoholic drinks have doubled over the past 30 years and now bring in taxes worth £6,000 million billion.

because they are unconfident, unhappy, lonely and have little support. They warn that women's bodies are more easily damaged by drink than men's.

The costs to society are enormous. It is reckoned that a violent crime is committed every eight minutes by people who have been drinking.

Dr Bruce Ritson, a member of the Royal College of Psychatrists' alcohol working party, critizing the Government's plans to extend licensing hours, said that he wondered why the law was being liberalized when there was good evidence that the existing laws, for example on underage drinking, were poorly enforced.

Dr John Havard, secretary of the British Medical Association, said even existing drink-drive laws were not enforced properly. He said: "Unfortunately the risk of being caught at current levels of enforcement is remote, and is known to be so by those who regularly drink and drive without being caught."

The Press Association survey showed in London the number of problem drinkers has trebled over the past 25 years, to 750,000 with many in their twenties and thirties. Dr David Marjot, consultant psychiatrist at St Bernard's Hospital, Ealing, said that

five boys aged 14 questioned drank up to ten pints of beer a week or 20 glasses of wine or spirits, and that half the children aged 11 questioned drank some alcohol each week.

The Ministerial alcohol abuse group is expected to study plans for a drink-free zone in Coventry, West Midlands, where 12 per cent of men and 2 per cent of women are estimated to be drinking at levels harmful to their health. The city council, magistrates and the police all want to ban drinking in the open air in the city centre.

Mrs Margot Jenyon, executive director of the Merseyside, Lancashire and Cheshire Council on Alcoholism, said that alcoholism among young people was often a symptom of of underlying causes such as unemployment.

She believes sporting figures and celebrities they look up to should actively encourage a non-drinking lifestyle.

The North-west has one of the highest levels of alcohol consumption in Britain, 25 per cent above the national average.

Mrs Liz Smith, director of the Greater Manchester and Lancashire Regional Council on Alcohol, saidz; "The major problem today is not drugs and it is not AIDS. It is

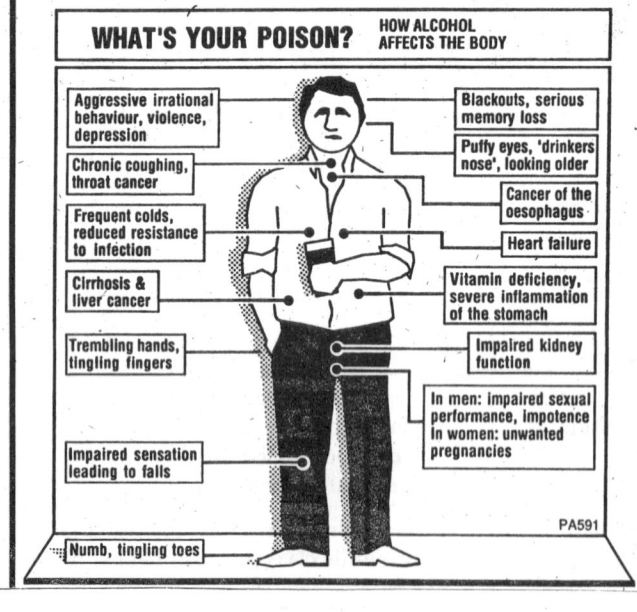

WHAT'S YOUR POISON? **HOW ALCOHOL AFFECTS THE BODY**

- Aggressive irrational behaviour, violence, depression
- Chronic coughing, throat cancer
- Frequent colds, reduced resistance to infection
- Cirrhosis & liver cancer
- Trembling hands, tingling fingers
- Impaired sensation leading to falls
- Numb, tingling toes
- Blackouts, serious memory loss
- Puffy eyes, 'drinkers nose', looking older
- Cancer of the oesophagus
- Heart failure
- Vitamin deficiency, severe inflammation of the stomach
- Impaired kidney function
- In men: impaired sexual performance, impotence In women: unwanted pregnancies

PA591

Fig. 8.4 Popular and quality: different styles of presentation at work in *The Times* and the *Daily Mirror*

	Socio-Economic Grades in the UK	
A	Higher managerial, administrative or professional	
B	Intermediate managerial, administrative or professional	
C1	Supervisory or clerical, and junior managerial, administrative or professional	
C2	Skilled manual worker	
D	Semi and unskilled manual workers	
E	State pensioners or widows (no other earner in household), casual or lower grade workers, and unemployed	

Fig. 8.5 ABC1C2DE

The following statistics (Fig. 8.6) are taken from a *National Readership Survey* undertaken in 1985 and support the notion that British newspapers are founded on the rock of social class. This chart also gives us much useful information concerning the readership of newspapers by **age** and **sex**. The information contained in this chart would be of special interest to potential advertisers (see Case Study 4: Medicheck, p. 187).

TITLES	SOCIO-ECONOMIC GROUP						AGE					SEX	
	A %	B %	C1 %	C2 %	D %	E %	15/24 %	25/34 %	35/44 %	45/54 %	55+ %	M %	F %
DAILY TELEGRAPH	14	40	29	10	5	3	13	9	19	19	39	55	45
GUARDIAN	9	43	26	13	6	3	25	24	20	16	15	61	39
THE TIMES	17	41	28	9	3	2	24	18	22	18	18	60	40
FINANCIAL TIMES	17	38	31	8	4	1	19	19	30	16	16	71	29
SUN	0	5	17	37	26	14	26	19	17	14	24	54	46
DAILY MIRROR	1	7	19	35	26	13	22	17	16	14	29	55	45
DAILY EXPRESS	4	19	30	27	14	7	18	14	17	14	37	52	48
DAILY MAIL	4	22	32	26	9	6	17	15	17	16	35	49	51
DAILY STAR	1	4	15	37	30	14	29	22	17	12	21	59	41

Source: A National Readership Survey, 1985

Fig. 8.6 A National Readership Survey

 **TASK 3** Study Fig. 8.6 carefully and answer the following questions.

1. Which newspaper has the highest proportion of As and Bs amongst its readers?
2. Which has the highest proportion of C1s and C2s?
3. Which newspaper can boast the highest proportion of Ds and Es?
4. Which newspaper has the highest *number* of ABC1s in its readership?
5. Which is the only newspaper to have more female than male readers?
6. Which newspapers have the oldest and youngest readership profiles?

The power of the audience

It could be argued that power in the newspaper industry lies with the **audience**, who can decide each day which paper to buy. If a newspaper loses its readers to a rival it may go out of business or it may have to modify its format or style like the *Sun* did after it was acquired by Rupert Murdoch in the 1960s. However, newspapers cannot change *too* much. We can predict that if the *Sun* started to include two page articles on the Stock Exchange or the *Guardian* began using three inch high headlines, a large proportion of their loyal audiences would probably switch to another paper. In this sense, perhaps we do get 'the newspapers we deserve'?

Ownership and control

At the turn of this century newspaper ownership was dominated by powerful men known as **Press Barons**, like Alfred Harmsworth. They were in the newspaper business for reasons of social status and to influence 'the masses' as well as to make money. However, the most important trend in the 20th century has been towards **corporate** ownership by large, sometimes multinational, corporations, with a corresponding decline in the number of titles on offer to the audience. The national newspaper market in Britain is dominated by four such corporations. Fig. 8.7 lists the titles they own, their total circulations and their percentage share of the market. They control almost 80% of the national daily market and are 90% of the Sunday market.

CORPORATION	TITLES	TOTAL CIRCULATION (MILLIONS)	% OF MARKET
NEWS INTERNATIONAL	*Sun, The Times, The Sunday Times, News of the World, Today*	10.96	34
PERGAMON	*Mirror, Sunday Mirror, People*	9.00	27
UNITED NEWSPAPERS	*Daily Express, Daily Star, Sunday Express*	5.80	17
ASSOCIATED NEWSPAPERS	*Daily Mail, Mail on Sunday*	3.44 ⎯⎯ 29.20m	10 ⎯⎯ 88%

Fig. 8.7 Corporate ownership

We must also remember that companies like Associated Newspapers also have significant interests in the local press in Britain. One major exception to the rule of corporate ownership is the *Guardian* which is owned by a Trust which, it argues, guarantees its independence from an interfering owner.

Many critics argue that such a concentration of press ownership has negative effects, especially with regard to the narrow range of opinions which results from this state of affairs.

Who pays for the press?

We have seen that the press in Britain is mainly privately owned by large corporations. They do not rely on public subsidy; hence they are free from formal governmental control. In some countries like the Soviet Union newspapers like *Pravda* are under strict State control. British newspapers obtain their **revenue** from two sources:

— The **cover price:** Popular newspapers like the *Sun* are cheaper to buy than the qualities because they use less newsprint but also because their readers come from lower socio-economic groups and have smaller incomes.

— **Advertising**: According to the Report of the last Royal Commission on the Press (1977) advertising is the 'most important source of revenue for all classes of publication', except for the tabloids.

Who depends on advertising the most? Fig. 8.8 shows the relative dependence of different kinds of newspaper on advertising.

TYPE OF PUBLICATION	% FROM ADVERTISING	% FROM SALES
POPULAR DAILIES	27	73
POPULAR SUNDAYS	31	69
QUALITY DAILIES	58	42
QUALITY SUNDAYS	66	34
REGIONAL DAILIES	61	39
REGIONAL WEEKLIES	84	16

Source: Advertising Association

Fig. 8.8 Reliance on advertising

Types of advertising

There are *three* types of advertising in the press:

— **Classified** These are columns of tightly-packed ads composed only of words and used by private individuals, employers, small businesses etc. The advertiser chooses the wording but does not have control over the layout.

— **Display** These are larger ads from quarter page size to double page spreads. The most important characteristic of display ads is that the advertising agency buys the space from the newspaper and then has control over what is actually put into that space.

— **Semi-display** The size of this ad is in between classified and display. Again, the advertiser has a degree of control over the nature of the ad but it will be composed mainly of type inserted by the newspaper.

 TASK *4* Find out how much a **full page display ad** costs in your local evening paper.

Different types of advert are more important for different types of publication. The last Royal Commission on the press found that display ads were more important for the national populars (accounting for 85% of ads in 1975) whilst classified ads contributed to over 60% of the revenue coming in to the provincial evening press in the same year.

How does advertising affect the press?

Some people argue that a reliance on advertising can affect what is written in a newspaper. For example, if a large food manufacturer advertises in a popular newspaper is that paper likely to publish a report about the dangers of food additives if there is the possibility that the company will withdraw its lucrative advertising and switch to a rival publication? Or are newspapers wary about supporting controversial viewpoints for fear of driving away present or potential advertisers? To take a case in point, if the labour movement were to start their own left-wing daily newspaper would the large food, drink and motor car manufacturers be willing to advertise in it?

It could also be true that in their search for the highest possible mass readership (and, therefore, advertisers) the popular press 'play safe' and appeal to the **lowest common denominator** of public taste. The press is a medium in which there is very little regulation of content. The proprietors and editors are allowed to give the public what they want, within certain legal constraints and there is no obligation to provide a balanced account.

Competition for advertising

Of course, the press has to **compete** for advertising with other media, especially commercial television. It is difficult to gauge the precise effect on press advertising since the arrival of ITV in 1955, although the last Royal Commission noted that TV advertising has grown faster than display advertising in the press. In 1985 press advertising accounted for 63% of all advertising in Britain, compared to 31% for broadcasting.

Another powerful competitor (especially for the local press) is the web of free newspapers/freesheets developed since the 1970s which now take 10% of all press advertising.

Fig. 8.9 Types of advert

The press and politics

Political bias is a fact of life in Fleet Street, with the majority of the national press showing a distinct bias towards conservative values in general and the Conservative Party in particular. This is especially true of newspapers like the *Daily Telegraph, Daily Mail, Daily Express* and *Sun*. Other titles like *The Times* and *Financial Times* support conservatism without necessarily being quite so strident as the others. In fact, only the *Daily Mirror* has consistently supported the ideas associated with the Labour Party, whilst the *Guardian, Independent* and *Today* like to feel they are 'non-aligned', operating in the middle ground of the political spectrum. Figs. 8.10 and 8.11 are front pages from the *Sun* and the *Mirror*.

LES DAWSON WIFE DIES OF CANCER See Page 7

Wednesday, April 16, 1986 · 18p   TODAY'S TV IS ON PAGE 14

THRILLED TO BLITZ!

Bombing Gaddafi was my greatest day says US airman

By KIERON SAUNDERS

JUBILANT American bomber pilots were walking on air last night after the revenge mission aimed at wiping out Libya's "Mad Dog" Colonel Gaddafi.

One airman described the hit-and-run raid as the "greatest thrill of my life." But another crewman said he regretted the crazed dictator had escaped with his life and that "we didn't nail the bastard."

The raid early yesterday was spearheaded by 18 F-111 bombers based in Britain—backed by 15 warplanes from U.S. carriers in the Mediterranean.

The attack was ordered by President Reagan as a reprisal against recent outrages by Libyan bomb squads.

One airman, relaxing in a bar near his base at Mildenhall, Suffolk, said: "We were not told until the last minute we were taking part."

The fuel tanker flier added that Gaddafi was "a schizo."

Gaddafi . . . escape

SUN NEWS SPECIAL
See Pages 2,3,4,5 and 6

"How else do you deal with a guy like him?"

Gaddafi's adopted year-old daughter Hanna died in a direct hit on his HQ, Libyan doctors claimed. Another 13 people are said to have been killed with about 100 injured.

Two F-111s failed to get back from the mission—the biggest air strike by the Americans since Vietnam.

A search for one that ditched in the Mediterranean was going on last night. A second F-111 landed in Spain after its engine overheated.

Mission accomplished . . . smiling Americans at Lakenheath, Suffolk, yesterday after the raid

Fig. 8.10 'Thrilled to Blitz'

OUR NHS
—AND THE GREAT TORY LIE

Upside down world of the Rt. Hon. Norman Fowlup PC. MP.

NORMAN FOWLER, the man responsible for the appalling state of the Health Service, yesterday attacked the Mirror for our campaign against his cuts.

That was a tribute to us, an indictment of him.

He attacked Joe Haines, our group political editor and columnist, for daring to write about the terrible state of a service that was once the envy of the world.

That was a tribute to Joe.

The Mirror's campaign has already brought about the political downfall of Barney H.yhoe and Ray Whitney, the men formerly responsible for running the NHS.

BY THE EDITOR

They were sacked because they couldn't convince anyone that they were right and the Mirror was wrong. Mr Fowler should take note of that.

Smug

His attack on us yesterday was smug, self-satisfied and arrogant. But then he doesn't live in the real world.

During the past nine months, we have run many stories illustrating how the Tories are destroying the NHS.

The evidence against Mrs

Thatcher and Mr Fowler is overwhelming.

Ask those who cannot get a hospital bed. Ask those who cannot get a dialysis machine. Ask those who cannot get adequate screening for cervical cancer.

Caring Tories? Their world is tawdry and tatty, a world dominated by Number One. A world that cynically turns the truth on its head.

That is why today the Mirror is the only paper to show you Mr Fowler in his true perspective.

FOWLER UPROAR: *Page 2*

Fig. 8.11 'The Great Tory Lie', *Daily Mirror*, 9 October 1986

TASK 5 Discuss the ways in which these two front pages could be said to be examples of biased press coverage.

In a wider context it could be argued that one of the main functions of the press in a liberal-democratic society like ours is to support the **status quo** or **consensus** that is supposed to exist in Britain about how we should organise our political and economic systems. As James Curran (see Further reading) has argued, the modern press:

> 'tends to construct reality as a series of more or less discrete events that encourage the belief that the social and political structure is "natural" — the way things are — whilst blocking out alternative, radical perspectives'.

The press often defends itself by arguing that it is only really representing society 'as it is', and that it is not its job to offer radical alternatives or solutions to the nation's problems. But many people believe that those individuals and organisations who offer 'non-consensus' ideas do not receive anything like a fair chance to put over their views. Those on the left often point to the media's treatment of Tony Benn and Peter Tatchell in the Chesterfield and Bermondsey by-elections of 1984 and 1983, during which a campaign was waged by the conservative popular press to discredit the left-wing Labour candidates.

Critics also point to the language used in news reports which often betrays the paper's political stance. For example when conservative papers report trade union affairs they usually label the people whose views they agree with 'moderates'. Alternatively, if other individuals or groups are offering radical viewpoints they are often called 'extremists', or 'militants'.

Is the solution to this massive pro-Conservative bias the creation of more left-wing newspapers, along the lines of the now defunct *Daily Herald* and *News Chronicle*? A national daily newspaper has been a dream of the labour and trade union movement over the past two decades but this dream has not yet become reality because of the massive costs involved in launching an entirely new newspaper. However, modern technology will probably bring these costs down considerably (especially the cost of labour) meaning that newspapers could become financially viable on much lower circulations than in the past.

The future of the press

What, then, does the future hold for the press in Britain in the late 1980s? The statistics show that people today are reading fewer newspapers than they did in the post-war period. The average number of national newspapers read by adults per issue has declined steadily since 1951. Even so, the **reach** of newspapers in society is still very high, despite the challenge of radio and television since the 1950s. The press may have weathered the challenge of broadcasting but there will probably be fresh competition in the 1990s. Perhaps the most important will be the new electronic information media. **Viewdata** systems such as Prestel are interactive in that they allow the consumer to 'interrogate' databases full of constantly updated information through the telephone system. The information required is then displayed on a TV monitor. Prestel is used mostly by business at the moment but home use is likely to grow over the next ten years.

The newspapers themselves are, of course, finally in the process of introducing **new printing technology** into their own operations. News International, publishers of the *Sun* and *The Times,* have already moved, amid much controversy, to a new high-tech plant at Wapping in London's Dockland, and other titles also have plans to move towards **computerised** typesetting and other innovations like 'direct entry' by journalists from Visual Display Units (VDUs).

As Anthony Smith (see Further reading) has argued,

> 'The newspaper is passing through an era of rapid and accelerating change from one technology to another.'

This 'computer revolution' has led to the development of entirely new production techniques which will obviously affect the social relationships that exist within a newspaper organisation. The most evident example is the relationship between labour, i.e. the unions, and capital, i.e. owners and management. Over the next few years the traditional craft printing unions (NGA, SOGAT 82) are likely to lose much of their influence in the industry since many of their skills are now no longer needed.

The newspaper, therefore, will change in the future as it has evolved and adapted throughout its history. Over the years our newspapers have altered their formats and revised their contents according to their audience's attitudes and expectations, their changing lifestyles and the technological advances available to them. The quality press, in particular, has been at great pains to address themselves to the rapidly-changing lifestyle of its professional, middle-class audience. The Sunday qualities especially are now characterised by a profusion of supplements and magazines which reflect the new concerns of the 1980s e.g. fashion, home improvements, motoring etc.

In conclusion, the newspaper is still a very important mass medium and a key source of information, stimulation and, above all, entertainment for millions of people. In the age of the mass society the newspaper is still one of the most highly **personalised** of the media, which people have **access** to as and when they wish.

Self-assessment

1. List *three* reasons why you think the press have declined in importance in society since 1945.
2. Define the terms 'popular' and 'quality' press and list the characteristics associated with each of them.
3. Briefly discuss the relationship which exists between newspapers and social class.
4. How are newspapers financed?
5. Define the terms 'classified', 'display' and 'semi-display'.
6. Discuss the reasons why many newspapers are biased in favour of the Conservatives.

Further work

1. Take one of the national tabloids or qualities and analyse its content and style in terms of the following questions. When the class have looked at all the titles collate your results and present them in the form of a chart.
   (a) What is the approximate ratio of written to visual material?
   (b) How large is the main headline (measured in square cm)?
   (c) What approximate percentage of the paper is devoted to advertising?

(d) What percentage of the paper is devoted to the following content areas: News and Current Affairs/Background articles/Sport/Lifestyle articles (hobbies, travel, holidays etc.), Sex/Crime/Soap-Operas etc.?

(e) Are there any examples of open political bias?

2. Discuss the role of the press in the formation of 'public opinion'. Illustrate your answer with specific references to *at least two* real-life press campaigns.

Further reading

Blake R.H and Haroldsen E.O, *A Taxonomy of Concepts in Communication* (Hasting House, 1975)

Boyce G (ed), *Newspaper History: from the seventeenth century to the present day* (Sage Constable, 1978)

Curran J and Seaton J, *Power Without Responsibility* (Methuen, 1985)

H.M.S.O. Final Report of the Royal Commission on the Press (H.M.S.O., 1977)

McQuail D, *Mass Communication Theory: an introduction* (Sage Publications, 1983)

Smith A, *Goodbye Gutenberg: The Newspaper Revolution of the 1980s* (Oxford University Press, 1980)

Tunstall J, *The Media in Britain* (Constable, 1983)

Baistow T, *Fourth Rate Estate* (Comedia, 1985)

CHAPTER 9 *Broadcasting*

This chapter contains the following sections:

- A brief history of radio and television
- Ownership and control
- The public service tradition
- Who pays for radio and television?
- Types of programme
- The audience
- The future of broadcasting
- Self-assessment
- Further work
- Further reading

A brief history of radio and television

Broadcasting is a phenomenon of the 20th century. Just as the printed word dominated mass communication in the 19th century, so radio, but especially television, have become the most powerful media in this century. Although radio technology had existed for some time, the first actual broadcast was not made in Britain (by the Marconi Company) until 1922, the Americans having led the way with broadcasts from KDKA Pittsburgh in 1921. In 1922, the British Broadcasting Company was formed, representing the six major radio manufacturers; in 1927 this became the British Broadcasting Corporation (BBC) established by Royal Charter.

When radio technology first developed there was little idea about what the broadcasts should actually contain. As Raymond Williams (see Further reading) has argued:

'Radio and television were systems primarily devised for transmission and reception as abstract processes with little or no definition of preceding content.'

Indeed, with radio, and later with television, it would appear that the supply came before the demand from the mass of the population. John Logie Baird had been experimenting with the emerging technology of television and the problems inherent in sending pictures from one place to another for a number of years. His (and other people's) labours came to fruition in 1936 when the BBC broadcast its first scheduled TV service from Alexandra Palace in London to a very small audience.

Television broadcasting was overtaken by the onset of World War II in 1939, and had to wait another 20 years for its next major expansion. The war years, however, were a boom time for BBC Radio, with the Overseas (later World) Service trusted and respected throughout the world as a source of impartial news about the progress of the war.

It was during the 1950s, however, that television really took off in Britain, fuelled by the economic boom and the rise of the consumer society. It was during this period that TV superseded the cinema as the major organ of mass entertainment for the working and middle classes.

During the 1950s certain interest groups in society had begun to lobby for the breaking of the BBC's monopoly of broadcasting. This campaign finally became successful in 1955 when Independent Television (ITV) first came on the air. (By this time, 90% of Britain had access to TV.) Britain now had a broadcasting 'duopoly', with an established public sector in competition with a new commercial sector. The first years of this competition saw the brash, populist ITV companies take the lion's share of the audience from the staid, conservative BBC (80% in 1957). To survive, the BBC had to learn to make popular programmes which appealed to the mass of the population.

Politically, TV came of age in Britain in 1959 with the first major coverage of a general election, whilst in terms of programming 1962 saw the first transmission of colour TV and the first live TV broadcast from America via the Telstar satellite. A new channel arrived on the scene in 1964 with the introduction of BBC 2 whilst the first broadcast of Radio Caroline, a 'pirate' radio station, signified the emergence of a new youth sub-culture and pointed the way towards the radical changes that would take place in the world of radio broadcasting over the next decade.

In fact, 1967 saw a major reorganisation of BBC Radio with the introduction of Radios 1, 2, 3 and 4, each catering for a specific audience in terms of age and taste. The Corporation also launched its first local radio station in this year, Radio Leicester, whilst in 1972 the foundations were laid for an Independent Local Radio network with the first broadcasts of LBC (London Broadcasting Company) and Capital Radio in London. Local radio continued to expand throughout the 1970s and 1980s although radio will now always be a 'secondary' broadcasting medium behind TV.

The technology had existed for some time for a fourth television channel but there had been major disagreement as to what form it should take. Should it be run by the BBC or ITV? What should its programming policy be? These issues were resolved in 1982 when Channel 4 arrived, as a separate ITV company, a subsidiary of the IBA. It has an obligation to provide distinctive programming aimed mainly at minority tastes and has proved relatively successful after a shaky start.

The most recent innovation in broadcasting has been the introduction of Breakfast Television in 1983 whilst popular TV programming throughout the mornings was introduced in 1987 as a first step, perhaps, towards 24 hour TV.

The next decade will witness a further expansion of the mass media with the probable introduction of both cable and satellite TV, which, along with the increasing use of the video recorder in the home, will bring a whole new dimension to the world of the media.

Ownership and control

As with other industries which aim at a mass market, broadcasting has both **public** and **private** sectors. The public sector takes the form of the BBC which is responsible for two television channels, four national radio channels, over 30 local radio stations and various external broadcasting services such as the World Service. According to the BBC's Annual Report and Handbook, the BBC is a **public corporation** set up by Royal Charter, operating under a Licence and Agreement granted by the Home Secretary. The BBC is obliged to provide a public broadcasting service both at home and overseas.

The BBC is 'owned' by the public in the same way that the British Steel Corporation or British Coal is under public ownership. There is no day-to-day governmental control of the BBC, although its Board of Governors is appointed by the Government of the day. In addition, pressure can always be exerted privately or publicly, as was the case during the *Real Lives* controversy in 1985.

The Corporation came under strong pressure from the Home Secretary to ban a programme that had been made about the views of supporters of Irish terrorism. The Licence and Agreement also gives the Government the power to take over the BBC in times of national crisis.

The public sector is under no obligation to 'make a profit' out of its activities, although it must obviously work within the financial constraints of its budget.

Commercial television, on the other hand, is privately owned by large capitalist organisations who aim to make a profit for their shareholders as well as providing a public service. The reference book *Who Owns Whom?*, for example, tells us that Thames Television is owned mainly by Thorn-EMI and British Electric Traction (BET), two of Britain's largest companies who both have interests in other media concerns as well.

Many people criticise capitalist ownership of the media because they believe it narrows the range of opinions expressed and leads to bias against certain groups in society who challenge the status quo. Others argue that the surest safeguard against State control of the media is private ownership. In Chapter 11 we will take a more thematic look at media ownership.

The ITV companies and independent local radio stations have to work within the constraints contained in the Broadcasting Act and the rules and regulations of the Independent Broadcasting Authority, the 'watchdog' of the independent system. The IBA is responsible for 15 ITV companies, over 40 ILR stations, TV-AM and Channel 4. Unlike the BBC, it does not actually make any programmes itself. Its main job is to award **franchises** to companies like Central and Granada who then make programmes for the ITV network. The IBA is also obliged to make sure that the ITV and ILR companies fulfil their public service obligations.

TASK /

Consult a copy of the reference book *Who Owns Whom?* from your local library and find out who owns the following media concerns:
— Capital Radio;
— Yorkshire Television;
— Goldcrest Films;
— Radio City.

The public service tradition

When broadcasting first developed in Britain in the 1920s a particular 'ethos' was also formulated which involved a consensus or agreement about the general aims of broadcasting in a modern society. The main reason was the involvement of the State from the earliest days; since wavelengths were limited, somebody had to decide who should have access to them. It was natural, therefore, that the State should also attempt to define what the content of broadcasting should be. The key personality during this formative period was John Reith, the first Director General of the BBC. It is Reith who is usually credited with developing the notion of broadcasting as a service to the community, although Asa Briggs, in his history of the BBC, quotes the American broadcaster Sarnoff, who argued that:

'Broadcasting represents a job of entertaining, informing and educating the nation, and should, therefore, be distinctly regarded as a public service.'

Broadcasting in the USA later came to be dominated by advertising but the consensus in Britain was that radio (and later TV) should be non-profit making, being funded by a licence fee system. Throughout its history, the BBC (and later,

ITV) has been obliged to fulfil two key public service requirements. These are contained in the documents the BBC's Royal Charter, its Licence and Agreement, the Television Act and the rules and regulations of the IBA. Let us now look at the broadcasters' obligations.

Range of programmes Both BBC and ITV are obliged to maintain a rough balance between informative, educational and entertainment-based programmes in their schedules. In this sense, they are asked to cater for a very wide range of attitudes, tastes and interests. Only in broadcasting are the practitioners obliged to do this. Imagine a bookshop where it is compulsory to buy a book by Dickens or Jane Austen if you want to purchase a Mills and Boon!

With regard to ITV, the IBA closely monitors the output of the ITV companies. The franchises for the ITV areas come up for renewal every ten years and the IBA has the power to take the franchise away from a company and award it to another if it believes it is failing to live up to its public service obligations.

Impartiality The other major aspect of the public service tradition has been the official stress on impartiality or neutrality in social and political affairs. Again, broadcasting is supposed to have higher standards than other media, especially newspapers. The BBC's 'Licence and Agreement' (contained in its Annual Report and Handbook) specifically says that:

> 'The Corporation shall at all times refrain from sending any broadcast matter expressing the opinion of the Corporation on current affairs or public policy.'

The Broadcasting Act contains a similar statement for ITV. The extent to which the broadcasters actually live up to these obligations is, of course, a matter of (often heated) debate. We will look at bias in the media in greater detail in Chapter 11.

This notion of impartiality has been modified slightly since the introduction of Channel 4 in 1982. BBC and ITV are both obliged to be impartial within programmes. Channel 4, on the other hand, is allowed to show its neutrality *across* a series of programmes, which allows it to show a film on nuclear weapons made by a committed socialist followed, the next week, by a programme made by an equally committed conservative.

Many people believe that it has been the public regulation of broadcasting over the last 60 years that has helped to make British radio and television respected throughout the world. They point to the dangers inherent in the totally commercialised system operating in the USA where the three major networks (NBC, CBS and ABC) are locked in a perpetual battle to win viewers and advertisers. However it is entirely possible that broadcasting in Britain will be **de-regulated** at some point in the future, if the recommendations of the *Peacock Report* are followed.

Who pays for radio and television?

The public and private sectors of broadcasting are funded by two different methods.

BBC BBC radio and television is financed by a **licence fee** paid by all owners and renters of televisions. Direct funding by the Government was rejected in the 1920s because it was felt that broadcasting would become an arm of the State, as is the case in many countries today. It was argued that a licence system would guarantee the **independence** of the fledgling BBC. The money paid by the audience for their licences is collected by the Post Office and handed over to the Corporation, minus collection costs.

The actual size of the licence fee is indexed to the Retail Price Index. However, for most of its history it was decided by the Government of the day. Many people argued that, during those periods when the licence was up for renewal, the BBC became very vulnerable to pressure from the Government.

In the mid 1980s there was a major debate about how the BBC should be financed in the future. In 1986 there was speculation that the *Peacock Report* would include a recommendation that the Corporation should be forced to take advertising. As it happened, this idea was rejected, after much lobbying from the BBC. The report did argue, however, for the privatisation of Radios 1 and 2.

ITV/ILR   **Advertising**, of course, is the main source of funding for commercial radio and television. The ITV and ILR companies finance their programme making by selling advertising time within and between programmes. The Broadcasting Act does not actually state exactly how much advertising is allowed. Instead it states:

> 'The amount of time given to advertising shall not be so great as to detract from the value of the programmes as a medium of information, education and entertainment.'

However, since the 1950s the IBA has allowed a maximum of six minutes per hour on TV (average throughout the day) and nine minutes on commercial radio. An important point to make here is that there will be no such restrictions placed on the new Cable TV stations by the Cable Authority.

According to the IBA, of 180 programmes broadcast during a typical week on ITV, 100 have no 'internal' advertising, 60 have one commercial break and 20 have two breaks. Some programmes like *World in Action* or 30-minute documentaries are not allowed any internal advertising. In addition, IBA rules state that there must be a total distinction between programmes and advertising, with sponsorship of individual programmes rarely being allowed on television.

How much does advertising cost on radio and television?

Obviously, it costs a lot more to advertise on TV than radio because the potential audience is so much larger (and, of course, national). Other factors affecting the cost will include:

— The **time** of the day. Peak-time, e.g. 8.00 am for radio will be much more expensive than off-peak, e.g. 11.00 pm.

— The **popularity** of the programme. A programme attracting 17 million viewers will attract more potential advertisers than one only being watched by 5 million.

Figs. 9.1 and 9.2 show the relative costs of broadcast advertising.

You may wonder, how do advertisers get to know these costs? The answer is that companies and advertising agencies are sent **rate cards** and other information about the advertising medium. Fig. 9.2 shows the current rate card for Piccadilly Radio, the ILR station which serves the Manchester area.

TASK *2*   Find out how much it costs to book a 10 sec, 30 sec and 60 sec advertising spot on *your* local ITV and ILR stations. Present your findings in the form of a chart.

COMPANY	POTENTIAL AUDIENCE	COST OF ADVERTISING
GRANADA TV	6.5 million	£17 000/30 secs, 17.20–23.00, Monday–Friday
ANGLIA TV	3.6 million	£6500/30 secs, 17.20–23.00, Monday–Friday
CHANNEL TV	120 000	£79/30 secs, 18.00–19.00, Monday–Friday
PICCADILLY RADIO (ILR STATION)	3.6 million	£445/30 secs, 07.00–10.00, Monday–Friday
RADIO TRENT (ILR STATION)	1.14 million	£58/30 secs, 07.00–10.00, Monday–Friday
MARCHER SOUND (ILR STATION)	570 000	£30/30 secs, 07.00–10.00, Monday–Friday

Fig. 9.1 The cost of broadcast advertising

Source: Company Rate Cards

Class/Code	Days	Time	10 secs	20 secs	30 secs	40 secs	50 secs	60 secs
			£	£	£	£	£	£
AMD	Mon–Fri Sat Sun	07.00–10.00 08.30–13.00 09.00–13.00	228	356	445	579	734	801
AAA	Mon–Fri Sun	10.00–14.00 13.00–15.00	190	304	380	494	627	684
AA	Mon–Fri Sat Sun	06.30–07.00 14.00–18.00 07.00–08.30 13.00–18.00 08.00–09.00 15.00–19.00	93	148	185	240	305	333
A	Mon–Fri Sat Sun	18.00–01.00 18.00–01.00 18.00–01.00 06.00–08.00 19.00–01.00	25	40	50	65	83	90
B	Mon–Fri Sat–Sun	01.00–06.30 01.00–07.00	5	8	10	13	17	18

Fig. 9.2 Piccadilly Radio rate card

Controls over advertising

As we have already seen, the IBA controls the amount and frequency of advertising on ITV. It also controls the nature of the adverts themselves. The Broadcasting Act (1981) gives the IBA the power to 'exclude any advertisement that could reasonably be said to be misleading'. The IBA has also formulated a 'Code of Advertising Standards and Practice' which aims to stop ads being broadcast which could cause offence to the listeners and viewers. The general practice is for advertising agencies to send proposed scripts to the IBA for clearance before production. Over 10 000 TV ads and 8000 radio ads are examined each year and over 80% of the TV ads are cleared.

Funding radio and television in the future

There may well be two important developments arising from the introduction of cable and satellite TV. Firstly, if the audience for the public service channels declines as a result of competition with the new media there will be increasing pressure to abolish the licence fee and introduce alternative methods of funding the BBC. Both the advertising agencies and parts of the popular press have campaigned for advertising on BBC, the former because it will probably bring down the cost of advertising on TV, and papers like the *Sun* and *The Times* because their owner (News International) controls the *Sky* satellite channel! The new media will also compete with ITV for advertising thus eroding its financial base.

Secondly, it is likely that new ways of financing TV will be introduced, the most important being **subscription** (viewers paying a monthly fee for the service) and **Pay-TV** (a system by which viewers pay for each programme they watch, with a bill being sent at regular intervals).

Types of programme

As we saw in an earlier section, both BBC and ITV are obliged to offer a wide range of programmes to their audiences. Broadly-speaking, we can classify the hundreds of programmes that are broadcast each week into what the IBA calls:

— **Informative** programmes: news, current affairs, religion, schools programmes, children's informative;

— **Narrative** programmes: plays, dramas, TV movies, feature films;

— **Entertainment** programmes: entertainment, variety, music, children's entertainment.

— **Sport**.

Fig. 9.3 shows how this works out in terms of the numbers of hours devoted to each type of programme during a typical week.

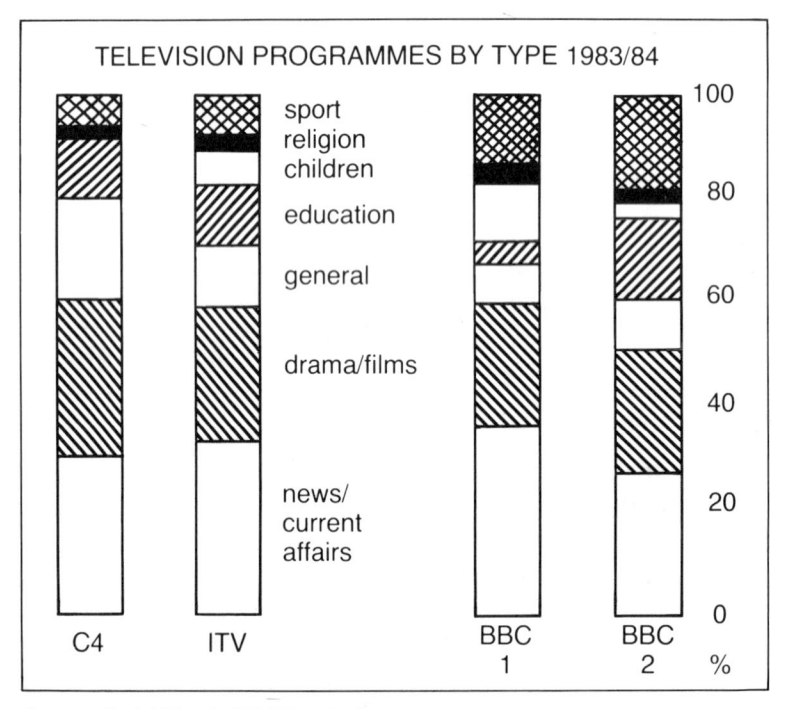

Source: *Social Trends* (HMSO, 1986)

Fig. 9.3 TV programmes by type 1983/84

 *3*   Using the TV page of a daily newspaper, make a study of the types of programme broadcast on all four channels during that day. Calculate (roughly) the percentages of air-time devoted to Informative, Narrative, Entertainment and Sports programmes. Present your findings in the form of a barchart, as in Fig. 9.3.

Broadcasting genres

TV and radio programmes can be further classified into a number of different **genres**. A genre is a way of classifying programmes together if they have certain characteristics or **conventions** in common. Just as the cinema has its genres (westerns, horror, science fiction, etc.) so TV and radio have their own genres. Fig. 9.4 is a checklist of some of the genres that exist in the world of broadcasting and examples of present and past programmes that represent them.

GENRE	PRESENT/RECENT	PAST
NEWS, CURRENT AFFAIRS	*Panorama, World in Action, The World at One (Radio 4)*	*24 Hours, Tonight*
DOCUMENTARIES	*First Tuesday, Life on Earth*	*The Ascent of Man, Civilisation*
DRAMA	*Jewel in the Crown, Reilly: Ace of Spies*	*Upstairs, Downstairs, The Forsyte Saga*
SITUATION COMEDIES	*Only Fools and Horses, Duty Free*	*Man about the House, Steptoe and Son*
SOAP OPERAS	*EastEnders, Crossroads, The Archers (Radio 4)*	*Emergency Ward Ten, Mrs Dale's Diary (Radio)*
QUIZ SHOWS	*The Price is Right, Blockbusters*	*Double Your Money, Criss Cross Quiz*

Fig. 9.4 Broadcasting genres

 *4*   Make a list of *two* more examples of present radio or TV programmes which can be classified according to the genres listed in Fig. 9.4.

The most popular genre amongst the general public, is, of course, the **soap opera**. This popularity can be illustrated by looking at the top ten programmes for a typical week's viewing.

Within each of these genres we can identify a set of characteristics or conventions which, taken together, help to create an image in the audience's mind of the typical quiz show or soap opera. Let us look at the concept of genre in greater detail by analysing that cornerstone of the television schedule, the soap opera. This particular type of programme has its origins in the USA in the 1950s when short popular dramas/melodramas were often broadcast in the afternoons to an audience of housewives. Soap powder companies often advertised during the shows, hence the origin of the term.

At the moment there are a number of British-made soaps running on radio and TV as well as various imports from the USA and Australia. Although there are obviously differences, we can list the following conventions that most soaps have in common:

− The plots and storylines are **never-ending** in that they chart the life of a particular community such as a street or a motel. As one storyline is coming to an end, another might be already developing.

− The storylines in an episode or set of episodes are usually **interwoven** without

Fig. 9.5 TV drama: *Brideshead Revisited* (Granada TV)

Fig. 9.6 Quiz show: *The Price is Right* (Central TV)

necessarily being related. The camera, and our attention, moves continuously from one set of characters to the next as the storylines are worked out.

— The content of these storylines is often of a **moral** nature. Should X be unfaithful to his wife? Should Y have an abortion or keep her baby? Only recently have the soaps attempted, with varying degrees of success, to tackle 'serious' social and political issues such as unemployment, rape and homosexuality. *Brookside* and *EastEnders* could be seen as pioneers of the 'new realism' in the soaps.

— The action usually takes place in **specific social locations** such as pubs or shops (since this allows the scriptwriters an almost infinite degree of possibilities) although *Brookside* is unconventional in this respect because most of the action takes place in the characters' 'real homes'.

— The characters are often simplified, sometimes to the point of being **stereotypes**.

Fig. 9.7 Soap opera: *Brookside* (Channel 4)

TASK 5 Take one soap opera you are familiar with and analyse it in terms of the conventions listed above.

Scheduling **Scheduling** is the creative process of placing programmes in such an order as to maximise the audience. It is an essential aspect of the healthy competition that has existed between the BBC and ITV since the 1950s. Central to the philosophy of broadcasting developed by John Reith was the notion that audiences could be encouraged to watch informative and educational programmes if they were scheduled amongst more popular ones. People have criticised this approach as being élitist in the sense of a centralised body thinking it knows what is best for the audience. However, its supporters point to the high standards which this policy has helped to bring about.

Christopher Dunkley (see Further reading) has discussed two scheduling strategies at the disposal of the broadcaster both of which can help to bolster audiences for less popular programmes. **Hammocking** involves placing higher-rated shows at either end of a weak programme whilst the **inheritance factor** refers to the practice of scheduling a lower-rated programme after a popular one. Probably the most successful example of scheduling in recent years was the launching of *Wogan* and *EastEnders* by the BBC in 1985. Michael Grade, then the newly-appointed Controller of BBC1, hoped that by scheduling these popular programes at fixed, early evening times, it would boost audience figures for the rest of the evening. The plan has been a success and the BBC has mounted a major fightback in its ratings battle with commercial television.

One further factor which must be taken into account when scheduling is the requirement to protect the interests of children, especially where programmes of a sexual or violent nature are concerned. The IBA, for example, has a **Family Viewing Policy** which states that nothing unsuitable for young children should be shown before 9.00 pm. The BBC also abides by this rule.

The future

The programming policies discussed earlier were developed in an age of *duopoly*, that is, limited competition between the public and private sectors of broadcasting. Both have had an obligation to provide a range of programmes to suit all interests and tastes. However, the trend is towards single theme channels, especially in the USA, where the MTV rock video channel and Ted Turner's 24 hour news channel are notable examples. One might argue that this is already the case with regard to BBC Radio which already has channels devoted to particular musical tastes or cultural interests. It is likely that the new Cable TV stations in Britain will also be devoted to single themes, e.g. light entertainment, rock music, news and children.

The audience

The numbers game In this section we shall consider the following questions, looking at radio first: how often does the audience experience radio and television, and what is the state of competition between the BBC and ITV/ILR?

Radio in Britain has a **reach** of around 85% (this refers to the proportion of potential listeners who actually listen). How often do people actually listen, though? IBA research tells us that the average radio listener has the radio on for nearly 21 hours every week. This averages out, according to *Social Trends* (HMSO), at 8½ hours per head of the population.

Nationally, the BBC takes nearly 70% of the total radio audience compared to ILR's 28%, although if we compare only local radio, ILR is easily more popular than BBC local radio. It is interesting to note how ILR's audience has declined since 1981, the main reason being the introduction of breakfast TV in 1983.

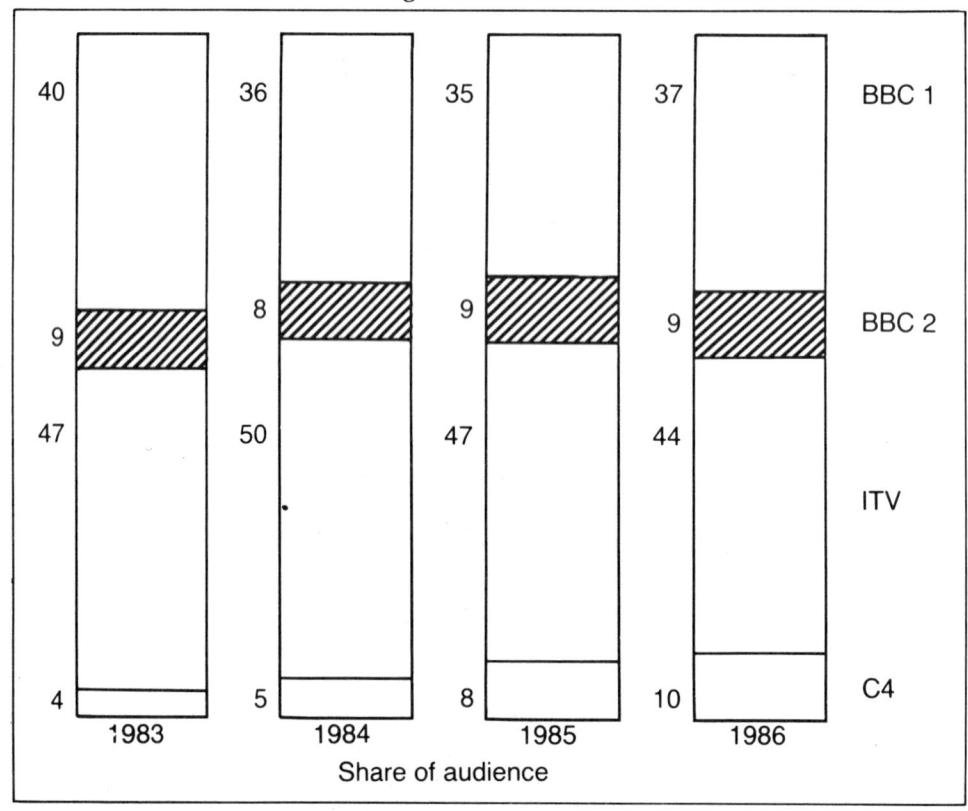

Source: BARB

Fig. 9.8 Who watches what

Television's reach is even higher, with 94% of the population having claimed to watch TV at some point during the first two months of 1985, according to *Social Trends*. During the same period, men watched over 26 hours per week, whilst the figure for women was over 31 hours.

It is the job of the Broadcasting Audience Research Bureau (BARB), an organisation funded jointly by the BBC and ITV, to undertake research into the radio and TV audience. Their figures for 1986 show that a rough parity exists between the public and private sectors in the battle for TV viewers.

Size of audiences is obviously important, especially to broadcasting hierarchies and advertisers, but just as worthy of study are the **reasons** why people listen to radio, watch TV or go and see films. We also need to know what they experience during this process.

Audience appreciation   Audience research does not merely concentrate on the numbers of people listening or viewing — it also looks at the audience's **perception** of programmes and services. BARB, the IBA and the BBC all take the trouble to measure public opinion about programmes and adverts. The IBA's tool is the Appreciation Index (AI). AIs are compiled by sending out Appreciation Diaries to a selected sample of the population. People are asked to rate each programme they are familiar with on a scale from 1–6. When the results are collated they are then converted into a percentage. According to the IBA, most programmes have an AI of between 70 and 80%, as Fig. 9.9 shows.

 **TASK 6**   Conduct an Audience Appreciation survey in your own class, choosing *six* different types of programmes. When you have worked out the AIs construct a chart like the one in Fig. 9.9.

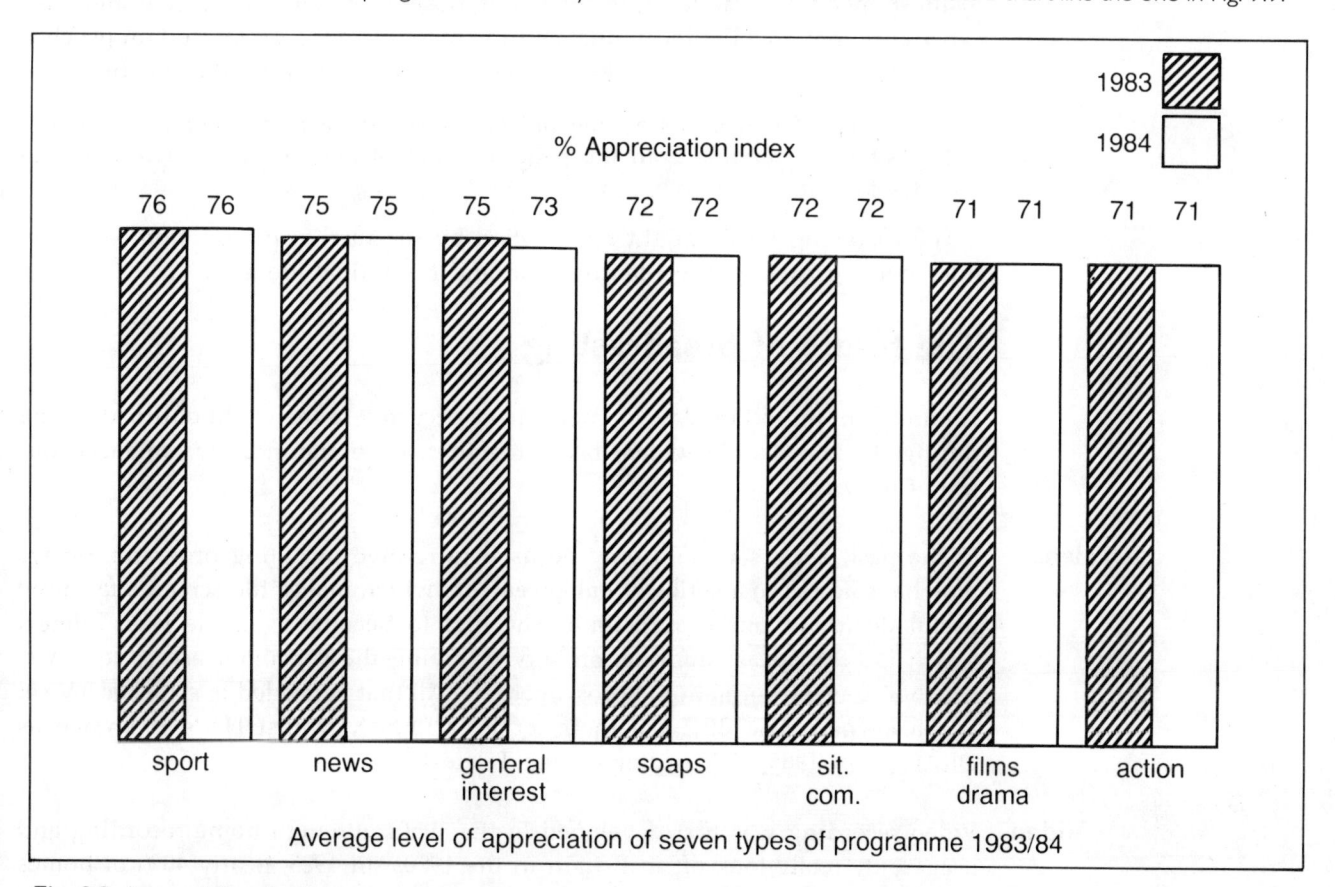

Fig. 9.9 Appreciation indexes

Research is also carried out into the public's perception of broadcasting in general. For example, each year the IBA conducts a major survey in this area, the most recent being 'Attitudes to Broadcasting in 1985'. The report of this survey tells us that:

— Almost 40% of the public thought standards of TV programmes had declined between 1984 and 1985 (the main cause for complaint being 'too many repeats').
— People believed that different channels were better at producing different types of programmes, with the BBC being preferred for plays, documentaries, current affairs and arts and science programmes and ITV getting the vote for entertainment, comedy, adventure programmes and national/regional news.
— Satisfaction with radio was 'generally high' amongst the population.

Approaches to the study of the audience

At this point we can consider two contrasting theoretical approaches which attempt to explain the relationship between sender and receiver in mass communications.

— **The hypodermic model.** This was an early and influential model of mass communication which viewed the audience as a mass of individuals passively receiving messages, the nature of which were decided by the source. It is as though information, ideas and values are being 'injected' into the audience. The logical result of this kind of pessimistic approach is the notion that the *effects* of the mass media on the audience can somehow be measured (along the lines of **stimulus-response** theory). Much of the popular debate about the relationship between television and violence is in line with this perspective.

— **Uses and gratifications theory.** This is a more up-to-date approach. Contrary to the hypodermic model, this theory proposes a much more active audience experience in which the individual *uses* the mass media to satisfy certain psychological and social needs. According to Denis McQuail (see Further reading):

'It is assumed that needs arising out of social circumstances and psychological dispositions determine both the pattern of use of mass media and response to media content.'

The following needs might be satisfied by the media: information, security, interaction, escape, group identification and individual identity.

The future of broadcasting

A number of important developments have occurred in the world of broadcasting during the last decade which, taken together, have significantly enhanced our use of television.

Teletext

In the past, a TV set could only be used to receive incoming programmes; we now have access to a series of **enhancements** which makes the screen a far more useful device in our leisure time. The first to become available was **Teletext** which is a broadcast information service giving the consumer access to news, weather, travel information, horoscopes, etc. All that is needed is a special TV set and a keypad. The BBC call their service CEEFAX, whilst ITV's is known as ORACLE. In 1985, 17% of .homes had Teletext sets.

Video

Video recording was first developed in the 1950s although home recording and usage only really took off in Britain in the 1970s. In 1985, nearly 40% of homes had videos, the highest proportion in the world. Video has two main uses:

Fig. 9.10 *St Elsewhere*
(Channel 4)

— **Time shifting:** this is the recording of programmes to be viewed at a later time, and is by far the most frequent use of home video.

— Viewing commercially pre-recorded films, usually rented from local video shops.

Video is important in communication studies because it is an example of the shift towards the **privatisation** of our leisure time, a trend which, perhaps, started with the arrival of television. The increasing popularity of video also hammers another nail into the coffin of cinema as a medium of mass entertainment. Video also illustrates the extent to which people are now able to control their access to the mass media in a way that was unthinkable 20 years ago.

Channel 4

The fourth channel, which came on the air in 1982, is a major development in programming policy. It is obliged to be distinctive and innovative in the service it offers, especially with regard to the needs of ethnic minorities, women and young people. Channel 4 is supposed to cater for a wider range of tastes and interests than BBC or ITV. It was also envisaged that a wider variety of viewpoints would be broadcast than on the existing public service channels; this approach has come to be known as **editorial television**.

Channel 4 is financed by a subsidy from the ITV companies who are then allowed to sell advertising time on the channel. The new channel attracted much criticism during its first year but is now firmly established with a share of the total audience of around the 10% mark.

Other innovations will be introduced over the next decade which could be even more influential than those already discussed.

Cable TV

Television transmitted through cables has been a fact of life in some parts of Britain for years. However, it is only recently that new channels like Sky, Premiere and Screensport have been established to bring programmes other than BBC or

ITV to the home. Having access to cable can, theoretically, give the viewer access to a multiplicity of TV channels in return for paying a monthly subscription on top of the normal TV licence.

The *Hunt Report* of 1983 pointed the way towards an expansion of cable in Britain during the next decade. The Government set up a Cable Authority to oversee the development of the industry. Many claims were made about how cable would 'take off', although a recent IBA survey showed that two thirds of the population are 'unlikely to subscribe' to cable (with less than 1% having subscribed at the moment). Cable differs from public service broadcasting in two main ways:

– There will be much less public control over the new cable stations; the Cable Authority will *oversee* rather than *regulate* and it will not have the same powers as the IBA.

– There will be no obligation to provide the range of programmes associated with the public service tradition. It is likely that most cable stations will, in the battle for audience maximisation, concentrate on crowd-pullers like quiz shows, comedies, soaps etc. It is also probable that much of the material will be of American origin since there will no longer be any restriction on foreign programmes.

Direct broadcasting by satellite (DBS)

This is, perhaps, the most ambitious and expensive development in broadcasting. By buying or renting a small satellite dish viewers will soon have the technical ability to receive a wide variety of new channels. In addition, they will be able to receive programmes from other countries. Another step in the direction of the 'global village'? In December 1986 the IBA announced that it had offered Britain's first DBS contract to the British Satellite Broadcasting (BSB) group. This consortium is made up of major media companies like Virgin, Granada, Amstrad, Pearson and Anglia Television. There are likely to be four programme services:

– NOW: a news, current affairs and sports channel;

– GALAXY: an entertainment channel full of dramas, serials, plays and quiz shows;

– ZIG-ZAG: a daytime family service.

These three channels will be free to viewers since they will be funded by advertising revenue, as with ITV. However, there will be one extra channel – SCREEN (an evening feature film service) – for which subscription will be compulsory.

How does DBS relate to the rest of public service broadcasting? The satellite channels will still have to have their programme schedules approved by the IBA but they will not be required to transmit the *range* of programmes that BBC and ITV are obliged to.

Community radio

Local radio first appeared on the scene in the 1960s and grew rapidly during the following decade. The 1990s are likely to witness a further expansion of radio on an even smaller, more localised scale. **Pirate** radio stations are already operating in certain areas (especially London) to small communities and it is likely that, at some point in the future, their activities will be legalised and they will be awarded licences to broadcast.

 TASK 7

Take *one* of the new developments discussed in this chapter and research it in detail. You should cover the following areas:

– How the technology works.

— How the industry is organised.
— How it is likely to affect the audience.

Present your findings in the form of a *handout* which could be distributed to the other members of your class.

Self-assessment

1. Why did State regulation of broadcasting exist from the outset?
2. Define the term 'public service tradition'.
3. Discuss the role of the IBA in broadcasting.
4. How are the BBC and ITV financed?
5. Why should the cost of advertising on ITV vary?
6. Define the term 'genre' and list *four* of the conventions associated with the soap opera genre.
7. Define the terms 'hammocking' and 'inheritance factor'.
8. Write definitions for the following terms or concepts:
   — Privatisation;
   — Deregulation;
   — Duopoly;
   — Reach;
   — Time-shifting.
9. Briefly discuss the hypodermic model and the uses and gratifications theory.

Further work

1. List the pros and cons of allowing advertising on the BBC.
2. Study carefully the programmes on offer on TV during an evening and discuss any examples of hammocking or the inheritance factor you think are at work.
3. Conduct a survey of the listening and viewing habits of the population of your school or college. Design a simple questionnaire to find out:
   — How many hours per week the sample listen to radio or watch TV.
   — Appreciation Indices for a selected number of programmes.
   — At what times of the day people listen or watch.
   — *Why* people make use of radio and TV (uses and gratifications approach?)
   Make sure your sample is *representative* of your school or college. For example, if there are 70% full-time and 30% part-time students, your sample should reflect this fact (and likewise with other variables such as sex, age etc.).
   Present your findings in the form of a Report, with visual presentations where appropriate.
4. Write an essay with the following title: What are the main likely social, cultural and economic effects of the introduction and expansion of cable television throughout Britain? (AEB 'A' Level, Communication Studies, Paper 1, 1984).
5. Write an essay with the following title: It is essential that *Television Literacy* should become a central component of the secondary school curriculum during the next decade.
   Discuss the implications of this statement and the reasons why you think the person made it.
6. Make a checklist of the criteria you would use to assess the effectiveness of a local radio station.

Further reading

BBC, *Annual Report and Handbook* (BBC, 1986)

Briggs A, *The BBC; The First Fifty Years* (Oxford University Press, 1985)

Curran J and Seaton J, *Power without Responsibility* (Methuen, 1986)

Dunkley C, *Television Today and Tomorrow* (Penguin, 1985)

Fiske J, *Introduction to Communication Studies* (Methuen, 1986)

Hartley J et al, *Making Sense of the Media* (Comedia, 1985)

Independent Broadcasting Authority, *Television and Radio 1986* (IBA, 1986)

Independent Broadcasting Authority, *The Audience for ILR* (IBA, 1984)

Independent Broadcasting Authority, *Attitudes to Broadcasting in 1985* (IBA, 1986)

Masterman L, *Teaching the Media* (Comedia, 1985)

McQuail D, *Mass Communication Theory* (Sage, 1983)

McQuail D, *Communication* (Longman, 1980)

Tunstall J, *The Media in Britain* (Constable, 1983)

Williams R, *Television: Technology and Cultural Form* (Fontana, 1979)

CHAPTER 10 *Persuasion in mass communication*

This chapter contains the following sections:

- Introduction
- Some key concepts and definitions
- The process of persuasion
- The techniques of persuasion
- The advertising industry
- Self-assessment
- Further work
- Further reading

Introduction

As we saw in Chapter 2, people communicate for a variety of different purposes. One of these purposes is that of **persuasion.** Much communication involves trying to influence someone's attitudes, opinions and behaviour. For example, there are manufacturers trying to persuade us to buy their products; politicians trying to win support for their vote; parents, teachers and friends trying to convince us of their point of view, etc.

In interpersonal communication this persuasion is sometimes a deliberate strategy. For example, a parent trying to persuade a small child to go willingly to bed may deliberately create the illusion of bedtime as a very special experience, a time when stories are told in a warm and intimate setting. Often though, the sender may not be fully aware that they are using a persuasive approach and that persuasive techniques are unwittingly being used. For example, during a discussion involving a difference of opinion, many people use expressions and phrases which imply that their point of view is inevitably correct, phrases such as: 'As I'm sure most intelligent people would agree, my view is . . .'.

In mass communication on the other hand, there are many examples where techniques of persuasion are used in a quite deliberate, well-organised and pre-planned manner. For example, a party political broadcast on television is a costly, thoroughly researched and finely orchestrated attempt to influence public opinion and ultimately voting behaviour. Similarly, a major advertising campaign to launch a new product will cost many thousands of pounds, involve a great deal of market research and will probably be organised through several different media.

In this chapter we will be looking at persuasion within the context of the mass media. In particular, we will be looking at **advertising** and **propaganda.**

Some key concepts and definitions

Advertising   Advertising can be defined as a controlled and pre-paid use of a medium to inform or persuade people. A key point in this definition is that advertising involves **paying** for the use of the medium. In this sense it is useful to distinguish between **advertising** and **publicity**. For example, if the organiser of a country fête is invited to be interviewed on local radio, this would be called 'publicity' and not 'advertising'. Although the organiser of the fête may well be able to advertise

119

the event by a careful choice of words in answering questions, the interview itself would not constitute an advertisement, in that it was not paid for, nor was it under the direct control of the fête organiser. The essential difference between advertising and publicity is that advertising is under the control of the advertiser. Subject to laws and agreed codes of practice, advertisers can say exactly what they want to say, where and when they want to, for as long as they can pay for it.

One final point about advertising which we should not forget is that a great deal of it is simply designed to inform people of basic facts. For example, a 'For Sale' small ad. does not primarily aim to persuade; it simply states that a particular item is for sale at a particular price. In practice many adverts attempt both to **inform** and **persuade**.

Propaganda

The word '**propaganda**' is often used to describe attempts to mislead people and deceive them into believing something which isn't true. Often, the word is associated with something 'evil', or 'alien' and 'foreign'. For example, the leaflet in Fig. 10.1 would be described by most of us as a clear example of propaganda. This leaflet was produced by the Japanese during World War II and was used in an attempt to weaken the morale of Australian troops fighting in South East Asia.

Fig. 10.1 Japanese propaganda from World War II

However, people do not always agree about what can correctly be described as propaganda. For example, would a Conservative voter describe the poster in Fig. 10.2 an example of propaganda, or just 'the truth'?

Equally, not all propaganda can be described as 'evil'. It could be argued that the Health Education Council poster in Fig. 10.3 is in fact an example of propaganda not because it is an 'evilly' inspired attempt at 'brain-washing', but because it is a deliberate attempt to influence the behaviour of pregnant women by playing on their emotions.

Although the distinction between what is and what is not propaganda is often blurred, there are three particular areas of life which most would recognise as the main sources of propaganda. These three areas are: **war, politics and religion.** In many ways these three areas of human activity are very different to each other,

Fig. 10.2 Conservative Party poster from the 1979 General Election Campaign

Fig. 10.3 Health Education
Council poster

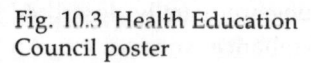

though interestingly they do have one thing in common. In each, there are rival groups, or communities of people, having very different beliefs and interests and competing with each other for supremacy of those beliefs and interests. It is precisely in situations like these that one group will assert that their pronouncements are the 'truth' and that those of their rivals are 'just propaganda'. Indeed, it is interesting to note how the very word itself — propaganda — can be used as a means of dismissing and devaluing the beliefs and pronouncements of a rival. For example, an extremist Ulster protestant might refer to 'the propaganda put out by the Pope'; a cigarette manufacturer might refer to 'the propaganda of the keep-fit fanatics', and so on.

In view of these various connotations which are associated with the word, it may appear difficult to offer a clear and accurate definition. However, one possibility would be to define propaganda simply as: 'a deliberate attempt to influence the opinions and behaviour of people, either by appealing directly to their emotions rather than their reason, or by deception'. This definition avoids connotations of 'evil', 'right/wrong', 'alien' etc., and instead invites us to focus on the techniques and the psychological processes which all propagandists, and some advertisers, make use of. Before we take a closer look at these techniques and processes it may be useful to ask the question: is advertising an example of propaganda?

Is advertising an example of propaganda?

This is an interesting question because it brings together many of the comments made earlier about the difficulties involved in defining the term 'propaganda'. For example, many advertisers would say propaganda sets out to change an individual's whole outlook on a major subject, whereas *they* are simply trying to encourage people to buy a certain product, or use a certain service; hardly an example of brain-washing, the advertiser would say. In addition, so the argument would go, each individual consumer is free to choose what to buy and what to do. On the other hand, there are those who would argue that advertising confronts us at every turn, on radio, on television, in newspapers and in the street, tempting us to consume and to compete for things which we would not normally want. These critics would say that much advertising is propaganda in that it actively and relentlessly promotes a system of greed and over-consumption. What do you think? Is advertising an example of propaganda?

 **TASK** /

Individually, produce *two* lists of points summarising the pro's and con's of advertising. For example, your lists could include the effect advertising may have upon the range and price of products available to consumers, the impact advertising may have upon the mass media, the influence of advertising upon society in general, and so on.

Share your points with those of other members of your group. Now try and produce a statement which summarises your view on the value of advertising.

The process of persuasion

Values, attitudes and opinions

In any study of the process of persuasion it is important to distinguish between a person's **values, attitudes** and **opinions**.

— **Values** are those fundamental beliefs which are so deep-seated that an individual may not always be conscious of them, or fully able to state them. Compared to attitudes and opinions, an individual's values are relatively few in number and form the 'core' of his or her beliefs and behaviour. Values are usually described in terms of abstract qualities, for example: honesty, self-reliance, success, etc. An individual's values are usually formed in early childhood and once acquired are very difficult to manipulate and change.

— **Attitudes** refer to the ways in which an individual's underlying values are expressed in the form of feelings and behaviour in given situations. A person's attitudes are best seen in the way he or she reacts and behaves to someone, or something, and not necessarily in what he or she says. This is one of the main differences between an attitude and an opinion. For example, someone may say (their opinion) that Rashid is as good as any man, but their uneasiness in the presence of Asian immigrants may belie their true feelings (their attitude). Attitudes are more numerous than values, and are more susceptible to change, precisely because they are the outward expression of values in response to people and issues.

— **Opinions** are the consciously-expressed thoughts, spoken or unspoken, which an individual has about specific incidents, issues and people. In one sense opinions can be regarded as the conscious and public expressions of underlying values and attitudes. However, two things must be stressed. Firstly, as illustrated in the earlier example, an individual's opinions may not always accurately reflect their true feelings. Secondly, an individual's opinions, unlike their values, can easily change and are susceptible to manipulation, social pressure and fashion.

A model representing the relationship between an individual's values, attitudes and opinions is given in Fig. 10.4.

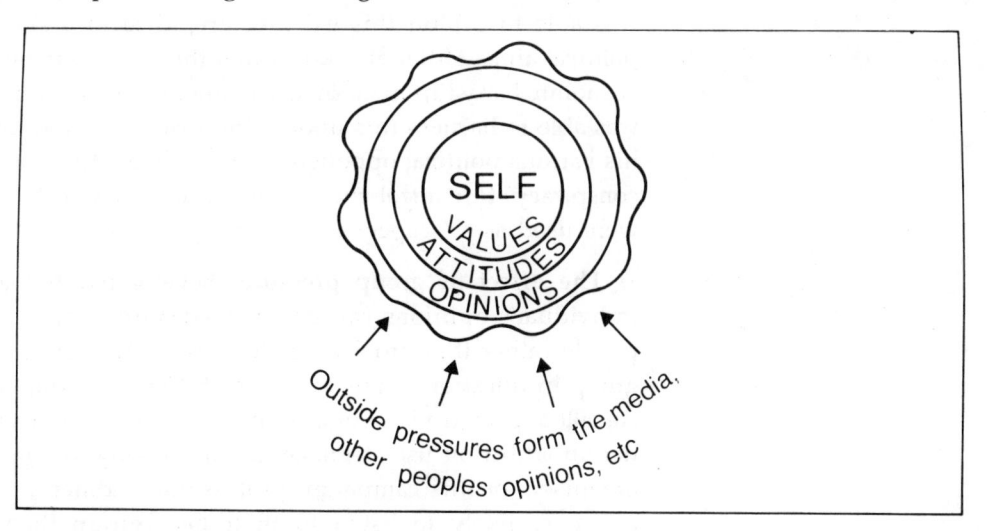

Fig. 10.4 Values, attitudes and opinions

As an example let us suppose that **respect for others** is very high on your list of core values. Examples of specific attitudes and opinions which could result from this might look as follows:

— **value:**   Respect for others;
— **attitudes:** Listening patiently to what others have to say, helping others less fortunate than oneself;
— **opinions:** 'I don't approve of Jack's behaviour because he seems so selfish'.

The interesting point here is how your opinion of Jack could easily be influenced and even be caused to change. For example, you may subsequently discover that you had made a rash and inaccurate judgement of Jack on the basis of just a brief acquaintance. Alternatively, you may find that some of your friends have a surprisingly good opinion of Jack and this may influence your own opinion. One final possibility might be if someone were to point out to you that if 'respect for others' were truly one of your core values then you ought to accept Jack for what he is, selfishness and all! This final approach recognises that it would be futile to try and change your opinion of Jack by trying to convince you that 'selfishness' didn't really matter. After all, 'respect for others' is one of your core values. Instead this approach acknowledges your underlying values and attempts to exploit one of them in a positive way to bring about a change of opinion. This possibility of exploiting an individual's values, rather than crudely trying to change them in order to influence opinions and behaviour, is one which has not been overlooked by the propagandist, as we shall see in the next section.

Factors involved in changing attitudes and opinions

In his book *Techniques of Persuasion*, JAC Brown discusses a number of studies which have attempted to identify those factors which make the process of persuasion possible. These studies suggest that there are three main factors which can be manipulated by the propagandist to help change attitudes and opinions.

— **Using existing values and prejudices.** As we have already seen, values are formed early in childhood, are deep-seated and are therefore difficult to change. The propagandist recognises this and exploits existing values and prejudices to his own ends. For example, it is often thought that Adolf Hitler and the Nazi party single-handedly 'brain-washed' the German nation into hating the Jews. In fact there had been a well-documented prejudice against the Jews for centuries throughout most countries in Europe, including England. Hitler knew this and was able to exploit this existing prejudice in a skilful way to further his own political aims. Hitler also knew that there was a great deal of fear, insecurity and economic hardship in Germany following its defeat in World War I. Again, Hitler was able to harness this underlying insecurity and direct it against the Jews and his various political opponents. In this way Hitler spoke of a 'communist Jewish conspiracy' to control the world. In an example like this we say that the Jews were used as a 'scapegoat'; as victims on whom all of the blame could be laid.

— **The effect of group pressure.** Several psychological studies show that an individual's opinions can be changed more easily by pressure from a group of people rather than from a single person. This effect is particularly strong if the group in question is one with which the individual can personally identify, the so-called 'peer group'. For example, the government's television campaign against heroin addiction uses teenage junkies talking to a mainly teenage audience. The organisers of this campaign, professional 'admen', recognise that young people are more likely to listen to their peer group than to older, well-established authority figures.

— **Subtle persuasion versus direct attack.** Further studies show that trying to persuade someone by directly confronting them and telling them to change their opinions is almost always bound to fail. Direct confrontation makes a person feel that they are under attack and that they must therefore defend themselves by automatically disagreeing with the point which is being thrust upon them, irrespective of the actual merit of the point. Phrases like 'getting someone's back up' and 'ramming a point down someone's throat' adequately describe this. A much more effective alternative is to persuade people gently and subtly by allowing them to feel that they themselves are making the decision to change their own opinion. This technique is well understood by professional counsellors who work with people who have behavioural problems or problems with their personal relationships. For example, a good marriage guidance counsellor would try and bring a problem out into the open by skilfully guiding a husband or wife to the point where they were able to admit freely to mistakes and difficulties.

Here is an example from the book *Techniques of Persuasion* (see Further reading) which illustrates some of those factors involved in changing attitudes and opinions discussed above.

'Experiments during the last war showed that lecturing mothers on the importance of feeding their children orange juice yielded singularly poor results and after a few months only a small number were still following the practice. On the other hand, when they were formed into a group and invited to discuss the problem, with the doctor sitting in merely as a source of information when this was desired, the great majority accepted and continued to follow the practice indefinitely.'

TASK 2 You have been approached by a teacher who is worried about the degree of racial prejudice he or she has heard expressed by fifth formers of a rural comprehensive school. The teacher asks for your opinion on how best to tackle this problem. You are given the following possible approaches to comment upon. Giving reasons, say how effective you think each approach might be in reducing the level of racial prejudice.

— Identify the most prejudiced members of the class and discuss the problem with each, privately and separately.

— Encourage the whole class as a group to discuss the issue of ethnic minorities in an open and free atmosphere with the teacher 'stepping in' only when necessary.

— Ask the most prejudiced members of the group to state and defend their opinions openly to the rest of the class.

— Organise activities such as sports fixtures, quizzes etc. which involve the fifth formers visiting schools which have a large number of pupils from ethnic minorities.

— State a firm and simple disagreement with each racially prejudiced comment as and when they arise naturally in class.

— Do nothing on the grounds that any positive course of action on the part of the teacher, no matter how subtle, is likely to be ineffective or counter-productive.

The techniques of persuasion

In this section we will look at the major types of techniques employed by the propagandist. This is not intended to be an exhaustive list, but simply an indication of those techniques most commonly used. It is interesting to note that most of these techniques can be related to one or more of the three major factors discussed above — 'using existing values and prejudices', 'the effect of group pressure' and 'subtle persuasion versus direct attack'.

Language As we have already discussed in Chapter 4, many words are capable of arousing in the receiver a whole range of associations and feelings. This emotive power of language is extensively used by the propagandist. Read the three extracts below and identify those words which are used because of the associations they arouse.

'Next slide please. This baby was 19 weeks old when he was killed by the method called "saline injection" (that is, salt poisoning). Though less popular than it used to be, this method is still widely employed in England for older and larger children.'

From a commentary to a set of slides on abortion produced by LIFE

All the human culture, all the results of arts, science and technology that we see before us today, are almost exclusively the product of the Aryan. This very fact admits to the not unfounded inference that he alone was the founder of all higher humanity, therefore representing the prototype of all that we understand by the term 'man'. He is the Prometheus of mankind from whose bright forehead the divine spark of genius has sprung at all times, forever kindling anew that fire of knowledge which illuminated the night of silent mysteries and thus caused man to climb the path to mastery over the other beings of the earth. Exclude him — and perhaps after a few thousand years darkness will once again descend upon the earth, human culture will pass and the world will turn to a desert.

From Mein Kampf, Adolf Hitler (Translated by Ralph Manheim) Hutchinson

'Now there's a new eyeshadow formula so silky-smooth, so luminous, it opens your eyes with colour. Choose from a luxurious array of jewel-toned brights, airy pastels, and classic neutrals — all shot with pearly highlights. You'll love the way it glides on. And stays on.'

From an Estee Lauder advert

In advertising, careful attention is given to choosing a 'brand name' which has connotations appropriate to the image which the manufacturer wishes to promote for a product. For example, 'Brut' is chosen for the brand name of a men's after-shave, whilst 'Je Reviens' is chosen for a perfume for women.

TASK 3

Below is a list of some familiar brand names. Discuss the connotations which these names have for the members of your group:

YORKIE; CHANEL; RADIENT; JAGUAR XJ6; CREAM E45; EMBASSY; LUX.

For each product say why you think the manufacturer may have chosen its particular brand name.

Fig. 10.5 Key words commonly used by the propagandist

Fig. 10.5 is a montage of key words which are commonly, almost predictably, used by the propagandist. Can you add to this montage?

Group pressure and group identification

Most extremist political groups with a strong nationalistic feeling exploit the powerful desire of wanting to belong to an elite group, race or nation. The British

National Front stresses the 'purity' of the so-called 'Anglo-Saxon' race, even though the white people of England are a complex mixture of genetic influences from across the whole European continent. Allied to this technique of glorifying a particular group is the notion of an 'out group'. To enhance a sense of belonging, a sense of patriotism for example, it is useful to have a second, contrasting group to use as a rival and as a possible scapegoat. For the English Fascist party during the thirties it was the Jews; now, for the National Front, it is 'the blacks'. For the French National Front it is the migrant workers from Morocco and Algiers. In this sense for every 'in group' there must be an 'out group'.

Many advertisers cultivate the image of a product around a clearly identifiable group. For example, many items of teenage fashion such as clothes and cosmetics are marketed through a strong image of belonging to a young, vital 'trendy' generation. In addition, slogans such as 'We're with the Woolwich' and 'The Martini People' imply that using a particular service or product confers membership to the group. So much better, then, if this group can be made to appear exclusive, for example: 'Mine's a Renault — what's yours called?'

Stereotypes, caricatures and heroes

Stereotypes, caricatures and heroes are all examples of images of individuals, or groups of individuals, which can be used by the propagandist in a variety of different ways for a variety of different purposes.

Stereotypes are commonly used by advertisers for two main reasons. Firstly, they can be used to introduce humour into an advert and therefore make it more noticeable and more memorable. An example of this would be a 'stuffy' pin-stripe-suited bank manager in a banking advertisement. Secondly, stereotypes are often used in adverts to enable the advertiser to communicate a relatively complex message simply and quickly. For example, an advert for washing-up liquid showing a kind and gentle mother and a small vulnerable daughter quickly and effectively establishes the necessary images of softness and domesticity. Using stereotypes of the 'typical mum', 'typical dad', etc., the advertiser can save a lot of time by bringing well-established meanings already pre-packaged, as it were, within the image.

A **caricature** is when an image of an individual, or group of individuals, is distorted to the point that it appears ridiculous, evil or grotesque. Caricatures can be conveyed verbally, as in this example taken from a German school textbook used during the Nazi regime:

> The Near-Eastern race, from which the Jews partly originate, can be found mainly in Armenia. It consists of people who are of medium height, squat, dark-haired, dark-eyed, and have a short head. Members of this race characteristically have a hooked nose, a strongly formed lower lip, and a barely emphasised chin. They also have bad tempers and a strong commercial talent which results in their minds being occupied by thoughts of the acquisition of material goods. This contrasts strongly with the mind of the German.

> From *Biologie: fur Oberschulen und Gymnasium* (Berlin, 1941) (Biology: for Grammar Schools.)

Normally, caricatures are best conveyed visually as in *Spitting Image* shown in Fig. 10.6.

Idealised or glorified images of individuals, or groups of individuals — **heroes** — are in a sense the opposite of caricatures. A good example of the use of heroic figures was Hitler's glorification of the blond German as 'the saviour of the purity of mankind'. Fig. 10.7 is a good, visual example of the idealisation of individuals by the British during World War II. Can you identify any elements of this poster which make it particularly effective?

Fig. 10.6 A *Spitting Image* caricature (Central TV)

Fig. 10.7 British poster from World War II

Appeals to authority

Propagandists can attempt to make their statements more powerful and believable by connecting them with some well-known and well-respected outside authority. For example, a politician may say during a television or radio interview: 'As Winston Churchill once said, I believe that . . .' In this way the politician effectively attempts to enhance the status and credibility of his or her own position by associating it with a well-respected name. In advertising 'experts' are often used in a similar manner. For example, an ex-Wimbledon champion may be used to advertise a particular brand of tennis racket. The use of such a well-known figure not only draws our attention to the advert but, by a process of 'status by association', attempts to confer a special quality on the product.

Appeals to emotions, needs and values

Insecurity is a key emotion which the propagandist often plays upon. For example, advertisements for slimming aids, deodorants and acne treatments often exploit the need to look and smell socially acceptable. A not-too-subtle example of this is shown in Fig. 10.8. Politicians can exploit the insecurity the electorate may feel about basic issues such as jobs, war and civil unrest and crime.

Guilt is another key emotion often exploited by the propagandist. For example, in advertising a mother may be encouraged to feel that if she really cared about her children she would feed them a particular brand of breakfast cereal.

In politics, abstract qualities such as honesty, integrity, self reliance, etc., are often highlighted not only to distinguish a particular policy from its rivals, but also in an attempt to appeal to the electorate's underlying core values. For example, Margaret Thatcher often uses the image of the good housewife living sensibly and cautiously within her weekly allowance as a means of depicting her

Fig. 10.8 'Bad breath and how to cure it'

own government's management of the economy. In this way Mrs Thatcher effectively draws our attention to values of common sense, thrift, caution — values which in abstract form most of us would have some difficulty in disagreeing with. Equally, Neil Kinnock frequently refers to a tolerant, caring society, a society which listens and offers help. Here again, qualities are being used which in abstract form few would disagree with.

Appeals to the senses

In political rallies and religious ceremonies there are many devices which are used to appeal to our emotions directly through our senses. The 'razzamatazz' of the American political convention, with its flags, banners and bands, is a good example of this. In religious ceremony the high-vaulted church with its stained glass, the use of incense, and the distinctive dress of the priest all help to create an atmosphere of something extraordinary, of something outside normal experience.

A more subtle but no less effective technique is the use of the power and rhythm of the human voice. In political speeches for example, is the use of the so-called 'three part trick' where a speaker repeats a word or phrase three times. Most of the memorable quotations from politics are of this kind. Here are a few:

'Never in the field of human conflict was so much owed by so many to so few.'

Winston Churchill. 1940

'There are some of us who will fight and fight and fight again to save the party we love.'

Hugh Gaitskell. 1960

'Government of the people, by the people, and for the people.'

Abraham Lincoln. 1863

'Ein Reich, Ein Volk, Ein Fuhrer.' ('One state, one people, one leader.')

Adolf Hitler

There is something curiously compelling and emotional about this sequence of three, something which affects our senses directly. It's not surprising therefore to find that its use is not confined to politics. Consider the following examples:

'In the Name of the Father, and of the Son, and of the Holy Ghost.'

'With this ring I thee wed, with my body I thee worship, and with all my worldly goods I thee endow.'

The Book of Common Prayer

Other examples of direct appeals to the senses, especially in television and cinema advertising, involve the use of fast-moving, rhythmical sequences of colour. With still photography, in magazines especially, the advertiser continues to appeal directly to our senses. The cool refreshing quality of lager can be enhanced by clear 'sharp' images of condensation dripping down the side of a misted glass.

Control of information

This is the technique which is most popularly associated with the activities of the propagandist — the notion of withholding, slanting and distorting information.

In times of war or national unrest and tension, **censorship** is perhaps the most blatant example of this technique. In South Africa during the state of 'national emergency', the Pretoria government kept a rigorous control over what journalists could and could not report. As in this case, censorship is usually backed up by the rule of law.

A more subtle form of controlling information is when the propagandist draws the audience's attention to the strong points in his/her argument, whilst conveniently underplaying, or ignoring its weaknesses. This **slanting** of information is a standard technique used by politicians when being interviewed on television or radio. An interesting example of this from advertising was when the manufacturer of a famous 'biological' washing powder claimed that 'Stains do come out when soaked in Ariel, but don't wash out in ordinary powders.' What the manufacturer conveniently forgot to point out was that stains come out when they are 'soaked' — as opposed to just 'washed' — in any washing powder!

Fig. 10.9 An example of photographic censorship

Finally, an interesting visual example of controlling information is shown in Fig. 10.9. This shows how the figure of Alexander Dubcek was removed from an official Communist Party photograph following the invasion of the Russian tanks into Czechoslovakia and Dubcek's fall from office. More subtle examples of slanting information by photographic editing are shown in Harold Evans' book *Pictures on a Page* (Heinemann, 1978).

TASK 4 Several examples of communication which set out to influence opinion and behaviour are shown in Fig. 10.10 a)—e). Study these examples carefully and for each:

— Identify and describe any specific techniques of persuasion which you feel are being used. For this you may wish to refer to the examples of techniques discussed above.

— Assess its likely effectiveness in influencing the opinions of specific groups of people, or 'audiences'. (For this you should bear in mind that different receivers may be influenced differently, depending on their individual values and beliefs. In other words, an example of communication which sets out to persuade may be effective for one audience, but not for another.)

(a)

(b)

(c)

Fig. 10.10 Influencing opinion and behaviour

(d)

Did I kick too hard ?

a child of about
15 weeks killed
under the 1967
Abortion Act

Save the Unborn Child
Life

7 Parade
Leamington Spa
Warwickshire
0926 21687

Fig. 10.10

(e)

CURIOSITY WILL KILL THIS CAT

This cat may be dead
already. It is part of a
British experiment where
electrodes are put into
cats' brains and the animals
are subjected to tests – just to see what
happens. After three years the cats are
killed.

No civilised country should allow this
suffering. The animals can't protest, but you can.
**Join us now in our campaign to end
behavioural experiments in 1985.**

BUAV AGAINST ALL ANIMAL EXPERIMENTS
BUAV. 16a Crane Grove, Islington, London N7 8LB 01-607 1545/1892

The advertising industry

The cost and effectiveness of advertising

Advertising is big business. For example, Fig. 10.11 shows that £3126 million were spent buying advertising space in all forms of the media in Britain in 1982. One of the most expensive media to use is television. The reason for this is not that television is in itself so costly to use, but that it attracts such large viewing audiences and so is a much sought-after medium. Typical costs of using television for advertising are illustrated in Fig. 10.12.

	1960		1975		1980		1982	
	£m	%	£m	%	£m	%	£m	%
National newspapers	64	19.8	162	16.8	426	16.7	515	16.5
Regional newspapers	77	23.8	283	29.3	640	25.0	737	23.6
Magazines and periodicals	40	12.4	79	8.2	192	7.5	209	6.7
Trade and technical	31	9.6	86	8.9	214	8.4	247	7.9
Other	17	5.2	69	7.2	212	8.3	278	8.9
TOTAL PRESS	229	70.9	679	70.2	1684	65.9	1986	63.5
TV	72	22.3	236	24.4	692	27.1	928	29.7
Poster and transport	16	5.0	35	3.6	107	4.2	124	4.0
Cinema	5	1.5	7	0.7	18	0.7	18	0.6
Radio	1	0.3	10	1.0	54	2.1	70	2.2
TOTAL	323	100	967	100	2555	100	3126	100

Source: *Statistical Yearbook* Advertising Association

Fig. 10.11 Total advertising expenditure by media

Anglia Television Ltd

PEAK TIME
(Monday to Saturday 17.25–22.25 and Sunday 19.00–22.25)
30 seconds £6,000
60 seconds £12,000
OFF PEAK TIME
(all other times)
30 seconds £1,300
60 seconds £2,600

Central Independent Television plc

Central sets its advertising rates not by the time of day but by the number and type of people likely to be watching.
30 HOUSEWIFE RATING (*HIGH*)
30 seconds £9,100   60 seconds £18,200
10 HOUSEWIFE RATING (*LOW*)
30 seconds £2,100   60 seconds £4,200
(1983 prices)

Thames Television Ltd

PEAK TIME
(Monday to Friday 18.00–23.05)
30 seconds £10,360
60 seconds £20,720
OFF PEAK TIME
(for example, Monday to Friday 17.10–18.00)
30 seconds £4,770
60 seconds £9,540

Source: Company Rate Cards

Fig. 10.12 The cost of advertising on TV

Since advertising is so costly, and since it inevitably adds to the retail price of products, is it really necessary, does it really work? Some critics of advertising may say that a good product will sell itself. Others might argue that advertising techniques, no matter how subtle, can never really influence the behaviour of the intelligent and rational consumer. What are the facts? Is advertising effective? Obviously, if a product is badly designed or of little value to anyone, then no amount of advertising could make the public buy it. However, most advertising is concerned with increasing the popularity of a particular brand of a well-established commodity, e.g. clothes, drink, household goods, etc. compared with other, competing brands. This popularity of a brand against its rivals is described as its **market share**. Several studies clearly show how advertising can be very

Fig. 10.13 The 'Turtle Wax Campaign'

effective in increasing the market share of a product. The more money which is spent on an advertising campaign, and the more media which are used, the more the market share can be made to increase. A dramatic example of this effect of advertising can be seen in Fig. 10.13 describing the launch of the 'Turtle wax campaign'.

BRAND LEADER IN 3 MONTHS

CAMPAIGN STRATEGY

Foster McMillan Smith recommended a drip campaign as opposed to the more traditional burst campaign, thus extending the advertising period over nine weeks and helping to offset variable weather conditions. The £380,000 national campaign was rolled out on ITV and Channel Four from late April to July 2. Channel Four was used primarily to influence the young and upmarket profile especially among men. Also coverage and frequency analyses run on a hypothetical schedule prior to final planning clearly revealed the extent to which Channel Four contributed towards building coverage at a cost effective level, especially among ABC1 men aged 25-34. Programme selection played a major role in all respects, and especially with the extra planning time that a drip campaign provided. Advertising on ITV was deployed in alternate weeks whilst Channel Four ran continuously to give a greater impression of repetition than the spot deployment pattern itself warranted. To reach the prime target effectively, ITV was restricted to peak time except Wednesday, Thursday and Friday, whereas airtime on Channel Four was spread across the week achieving a combined ITV plus 4 total of 360 male television ratings, 85 per cent coverage and just on 5.0 opportunities to see.

THE COMMERCIAL

The 30 second commercial took a hard sell, no nonsense approach to demonstrate Minute Wax's unique ability to wax a car in less than 15 minutes. It was decided to stage the 'Turtle Wax challenge' in which members of the public were invited to wax their cars in a race against the stop watch. In order to demonstrate that the challenge was fair and above board, the whole operation was carried out in the most public of places — Trafalgar Square.

CAMPAIGN RESULTS

★ An established 19 per cent £ market share in 1983 making Minute Wax brand leader (up to 35 per cent sterling share was achieved during the television advertising).
★ 75 per cent sterling distribution within 12 months.
★ A dominant 41 per cent total Turtle Wax market share (all Turtle Wax polish brands) in 1983.
★ The market experienced growth of 7 per cent 1983/ 1982 following four years of decline.
★ The television advertising not only exceeded the objectives for Minute Wax but also helped to increase market share for existing Turtle Wax polish brands. In addition, sales and distribution levels across the entire range of Turtle Wax automotive products improved.
★ Line extensions and new product launches are benefitting from the 'halo' effect of television advertising for Minute Wax.
★ All this was achieved profitably and price became of secondary importance to product benefit among consumers.

THE FUTURE

Roy Line, managing director of Turtle Wax, states, 'Following our spectacular sales success on television in 1983, we are deploying nearly 100 per cent of an increased advertising budget on television in 1984 to support Minute Wax and help the launch of further Minute brands. We are confident that television advertising will translate the high consumer appeal of our brands into profitable sales.'

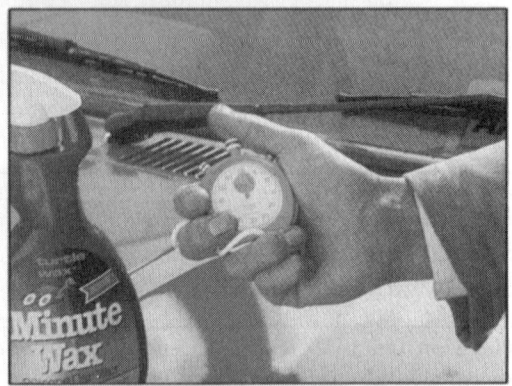

The advertising agency Anyone can buy advertising space. Private individuals often put adverts in local newspapers for selling and buying things. Businesses can put adverts directly into the press for job vacancies and for their goods and services. However, most of the money spent on advertising is spent by special **advertising agencies** working on behalf of their clients, the manufacturers of goods and services.

A large manufacturer like British Petroleum, for example, would not advertise its own products, nor would it deal directly with the media. Instead, it would hire the services of an advertising agency which would plan, organise and carry out a complete campaign on its behalf. The work of a typical agency covers both the financial aspects of a campaign, e.g. researching costs, buying space on television etc. and the creative aspects e.g. designing artwork, inventing jingles/slogans etc. This is illustrated in Fig. 10.14.

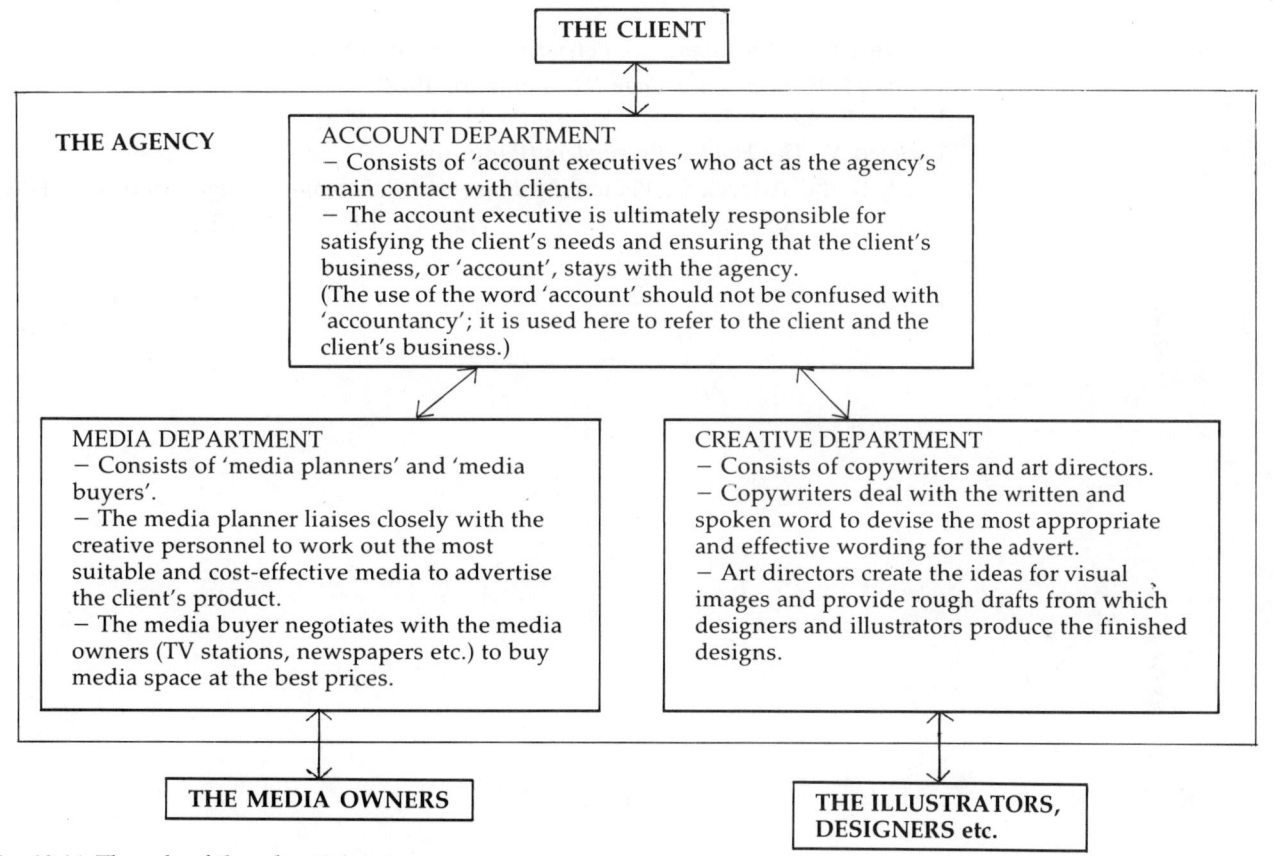

Fig. 10.14 The role of the advertising agency

Self-assessment

1. Using examples, illustrate the difference between advertising and publicity.
2. Using examples, explain why people may disagree with specific uses of the word 'propaganda'.
3. Distinguish between attitudes, values and opinions.
4. What are the *three* main psychological factors involved in effective persuasion?
5. Write notes on the main techniques employed by the propagandist. For each give your own example.
6. Explain why advertising space on television is so costly compared with that of other media.
7. What is an advertising agency and what are its main activities?

Further work

1. Compile a scrapbook of items selected from back-copies of magazines and newspapers to illustrate the techniques of persuasion discussed in this chapter. Try and include items from a wide range of material such as: adverts, cartoons, editorials, headlines, etc.
2. Write an essay with the following title: Discuss the proposition that advertising is a form of propaganda.
3. Produce a checklist of 'do's' and 'don'ts' which could act as a guide to effective persuasion for the would-be propagandist.

Further reading

Brown J.A.C, *Techniques of Persuasion* (Pelican, 1963)

Evans H, *Pictures on a Page* (Heinemann, 1978)

Jefkins F, *Advertising Made Simple* (W.H.Allen, 1973)

Packard V, *The Hidden Persuaders* (Penguin)

Reich B and Adcock C, *Values, Attitudes and Behaviour Change* (Methuen, 1976)

Rhodes A, *Propaganda – The Art of Persuasion, 1933–1945* (Chelsea House, 1979)

11 Control and accountability in the media

This chapter contains the following sections:
- **Ownership of the media**
- **Bias in the media**
- **Accountability**
- **Censorship**
- **Self-assessment**
- **Further work**
- **Further reading**

Ownership of the media

In Chapters 8 and 9 we briefly discussed who owns our press and broadcasting industries. We noted that, with the exception of the BBC, capitalist private ownership was the rule. (NB. The *Peacock Committee,* which reported in July 1986, even recommended that Radio 1 and 2 should be *privatised.*) We also saw how press ownership, in particular, was becoming more and more concentrated into fewer and fewer hands. We can now point to two other trends in media ownership.

Diversification   James Curran and Jean Seaton (*Power without Responsibility*) show how corporations like Associated Newspapers (whose origins lie in the newspaper industry) have attempted to **diversify**, and widen their power base, by taking interests in other media enterprises. This company, for example, has a stake in the London Broadcasting Company (LBC) and Plymouth Sound, both independent local radio stations. The other top three press companies also have interests in TV-AM and Capital Radio (Fleet Holdings), Central Television and Rediffusion Cablevision (Pergamon) and the SKY satellite channel (News International). Diversification has also occurred into non-media industries. Examples include Fleet Holdings moving into insurance and Associated Newspapers into oil and gas. Of course, non-media companies have also taken control of newspapers in the past. The most widely-quoted example is that of the *Observer*, which was taken over by the multinational giant, Lonhro, in the 1970s. Fig. 11.1 shows how multi-dimensional media ownership has become, taking the company S.Pearson and Son as an example.

Foreign ownership   **Foreign ownership** and influence on the mass media is a fact of life in Britain. The most obvious example is, of course, News International, controlled by the Australian Rupert Murdoch, which owns the *Sun, The Times, News of the World, Sunday Times* and *Today.* In 1985, the *Daily Telegraph* also passed into Canadian ownership.

Many critics argue that it is the private ownership of most of the mass media which guarantees its independence from the State. This is usually known as the 'freedom of the press'. They point to societies like the Soviet Union, where the media is merely a branch of the Communist government, to support their view. However, radical critics like the Campaign for Press and Broadcasting Freedom (CPBF) reject this and 'challenge the view that only private ownership ...

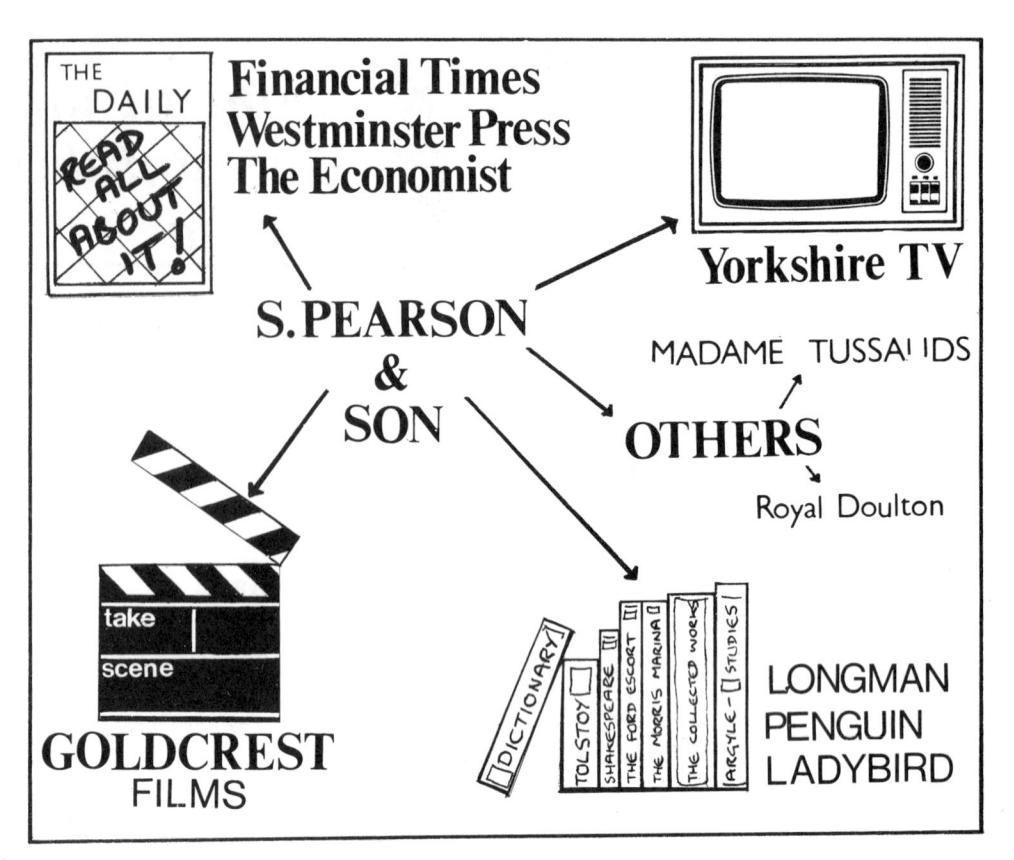

Fig. 11.1 Multi-dimensional ownership

provides genuine freedom, diversity or access'. The CPBF, in particular, are keen to arouse debate about alternative forms of media ownership and would like to see a National Printing Corporation set up to provide a public sector which could assist the launching of new publications (especially those sympathetic to the labour movement). In terms of *control* of the media, they also propose a greater degree of *industrial democracy* (worker participation) within media industries.

 TASK /

Imagine that a National Printing Corporation (NPC) has recently been set up. You are the spokesperson for a group of people who want to publish a regional weekly newspaper with a left-wing leaning. Since you have very little capital you need to approach the NPC for funds and assistance. Write a detailed submission to the Secretary of the NPC outlining your plans for your regional newspaper. Include details of:

— Your target audience (nature and size of);
— How much start-up capital you would need (you will have to contact existing newspapers to find out these details);
— Your proposed editorial policy on major issues of the day;
— How you would intend to satisfy the needs of your region;
— The style you will intend to adopt (sensational or sober?);
— Why you think your proposal should be favoured instead of others.

Bias in the media

We saw in Chapter 8 that there is no pretence of impartiality in the press industry. Newspapers openly express political **bias** in their news reporting and editorials. The broadcasters, on the other hand, do claim that they are impartial in their presentation of social and political issues. But how biased are the mass media, and who are they biased against?

Access to the media   Many people on the Left in politics argue that there is a pronounced and continuous bias in broadcasting against unconventional ideas, policies and political movements. The trade unions, the labour movement, peace activists, ethnic minorities and homosexuals are usually seen as the main victims of this media bias. One of the main criticisms is that these kinds of groups are denied **access** to the media – the end result being an inadequate representation of the complex nature of our society (since they are unable to put across their views effectively to the public). Likewise, it is argued, moderate politicians, employers, whites etc. find the media much more accessible to their particular viewpoints.

One aim of the radical Campaign for Press and Broadcasting Freedom is:

> 'to challenge the myth of "impartiality" and "balance" in broadcasting, and "objectivity" in newspapers, by campaigning for the genuine representation of the diversity and plurality of society.'

This organisation argues that media content ought to be 'free of material detrimental to any individual or group on the grounds of gender, race, class, religion, sexual preference, age or physical or mental ability'. There has always been a left-wing distrust of the media; it has been viewed, especially by those who subscribe to the Marxist interpretation of society, as a means of supporting and sustaining the status quo in society.

Bad news   However, it is only recently that critics have moved the debate on from generalisations to detailed factual research. This process, of attempting to prove media bias through the detailed analysis of media texts, was started by the Glasgow University Media Group. This radical group of media researchers have published a series of critical books on media bias during the last decade, starting with the influential *Bad News*. The focus of this first research project was the **decoding** of television news, and the group monitored all TV news broadcasts between January and June in 1975. The main conclusions reached in *Bad News* were:

– Through a process of constant *selection*, the media set the *agenda* and define what is 'news'.

– Television news is no more neutral or objective than the press.

– Television news (whether BBC or ITN) is engaged in a process of **cultural legitimation** and the maintenance of the status quo. This means that the media support and project the dominant values of our society and reject values that conflict with those of the *Establishment*.

As the Group argued:

> 'news is not a neutral product. For TV news is a cultural artefact; it is a sequence of socially manufactured messages which carry many of the culturally dominant assumptions of our society.'

However, criticism of the media does not just originate from the Left. In June 1986 the Conservative Party set up a Media Monitoring Unit to focus attention on what they believe is anti-Conservative bias in broadcasting. The particular targets of the Unit are *Panorama* (BBC1), *Newsnight* (BBC2), *Today* (Radio 4) and news bulletins.

Media professionals have, of course, always denied that they consciously engage in biased treatment of news. Indeed, not all research has supported the view that broadcasting is biased. In 1986 the Broadcasting Research Unit published a study of television news reporting of the recent miners' strike. Whilst by no means completely exonerating the broadcasters, they did (after a detailed analysis of all major news bulletins backed up by three national opinion surveys) conclude that 'balance was usually demonstrated'.

What do the viewers think?

The perception of the audience would appear to be a key element in this debate. One might argue that just as beauty is in the eye of the beholder, so too is alleged bias. Audience research can help us to find out the views of those who are at the receiving end of media representations. The study referred to above also found that nearly 60% of the sample believed that BBC and ITN's coverage of the dispute had been impartial. The IBA also regularly commissions detailed attitudinal surveys of the population, the most recent one being *Attitudes to Broadcasting*. This report showed that over 60% of the population believed that television was generally 'fair and balanced' (although 20% of viewers believed that BBC1 favoured the Conservatives). However, the report did point out that there had been a 10% decline in the 'trust factor' since 1984.

Conclusions

Bias in the press is accepted by most people as a fact of life whilst broadcasting partiality is a matter of heated debate. The evidence to support the view that radio and television are equally biased would appear to be inconclusive and open to individual perception. However, it is valid to argue that, in a very general sense at least, the media are in the business of supporting the status quo in any society. They do this through a constant attempt to express a social and political **consensus** or agreement about the way society should be ordered. Whether or not the media actually helps to create this consensus is, of course, a whole new debate.

TASK *2*

Below are some factual statements about a fictitious event. Write a strongly *emotive* front page article for the *Sun* which would accurately reflect that paper's Conservative viewpoint.

. . . Mass demonstration by National Union of Students outside American Embassy in London . . . students protesting about US policy in Central America . . . Police estimate crowd at 5000 . . . NUS believes 15000 took part . . . Violent clash between police and small section of crowd . . . took place towards end of peaceful demonstration . . . 5 police and 25 demonstrators taken to hospital . . . one policeman seriously ill . . . 13 demonstrators arrested . . .

Accountability

In this section we discuss the complicated, and controversial, question: 'To whom are the media **accountable** for their actions?' This question is asked of relatively few large enterprises in society. However, since the mass media are public, easily accessible and able to influence the attitudes and behaviour of the public, we are concerned that there should be constraints on their behaviour.

Some critics believe the media are centralised, bureaucratic organisations which are accountable to nobody but themselves. For our purposes, though, we will argue that the media could be held to be accountable in the following ways.

The State

As we saw in Chapter 9, the **State** has always been heavily involved in the development of broadcasting in Britain. Although there was an early decision to give the fledgling BBC a degree of independence, the State has always felt that the Corporation (and, later, ITV) should be accountable for their actions and output. Since the State has appointed the BBC and the IBA to be 'servants of the community', it follows that these organisations should be accountable to the general public, through the medium of the State. This accountability, as we have seen in earlier chapters, is exercised mainly through the terms of the BBC's **Charter and Licence** and the terms of the **Broadcasting Act**, which set out the regulations covering broadcasting in Britain. The problem here is the extent to which the **national** interest (which often just means the interests of the Government in power) is synonymous with the **public** interest.

In terms of accountability, the Governors of the BBC and the members of the IBA are seen as occupying key positions. Legally, for example, the Governors are responsible for the programmes broadcast on the BBC. It is they who must defend controversial programmes to the Home Secretary (who has a Governmental responsibility for broadcasting). In the *Real Lives* controversy of 1985 they stopped the transmission of a politically sensitive programme as a result of pressure from the Government. Perhaps this episode showed that one man's accountability is another man's censorship?

These broadcasting watchdogs, however, are usually amateurs and appointed by the Government of the day. Events over the past decade have shown that they find it difficult to stand up to what some might call intimidation from the Government. The equation between accountability on the one hand, and independence on the other, is a problematical one and often a subject of heated debate.

Legal constraints   Like all organisations, media industries have to be accountable to the laws of the land. Some laws are applicable to everybody, whilst others are specifically media-orientated. Here are details of some of the most important **legal constraints** on the media in Britain:

– **Broadcasting Act (1981).** This outlines a legal framework for the independent broadcasting system in Britain and gives the IBA the responsibility of providing a high quality radio and TV service, including a range of programmes, presented in a balanced way.

– **Contempt of Court Act (1981).** This very important constraint on the activities of the media prevents journalists from publishing anything which might, for example, interfere with the outcome of a trial. The media are not allowed to comment on the progress of a trial or 'take sides'. Again, we have a conflict – between the 'freedom of the press' and the interests of the legal system. A well-known case of contempt occurred in the 1970s during the Thalidomide affair. The *Sunday Times* was running a campaign in its pages against the Distillers corporation (makers of the drug), aimed at getting the best possible financial deal for the families affected. The articles were deemed to be in contempt of the court cases occurring at the time.

– **Official Secrets Act (1912).** It is often argued that Britain is one of the most secretive societies in the world. Unlike in the USA, which has passed a Freedom of Information Act, journalists in Britain often find it very difficult to report on matters of state if the Government decides that publication would be against the 'national interest'. The Official Secrets Act covers a wide variety of possible offences – an example of contravention would be if a journalist received information from a civil servant in a sensitive government department like defence, which was unauthorised. This is what happened in the Sarah Tisdall affair in 1984, although it was the civil servant, rather than the *Guardian* newspaper, who was prosecuted and sent to gaol. This Act is a matter of intense debate and many people argue that it should be replaced by a much less restrictive piece of legislation.

– **Defamation Laws.** There are two ways the media can engage in defamation; **libel** is written defamation and **slander** is spoken defamation. If a person can prove in a court that an article in a newspaper has damaged his or her reputation,

ABBEY NATIONAL BUILDING SOCIETY
Abbey House
Baker Street
London NW1 6XL

(Previous complaints upheld during last 12 months: 1)

Complaint from: Birmingham

Basis of Complaint: A member of the public objected to a promotional brochure for the Abbeylink service which claimed "The Abbeylink card is issued free to Abbey National savers with Share or Cheque-Save Accounts. There is no charge when you use the card to deposit or withdraw money or make balance enquiries (unlike most banks where a charge is made for using the service)". The complainant pointed out however that balance enquiries were free to bank customers as were withdrawals provided that their accounts remained in credit. Similarly, no charge would be made where deposit facilities were available. He therefore questioned the validity of the comparison. (B.21.2)

Conclusion: Complaint upheld. The advertisers stated that the leaflet had been printed in early December, and that the claim had been correct at that time. The Authority noted, however, that the major banks had announced changes in their charging policy for those customers remaining in credit at this time, and was concerned therefore that the advertisers had proceeded with the distribution of the leaflet. The advertisers confirmed that the claim would be amended.

NIREX
Building 173
Harwell, Didcot
Oxon OX11 0RA

Agency: Foster, Turner & Benson

Complaints from: Amptill, Beds; Shefford, Beds

Basis of Complaint: Two members of the public objected to a local press advertisement headlined "Hands up if you know what low level nuclear waste is" and which claimed that waste would be buried "in concrete boxes or steel drums". The complainants pointed out however, that a fact sheet prepared by the advertisers stated that such waste would be "transported in metal containers or in plastic bags and no additional precautions need be taken before it is buried in the trenches". (Section II.4.2)

Conclusion: Complaints not upheld. The advertisers stated that the references in the fact sheet described the present practices at Drigg. While they believed this to be perfectly safe and satisfactory practice, they nonetheless always endeavoured to introduce ever increasing levels of precaution and the advertisement, which related specifically to a proposed repository at Elstow, accurately reflected their proposals for the disposal of waste at that site.

NIGHT-VIEW TV SERVICES
15 High Street
Welwyn
Herts

Complaint from: Welwyn, Herts

Basis of Complaint: A member of the public objected to a local press advertisement which stated "Buy a video for Christmas and get 40 film rentals free . . .". The complainant responded to the advertisement but discovered that the offer did not apply to all the films in stock but only to a limited range. The complainant considered that this restriction to the offer should have been made clear in the advertisement. (BCSPP 5.9.1)

Conclusion: Complaint upheld. The advertisers stated that the offer was limited to those videos for which the normal nightly rental was £1.00. These videos were generally older stock but, they stated, comprised a substantial proportion of their total range. The Authority noted the advertisers' comments but considered that the advertisement should have made clear the terms under which free videos were supplied. The advertisers agreed to modify future advertisements accordingly.

The Advertising Standards Authority

Brook House, 2-16 Torrington Place, London WC1E 7HN. Telephone 01-580 5555 (9 lines)
Telex: No. 27950 MONOREF G 1020

NISSAN U.K. LTD
Nissan House
Columbia Drive
Durrington
Worthing
West Sussex BN13 3HD

Agency: Saatchi & Saatchi Compton Ltd

(Previous complaints upheld during last 12 months: 3)

Complaints from: Rotherham, South Yorkshire; Leigh; Worthing, West Sussex

Basis of Complaint: Three members of the public objected to advertisements claiming that all Nissan cars possessed "a 3 year/100,000 mile warranty". The complainants, who had bought Nissan cars, found that the advertisers' liability during the 2nd and 3rd year of the warranty was limited to £300 for any single claim and a maximum of £600 for the total of claims during that period. They considered that the advertisements exaggerated the extent of cover that would be provided. (B.13.4; B.13.5)

Conclusion: Complaints not upheld. The advertisers stated that the conditions referred to by the complainants had been superseded by new conditions for vehicles purchased after January 1st 1986. They submitted a copy of the current warranty document and it was noted that there were no financial limitations in the conditions.

Fig. 11.2 Recent adjudications

he or she can sue the paper and claim damages. Probably the 'most-sued' publication is the satirical magazine *Private Eye*, whose former editor Richard Ingrams lists 'litigation' as his main leisure pursuit in *Who's Who*. The libel and slander laws are a constant constraint on the activities of the mass media and could be said to give power to the individual vis-à-vis powerful media organisations. Litigation costs a lot of money, however, which rules it out as a course of action for most ordinary people.

— **Obscene Publications Act (1959).** This covers the print and cinema industries, but not broadcasting. The Act allows for the prosecution of anybody who, by their actions, is 'likely to deprave and corrupt'. Of course, once we enter the arena of public taste, decency and morality things become very subjective indeed. A magazine or film may appear obscene to one person but tame to another. Legislation of this kind often tends to lag behind movements in public opinion.

Self-accountability   The media have themselves taken steps to create mechanisms through which public opinion of the media can be channelled (and, to a certain extent, controlled). Two main bodies have been set up to fulfil this objective:

— **The Press Council.** This organisation, set up by the newspaper industry in 1963, has the job of adjudicating complaints from the public about press content and treatment. The Press Council has not had a happy history, since it has been criticised for not having any legal powers to enforce its adjudications. More radical critics of the media insist that people who have been misrepresented in the media ought to have a statutory **right of reply.**

— **Advertising Standards Authority.** This body was set up by the advertising industry in 1962 in order to monitor its Code of Practice. The ASA has more 'teeth' than the Press Council and its decisions are much more likely to be followed, since it has the support of the industry. Fig. 11.2 contains some recent adjudications by the ASA.

(Members of the public can also complain to a body called the Broadcasting Complaints Commission, set up in 1981, if they believe they have been the victim of unfair treatment or if their personal privacy has been invaded. However, as with the Press Council, the Commission is seen by many people as an ineffectual organisation in terms of making the media more accountable to the general public.)

Codes of practice and conduct   Media practitioners have also made the effort to develop professional standards and codes of ethical behaviour in their particular industries. This has taken place through the adoption of *Codes of Practice and Conduct*. Two examples are discussed below.

— **The IBA's Television Programme Guidelines.** This is a collection of documents produced by the IBA which aims 'to see that the requirements of the Broadcasting Act and of the programme contracts are observed and that fair practices are established'. They cover areas such as offence to good taste, fairness and impartiality, privacy, party politics and feature films. Fig. 11.3 illustrates the IBA's 'Family Viewing Policy' and its guidelines on the 'Portrayal of Violence'.

— **National Union of Journalists Code of Conduct.** All members of the main journalists union are asked to comply with this Code which seeks to uphold high journalistic standards and ethical behaviour. In theory, failure to do so could involve expulsion from the union (which might cost journalists their job). However, the Code is notoriously difficult to operate as the experience of the *Sun's* con-

The Portrayal of Violence

11.4 Family Viewing Policy

It is the IBA's aim so far as possible not to broadcast material unsuitable for children at times when large numbers of children are viewing. Constraints on this policy arise from two factors: first there is no time of the evening when there are not some children viewing, perhaps even in quite substantial numbers; and secondly any attempt to provide a wide range of programmes appropriate for adults and including serious subject-matter will entail the broadcasting of some material that might be considered unsuitable for children. The IBA does not accept that, because some children are always likely to be present in the audience, there should be no adult material included in the programme output of Independent Television. The necessary compromise between these constraints and the IBA's general aim is embodied in the IBA's Family Viewing Policy for evening viewing.

The policy assumes a progressive decline throughout the evening in the proportion of children present in the audience. It expects a similar progression in the successive programmes scheduled from early evening until closedown; the earlier in the evening the more suitable, the later in the evening the less suitable. Within the progression, 9.00p.m. is fixed as the point up to which the broadcasters will normally regard themselves as responsible for ensuring that nothing is shown that is unsuitable for children. After nine o'clock progressively less suitable (i.e. more adult) material may be shown, and it may be that a programme will be acceptable for example at 10.30p.m. that would not be suitable at 9.00p.m. But it is assumed that from 9.00p.m. onwards parents may reasonably be expected to share responsibility for what their children are permitted to see. Violence is not the only reason why a programme may be unsuitable for family viewing. Other factors include bad language, innuendo, blasphemy, explicit sexual behaviour, and scenes of extreme distress.

All concerned in the planning, production and scheduling of television programmes must keep in mind the following considerations:

The Content of the Programme Schedules as a Whole

(a) People seldom view just one programme. An acceptable minimum of violence in each individual programme may add up to an intolerable level over a period.
(b) The time of screening of each programme is important. The IBA policy of 'family viewing time' until 9.00p.m. entails special concern for younger viewers.

The Ends and the Means

(c) There is no evidence that the portrayal of violence for good or 'legitimate' ends is likely to be less harmful to the individual, or to society, than the portrayal of violence for evil ends.

Presentation

(d) There is no evidence that 'sanitised' or 'conventional' violence, in which the consequences are concealed, minimised or presented in a ritualistic way, is innocuous. It may be just as dangerous to society to conceal the results of violence or to minimise them as to let people see clearly the full consequences of violent behaviour, however gruesome: what may be better for society may be emotionally more upsetting or more offensive for the individual viewer.
(e) Violence which is shown as happening long ago or far away may seem to have less impact on the viewer, but it remains violence. Horror in costume remains horror.
(f) Dramatic truth may occasionally demand the portrayal of a sadistic character, but there can be no defence of violence shown solely for its own sake, or of the gratuitous exploitation of sadistic or other perverted practices.
(g) Ingenious and unfamiliar methods of inflicting pain or injury – particularly if capable of easy imitation – should not be shown without the most careful consideration.
(h) Violence has always been and still is widespread throughout the world, so violent scenes in news and current affairs programmes are inevitable. But the editor or producer must be sure that the *degree* of violence shown is essential to the integrity and completeness of his or her programme.

Fig. 11.3 The IBA guidelines

troversial coverage of the Falklands War showed. Recent history suggests that, if anything, journalistic standards have declined.

The audience We have already noted how members of the public can make representations to various organisations if they feel they have a grievance against the media. However, the way the public gets its real power is through its role as the **audience** and **market** for media output.

Few newspapers can survive long with a falling circulation, and if people feel they are not getting value for money they will switch to another. Similarly, consumers will change TV channels if they feel a programme is boring or un-

NATIONAL UNION OF JOURNALISTS
Acorn House, 314 Gray's Inn Road, London WC1X 8DP
Telephone: 01-278 7916

CODE OF PROFESSIONAL CONDUCT

Like other trade unions, formed for mutual protection and economic betterment, the National Union of Journalists desires and encourages its members to maintain good quality of work and high standards of conduct.

Through the years of courageous struggle for better wages and working conditions its pioneers and their successors have kept these aims in mind, and have made provision in Union rules not only for penalties on offenders, but for the guidance and financial support of members who may suffer loss of work for conforming to Union principles.

While punishment by fine, suspension or expulsion is provided for in cases of "conduct detrimental to the interests of the Union or of the profession," any member who is victimised [Rule 20, clause (g)] for refusing to do work . . . "incompatible with the honour and interests of the profession." may rely on adequate support from Union funds.

A member of the Union has two claims on his/her loyalty – one by his/her Union and one by his/her employer. These need not clash so long as the employer complies with the agreed Union conditions and make no demand for forms of service incompatible with the honour of the profession or with the principle of trade unionism.

1. A journalist has a duty to maintain the highest professional and ethical standards.
2. A journalist shall at all times defend the principle of the freedom of the Press and other media in relation to the collection of information and the expression of comment and criticism. He/she shall strive to eliminate distortion, news suppression and censorship.

3. A journalist shall strive to ensure that the information he/she disseminates is fair and accurate, avoid the expression of comment and conjecture as established fact and falsification by distortion, selection or misrepresentation.

4. A journalist shall rectify promptly any harmful inaccuracies, ensure that correction and apologies receive due prominence and afford the right of reply to persons criticised when the issue is of sufficient importance.

5. A journalist shall obtain information, photographs and illustrations only by straightforward means. The use of other means can be justified only by over-riding consideration of the public interest. The journalist is entitled to exercise a personal conscientious objection to the use of such means.

6. Subject to justification by over-riding considerations of the public interest, a journalist shall do nothing which entails intrusion into private grief and distress.

7   A journalist shall protect confidential sources of information.

8. A journalist shall not accept bribes nor shall he/she allow other inducements to influence the performance of his/her professional duties.

9. A journalist shall not lend himself/herself to the distortion or suppression of the truth because of advertising or other considerations.

10. A journalist shall only mention a person's race, colour, creed, illegitimacy, marital status or lack of it, gender or sexual orientation if this information is strictly relevant. A journalist shall neither originate nor process material which encourages discrimination on any of the above-mentioned grounds.

11. A journalist shall not take private advantage of information gained in the course of his/her duties, before the information is public knowledge.

12. A journalist shall not by way of statement, voice or appearance endorse by advertisement any commercial product or service save for the promotion of his/her own work or of the medium by which he/she is employed.

Fig. 11.4 The NUJ Code of Conduct

interesting. The power of the audience is revealed by the close attention paid by media hierarchies to the audience figures produced by organisations like BARB (Television) and ABC (Press). As a result of changing fortunes in the market place, newspapers can be closed down or redesigned, or TV programmes can be shifted to an off-peak slot in the schedule.

Other ways in which the audience can influence and exert pressure on the media are through participation in 'access' programmes like Channel 4's *Right to Reply*, writing letters to newspapers, and attendance at the various public meetings held by the BBC and IBA each year. The usefulness of this kind of criticism has to be questioned, however, since the process is controlled by the media themselves.

Fig. 11.5 Channel 4's *Right to Reply*

 **3** You have agreed to take part in a formal debate in which the motion is 'This House believes that the media are accountable to no-one but themselves'. You are going to speak *against* this motion. Produce a set of detailed notes to aid you in your speech.

Censorship

Definitions Censorship has been called:

> 'the deliberate exclusion of material from the flow of information in order to shape the opinion and action of others'

(Blake and Haroldsen, *A Taxonomy of Concepts in Communication*)

and:

> 'a process involving the blocking, regulation and manipulation of all or part of some original message'

(O'Sullivan et al *Key Concepts in Communication*)

In one sense, censorship is inevitable since no society could allow total freedom of action or information, because everybody has to operate within the constraints of the legal system. However, the term censorship has come to have negative connotations and has been seen, especially by its victims, as an infringement on the rights of publishers and broadcasters. Here are details of two types of censorship.

Official censorship

In extreme circumstances (especially during times of war) the State can take direct control of broadcasting. For example, under the terms of its Licence and Agreement the BBC is liable to be taken over by the Government in time of national crisis. Section 15(4) of this Licence also gives the Government the power to prohibit the Corporation from broadcasting *any* item or programme. Likewise, the powers of the IBA are laid down by law. Under the terms of its contracts with the ITV companies it has the power to vet all programmes to make sure that they do not offend people's good taste (and other subjective criteria). Censorship is often used when programmes are made about sensitive issues like defence or terrorism which conflict with the political consensus in our society. For example, programmes about the 'troubles' in Northern Ireland have been a constant victim of censorship since 1969.

The State is often a perpetrator of censorship in the way it restricts or manages the flow of information to the mass media. This was clearly seen during the

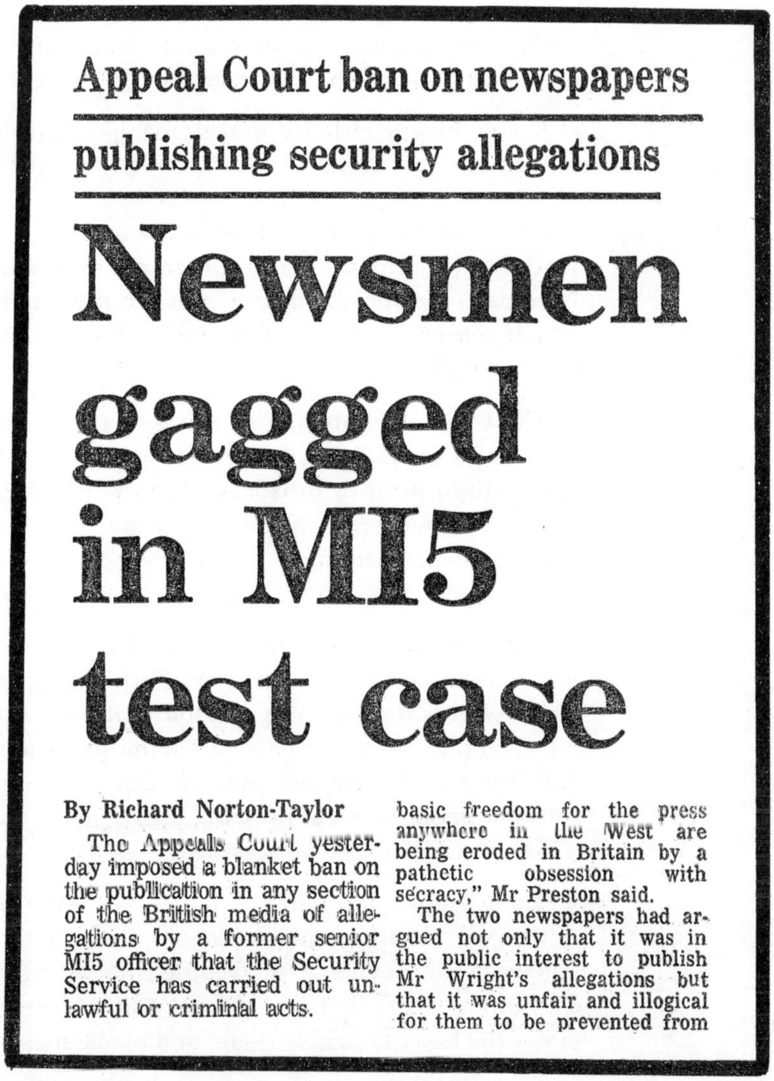

Appeal Court ban on newspapers
publishing security allegations

Newsmen gagged in MI5 test case

By Richard Norton-Taylor

The Appeals Court yesterday imposed a blanket ban on the publication in any section of the British media of allegations by a former senior MI5 officer that the Security Service has carried out unlawful or criminal acts.

basic freedom for the press anywhere in the West are being eroded in Britain by a pathetic obsession with secrecy," Mr Preston said.

The two newspapers had argued not only that it was in the public interest to publish Mr Wright's allegations but that it was unfair and illogical for them to be prevented from

Fig. 11.6 Censorship in action?

Falklands War, during which the British media was subjected to official censorship. This took the form of censorship of reports sent back from the South Atlantic as well as censorship in London. The Government also made use of **misinformation** by supplying the media with false or misleading information.

In the world of film there has been a long-standing system of official censorship since 1912 when the British Board of Film Classification was set up by the film industry. The Board has the power to issue films with certificates which indicate their suitability for particular audiences (as well as being a rough guide to the degree of sex and violence contained in the films). The certification system used is as follows:
- 'U': Universal viewing;
- 'PG': Parental Guidance needed;
- '15': Viewers need to be at least 15 years old;
- '18': Age requirement is 18+.

In the early 1980s there was a growing public outcry, orchestrated in part by the tabloid press, against *video nasties* — films on video that contain very explicit sex or violence. The result of this campaign was the Video Recording Act. This restrictive piece of legislation has given the BBFC the responsibility of certificating most video cassettes intended for home viewing. Many people have criticised the Government's response to the threat of video nasties as a classic case of over-reaction.

In Chapter 9 we saw how cable television is likely to expand in Britain in the 1990s. Even though the new Cable Authority will not be expected to regulate cable as tightly as the IBA regulates TV, it will still be expected to make sure:

> 'that nothing is included in the programmes which offends against good taste or is likely to incite crime or lead to disorder or to be offensive to public feeling'.

Self censorship

Official censorship, or at least those aspects of it which attract most publicity, tends to be *reactive* — that is, programmes or publications are censored after they have been produced. Perhaps an even more powerful form of censorship is that of **self censorship** by those in the media themselves. Here are some examples of self censorship.

— **The D Notice system.** This refers to a long-standing arrangement between the media and the Defence Press and Broadcasting Committee. Basically, the media agree not to print or broadcast material which might be detrimental to national security. However, D Notices have no legal basis and are often flouted, since many media practitioners believe they are an outdated constraint on the *freedom of the press*.

— **Pre-emptive censorship.** Broadcasting organisations, because of the tighter constraints they work under, are particularly prone to **pre-emptive censorship**. This involves the blocking, or modification of one's own material out of a fear of the Government or, perhaps, a feeling that the material will be vetted at a later date by a body like the IBA. Newspapers might also engage in pre-emptive censorship out of a fear of being prosecuted under the libel or contempt laws, or a fear of trade union censorship.

— **Trade union censorship.** A more overt form of self censorship is the fact that, in the past, printing unions like the National Graphical Association (NGA) have believed that they have the right to intervene in the production of newspapers if they do not agree with a particular editorial, story or advertisement. The result is either the loss of a whole issue, or a blank space where the offending item would have appeared. The following news story was taken from an issue of *Free Press*, the journal of the Campaign for Press and Broadcasting Freedom.

PRINTERS BAN APARTHEID ADS

Action by advertising clerks and NGA compositors at the Daily Mail, has stopped the appearance of S. African adverts in the paper.

Printers plan to keep up the action and are encouraging members to boycott all goods and services emanating from the apartheid regime, in solidarity with their colleagues in the black South African unions.

Of course, it is impossible to gauge the extent to which self censorship is actually practised.

TASK *4* Produce a chart containing points *for* and *against* the idea of censorship.

Self-assessment

1. Define the following key terms:
   - Bias;
   - Accountability;
   - Censorship.
2. What do you understand by the phrase 'multi-dimensional ownership'? Give a real-life example.
3. Briefly discuss the aims of the Campaign for Press and Broadcasting Freedom.
4. Summarise the main findings of the Glasgow University Media Group's *Bad News* on bias in TV news.
5. In what ways, and to whom, are the media accountable for their actions?
6. What is the difference between libel and slander?
7. Summarise the roles of the Press Council, the Advertising Standards Authority and the Broadcasting Complaints Commission.
8. What is a Code of Conduct?
9. Define the term 'misinformation'.
10. What does the term 'self censorship' refer to?

Further work

1. Consult a copy of the reference book *Who Owns Whom?* (see Further reading) in your local reference library. Find the entry for Pergamon Press and note down details of all the main interests owned by this holding company. Classify them into publishing, newspapers, broadcasting etc. and produce a diagram similar to Fig. 11.1 p.138.
2. Make a video recording of BBC1's *Nine O'Clock News* and ITN's *News at Ten* on a given night. Conduct a study of possible bias in these two news programmes. You will need to write a checklist to aid you in your study. Make sure you include an analysis of the language used in the broadcasts and a comparison between the treatment of the same event in the two programmes. Present your findings in essay form.
3. Write an essay with the following title: 'Censorship is both inevitable and desirable'. Discuss.

Further reading

BBC, *Annual Report and Handbook* (BBC, 1986)

Blake R.H and Haroldsen E.O, *A Taxonomy of Concepts in Communication* (Hastings House, 1975)

Dun and Bradstreet, *Who Owns Whom?* (Dun and Bradstreet, 1985)

Garnham N, *Structures of Television* (British Film Institute, 1980)

Glasgow University Media Group, *Bad News* (Routledge and Kegan Paul, 1976)

Hartley J et al, *Making Sense of the Media* (Comedia, 1985)

IBA, *Attitudes to Broadcasting* (IBA, 1980)

Masterman L, *Teaching the Media* (Comedia, 1985)

O'Sullivan T et al, *Key Concepts in Communication* (Methuen, 1985)

Robertson G and Nicol A, *Media Law* (Sage, 1985)

PART 2 Case Studies

CASE STUDY 1 Buster's Last Stand: writing a press release

This case study contains the following sections:

- **Introduction to press releases**
- **Writing a press release**
- **Main task**
- **Self-assessment**

Introduction to press releases

This case study takes a close look at a fairly simple and straightforward communication artefact: the press release. There is nothing terribly complicated about writing and presenting a press release, but applying a number of fundamental rules makes for the most effective communication.

Definition

A **press release** or a **press handout** consists of one or more sheets of paper giving details of a product, e.g. a book recently published, or an event, e.g. a computer hardware exhibition, in such a way that a journalist can make use of it and help provide publicity for the sender.

The various news media – newspapers, magazines, radio and television – receive a very large number of such press releases every day; a company or organisation would need to make sure that its own press release was an effective piece of communication in order to stand a chance of its being used.

Empathy with audience

Imagine you are a hard-working and busy journalist employed by a glossy county magazine called *Derbyshire Life and Countryside*. One morning a press release arrives in the post looking like Fig. 1A. What overall impression would it make on you? Would you consider using the 'material' in your magazine?

Empathy with your audience – that is, trying to imagine things from somebody else's point of view is fundamental to effective communication.

Journalists are busy people; you owe it to yourself as a writer of a press release, both to attract their attention with something special, and also to make things as easy as possible for them. If you don't, you won't get the free publicity which they can offer you. You may need such publicity, and they do need stories – but your chances of success are greater if you apply sensible communication techniques to the construction of a press release.

Writing a press release

Bearing your audience in mind

Journalists like an **angle** – that is, some special feature they can use to give your material some

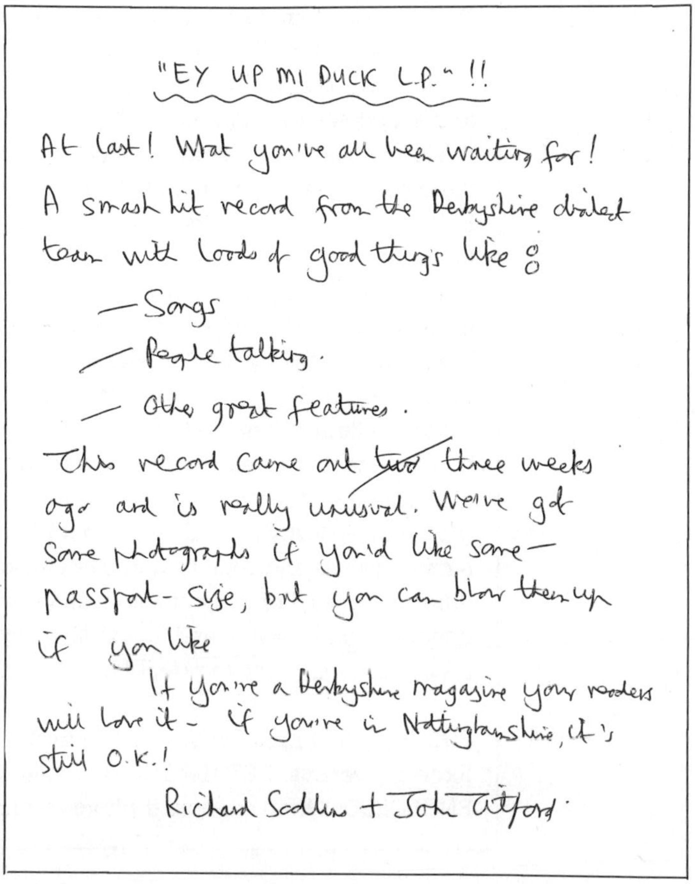

"EY UP MI DUCK L.P." !!

At last! What you've all been waiting for!
A smash hit record from the Derbyshire dialect team with loads of good things like:
— Songs
— People talking.
— Other great features.
This record came out ~~two~~ three weeks ago and is really unusual. We've got some photographs if you'd like some – passport-size, but you can blow them up if you like
If you're a Derbyshire magazine your readers will love it - if you're in Nottinghamshire, it's still O.K.!
Richard Scollins + John Titford.

Fig. 1A A handwritten press release

impact. You may need to write more than one press release with different angles: a story about a badger being struck and killed by a steam locomotive, for example, would need a different treatment if it were aimed at a Natural History Journal or a Locomotive Enthusiasts' Magazine.

You may need to re-write your story for a local or national newspaper or magazine — stressing the local or the national importance of what you have to say.

Try not to send a photocopied press release if you can — and certainly not a carbon copy! Make your audience feel wanted.

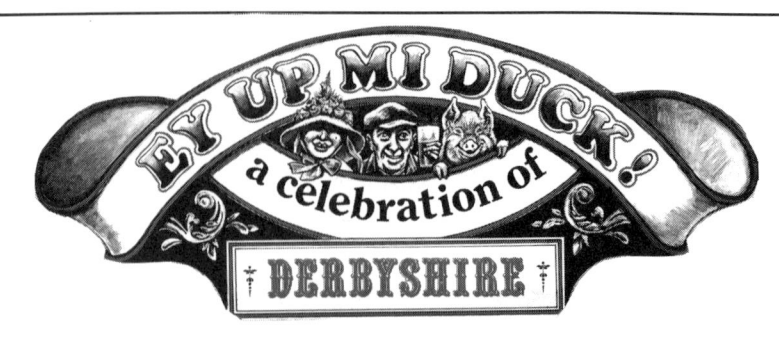

THE 'EY UP MI DUCK!' L.P. RECORD

FOR THE ATTENTION OF: The Editor, 'Derbyshire Life and Countryside', Lodge Lane, Derby.
FROM: John Titford, 5, Appleby Close Ilkeston, Derbys. DE7 4LP
DATE: 4th June, 1987.
DETAILS OF L.P. RECORD: 12″ Long-Playing Record. Available from all major record shops in Derbyshire. Price: £6.50.
RECORD ON SALE FROM: 26th June, 1987.

Derbyshire's own distinctive dialect, featured in a series of books called 'Ey Up Mi Duck!' by Richard Scollins and John Titford, can now be heard for the first time on an L.P. record. The 'EY UP MI DUCK!' L.P. offers a mixture of stories, songs, poems, jokes and anecdotes to celebrate Derbyshire's own very special identity.

Variety has been the main concern: there are contributions from the larger towns in the county — Derby, Chesterfield and Ilkeston — but smaller settlements like Hope, Holloway, Tideswell, Horsley Woodhouse, Marlpool and Stanton-by-Dale also have an important part to play.

There are young people as well as old on this L.P., women as well as men, and musical offerings ranging from traditional songs and dance music by 'Ram's Bottom' to brass band items by the Shirland Miners' Welfare Band, Ashbourne Town Band and Ilkeston Brass. Live recordings of Derby Morris Men on tour are also included.

Every attempt is made to present Derbyshire people as they really are in their own homes — telling an exciting story with great skill, giving a dramatic rendering of a long-cherished poem or monologue, or just reminiscing about the old days.

Lovers of Derbyshire dialect should find much to fascinate them here — recognizing familiar words and sounds, and even making comparisons between speakers from different areas. For those not so well versed in local speech, there is nothing very difficult to understand, and an explanatory illustrated booklet is included in the record to make things as clear as possible.

FURTHER DETAILS FROM: John Titford, 5, Appleby Close,
Ilkeston, Derbys. DE7 4LP TEL.: Ilkeston (0602) 301294.
ENCLOSED: Three captioned photographs of individuals featured on the L.P.

Fig. 1B A typed press release

Hints

Press releases are written and presented in a variety of ways. There are no rigid rules, but the following three areas are important to consider: giving information; using an appropriate layout and style; thinking in pictures as well as words.

Giving information

− Date your press release.
− Give your name and address and details of where the journalist may phone for more information. Journalists are great users of phones − they may well not have the time to write to you.
− Give the full names of people you refer to − not just 'Mrs. Smith'.
− If the press release refers to something which will happen on a particular day − a school play, a fashion show, the publication of a book and so on − then give the date or dates clearly. Send out your press release in advance − but not too far in advance or it may get filed away and forgotten.

Using an appropriate layout and style

− Use short paragraphs.
− Put all the main facts in the first paragraph − it should be possible, in a good press release, both for the sub-editor to use it exactly as it is without rewriting, and for him or her to prune your information from the last paragraph upwards. So even if all your later paragraphs have to be cut because of lack of space in the paper or magazine, at least make sure that the first paragraph will stand on its own.
− Be aware of the need to use a language register appropriate to your audience. Keep to a plain style of English − don't be racy or colloquial but remember to look for that interesting angle!
− Use one side of the paper only.
− Use double spacing between lines if you are typing, and four spaces between paragraphs.
− Be consistent − indent all paragraphs, or indent none.
− Leave decent margins all around your typed information − approximately 1½ inches on both sides, and about 2 inches at top and bottom.
− If you need to run onto a second page, write 'continued' at the bottom of the first page. Never run a paragraph over from one page to the next.

Thinking in pictures as well as words

As you write your press release, try and mention some aspect which would lend itself to a press photograph − a picture in a newspaper or magazine really attracts the reader's attention.

If you include a photograph or photographs of your own, bear the following hints in mind.
− Send a large photograph if you can.
− Stick a **caption** to the back of the photograph; this should be a kind of mini-press release of about 40 or 50 words in length, with a headline.
− Give names and initials or Christian names of the people in the photograph, clearly indicating who is who. List groups left to right, front to back.
− **Attach the name and address of the person sending the press release**; preferably write it on the photograph itself, as captions are sometimes removed.
− If you can't afford to send out photographs to everyone, add 'Photographs available on request' at the end of the press release.

FINALLY ... Reinforce your message! Having sent a press release and waited a few days, telephone the newspaper or publication concerned and ask if you can be of any further help to them − and draw your press release to their attention. Papers like to have a 'live' comment from someone to brighten up their articles.

TASK 1

Write *two* or *three* paragraphs analysing the press release Fig. 1B. It is not meant to be a perfect example, but the writer has tried to bear in mind the advice you have just read.

Go through the hints on writing press releases and see whether the writer has followed them or not.

Return briefly to the earlier handwritten press release; make as full a list as you can of its failures in the light of what you have learned since.

MAIN TASK

You are working as a Publicity Assistant at Nottingham Playhouse. The Publicity Manager is keen to inform the local media about a forthcoming World Première of a play called *Buster's Last Stand*.

You have been given the task of writing a 300 word press release for the local Nottingham evening paper, publicising this play. The first performance will take place in ten days' time.

To help you, the Publicity Manager has given you:
− A copy of a previous Nottingham Playhouse Press Release, Fig. 1C, for a production of *The Price of Coal* by Barry Hines. You may use or modify the layout and style of this Press Release in any way you think appropriate for your present task.
− Four photocopied sheets from the programme for *Buster's Last Stand*, Fig. 1D, which has already been printed. Note that the author, Peter Fieldson, is prepared to say very little about his play in advance of its first performance; you need to excite the public's interest by using whatever other information is available to you.

NOTTINGHAM Press PLAYHOUSE Release

T.V. SUCCESS TAKES TO THE STAGE

Nottingham Playhouse is poised to present the Stage Premiere of THE PRICE OF COAL by 'Kes' author BARRY HINES. It was originally seen as a BBC Play For Today four years ago and has now been adapted for the stage. It will form the Playhouse's main contribution to the Nottingham Festival opening with a Preview on Wednesday 16 May at 7.30pm (running until 9 June).

Set in a local colliery, this mixture of comedy and suspense introduces us to a group and miners and their families. Preparations are in hand for a visit by Prince Charles and the rule seems to be "If it doesn't move, paint it white!". It's chaos at the colliery then life returns to normal, but not for long! The characters in this hilarious but often moving play will be instantly recognised by the people of Nottingham and the surrounding areas!

Playing Sid Storey, the anti-royalist miner, is actor/comedian DUGGIE BROWN who also appeared in the television version of the play. His numerous television credits include 'The Comedians', 'Glamour Girls' and 'The Enigma Files' and he was seen in the film 'Kes'. He is also well-known as a cabaret entertainer.

Four local children will appear in the show playing Sid's son and daughter, Mark and Janet. Craig and Sharon Yates (whose father is a miner) and Lee Porter and Charlotte Marsh who auditioned along with about sixty other children, will play on alternate nights throughout the run.

The cast is completed by JOAN CAMPION, DAVID GILLESPIE, ELLIE HADDINGTON, ANDY HAY, TIM KILLICK, TED MORRIS, FENELLA NORMAN, PAUL OLDHAM, KAREN PETRIE, CARL PROCTOR, TED RICHARDS, BRIAN SOUTHWOOD, TERRY TAPLIN, JAMES TOMLINSON and EDWARD YORK.

Directing his first production for the Playhouse is KENNETH ALAN TAYLOR. Design is by ROBERT JONES and Lighting by STEFFAN ADDERTON.

We are very grateful to C.I.S.W.O. for their sponsorship of THE PRICE OF COAL.

* *

For further information contact: SHEILA POPPLE/TRICIA ALVEY
Press & Publicity Officers. Tel. (0602) 474361/470882

Fig. 1C A Nottingham Playhouse press release

Buster Keaton

It was not until the late fifties that Buster Keaton was rediscovered and acknowledged as Chaplin's only serious rival among the great masters of silent film comedy. Since then Keaton has emerged in the eyes of many as at least Chaplin's equal, if not his superior. His now legendary reputation rests mainly on the work he did in the short time span of 1920 through 1929, a period of incredible creative achievement in which he made twelve feature films and nineteen two-reel comedies, nearly all of them superb by any standard. This rediscovery of Keaton has also had its miraculous side, for many of his films, believed lost forever, were found only as late as 1960.

After twenty-five years of neglect, Keaton has been totally rehabilitated as a great comic actor and discovered as one of the great filmmakers. In the 1960s and 1970s the incomparable comic gloom of Keaton's art has seemed extraordinarily contemporary in spirit. His fame has produced a flourishing Keaton industry, and half a dozen books have been published about a man who had been almost completely forgotten by the end of the 1930s. American universities give courses entirely devoted to Buster's films, while hundreds of articles have appeared that deal with the infinite subtleties to be found in his best work. Unlike Chaplin, Keaton always refused to identify himself as an artist, preferring to be regarded as a technician of laughter, a master of pratfalls. To Keaton, who attended school for only one day in his entire life, artists were people with an education.

Perhaps the most disconcerting thing about Buster Keaton was the deadly seriousness with which he undertook the art of being funny. Unlike other famous comedians, Buster was convinced that humour is a very serious business. His work was always the greatest single passion of his life.

Buster possessed all the wrong character traits for a successful comedian. He was pathologically shy, he detested what he called low comedy, and he had a terror of crowds. He was totally uninterested in money; although he made an immense amount of it, he lost every penny. His first two wives were absolutely unsuitable, and he was very much his own worst enemy. He exhibited a curious mixture of extreme shyness and testy arrogance in his dealings with the world. Buster was a truly private person, and none of his close friends ever claimed to know what he really felt about anything except his work. The "Great Stone Face" was an enigma to everyone who knew him well.

Fig. 1D Buster's Last Stand

Born with a Show

Maybe you think you
were handled roughly
when you were a kid -
Watch the way they
handle Buster!

- Ad for "The Three Keatons" in Myra Keaton's
Scrapbook, 1905

Joseph Frank Keaton literally crawled his way onto a stage for the first time at the age of nine months. He had escaped from the theatrical trunk that served as a backstage crib and scuttled out to the stage where his father, Joe Keaton, was warming up that night's audience with a flow of comical chatter. Joe suddenly noticed that the audience had really begun to laugh its head off; he felt a strong tug on his right leg and looked down to see his infant child sitting between his legs, staring out, wide-eyed, at the laughing crowd. Joe immediately held the child up in his arms to take a bow, receiving a wild round of applause.

In the next three years there was nothing the Keaton parents could do to keep their child from getting back on that stage. By the age of four he had become a regular part of the Keaton family's unique vaudeville act, had special costumes designed for him, and was the talk of American show business. Audiences couldn't get enough of this strange nonsmiling kid who made them laugh so much. Buster soon became a real professional at the rate of ten dollars a week, appearing regularly in the knock-about comedy act that his father had designed for his unique talents. Or, as Buster later put it, "I'd just simply get in my father's way all the time and get kicked all over the stage". By the time Buster was five he was appearing at Tony Pastor's famous vaudeville theater in New York; by the age of six he had played the entire Orpheum theater circuit all over the United States.

Throughout his life Buster loved to talk about his childhood on the vaudeville stage, relating in great detail amazingly vivid tales of disastrous encounters with fires and storms, regularly punctuated by terrifyingly close calls with violent death. It is more than likely that many of these marvellous stories are apocryphal, or the products of his father's inspired imagination. But Buster firmly believed in them and they soon became a central part of his life. In contrast, he was reticent about the brutality he received at the hands of his father, who was frequently drunk.

When Keaton recalled these years, he did so in a mood of complete detachment about the regular beatings he received both on stage and off; they too had become an accepted part of his life. Early photographs reveal a sullen face that glares back at the camera with the expression of someone who has undergone a terrible violation. It is a face that asks to be left alone.

Some of the old tales about Buster's early life have become as legendary in their own way as Parson Weems's account of George Washington and the cherry tree. One of the most famous of all the Buster Keaton stories is about how he got his name. Shortly after his birth in the tiny town of Pickway, Kansas, on the fourth of October, 1895, young Buster at the age of only six months topples down an entire flight of stairs in the theatrical boarding house where his parents are staying with a travelling "medicine show" troupe. Another member of the troupe is the man who later became the supreme magician of the age, the famous magus himself, Harry Houdini. The great Houdini is fated to be present at the very moment when the tiny infant rolls down the stairs. After quickly picking the baby up, Houdini is deeply shocked to discover that it is not only totally unharmed but is actually *laughing*. Houdini gasps at the apparent miracle; he tells the anxious parents, Myra and Joe Keaton, what they have just seen with their own eyes: *"That's some buster your baby took!"*. Most versions of this story conclude with young Joseph Frank Keaton being promptly dubbed Buster by his father.

Fig. 1D

THE COMPANY

PETER ALEXANDER   JOE KEATON

Peter trained at the Guildford School of Acting and his career has covered most aspects of the profession. In the theatre he has played parts as diverse as Freddie in Rattigan's *Deep Blue Sea* to Ugly Sister in *Cinderella* and at such theatres as Windsor Theatre Royal, Bath Theatre Royal, Glasgow Theatre Royal and Norwich Theatre Royal but has still not met the Queen! In the West End Peter played the lead in the long running comedy *No Sex Please We're British* at the Strand Theatre and the juvenile lead in the musical *Beyond The Rainbow* at the Adelphi with Roy Kinnear. For the BBC he has recorded many radio plays and on television his credits include *Chessgame* with Terence Stamp for Granada, *Family Man* opposite Julie Walters for YTV, a new comedy series with Derek Fowlds called *Affairs of the heart*, due to be shown this autumn and *Group Practice*, also for Granada. Interests include classical music and he plays the piano, flute and the fool. After *Buster's Last Stand!* Peter will be returning to the Pennines where he lives with his wife, children and numerous animals and is directing a Kenneth Alan Taylor pantomime for the Oldham Coliseum.

NICKY CROYDON   MAE SCRIBBENS

Nicky began her professional career with the New Shakespeare Company in Regent's Park. She made her West End debut in *Leave Him to Heaven* and went on to play Diana Morales in *A Chorus Line* at Drury Lane. Other West End credits include the much acclaimed British musical *Songbook* at the Globe, Cheryl in *I'm Getting My Act Together and Taking it on the Road* at the Apollo, *These Men* at the Bush, *Nitrogen* at the Spice of Life and *Not in Front of the Audience* at the Theatre Royal Drury Lane. Most recently she played Raquel Scrimmett in *Andy Capp* at the Aldwych and Peppermint Patty in *Snoopy* at the Duchess Theatre. Nicky's regional credits include a national tour of *Hair, The Italian Straw Hat* and Ken Hill's *Robin Hood* at Stratford East and Chicago, *Maria Marten* and *Temple of Reason* in *True Love's Gutter* all at the Sheffield Crucible. On television Nicky has been seen in the first series of *Russ Abbott's Madhouse* (LWT), four episodes of *Wainwright's Law* (BBC) and two series of *Dear Heart* for the BBC playing a wide range of characters. Her recent BBC radio broadcasts are *Living Language, The Godwulf Manuscript* and *Miss Anderson and Captain Oats*.

PHILIP HERBERT   ROSCOE ARBUCKLE

Last year Philip worked here with the Roundabout Company in *Oh What a Lovely War* and *School for Clowns*. He returned at Christmas to play Prince Bulbo in the panto tour *The Rose and the Ring*. Recent theatre work includes Falstaff in Henry IV Part I at Manchester Contact, Osric in Birmingham Rep's *Hamlet* and Councillor Large in Liverpool Playhouse's musical version of *The Piper of Hamelin*. He also toured as the Miller in *The Canterbury Tales*, Humpty Dumpty in *Alice Through The Looking Glass* (Plymouth Theatre Royal) and has had two seasons at Leicester Phoenix. Television work this year includes *Pickwick Papers* for the BBC (to be screened early '85) and Central's drama/ documentary *Take 30* playing Dr. J. F. Hackenbush, a compulsive gambler. Philip worked on *For Four Tonight* (for Channel 4), *On the Fringe* (HTV) performing his own self-devised comedy fire-eating act *Randolf the Remarkable*. He also works on London's alternative cabaret circuit with a cod-glamour act called *The Haddocks* and appeared on *Mondas Bursan (Monday Purse)* for Swedish TV transmitted live to Finland, Sweden and Denmark. His film work includes *Victor Victoria, Star Wars 3-Return of the Jedi* and *Fanny Hill*. Philip's ambitions include wanting to do a rum commercial in Jamaica (or Barbados) and playing Nicely Nicely in *Guys and Dolls*.

MELANIE KILBURN   NATALIE TALMADGE

 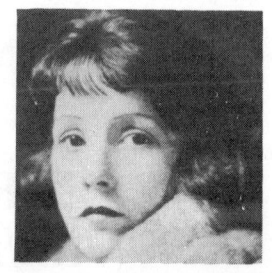

Melanie trained at the Guildhall School of Music and Drama. Since leaving she has worked with ATC playing various parts in *Don Quixote*, toured with Triumph Productions in *Cure For Love* and played a spider in *Plotters of Cabbage Patch Corner*. She has appeared at Milford Haven, Harrogate, York, Lancaster and Birmingham Repertories, at the Royal Exchange in *La Ronde, Hope Against Hope* and *The Government Inspector*, and in *Sexual Perversity in Chicago*. Melanie's most recent performance was as Bianca in *Othello* at The Young Vic. Her television appearances include Maureen in *Last Company Car* for Central TV. Her first film *The Little Drummer Girl* for Warner Bros. has yet to be released. Following *Buster's Last Stand!* Melanie will be appearing here as Mrs. Kay in *Our Day Out*.

SYLVESTER McCOY   BUSTER KEATON

Sylvester has just appeared in the Beckett Festival at the Edinburgh International Festival in a production called *From Its Beginning To Its End* and has recently completed playing Bowers in the TV film series by Trevor Griffiths called *Last Place on Earth*. Other TV credits include *Starstrider, Eureka, Big Jim and the Figaro Club, Tiny Revolutions* and *Jigsaw*. He has recently completed a long period of theatre work in London in productions which include *Pirates of Penzance* at Drury Lane, *Can't Pay, Won't Pay* at the Criterion, *Abracadabra* at the Lyric and playing Stan Laurel in *Gone With Hardy* which he also took to Canada. Sylvester has previously appeared at Nottingham Playhouse in several productions including *Servant of Two Masters, A Flea in Her Ear, Bartholomew Fair, White Suit Blues, Walking Like Geoffrey* and *Gone With Hardy*. His other theatre work includes *Robin Hood* at Stratford East, *School For Clowns* at the Half Moon, *Hoagy Bix and Wolfgang Beethoven Bunkhouse* at the King's Head, *A Midsummer Night's Dream* with the Welsh National Opera and many productions with Ken Campbell's Roadshow. Sylvester has also been seen on television in *Tiswas, Vision On, Lucky Fella, All the Fun of the Fair* and *Electric in the City*. He also appears in the films *Dracula* and *The Secret Policeman's Ball*.

Fig. 1D

PETER FIELDSON
(Author)

Buster's Last Stand! is Peter's fifth stage play, the others having been *Black and Blue,* commisioned by The Horseshoe,Basingstoke, *Brecht* and *Positively The Last Supper* for Contact Theatre, Manchester and his adaptation of *The Wind in the Willows* which was performed at The Chester Gateway last Christmas. Having started writing in 1970, Peter worked exclusively in radio up until 1975 during which time he has some forty plays produced both in this country and abroad. In 1975 he gained a place at Manchester University from which he graduated with a first class Honours degree in drama in 1978. A soon as he leaves Nottingham Playhouse, Peter will be going to the Coliseum Theatre, Oldham, to direct a new adaptation of *The Railway Children.*

"In the summer of 1983 Brian Wheeler approached me with the idea of writing a show based on the life of Buster Keaton, for his client Sylvester McCoy. I had already had three biographical plays produced at that time — Brecht, Black and Blue (based on the death of Joe Orton) and Positively the Last Supper (which was concerned with James O' Neil) and this, coupled with Sylvester's enthusiasm for the project sold me on the scheme. The next step was to approach Kenneth Alan Taylor who subsequently commisioned the play for the Nottingham Playhouse.

As to the nature of the piece itself, I wish to say nothing. It, like any other stage play, must stand or fall on its own. I will just mention however that during the last year I have come to admire and love Buster Keaton, the man, the comic genius, and the drunk. I hope my play has done him justice".

Peter Fieldson

Fig. 1D

Self-assessment

1. Explain in your own words what 'empathy with your audience' has to do with the design and content of a press release.
2. In what ways can you make the information contained in a press release helpful to the journalist who is to read it?
3. List the features of layout and style which will give your press release maximum impact; explain *why* each of these is important.

CASE STUDY 2 *Heathrow: designing a leaflet for children*

This case study contains the following sections:

- The Massachusetts State House: extracts from two booklets
- Design and layout
- Use of language
- Main task
- Self-assessment

The Massachusetts State House: extracts from two booklets

It would be useful to use this case study in conjunction with Part 3 of this book in which you will find information and tasks dealing with the production of leaflets and booklets.

The material used in this case study has been taken from two booklet guides to the Massachusetts State House, Boston, USA; one of the two guides is designed to be read by adults, and the other has been specially prepared for children.

Here we focus upon ways in which a printed artefact such as a booklet can be designed with a specific audience in mind and we consider how the two booklets (from which you are given extracts) reflect an awareness of the different perceptions and expectations of adults and children. First we will consider **design and layout** and then the **use of language**.

Design and layout

Page format

A book or leaflet may be printed on paper which is square or nearly square, or it may be oblong, with one edge significantly longer than the other.

A page format which is significantly taller than it is wide is said to be in a **portrait format**.

A page format which is significantly wider than it is tall is said to be in **landscape format**. The adults' guide (Fig. 2A) is landscape in format.

Style and placing of picture and text

We can usefully divide printed illustrations into two categories:
− **Line** illustrations use black lines on a white background (or brown on a blue background, and so on, according to which colours have been chosen). When

Fig. 2A Adults' guide

2  DORIC HALL

Doric Hall derives its name from the architectural style of its ten columns. It is located two floors beneath the dome and its appearance, although close to the original, was changed by the major restoration of the Bulfinch Front at the turn of the 20th century. The original Doric columns were pine tree trunks which were carved on the front lawn of the State House. The present columns, installed as a fireproofing measure, are copies made of practical iron and plaster.

As a main reception room, Doric Hall has served as the setting for uncounted formal and informal gatherings including banquets, press conferences, swearing-in ceremonies, and other special events. It was here, at the beginning of the Civil War, that arms, ammunition, and other equipment were distributed to company after company of volunteers to the Sixth Massachusetts. The men of the Sixth assembled in front of the State House and received their colors from Governor John Andrew; the units which arrived on April 19, 1861 in Washington, D.C. were the first organized military assistance President Lincoln received in the Civil War.

Doric Hall contains portraits, statues, and military artifacts recalling many periods of Massachusetts history. The 1826 marble statue of George Washington by Sir Frances Chantrey was the first to be placed in the State House. Governor Andrew is memorialized in Thomas Ball's marble sculpture, located to the left of Washington. Across the room is a rare full-length portrait of Abraham Lincoln, painted around 1900 by Albion Bicknell.

The two cannons beneath the Lincoln portrait commemorate the Concord Minutemen at the Battle of the North Bridge on April 19, 1775. The cannons on the opposite wall were used by the British East India Marine Company and are said to have been captured in the War of 1812. Between these cannons is a bronze bust of John Hancock, the first signer of the Declaration of Independence and the first governor elected after the adoption of the Constitution of the Commonwealth in 1780.

3 NURSES HALL

Climbing the stairs at the end of Doric Hall you will leave the 1798 Bulfinch Front and enter the 1895 Brigham addition to the State House. The small hall you have entered contains a Daniel Chester French bronze statue of the Massachusetts Civil War hero, William Francis Bartlett.

The next, larger room, built largely of Pavonazzo marble, is called Nurses' Hall because of the statue of an Army war nurse located on your right. Sculpted in 1914 by Bela Pratt, it was the first statue erected in honor of the women of the North after the Civil War.

Nurses' Hall also features several murals by Robert Reid depicting events crucial to the start of the American Revolution. Paul Revere's ride of April 19, 1775 is on the left, the Boston Tea Party is on the right. The central panel portrays the true beginning of the colonists' break with England. Fiery orator James Otis is pictured arguing against the Writs of Assistance, which allowed British soldiers to enter private homes and shops in search of smuggled goods. Refusing payment from the Boston merchants who retained him, Otis presented his case in February 1761. Although he did not win the case, Otis was described by John Adams as "a flame of fire . . . then and there the child Independence was born."

Bela Pratt's statue of a Civil War Nurse

Fig. 2A Adults' guide

4 HALL OF FLAGS

"The Return of the Colors," shown in Edward Simmons' mural on your right, depicts the return of the flags that Governor Andrew had given the Massachusetts companies as they departed to fight in the Civil War. This ceremony, which took place in December 1865, started a significant tradition.

Flags have been returned after duty in every war since then including the Spanish-American War, World Wars I and II, the Korean War, the Berlin emergency, and the Vietnam War. Today there are over 300 flags in this hall, which was built to preserve and appropriately display them. If you take a close look you will see that some of the older flags have been preserved with a linen backing stitched to the tattered and disintegrating material.

Edward Simmons depicted the Battle of Concord in the mural to your left. In front of you is Henry Walker's portrayal of the Mayflower Pilgrims as they first sighted land. Behind you is Walker's interpretation of John Eliot preaching to the Indians. Eliot learned the Algonquin dialect, translated the Bible for the Indians, and established fourteen villages of "praying" Indians.

The stained glass skylight above contains the seals of the original thirteen colonies of the United States. The Massachusetts seal is in the center.

The Return of the Colors

Fig. 2A

we look at such a picture we either see a line of some description or the absence of such a line. There are no tones in between the black of a line and the white of the page — there are no grey tones. A line illustration can give the impression of grey tones by skilful use of fine lines used side-by-side or in a criss-cross pattern — this is a technique known as **hatching.**

— **Half-tone** illustrations are reproduced by the printer in such a way that the reader sees a range of grey tones between pure black and pure white. These are half-tone illustrations, and include most reproductions of photographs.

The adult guide to the Massachusetts State House (Fig. 2A) uses a half-tone illustration, a photograph, for its front cover.

If you had decided to use such a photograph as a cover illustration, and the photograph was to be the single dominant feature, you would have at least three main alternative layouts available to you, as Fig. 2B shows.

Those responsible for the cover of Fig. 2A have chosen the third of these alternatives — the photograph bleeds off the edges of the page. Filling the page, it shows the main Massachusetts State House building centrally and leaves an area of sky at top-left and top-right. The sky area at top-left has been filled with a cluster of leaves; might these have been added later, to give the picture balance?

The booklet title fills the sky area top-right but both it and its sub-title are **centred,** i.e. the text is balanced equally left and right of an invisible centre line. You can imagine a central line running vertically through the 'h' in the word 'The' and the 'h' in the word 'Massachusetts'; either side of this line the text is symmetrical.

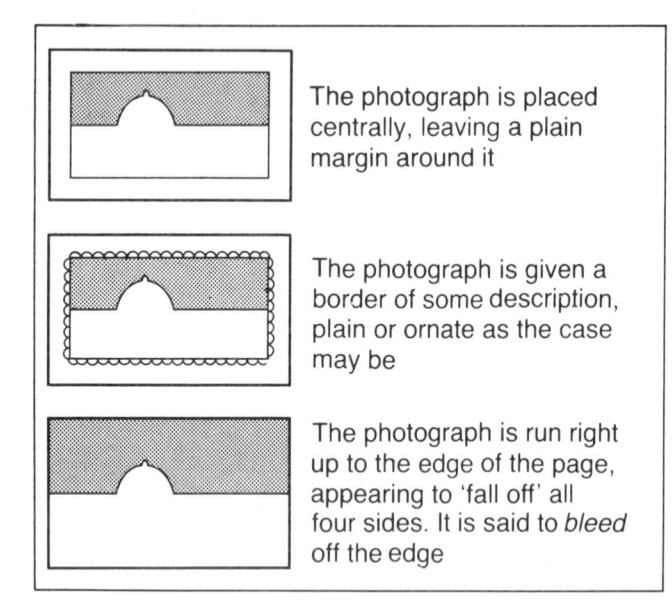

The photograph is placed centrally, leaving a plain margin around it

The photograph is given a border of some description, plain or ornate as the case may be

The photograph is run right up to the edge of the page, appearing to 'fall off' all four sides. It is said to *bleed* off the edge

Fig. 2B Cover photographs

The sub-title to the children's guide, however, is **ranged left.** This time you can imagine a straight vertical line running down the left-hand side of the title; each line begins against this imaginary left-hand line. It would be equally possible to set the text **ranged right** if that were more appropriate to your page layout.

The designers of the cover in Fig. 2A have used two distinct styles of type: large **bold** i.e. heavy, letters for the main title, with much smaller leaning type called *italic* for the sub-title.

The print at the bottom-right of the page is **reversed out** i.e. it appears as white text on a dark background.

Now consider the page layout and design of the cover to the children's guide in Fig. 2C. How has the designer of this cover kept the young audience in mind?

The original booklet cover uses two colours, blue and yellow, to give a cheerful and attractive appearance. The adult guide, by contrast, uses only the black, white and grey tones of its photograph.

Instead of a detailed photograph of the dome, we have a simple, bold sketch which catches the eye immediately and is not too 'fussy'. The designer has not been afraid to use a lot of 'sky' as plain space, not wishing to produce a cluttered cover.

The lettering is large, cheerful and easy to read.

It would be a mistake to think that bold, simple designs were the only means available to an artist who wished to appeal to children. Just as it is possible to 'talk down' to children, underestimating their maturity, so it is possible to make a design too 'childish' in its simplicity to the point where some children might feel they were being patronised. If you look at comic books aimed at children, you will find that many of them use colourful and clear illustrations, but these might be quite 'realistic' and complex, full

of detail to which the reader can return again and again to spot new things. Most children can cope with pictures containing quite sophisticated perspective and detail.

TASK /

Find *two* or *three* examples of printed material designed to be read by children, including at least one comic. Using these and the cover of the children's guide in Fig. 2C, compile a list of guidelines to be used by anyone designing a printed artefact for children. Include as many topics as you can, e.g. page layout, use of space, colour, size and style of print and of illustrations, etc.

Use of language

Speaking to children or writing for children is not quite such an easy activity as it may seem at first. If language is too complex, the child will not understand; if it is oversimplified the child will feel that he or she is being talked down to. In addition the linguistic ability of a child of ten is very much more sophisticated than that of a five-year old, and so we must be careful not to categorise all children as one indivisible audience.

There are two ways in which our language use may be more or less complex: there is the vocabulary we use (the **lexical** aspect of language) and the grammatical structures we employ (the **syntactical** dimension).

Let us consider each of these in turn by comparing passages from Figs. 2A and 2C, the one written for an adult audience, the other for children.

Vocabulary

An average child of two years of age has a vocabulary of some 300 words; a child of five uses over 2000 words, while an adult normally has a passive vocabulary (words that can be understood) of 8000 words and an active vocabulary (words actually used in everyday situations) of 6000 words. Remember that it is not necessarily long words as such which might give a child problems; 'hippopotamus' might present no difficulty to a seven-year-old, while a shorter word like 'irony' might be beyond his or her understanding.

Consider the two opening sentences in each booklet:

ADULTS' VERSION	CHILDREN'S VERSION
Doric Hall derives its name from the architectural style of its ten columns.	Doric Hall is named for the ten tall columns in the room ('Doric' is the name of the design).

What's under the Golden Dome?

A NEW
CHILDREN'S GUIDE
TO THE
MASSACHUSETTS
STATE HOUSE

PRINTED ESPECIALLY
FOR CHILDREN BY THE
OFFICE OF THE
MASSACHUSETTS
SECRETARY OF STATE
CHAEL JOSEPH CONNOLLY,
SECRETARY

Nurses' Hall

When you walk out of Doric Hall and into Nurse's Hall you have left the part of the State House designed by Bulfinch and entered a "new" addition which is quite old now. Built in 1895 and designed by Charles Brigham, it has a very different feeling with its ornate mosaic floors, marble columns, and large murals.

One of the most inspiring sculptures in the State House is in this room. It is a statue of a nurse and a wounded soldier which was carved to honor the women who served as nurses during the Civil War.

In this room too are paintings of Paul Revere's ride and the Boston Tea Party.

Hall of Flags

The fighters bold
pledged flags of old
marching along
when days were cold.
Down the lane
in pouring rain
some held flags
with aching pain.
Flags have stars of blue
red and white stripes too
carried for America.
This we all knew.
    Lisa Ohman
    North Weymouth

Dean Darr
Leominster

The Hall of Flags is a very special room. It was built just to preserve and display the flags brought back from war by soldiers from Massachusetts. There are flags from the Civil War, the Spanish-American War,

World Wars I and II, the Korean War, the Berlin Emergency, and the Vietnam War.

In the center of the stained glass window in the ceiling is the Massachusetts state seal, surrounded by the seals of the twelve other original colonies.

Tricia
Aliberti
Boston

Doric Hall

Doric Hall is named for the ten tall columns in the room (*Doric* is the name of the design). In this very room, Governor John Andrew passed out guns and ammunition and flags to the men who had volunteered to fight in the Civil War. The first military unit to arrive in Washington to help President Abraham Lincoln were part of the Sixth Massachusetts Division.

Inside the room you will see a painting of Abraham Lincoln, a statue of George Washington, historic cannons, and copies of gravestones.

It is interesting to know that the main doors of Doric Hall are only opened on two special occasions—when the President of the United States comes to visit, and when a Governor leaves the State House for the last time.

I went on a State House tour
and opened a side door
to see a marble floor.
    James Passa
    Boston

Fig. 2C Children's guide

Notice that the author of the booklet for children has decided to simplify or omit the words 'derived' and 'architectural', probably deciding that each would be beyond the comprehension of most children. The writer of the adult version pays his readers the compliment of assuming they will understand the architectural term 'Doric', while the children's version adds a word of explanation in brackets.

Which other words in the adult booklet would prove difficult for a young child to understand: 'installed'; 'artefacts'; 'memorialized'?

Notice that American and English spelling and use of language vary in some instances. 'Colors' in the adult booklet is an acceptable American spelling — and an English writer would not say that 'Doric Hall is named *for* the ten tall columns in the room'. Which word would an English writer substitute for the word 'for'?

Grammatical structure

Children not only use a more restricted vocabulary than adults; they also tend to use shorter and simpler statements expressed with a minimum of grammatical complexity.

Consider the second sentence from Fig. 2A:

'It is located two floors beneath the dome and its appearance, although close to the original, was changed by the major restoration of the Bullfinch Front at the turn of the 20th century.'

Three separate statements are being made here, as follows:

1. It is located two floors beneath the dome;
2. Its appearance is close to the original;
3. Its appearance was changed by the major restoration of the Bullfinch Front at the turn of the 20th century.

Each of the above statements is a complete **clause** in its own right, i.e. each contains a main verb ('is located' in 1; 'is' in 2; 'was changed' in 3). Each could stand as a separate sentence if necessary, but the author has chosen to combine the three statements into one long sentence, using two **conjunctions** to join them together (the words 'and' and 'although'), and commas where appropriate. The result is a fairly complicated grammatical structure, and one that might be beyond the comprehension of a child. In the event, the children's guide chooses to omit this particular reference to the restoration of the Bullfinch Front entirely; those statements it *does* make tend to be presented one at a time, each as a single sentence, avoiding commas wherever possible.

Also compare:

ADULTS' VERSION	CHILDREN'S VERSION
'It was here, at the beginning of the Civil War, that arms, ammunition and other equipment were distributed to company after company of volunteers to the Sixth Massachusetts.'	'In this very room, Governor John Andrew passed out guns and ammunition and flags to the men who had volunteered to fight in the Civil War.'

The children's version prefers the direct statement, 'Governor John Andrew *passed out* guns and ammunition', to the less direct adult version, 'arms, ammunition and other equipment *were distributed* to company after company . . .'

Notice also the use of a semi-colon in the second paragraph: 'The men of the Sixth assembled in front of the State House and received their colors from Governor John Andrew; the units which arrived on April 19, 1861 in Washington, D.C. were the first organized military assistance President Lincoln received in the Civil War.'

The great advantage of using a semi-colon is that the writer can introduce a second idea to modify or supplement his or her first statement, without bringing the sentence to a complete close by the use of a full stop. The children's version uses no semi-colons or colons.

Complexity in language, then, is not simply a matter of the length of words and the length of sentences — although we could say as a general guide that long words and long sentences tend to be more 'difficult' than short ones.

TASK 2

Read both the adult and the children's version of 'Nurses Hall' and 'Hall of Flags' from Figs. 2A and 2C and produce an analysis table which identifies contrasting examples of language from the two versions and attempts to describe these differences.

Using what you now know about elements of design and language appropriate to printed artefacts for children, carry out the MAIN TASK which follows. You are asked to design a draft leaflet, rather than a draft for a full booklet; the rules of good practice are exactly the same for such a leaflet as for the booklet in Fig. 2C.

MAIN TASK

A teacher working with nine and ten year-old children in a Primary School is planning to take her class to Heathrow Airport in London on a day trip. She has obtained copies of two Heathrow Airport Guides which are aimed at adult visitors. She has asked you to design a short leaflet which she can use with her children, giving them some idea about what an airport is, what happens there, and what there is to see and do during a day visit.

Using the extracts from the adult guides given in Fig. 2D (pages 167–174) as your information source, design a draft leaflet which could be the basis for something she could produce and give to her children. Include any notes or annotations you think necessary to make clear all details of layout, type style and so on. The teacher wishes the final leaflet to be printed on both sides of a single sheet of A4 paper, folded to give four A5-size pages of text.

Self-assessment

1. Distinguish between the following:
   Portrait format/Landscape format; Line illustration/Half-tone illustration; Text centred/Text ranged left.
2. What guidelines would you give to someone who asked you for advice on the design and layout of a printed artefact for children?
3. What steps would you need to take to make sure that a written text did not use language that was too complicated for children to understand?

Heathrow Airport
Facts and Figures

THE WORLD'S MOST SUCCESSFUL INTERNATIONAL AIRPORT THE WORLD'S MOST SUCCESSFUL INTERNATIONAL AIRPORT

Fig. 2D Heathrow: extracts from a guide

General Information

Full Postal Address
Heathrow Airport – London
Hounslow
Middlesex TW6 IJH

Telephones
(See London telephone directory E-K for details)
01-759 4321
or 01-897 6711 (travel tips – recorded information)

Telex
934982 (BAA – D'Albiac House)

Hours of opening
24 hours daily

Position
Latitude – 51° 28' 11" N
Longitude – 00° 27' 08" W
Elevation – 80' above sea level

Area
The airport covers 2,958 acres (1,197 hectares)
The perimeter road is more than 9½ miles long

Location
15 road miles west of London

Runway Dimensions
28R/10L – 3902m × 46m (12,800ft × 150ft)
05/23 – 2357m × 46m (7,734ft × 150ft)
28L/10R – 3658m × 46m (12,000ft × 150ft)

Navigational Aids
British Airports have responsibility for:
    Calvert Centreline & Crossbar Approach Lighting System
    Visual Approach Slope Indicators (VASI)
    Precision Approach Path Indicators (PAPI)
The Civil Aviation Authority is responsible for:
    1 – VDF (Very high frequency direction finding)
    2 – ILS (Instrument Landing System)
    3 – Surveillance radars
    4 – Radio Beacons

Airlines
More than 70 airlines fly direct scheduled services to well over 200 destinations.

Aircraft Stands
There are 125 aircraft parking stands in the central area and 70 are big enough to take wide-bodied aircraft. There are 26 aircraft parking stands in the cargo area of which 6 are suitable for Boeing 747Fs and a further 6 for wide-bodied aircraft.

Passengers
Last year nearly 30 million passengers used Heathrow. More than 24 million were international passengers, making Heathrow the busiest international airport in the world.

Staff
The airport has a workforce of 45,000 – roughly the population of a county town – consisting of 32,000 airline staff, nearly 7,000 people working for concessionaires, 3,600 BAA staff and 2,600 employed by various government departments and other control authorities.

Fig. 2D

Spectators
Visitors can watch airport activities from the roof gardens of the Queens Building.

Main Tunnel
Entry to the Central Terminal Area is via the main tunnel, under runway 28R/10L. The tunnel is 2080 feet long and 86 feet wide. More than 12 million vehicles pass through it each year and it has a capacity of 3,000 vehicles per hour in each direction.

Nurseries
Nursing mothers' rooms are provided free of charge in each terminal by the British Airports Authority.

Animal Quarantine Station (and RSPCA)
Built and operated by the Corporation of London to implement the quarantine laws (including the Rabies order of 1974).

Customs and Immigration
Departure and Arrival Halls are staffed by H.M. Customs and Immigration for the control of all international flights.

Police and Fire Service
The Metropolitan Police have overall responsibility for security and law enforcement. A full Airport Fire and Rescue Service is provided by the British Airports Authority.

Chapel
The Chapel of St. George, dedicated on 11 October 1968 is situated between the Control Tower and Terminal 2 Car Park. The chapel is open 24 hours per day. Regular services for Church of England, Roman Catholic and Free Church worshippers are held throughout the week.

Car Parking
There are four multi-storey car parks in the Central Area and for longer stay users a long-term car park on the airport's Northside. These car parks are operated for the BAA by National Car Parks Limited. During the summer months there is a special spectator's car park, which is on the northside of the airport, just off the A4 road.

Information
A Heathrow Information booklet giving details of passenger facilities can be obtained from the Public Relations Department, British Airports Authority. Queen's Building, Heathrow Airport, Hounslow, Middlesex TW6 1JH.

Historical Notes
Heathrow Airport – London was named after the village or hamlet of Heathrow located approximately where Terminal 3 now stands.

The origin of the name itself is more obscure. Some historians say that it was originally "Heath Row" or road to the Heath. Hounslow Heath is two miles to the East, and an area just North of the airport was once known as Heath End.

Others say that Heathrow is a corruption of "Hithero" which was the original name of the village. This is certainly born out by old maps of the area.

In the eighteenth century, of course, spelling of place-names was often erratic, and Hithero could also originate from a local heath.

The first Ordnance Survey base line, surveyed by General Roy in 1784, was from a point on the Northside of the Airport to Hampton, a distance of 27,402 feet. Both points were marked by cannons, the one used at Heathrow being discovered during the excavations for the Airport and later removed to the Ordnance Survey Museum at Chessington, Surrey. The cannon was returned to Heathrow in 1968 and is now on display on the Northside of the Airport.

Fig. 2D

Commercial Aircraft

Many types of aircraft are operated through Heathrow Airport on regular scheduled services by over 70 airlines.

Listed below are some of the aircraft to be seen now at Heathrow. The aircraft are listed under the country(s) of manufacture.

AIRCRAFT	RANGE in miles	SPAN in metres	LENGTH in metres	MAX. SEATS	CRUISE SPEED	NO. OF ENGINES
UK & Europe						
Concorde	3,915	25.56m	61.66m	128	Mach 2	4 Jet
BAe One-Eleven	1,865	28.50m	32.61m	119	540 mph	2 Jet
BAe 146	1,704	26.34m	26.16m	109	436mph	4 Jet
BAe Trident	2,464	29.87m	39.98m	180	600 mph	3 Jet
Airbus Industrie A300	2,530	44.84m	53.62m	330	578 mph	2 Jet
Airbus Industrie A310	2,540	43.9m	46.6m	292	514 mph	2 Jet
Short 330	450	22.76m	17.69m	30	190 mph	2 Prop
Short 360	655	22.75m	21.49m	36	243 mph	2 Prop
Fokker F-28 Fellowship	760	25.07m	26.76m	85	416 mph	2 Jet
Fokker F-27 Friendship	1,082	29m	25.06m	52	298 mph	2 Prop
Soviet Union						
Ilyushin IL62m	6,400	43.2m	53.12m	198	560 mph	4 Jet
Ilyushin IL86	2,858	48.06m	59.54m	350	590 mph	4 Jet
Tupolev TU134A	1,490	29m	34.35m	80	540 mph	2 Jet
Tupolev TU154B	3,280	37.55m	47.9m	180	560 mph	3 Jet
Yakovlev YAK-42	1,243	34.90m	36.38m	120	466 mph	3 Jet
Canada						
DHC Dash 7	696	28.35m	24.58m	50	235 mph	4 Prop
DHC Twin Otter	1,103	19.81m	15.77m	20	210 mph	2 Prop
United States						
Boeing 707	6,240	44.2m	46.61m	195	605 mph	4 Jet
Boeing 727	2,645	32.92m	46.69m	189	570 mph	3 Jet
Boeing 737	2,370	28.35m	30.48m	130	576 mph	2 Jet
Boeing 747	7,080	59.64m	70.51m	490	589 mph	4 Jet
Boeing 757	2,476	37.95m	47.32m	204	528 mph	2 Jet
Boeing 767	2,554	47.65m	48.5m	255	528 mph	2 Jet
Lockheed L-1011 TriStar	6,100	47.35m	54.17m	400	595 mph	3 Jet
McDonnell Douglas DC8	5,720	43.41m	45.87m	173	520 mph	4 Jet
McDonnell DC8 Super Sixty	6,500	45.23m	57.12m	259	600 mph	4 Jet
McDonnell Douglas DC9	1,070	28.47m	32.28m	139	510 mph	2 Jet
McDonnell DC9 Super 80	3,280	32.85m	45.08m	172	522 mph	2 Jet
McDonnell Douglas DC10	7,197	50.41m	55.5m	380	570 mph	3 Jet
SAAB-Fairchild 340	1,115	21.44m	19.72m	34	243 mph	2 Prop

10 | Concorde

Fig. 2D

Statistics

Calendar Year	Total Passengers	Commercial Air Movements	Cargo and Mail (Metric Tonnes)
1946 (June-Dec)	63,151	2,046	2,164
1950	523,351	25,450	14,341
1955	2,683,605	109,046	44,520
1960	5,380,937	135,468	93,490
1965	10,662,395	192,368	214,389
1970	15,606,719	246,447	372,502
1975	21,642,393	254,106	450,273
1978	26,910,068	268,848	513,783
1979	28,357,856	276,277	556,525
1980	27,770,643	273,133	531,271
1981	26,770,813	247,073	513,217
1982	26,740,784	250,839	497,328
1983	27,063,183	260,100	533,584
1984	29,457,227	272,906	612,157

Did you know that . . .?

* Highest number of aircraft movements at Heathrow in any one day was 1,007 on 7 June 1985.

* Peak number of passengers handled at Heathrow on any one day was 115,570 on Sunday, 2 September 1984.

* On the same day, the busiest single hour of two-way passenger flow was recorded, when over 11,169 passengers passed through Heathrow's terminal buildings.

* Peak rate of landing and take-offs recorded during a complete hour was 80 aircraft movements, on 10 September 1976 between 1100-1200 hours GMT – more than one per minute!

* Heathrow Airport handles two-thirds of *all* airline passenger arrivals in the U.K.

* Heathrow is the busiest international airport in the world. In terms of total traffic, including *domestic* traffic, it is the sixth busiest, behind five American airports.

* The average number of passengers per aircraft at Heathrow rose from 83 in 1972 to 108 in 1983.

* Terminal 1 handles a volume of traffic which would make it Europe's fifth busiest airport in its own right!

* Judged by the value of goods passing through it, Heathrow has become Britain's most important port – handling 13 per cent of the nation's total trade, in 1983.

* Over 70 different airlines fly from Heathrow to over 200 direct destinations.

* The average rate of landings and take-offs recorded in August 1984 was 802 per day, and 68 per hour during the peak hours.

* The longest runway at Heathrow is about 2½ miles long.

* There are 125 aircraft stands in the centre of Heathrow and 26 stands in the cargo area.

* There are about 30,000 meeters and greeters together with some 2,000 spectators or business callers at Heathrow *per day.*

* Heathrow has over 40 miles of roads and nearly 12 million vehicles enter the airport's central area, via the main tunnel each year.

* Heathrow has 4,500 baggage trolleys – more than any other airport in the world.

* Heathrow Airport employs 45,880 people.

* At peak times, trains run every four minutes to Central London.

* Heathrow currently handles on average 81,825 passengers *every day* – that's almost the size of a Wembley Cup Final crowd!

* Every day, Heathrow Airport serves the public over 22,600 cups of tea and coffee, more than 6,500 pints of beer and 3,400 sandwiches!

* Every year, Heathrow Airport duty-free shops sell 500 million cigarettes, 4 million bottles of liquor (1,000,000 gallons!), 10 million cigars, 40 tons of pipe tobacco and 1.3 million bottles of perfume.

* For every 4 inches (10 cms) of snow to fall on Heathrow Airport, the British Airports authority has to remove about 75,000 tonnes of snow to keep the airport open.

14

Fig. 2D

Airline Operators

AIRLINE	COUNTRY OF ORIGIN	TERMINAL USED
Aer Lingus	Eire	1
Aeroflot – Soviet Airlines	Soviet Union	2
Air Algerie	Algeria	2
Air Canada	Canada	3
Air France	France	2
Air India	India	3
Air Jamaica	Jamaica	3
Air Malta	Malta	2
Air Mauritius	Mauritius	3
Air U.K.	United Kingdom	1
Alia	Jordan	3
Alitalia	Italy	2
Austrian Airlines	Austria	2
Balkan-Bulgarian Airlines	Bulgaria	2
Bangladesh Biman	Bangladesh	3
British Airways	United Kingdom	1 and 3
British Caledonian	United Kingdom	Cargo
British Midland Airways	United Kingdom	1
British West Indian Airways	Trinidad	3
Brymon Airways	United Kingdom	1
Cyprus Airways	Cyprus	2
Czechoslovak Airlines	Czechoslovakia	2
Dan Air	United Kingdom	1
Egyptair	Egypt	3
El Al	Israel	3
Ethiopian Airlines	Ethiopia	3
Finnair	Finland	2
Flying Tigers	U.S.A.	Cargo
Ghana Airways	Ghana	3
Gulf Air	Bahrain	3
Iberia Airlines	Spain	2
Icelandair	Iceland	2
Iranair	Iran	3
Iraqi Airways	Iraq	3
Japan Air Lines	Japan	3
Jugoslav Airlines	Yugoslavia	2
Kenya Airways	Kenya	3
KLM Royal Dutch Airlines	Netherlands	2
Kuwait Airways	Kuwait	3
Libyan Arab Airlines	Libya	2
LOT-Polish Airlines	Poland	2
Lufthansa	Federal Republic of Germany	2
Luxair	Luxembourg	2
Malaysian Airline System	Malaysia	3
Malev-Hungarian Airlines	Hungary	2
Manx Airlines	United Kingdom	1
Middle East Airlines	Lebanon	3
Nigerian Airways	Nigeria	3
NLM City Hopper	Netherlands	2
Olympic Airways	Greece	2
Pan American World Airways	U.S.A.	3
PIA Pakistan International Airlines	Pakistan	3
Qantas	Australia	3
Royal Air Maroc	Morocco	2
Sabena Belgian Airlines	Belgium	2
SAS-Scandinavian Airlines	Sweden-Denmark-Norway	2
Saudia Saudi-Arabian Airlines	Saudi Arabia	3
Singapore Airlines	Singapore	3
South African Airlines	South Africa	3
Sudan Airways	Sudan	3
Swissair	Switzerland	2
Syrian Arab Airlines	Syria	3
TAP Air Portugal	Portugal	2
Tarom-Romanian Air Transport	Romania	2
Thai International	Thailand	3
Trans Mediterranean	Lebanon	Cargo
Trans World Airlines	U.S.A.	3
Tunis Air	Tunisia	2
Turkish Airlines	Turkey	2
Varig Brazilian Airlines	Brazil	3
Viasa Venezuelan Airlines	Venezuela	3
Zambia Airways	Zambia	3

19

Fig. 2D

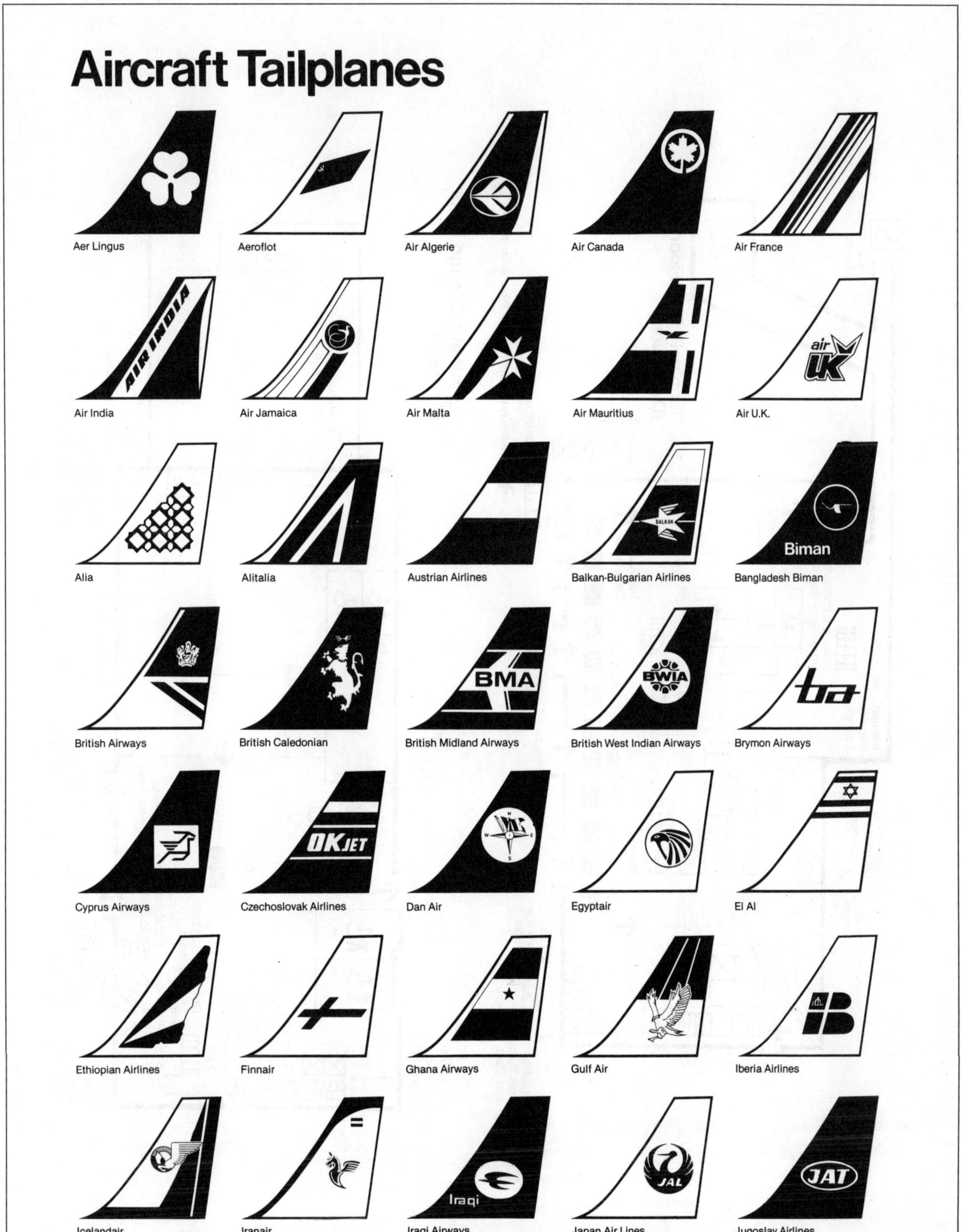

Aircraft Tailplanes
Aer Lingus
Aeroflot
Air Algerie
Air Canada
Air France
AIR INDIA
Air India
Air Jamaica
Air Malta
Air Mauritius
air UK
Air U.K.
Alia
Alitalia
Austrian Airlines
BALKAN
Balkan-Bulgarian Airlines
Biman
Bangladesh Biman
British Airways
British Caledonian
BMA
British Midland Airways
BWIA
British West Indian Airways
ba
Brymon Airways
Cyprus Airways
OKJET
Czechoslovak Airlines
Dan Air
Egyptair
El Al
Ethiopian Airlines
Finnair
Ghana Airways
Gulf Air
Iberia Airlines
Icelandair
Iranair
Iraqi
Iraqi Airways
JAL
Japan Air Lines
JAT
Jugoslav Airlines
20

Fig. 2D

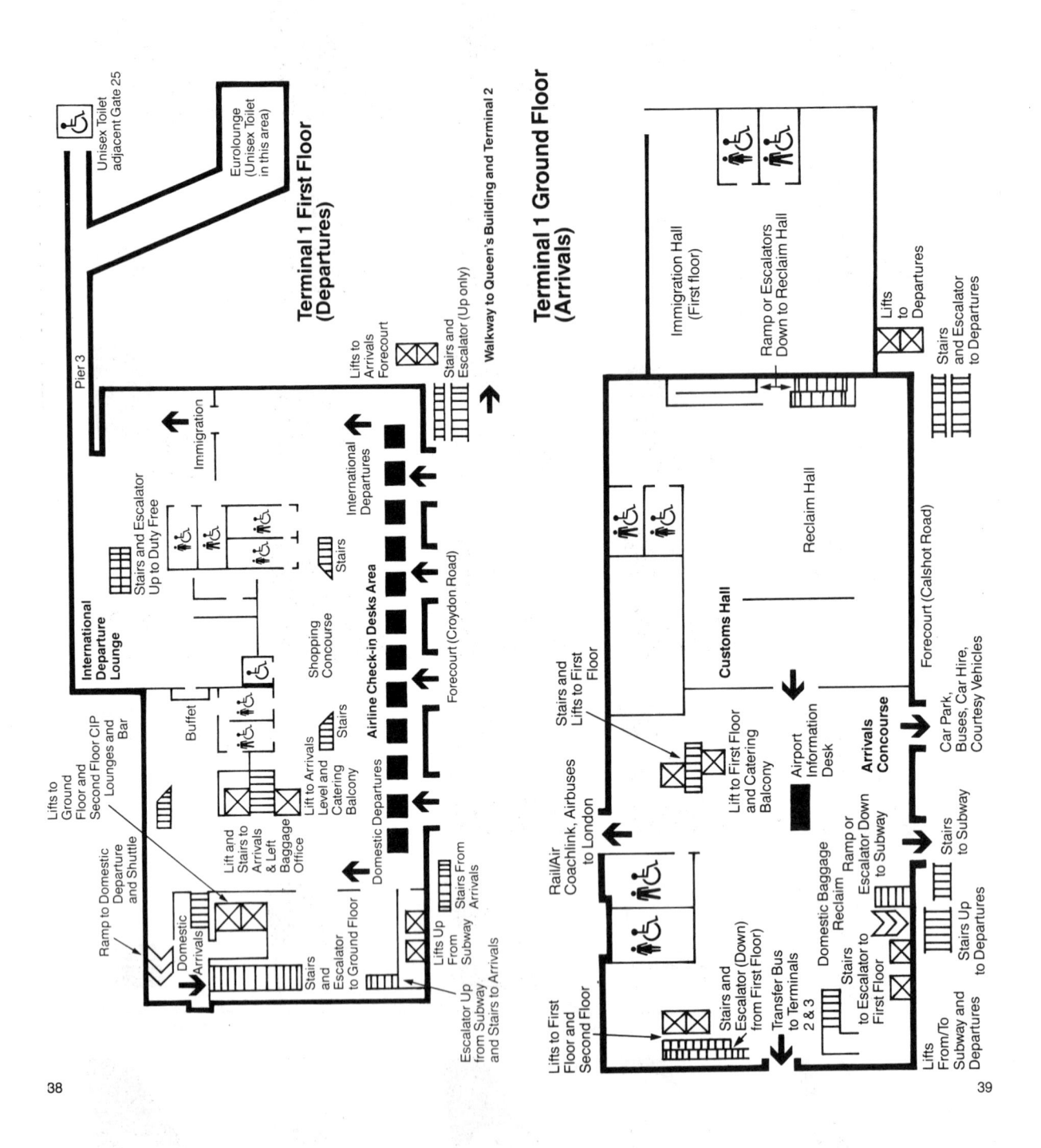

Terminal 1 First Floor (Departures)

Unisex Toilet adjacent Gate 25

Pier 3

Eurolounge (Unisex Toilet in this area)

Walkway to Queen's Building and Terminal 2

Immigration

International Departure Lounge

Stairs and Escalator Up to Duty Free

Shopping Concourse

International Departures

Stairs

Airline Check-in Desks Area

Forecourt (Croydon Road)

Buffet

Lifts to Ground Floor and Second Floor CIP Lounges and Bar

Lift to Arrivals Level and Catering Balcony

Stairs

Domestic Departures

Lift and Stairs to Arrivals & Left Baggage Office

Ramp to Domestic Departure and Shuttle

Domestic Arrivals

Stairs and Escalator to Ground Floor

Stairs From Arrivals

Lifts Up From Subway

Lifts to Arrivals Forecourt

Stairs and Escalator (Up only)

Escalator Up from Subway and Stairs to Arrivals

38

Terminal 1 Ground Floor (Arrivals)

Immigration Hall (First floor)

Ramp or Escalators Down to Reclaim Hall

Lifts to Departures

Stairs and Escalator to Departures

Customs Hall

Reclaim Hall

Forecourt (Calshot Road)

Stairs and Lifts to First Floor

Airport Information Desk

Arrivals Concourse

Car Park, Buses, Car Hire, Courtesy Vehicles

Lift to First Floor and Catering Balcony

Rail/Air Coachlink, Airbuses to London

Stairs to Subway

Lifts to First Floor and Second Floor

Domestic Baggage Reclaim

Ramp or Escalator Down to Subway

Transfer Bus to Terminals 2 & 3

Stairs to Escalator to First Floor

Stairs and Escalator (Down) from First Floor

Stairs Up to Departures

Lifts From/To Subway and Departures

39

Fig. 2D

This case study contains the following sections:

- Interviewers and interviewees
- The skills of the interviewer
  – before the interview
- The skills of the interviewer
  – during the interview
- Main task
- Self-assessment

Interviewers and interviewees

An interview which involves selecting someone for a job – the recruitment interview – is a situation which illustrates many of the key interpersonal communication skills discussed in this book. For example, the person conducting the interview will be busy asking questions, interpreting answers, assessing non-verbal communication cues and forming impressions. The other person involved in the interview – the candidate – will also be busy, trying to think clearly under stress, listening intently to questions, being careful to project the appropriate image, and so on.

In this case study we will be looking at recruitment interviews and we will be looking specifically at the skills of the **interviewer,** as opposed to those of the **interviewee**. The interviewer is the name we give to the person conducting the interview, the person 'in charge', whereas the interviewee is the person who is being interviewed. Interestingly, there are other situations which have similar terms to describe the working relationship between two contrasting roles. For example, we have 'employer' and 'employee'; 'tutor' and 'tutee'. Can you think of other examples?

At the end of this case study you will be asked to complete a MAIN TASK in which you are required to help prepare material for a business management training course on interviewing skills. To help you with this final task you should now work through the following pages and exercises.

What is a 'good interviewer'?

Those of us who have been interviewees can probably quote examples of 'bad interviews'. Sometimes we may say that an interview was 'bad' because we felt that we performed poorly, that we failed to answer

questions adequately, and that we were so nervous that we made ourselves look silly. Sometimes we may say that an interview was 'bad' because the interviewing panel gave us a 'rough ride', that they were aggressive and asked awkward and stupid questions. As experienced interviewees, whatever examples of 'bad' interviews we give, we would probably all agree that an interview is normally a tense and unpleasant experience.

Some people would say that it is perfectly right and proper that an interview should be a tense and difficult experience. According to this view, an interview should be a trial, a test of how well the individual can perform under pressure. After all, they may say, most jobs require an ability to cope under pressure, so why not put the candidates to the test during the interview? Fig. 3A shows this particular view of the interview as a kind of interrogation.

Fig. 3A The interview as interrogation

175

The truth is that most jobs simply do not place people under the kind of pressure and tension they may be made to experience during an interview. In this case study we take the view that although it is normal for the interview to be a tense experience because of what may be at stake, it is a responsibility of the interviewer to develop a relaxed atmosphere so that information can be freely obtained from the interviewee. After all, the main job of the interviewer is to get as full and as accurate a picture of the candidates as possible, so that a decision can be made about who is the right person for the job. A 'bad' interview would be one where the most suitable candidate was intimidated to the point where his or her qualities were not allowed to become apparent, and he or she as a consequence, was not selected.

According to the view taken in this case study a 'good' interviewer is one who:
— creates a relaxed atmosphere;
— encourages interviewees to answer questions freely;
— makes clear statements and asks intelligible questions;
— listens carefully and attentively.
A 'bad' interviewer is one who:
— creates a tense atmosphere;
— discourages candidates from talking;
— makes unclear statements and asks unintelligible questions;
— does not listen carefully and attentively.

Having described what we mean by a 'good' interviewer, let us now have a closer look at the specific skills which are involved in interviewing.

The skills of the interviewer — before the interview

We have already said that important interviewing skills include those involved in creating a relaxed atmosphere during the interview. However, it would be wrong to assume that the only skills which matter are those involved in talking and listening to the candidate during the interview itself. It is important to appreciate that a good interviewer must also have the ability to prepare for an interview before it takes place. For this reason we will be looking at those skills involved both before and during the interview.

Skill 1: Studying the application forms and preparing an appropriate set of questions

It is important that the interviewer studies the application forms carefully and brings to the interview a clear idea of the approach to be taken with each candidate. Nothing is gained by the interviewer continually referring to the application form during the interview to work out what question to ask next. Obviously it would be wrong to go to the other extreme and prepare an interview plan which is so rigid that there is little room for either the interviewer, or the interviewee, to develop points as they arise. A good compromise is to identify a range of questions to put to the interviewee, some of which may be essential and some of which may be optional.

What should these questions be? Clearly, the precise questions will depend upon the nature of the vacancy and the background of the candidate. However, in general terms it is possible to say that there are two main types of question: those designed to help the candidate relax and generally 'lubricate' the flow of the interview, and those designed to draw from the candidate areas of knowledge and attitudes which are specific to the job.

Questions which are designed to put the candidate at ease are sometimes best left to the interview itself. A skilled and confident interviewer can often assess the situation 'on the spot', as it were, taking into account how confident the candidate appears, the odd amusing incident which may have occurred just before the interview, and so on. However, it is useful to identify some possible 'ice-breakers' from the candidate's application form. Forms designed for use mainly with school leavers will often have a 'hobbies' or 'interests' section for this purpose. Another possibility for putting candidates at ease might be to invite them to describe their previous work experience. This puts the candidate into familiar 'home territory', and can also serve to bring out possibilities for further questions.

Careful thought needs to be given to those questions which are designed to draw from the candidate areas of knowledge and attitudes specific to the needs of the job. It is essential that the interviewer has a clear grasp of what the job entails and what kind of qualities are needed for the particular vacancy. Many organisations use what are known as **job descriptions** and **job specifications** to spell out the duties and requirements of a vacancy. A job description is a clear, written statement of the duties, responsibilities and conditions of work for a particular post. In effect, it tells candidates what they would be expected to do if they succeeded in getting the job. A job specification (sometimes called a **personnel specification**) is a clear, written statement of the qualities, qualifications, and previous work experience which are needed for a particular post. In effect, it tells candidates what qualities they are likely to need to be in a position to get the job. If a job description and a job specification are available, the skilled interviewer will scrutinise each candidate's application form against these.

<u>CITY COUNCIL</u>

<u>COMMUNITY ARTS AND RECREATION DEPARTMENT</u>

<u>POST OF: DIRECTOR OF CANAL CENTRE</u>

<u>JOB DESCRIPTION</u>

The Centre is situated on the city canal system and serves as both a museum of canal history, and as an information centre for a variety of local activities, such as walks and tours along the waterways. The Centre has been particularly active in promoting and organising educational tours and visits for local school children.

In addition to the Director, the Centre also employs a caretaker/handyperson and a receptionist/secretary.

The person appointed will be directly responsible for the overall running of the Centre, including the supervision of the Centre personnel.

Specifically, the duties of this post include:-

i   Supervising the day-to-day running of the Centre, including supervision of the Centre personnel.

ii   Liaising with outside bodies such as schools, history societies and waterways' groups.

iii   Giving talks and tours for members of the public interested in the activities of the Centre.

iv   Attending meetings of the Council's Community Arts and Recreation Committee, and preparing any necessary documentation requested by the Committee.

v   Generally promoting and developing the activities of the Centre.

<u>PERSONNEL SPECIFICATION</u>

The person appointed should:

i   Have a good general education.

ii   Have managerial, or supervisory, experience and knowledge.

iii   Be an effective communicator.

iv   Have some interest in, and knowledge of, British waterways and waterway history.

Fig. 3B Job description

Name: David Burnside	Address: 13, Gladstone Street, Stockport.
Date of Birth: 27.6.46	
Marital Status: Divorced	Children: —

Education:

1957–1964 The Grammar School, Oswestry.
1966–1969 London School of Economics

Qualifications:

1964 Economics D; Statistics E; History C
1969 B.A. (Hons) Social Administration II

Present Post: Community Worker, Community Centre, Stockport.

Previous Employment:

1970–1975 Self Employed Builder
1976–1977 Voluntary Service Overseas Nigeria
1977–1985 Community Worker, Tameside Metropolitan Council

Hobbies and Interests: Industrial Architecture & Archaeology, Reading & Cycling

Referees:

J. Freeman, Director,
Community Centre,
Wall Lane, Stockport.

Additional Statement My general interest in Industrial Architecture and Archaeology should give me some insight into the work of the Canal Centre.

I have considerable experience of working with people of various backgrounds and ages and I feel that this should prove invaluable in dealing with the public. As for "supervision of other Centre employees" I must say that I don't like this expression. I prefer the idea of teamwork and I'm confident that my past experience should give me the ability to cope with this.

I would be able to prepare data for committee approval, and any other documentation required

Date: 2.5.86   Signature: David Burnside

Fig. 3C Application form

Name: Janice Grant
Address: 24, Maureen Aveneue, Norwich.
Date of Birth: 1.2.54
Marital Status: Single
Children: None

Education:

1964-1969 The Convent School, Norwich.
1969-1963 Norwich College of Further Education.

Qualifications:

1973: B'TEC National Diploma (Business Studies) "A" level Economics (B)
1975: Pitman Shorthand 100 wpm/Typing 100 wpm

Present Post: Senior Librarian, Norwich City Council

Previous Employment:

1973 -1976 MicroTec Plc, Norwich
1976 -1982 Assistant Librarian, Norwich City Council.
1982 -   Present post.

Hobbies and Interests:

Local History Society (1978- Committee member)

Reading

Referees:

Jane Dixon, Chief Librarian, Norwich City Library, Norwich.	A.W. Green, Chairman, Norwich History Soc. 12 Hunter Close, Norwich.

<u>Additional Statement</u>   My interest in this post is directly related to my present job as a Senior Librarian, and to my involvement in local history. I have a good general knowledge of canal and waterway history, though less of the technical aspects. Above all, I have a strong commitment to the need to preserve our local heritage, in all its forms, and a strong desire to share my knowledge with the community.

Another interest I have in this post is my desire to take on more individual responsibility and to move away from the security of the conventional library system. Although the Canal Centre is relatively small, as Director I would be able to make my own decisions and to develop some of my ideas about the community's involvement in its local history. I would welcome such a challenge if appointed.

One final feature of this post which attracts me involves my decision to move away from the Norwich area.

Date: 1.5.86

Signature: *Janice Grant*

Fig. 3D Application form

Exactly what should the interviewer be looking for when scrutinising an application form? There are two main possibilities. Firstly, there may be items of information given on the form which are incomplete or unclear. For example, in the 'Previous Employment' section a candidate may have listed the name of the firm and the name of the department in which he or she worked, without specifying the exact role and position. Another example might be a 'gap' in the employment record. A whole year which is unaccounted for may be something which the interviewer ought to pursue.

Secondly, there may be statements on the application form which the candidate has quoted as evidence of his or her suitability for the post. It is important that the interviewer should explore these points and, perhaps, subtly test their accuracy and credibility. For example, in the case of an application for a junior management post, a candidate may have written: 'Athough I was not employed at Brown's as a supervisor, I had considerable responsibility for day-to-day matters on the shop floor, and was often asked to make key decisions about production levels'. This sounds very interesting and impressive, and certainly something which the interviewer should follow up in more detail during the interview.

TASK *1*

Study the job description, Fig. 3B, and application forms, Figs. 3C and 3D, and produce a list of possible interview questions for each candidate. Be sure to bear in mind the points which have been discussed above.

Skill 2: Making arrangements for the interview day

There are a number of arrangements which an experienced and sensitive interviewer should make to ensure that the interview takes place smoothly and comfortably. For example, careful attention should be given to the choice of the interview room and the seating arrangements within it. Rooms should not be used in which the interview could be interrupted at any time, either by ringing telephones, opening doors, or noise from a nearby corridor. Equally, a room should not be used which is likely to set an excessively formal or 'heavy' atmosphere, e.g. avoid a room which is too large. The seating plan which is chosen will obviously depend upon such factors as the number of people on the interview panel and the shape and size of the room. However, a general rule would be to avoid any devices likely to intimidate the interviewee, e.g. avoid seating the interview panel in a straight line confronting the candidate; avoid the use of too many desks and tables which may act as barriers to effective communication; avoid the use of hard, uncomfortable chairs.

Adequate arrangements should also be made for a quiet place where the candidate can sit and wait before being called into the interview room. This is especially important if a number of candidates are to be interviewed by the same panel on the same day.

Finally, care should be taken to ensure that each candidate is notified in writing, in advance, as to exactly where and when the interview is to take place. A candidate who is notified of an interview just a day, or even hours, before it is due to take place, is hardly likely to arrive in a relaxed and responsive frame of mind.

TASK *2*

You are asked to make the rooming and seating arrangements for a series of interviews involving five candidates. The interview panel will consist of the following three people: the personnel manager, one of the company's directors and the head of the department in which the vacancy has arisen. Draw a plan of the arrangements which you would recommend. Assume you have complete access to whatever seating and rooming you think is appropriate. Include notes in your plan explaining the decisions you have made.

The skills of the interviewer — during the interview

Skill 3: Putting the candidate at ease

One of the prime attributes of the skilled interviewer is the ability to put the candidate at ease. As we have already mentioned, choosing one or two relevant opening questions, possibly based upon information on the application form, is a useful technique. However, above all else the interviewer should have the ability to empathise with the candidate, to assess the mood of the situation, and to be aware of his or her own effect on the candidate. In Chapter 3 we saw that body language is a very powerful means of establishing the nature of the relationship between people. In an interview, all participants should be aware both of their own body language and of that of the people with whom they are communicating. In particular, the good interviewer should try and ensure that his or her facial expressions, gestures and use of eye contact, are all used in a positive, rather than a negative, way. For example, a good interviewer would be sure to greet the candidate with an open gesture, such as a handshake or an outstretched hand, and with a ready smile.

TASK *3*

The photographs in Fig. 3E show excerpts from an informal job interview. The interviewee is the man; the interviewer is the woman. In all of the examples the interviewee is talking. Study the photographs carefully and for each write notes summarising the main features of the interviewer's body language and what this may be 'saying' to the interviewee. Be sure to include in your notes comments about eye contact, facial expression, gesture and posture. Also say whether you would describe the overall impression created in each photograph as 'emotionally and socially positive' or 'emotionally and socially negative'.

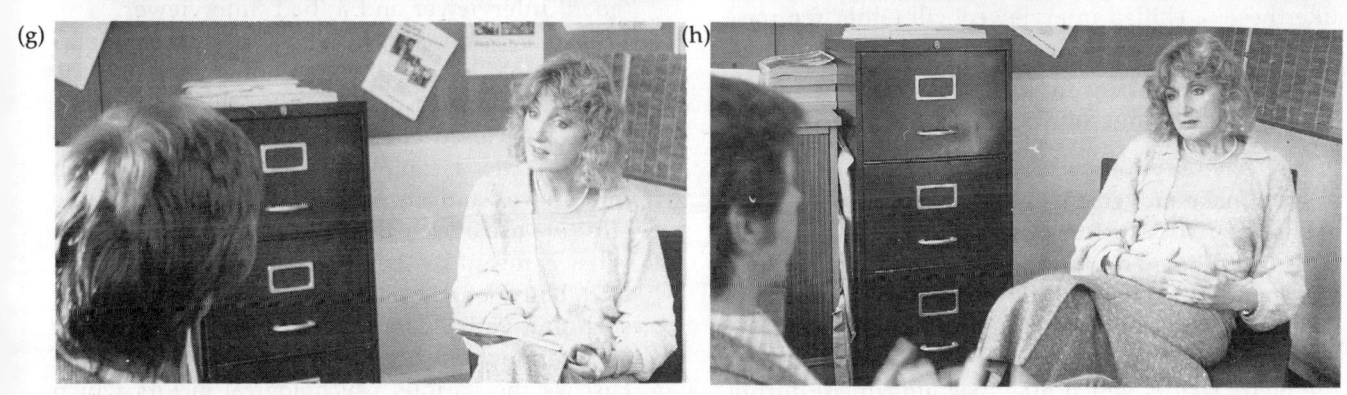

Fig. 3E Identifying positive and negative body language

Skill 4: Balancing the flow of the interview

There are many factors which will influence the flow of communication during an interview. Although not all of these factors are under the control of the interviewer, he or she will have some influence on the balance between the amount and types of question he or she asks and the amount and types of answer which the candidate gives. Specifically, the skilled interviewer will be aware of the following three points:

— Firstly, the interviewer should be careful not to monopolise the interview, either by talking too much or by interrupting the candidate unnecessarily

— Secondly, an interviewer should be aware of the uses of **open-ended** and **closed-ended** questions. An open-ended question is one which does not have a simple 'yes/no' type answer. For example, an open-ended question would be: 'Could you tell me something about your responsibilities as transport manager at Brown and Co?' A closed-ended question is one which invites a simple, factual answer. An example of this would be: 'Did you have much responsibility as transport manager at Brown and Co?' An unskilled interviewer may ask so many closed-ended questions in succession that the interview becomes little more than a sequence of brief and abrupt answers from the candidate. Using appropriately-phrased open-ended questions is a useful technique for getting a candidate to 'open up' and develop a point. However, it is possible to ask too many open-ended questions, or to ask questions which are so broad and general as to be very difficult for all but the very best candidates to answer. The skill is to balance open-ended and closed-ended questions to suit the flow of the interview, the ability of the candidate, and the information which the panel needs to know.

— Thirdly, a skilled interviewer should know how to handle those awkward moments in an interview when a candidate fails to understand a question, or when he or she answers too abruptly and briefly and so falls into an embarrassing silence. In moments like these, a skilled interviewer will either rephrase the question, or lead the candidate onto safer ground.

Skill 5: Avoiding making assumptions and premature judgements about the candidate

As we have seen elsewhere in this book, it is very easy to make judgements about people on the basis of characteristics such as physical appearance, accent, and dress. In many interviews it may be perfectly legitimate to make a careful note of the candidate's style of dress and general appearance. However, it is important that an interviewer should be aware of the many factors which may bias judgement during an interview. As well as the more obvious danger of stereotyping, such as 'people who have eyes close

together shouldn't be trusted', there may be more subtle influences at work. For example, there is the so-called 'halo effect'. Many psychological studies have shown that individuals who are perceived to be physically attractive also tend to be judged to be more intelligent, more able and more likeable than their less attractive peers. Clearly there is the danger that an unskilled, or inexperienced, interviewer could make judgements which have been influenced by such factors.

Finally, before you go on to the MAIN TASK of this case study, study the table in Fig. 3F which summarises the skills of the interviewer.

BEFORE THE INTERVIEW
SKILL 1: Studying the application forms and preparing an appropriate set of questions.
SKILL 2: Making arrangements for the interview day.
DURING THE INTERVIEW
SKILL 3: Putting the candidate at ease.
SKILL 4: Balancing the flow of the interview.
SKILL 5: Avoiding making assumptions and premature judgements about the candidate.

Fig. 3F The skills of the interviewer

MAIN TASK

You have been invited by Mr R.E. Evenden, the Deputy Director of Roffey Park Management College, to help prepare material for a residential course on interviewing skills. You have received a letter from Mr Evenden explaining in greater detail what your contribution should be. Read this letter (Fig. 3G), and the documents (Figs. 3H and 3I) which accompany it, very carefully. Prepare a finished copy of the material which Mr Evenden has asked for.

Self-assessment

1. Write a thumb-nail sketch of your own view of a 'good' interviewer and a 'bad' interviewer.
2. What is a 'job description' and a 'job specification'? How should both of these documents be used by the interviewer in preparing for the interview?
3. What are 'closed-ended' and 'open-ended' questions? Write a sample of dialogue between an interviewer and an interviewee to illustrate the effective use of closed and open-ended questions.
4. What is meant by 'emotionally and socially positive' body language? Explain the importance of such non-verbal communication in ensuring that an interview flows in a satisfactory manner.
5. Discuss the various psychological factors which may hinder the interviewer in trying to make an accurate assessment of a candidate.

ROFFEY PARK
MANAGEMENT COLLEGE

ROFFEY PARK INSTITUTE LIMITED
Forest Road, Horsham, West Sussex RH12 4TD
Telephone: Faygate 644 (STD Code 029 383)

Dear

Thank you for agreeing to help prepare material for use on our interviewing
skills course. I have included two extracts from our college prospectus
which you may wish to read as background information. The first extract
outlines the general structure of our course, entitled "Recruitment
Interviewing Skills". The second extract should give you an indication
of some of the facilities available at Roffey Park.

There are two things we would like to receive from you:-

i   An outline plan of an introductory talk on the key skills of
     the recruitment interviewer. The talk will be given at the
     start of our three day course, and it should last for between
     forty-five to sixty minutes.

     It should be fairly informal and should help to "map out"
     the main components of the course ahead in an interesting way.

     What we need from you is a written outline which includes
     the main points of the talk, supplementary notes, and a clear
     indication of the use of any visual aids or similar support
     material.

     Your outline should be detailed enough to give a clear sense
     of direction, whilst allowing the speaker to decide upon the
     precise wording and style of delivery.

ii   An "observation checklist" which course participants can use
     when watching video-taped recordings of their own interviewing
     performances from the practical sessions of the course. The
     purpose of the checklist is to provide participants with a
     "tool" to help them analyse and record aspects of their skills
     as interviewers.

     The checklist will probably take the form of a sheet which
     lists the main features of the interviewing process, with
     space for the user to assess their performance and to record
     appropriate comments.

contd./...

Chairman: John Hall.   Director & Secretary: John Giles, M.A.   Deputy Director: Robin Evenden, B.Sc.   Administrator: Diana Dodds, A.M.B.I.M.

Roffey Park Institute Limited is a charity registered No. 254591 and a company limited by guarantee registered in England No. 923975

Fig. 3G

ii (contd./...)

What we need from you is a detailed copy of such an "observation checklist", together with a set of "user's notes" explaining its purpose and how it is to be used.

Thanks once again for expressing such interest in our work at Roffey Park.

I look forward to receiving copies of your material.

Yours sincerely

ff R E Evenden

Assessment Centre Design

For Selection and Management Development

 Jointly sponsored by the College and the Institute of Personnel Management

Objectives:

- To examine the operation and uses of assessment centres.
- To enable members to learn skills for designing and running asessment centres tailored to fit their own organisation's requirements.
- To give members an understanding of the value of assessment centres, their limitations and associated problems.

For Whom:

People with responsibility in the areas of Selection and Management Development. These include Functional Managers as well as Personnel Specialists. No previous knowledge of assessment centres is required.

Method:

The course is divided into two parts, separated by a few weeks to enable project work to be done. It requires a very high level of participation, involving members in the design, operation and review of an assessment centre. 'Candidates' to be assessed are brought in from outside the course. Members are encouraged to examine the value of assessment centres to their own organisations with a critical eye.

Outline Programme:

Part 1

Day 1   Course Members arrive for dinner followed by introductory sessions.

Day 2   Outline of course content and method.
What are Assessment Centres?
Introduction to the process and 'mechanics'.
The Place of Assessment Centres
The uses of assessment centres and how they relate to appraisal schemes.
Management Abilities
The importance of identifying and defining the abilities to be measured.
The measurement question and subsequent use of criteria.

Day 3   Eliciting constructs: applying and practising the repertory grid method to determine criteria for effective performance.
Planning the Project Work
Course members identify the roles to be investigated.

Part 2

Monday: Reports on project work:
Selection and refinement of data to be used in the assessment centre workshop.

Tuesday: **Selecting the Exercises**
The value and limitations of various exercises.
Syndicates select exercises for use in the workshop.
Observation
The role of observers; selection and training.
Preparation for Workshop
Syndicates prepare for the workshop.

Wednesday: **Workshop**
Practical experience in running an assessment centre.
The follow-up and de-briefing.

Thursday: **Analysis**
Syndicates work as an evaluation committee to assess the candiates and test the effectiveness of the methods used.

Friday: **Pros and Cons**
Examination of advantages and problems.
Validity and the validation of methods used.
Course review.

Optimum membership: 8

Recruitment Interviewing Skills

A Short Course to Develop Skills in Recruitment Interviewing

Objectives:

- To provide an opportunity to review, practise and develop recruitment interviewing skills.
- To examine the context of the interview, including preparation, what the interviewer looks for, and additional sources of information.
- To help in making the right choice.

For Whom:

All managers and specialists who are involved in selecting staff and who wish to review, refresh or develop their skills in recruitment interviewing in a practical way.

Method:

The course is highly participative with every opportunity for all participants to practise recruitment interviewing situations with candidates brought in from outside the course. Extensive use of closed-circuit television and video-tape ensure that feedback and guidance from tutorial staff on individual interviewing styles is maximised for each individual. Preparation for effective recruitment interviewing is reviewed through practical activity.

Outline Programme:

- Identifying your requirements
- Preparing the ground
  - information needed before interview
  - short-listing
  - planning the interview
  - information to be sought during the interview
- Interviewing
  - Techniques to maximise the amount of relevant information: e.g. appropriate use of questions, non-verbal approaches, putting the candidate at ease.
  - Methods of dealing with difficult interviews: e.g. the unresponsive candidate, handling stress, dealing with personal issues.
  - Choosing the appropriate interviewing style: e.g. directive or non-directive, formal or informal, panel or one-to-one.
  - Evaluating the candidate: comparing information gained with requirements, productive use of intuition.
- Selecting the successful candidate: factors to take into account when making your choice; group decision-making.

Optimum membership: 10 Duration: 3 days

Dates and Fees: See card inside back cover

17

Fig. 3H

Facilities

The College is staffed and equipped exclusively to meet the needs of the people on the training programmes. The staff mount a range from highly structured to relatively unstructured learning events.

The College has three fully-equipped and adaptable training group rooms, eight syndicate rooms, a studio, projector room and several colour CCTV systems which can be linked in various combinations between all the rooms.

All course group sizes are kept deliberately small, none more than 15, some as few as eight. The larger groups do much of their work in syndicates of five or six. The tutor/course member ratio is high, never less than one to five, often no more than one to three.

The training rooms are centrally located within the premises and are supported by a reference library which is used by course members and staff within the programmes and also for private reading material. The library is often used for small group work.

30

Fig. 31

4 Medicheck: planning an advertising campaign

This case study contains the following sections:

- The importance of advertising
- Types of advertising campaign
- Marketing products
- The role of the media planner
- The candidate media list
- Main task
- Self-assessment

The importance of advertising

Advertising is a major industry in modern societies. This is illustrated by the following facts and figures:

– Total advertising expenditure in Britain stood at over £4 **billion** in 1985.

– Almost £3 billion was spent on advertising in the print media and over £1 billion on radio and television in that year.

– Over £300 million was spent advertising **food** alone.

– The three biggest advertisers in Britain were Proctor and Gamble (£47m), British Telecom (£41m) and Lever Brothers (£31m).

Advertising a product or service involves a variety of skills and professions. Graphic designers, copywriters, account executives and market researchers all have an important role to play. However, in this case study we are particularly concerned with the job of the **media planner,** whose main responsibility is to decide which of the mass media to use in an advertising campaign.

Types of advertising campaign

Colin Maclver (*Case Studies in Marketing, Advertising and Public Relations*) has argued that there are a variety of different types of advertising campaign, each with its own specific purpose. Here are four such examples:

Testing a product concept

This is a campaign based around the launch of a new product or service on to the market. The aim is to achieve a high 'recognition score' on the part of the target audience, which can be identified by **market research** carried out after the campaign has finished.

Revitalising an established brand

A company might feel that one of its established brands has an old-fashioned, out-of-date image. The purpose of this type of campaign is to give the product a more modern, progressive image.

A dash for brand leadership

In some industries, a number of products manufactured by different companies share a roughly equal chunk of the market. One of the companies might decide to invest heavily in an advertising campaign in an attempt to make their product the 'market leader'.

Waking a sleeping product

Sometimes, a product is launched onto the market but never really 'takes off', only achieving a low volume of sales. The manufacturer has two choices – either to cut the losses and withdraw the product, or make use of advertising to make it stronger in the market (perhaps by stressing one particular aspect of the product).

This case study is broadly concerned with the first of these types of campaign.

TASK 1

Identify and discuss in detail *two* real life examples of each of the above types of advertising campaign.

Marketing products

As an advertiser planning a campaign, there arc a number of important factors which you must take into account.

A mass audience

You must remember that you are aiming your message at a mass audience (perhaps over 17 million people if your adverts are to appear on commercial television) rather than individuals.

Choosing a target audience

As an advertiser, your message will not usually be aimed at a *single* mass audience. On the contrary, an advertising campaign will involve a degree of **market segmentation**. This term refers to the fact that the general public is composed of many different kinds of individuals and groups. In short, it is **heterogeneous**. As Colin MacIver has pointed out the advertiser's job is to:

'identify a reasonably homogeneous group of individuals with similar needs, attitudes and lifestyles'.

One of the most important aspects of our lifestyles, for the advertiser's purposes, is our use of the mass media — that is, what we read, watch and listen to, when and where.

This heterogeneity of the potential audience can best be analysed in terms of the dichotomies or opposites which exist within it. Simplistic examples include:
— Young vs Old People;
— Men vs Women;
— Single people vs Families;
— Rich vs Poor;
— North vs South.

The socio-economic group of the target audience is the single most important factor to take into account when planning a media campaign.

In Britain, advertisers, along with sociologists and market researchers, make use of a commonly-accepted (and simplified) series of socio-economic grades. Each job or occupation is placed in a band from A to E, from top managing directors down to unskilled workers and the unemployed.

	Socio-Economic Grades in the UK
A	Higher managerial, administrative or professional
B	Intermediate managerial, administrative or professional
C1	Supervisory or clerical and junior managerial, administrative or professional
C2	Skilled manual workers
D	Semi and unskilled manual workers
E	State pensioners or widows (no other earner in household), casual or lower grade workers, and unemployed

Fig. 4A Socio-economic grades

In most cases, a product or service will only be aimed at a relatively narrow audience. For example, a new perfume may be targeted at young women under the age of 25, whilst a new family saloon car will be aimed at high income families.

 TASK 2

What do you think are the 'target audiences' of the following products:
— Persil washing powder;
— Curly Wurlies;
— The *Guardian* newspaper;
— The Rover 3500 car;
— *Shoot* magazine?

Using an appropriate medium

You will also need to place your advertisements in a medium which is appropriate to your target audience. For example, if your target audience was 15-year-old girls, you would obviously decide to use *Jackie* rather than *Eagle*. Similarly, the following audiences might best be reached by adverts in these media:
— Housewives: *Woman, Woman's Own*;
— Feminists: *Spare Rib*;
— Computer buffs: *Sinclair User*;
— As, Bs, C1s: *Daily Telegraph, The Times*;
— C2s, Ds, Es: *Sun, Star*.

If you wanted to reach the *greatest number* of ABC1s you would use the *Daily Telegraph*, which has the highest circulation of the quality papers, as Fig. 4B illustrates.

But, advertising is not just about the *size* of the potential audience. Your target audience may well be a certain *type* of ABC1, for example a greater proportion of doctors might read the *Guardian* so you would tend to advertise in that publication. Advertising agencies are able to make use of a whole host of market research into the reading and viewing habits of every sector of the population. The most important, for their purposes, are the National Readership Surveys produced by the JICNARS organisation.

The principle is the same with radio and TV; a good example is the advertising of *Touchdown* magazine during the American Football programme on Channel 4. In this case, it is not merely a question of choosing an appropriate medium. One also has to choose a particular time-slot within the medium. This is known as **trafficking** your ads.

The role of the media planner

In this case study, we are concerned not with the creative side of advertising, but with the actual

| 2,614,000 ABC1 readers | 1,242,000 ABC1 readers | 909,000 ABC1 readers | 620,000 ABC1 readers |

Fig. 4B Reaching the ABC1s

planning of a media campaign. In advertising agencies, there is a person who is responsible for suggesting which of the mass media to use in a campaign. He or she is known as the **media planner**. The person who acts upon these recommendations and actually buys the space or time in the medium is called the **media buyer**. The agency's media planner is able to choose from the following advertising media:

— Television, e.g. Yorkshire Television;
— Independent radio, e.g. Capital Radio;
— National press, e.g. *Daily Mirror*;
— Regional press, e.g. *Yorkshire Post*;
— Local press, e.g. *Hereford Evening News*;
— Free press, e.g. *Burton Trader*;
— Trade and technical press, e.g. *The Grocer*;
— Magazines and periodicals, e.g. *Country Life*;
— Cinema, e.g. local Odeon;
— Transport, e.g. London underground, buses;
— Posters, e.g. local sites.

TASK *3*

Draw a chart to illustrate the main *advantages* and *disadvantages* of using each of the media listed above.

For example: Television.
Main advantage   — potentially massive audience.
Main disadvantage — high cost, relative to other media.

For example: Cinema.
Main advantage   — Ability to reach a localised audience.
Main disadvantage — Potential audience is small.

The media planner often proposes using a *mix* of different media when planning a campaign (although some products, like pet food, are almost exclusively advertised in one medium: in this case, television). For example, if your agency had recently won the

Vauxhall account and had been given the task of advertising cars like the Cavalier, Astra and Nova, you might well propose using 75% of your budget on ads on commercial TV whilst spending the rest on a press and poster campaign. Obviously, your budget would be a major factor in deciding on the particular media you would use.

Wendy Henson is a media planner with the Alexander Colbear agency in Nottingham:

'I have been working as a media planner with this agency in Nottingham for four years. My main job is to research the mass media and suggest which ones to use in advertising campaigns, depending upon the nature of the product and the type of target audience.

I receive my instructions from meetings with clients, but more often from the account director in charge of the particular account. At the moment, I am working on two major accounts (a building contractor and an electrical firm) as well as a few smaller ones. Some of the accounts are on-going whilst others last for a fixed period of time.

One of my most important jobs is to produce a **candidate media list** for each campaign I am involved with. This document lists the media I will propose to use, how often we will use them, and how much it will cost our client. For this job, I need to have access to a lot of detailed information about the mass media and I get this from two invaluable publications called *Brad* and *Where*. *Brad (British Rate and Data)* gives me up-to-date information about the costs of advertising in every medium, whereas *Where* tells me all I need to know about specific geographical areas of Britain. If I want to find out the percentage of Nottinghamshire families who own their own house or the percentage of ABC1s living in Gloucestershire I can get the answers from *Where*.

If I were asked to give students a set of guidelines for producing a candidate media list I would include the following:

— Always remember the nature of your product or service. For example, if you are advertising a service, how far can people be expected to travel to sample it? This would affect your choice of local newspaper as a possible advertising medium.

— Research the media thoroughly and choose the most appropriate for your product and audience.

— Remember to work within the constraints of your budget. A good guide to the cost-effectiveness of ads in newspapers is to work out the *cost per thousand* involved. This refers to the cost of reaching a thousand of the paper's readership. Here's a simple example:

— A full page display ad in the *Daily Mail* costs about £16 000.

— The average readership of the *Mail* is approximately 1.80m.

— There are 1800 thousands in 1.80m.

— Divide 16 000 by 1800 to give a cost per thousand of £8.88p.'

 TASK 4

Work out the following costs per thousand.

1. The *Guardian*:
   — Cost of full page display ad = £15 000
   — Readership of 524 000 (1986)
   — Cost per thousand?

2. *Daily Mirror*:
   — Cost of full page display ad = £22 000
   — Readership of 3.04m (1986)
   — Cost per thousand?

The candidate media list

As Wendy has told us, the accepted format for proposing which media to use in a campaign is the candidate media list or **media schedule**. Fig. 4C is a fictitious example which you can use as a model for the MAIN TASK.

MAIN TASK

During 1986 a private medical company called Medicheck based in Leicester and Nottingham decided it needed to raise its profile in the East Midlands. Obviously, they needed to have an effective advertising campaign planned for them. You will now have the opportunity to do this task. However, you will first need to know some basic facts about the campaign.

Length of campaign The campaign was planned to commence on 1 February and terminate on 26 April 1986.

Target audience and area The campaign was aimed at the general public in the cities of Derby, Nottingham and Leicester (and surrounding areas). See Fig. 4D.

Budget The advertising agency was allowed a budget of £13 000 for the campaign (you may assume that you can spend the full amount on media costs — disregard production costs).

Alexander Colbear Advertising

aca

REG. No. 1583738 ENGLAND
REGISTERED OFFICE Loversall Hall Loversall Doncaster S. Yorks. DN11 9DD
Vivian House, Vivian Avenue, Sherwood Rise, Nottingham. NG5 1AF.
Tel: 0602 602200 (6 lines)

MEDIA SCHEDULE

PROPOSED/REVISED/FINAL

CLIENT NORTHFIELDS MOTORS
PERIOD JULY 4th – AUGUST 8th
DATE TYPED MAY 6th

PUBLICATION	SIZE	COLOUR	POSITION	NO. OF INSERTS	COST PER INSERT	TOTAL COST	W/E	JULY 4	JULY 11	JULY 18	JULY 25	AUG 1	AUG 8						
MANCHESTER EVENING NEWS	11cm × 2cm	MONO	MOTOR TRADE	6	£183.70	£1102.20		X	X	X	X	X	X						
PICCADILLY RADIO	20 SECS	—	RATE AA 14.00 – 18.00	6	£148.00	£888			X	X	X	X	X						
GRANADA T.V.	20 SECS	—	LOCAL RATE (PEAK TIME) 17.20 – 23.00	2	£5440	£10,880		X					X						

Fig. 4C Northfield Motors: media schedule

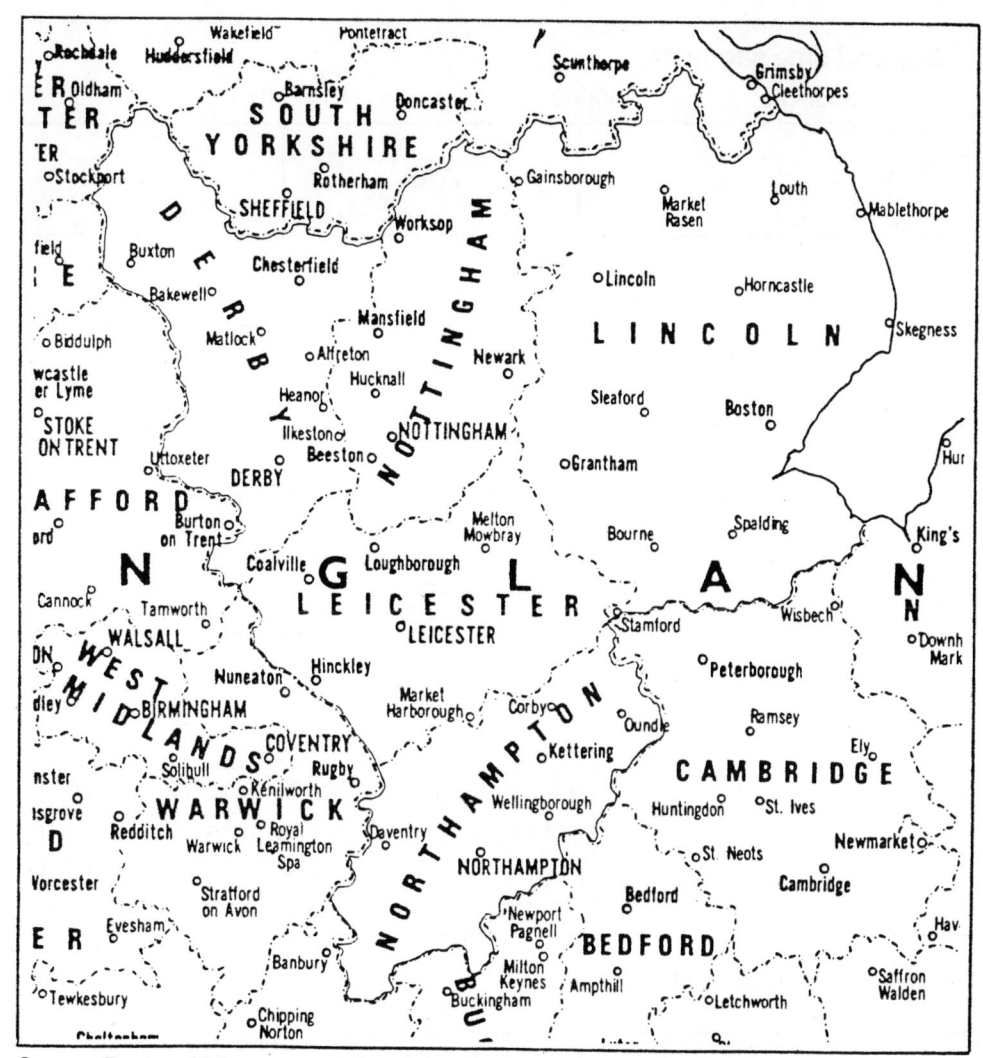

Source: Regional Newspaper Advertising Bureau
Fig. 4D The Medicheck target area

Publications available.

TITLE	CIRCULATION	COST OF ADVERTISEMENT
Nottingham Evening Post (Evening daily)	133 372	£174 for 11cm by 2cm Semidisplay ad (SD)
Nottingham Trader (Weekly freesheet)	171 400	£110 for 10cm by 2cm SD
Derby Evening Telegraph (Evening daily)	80 000	£98 for 11cm by 2cm SD
Derby Trader (Weekly freesheet)	120 000	£91 for 10cm by 2cm SD
Leicester Mercury (Evening daily)	156 954	£138 for 10cm by 2cm SD
Leicester Trader (Weekly freesheet)	163 000	£94 for 10cm by 2cm SD

Fig. 4E Local press in the target area

Broadcast media available If you feel that you need to widen your campaign you may decide to use independent radio and/or commercial television. In the East Midlands region this means using Radio Trent (incorporating Leicester Sound) and Central TV. Figs. 4F and 4G are the **rate cards** for each medium. They tell you how much it costs to advertise at certain times of the day.

As a media planner, your task is to plan a campaign for Medicheck using the most appropriate medium/media whilst keeping within your budget.

1. Make a copy of the candidate media list shown in Fig. 4C. Decide on the media you are going to use, the size/length of the individual adverts, what day they will be used and how much they will cost. When you have worked out your calculations in rough form, add them on to the list.

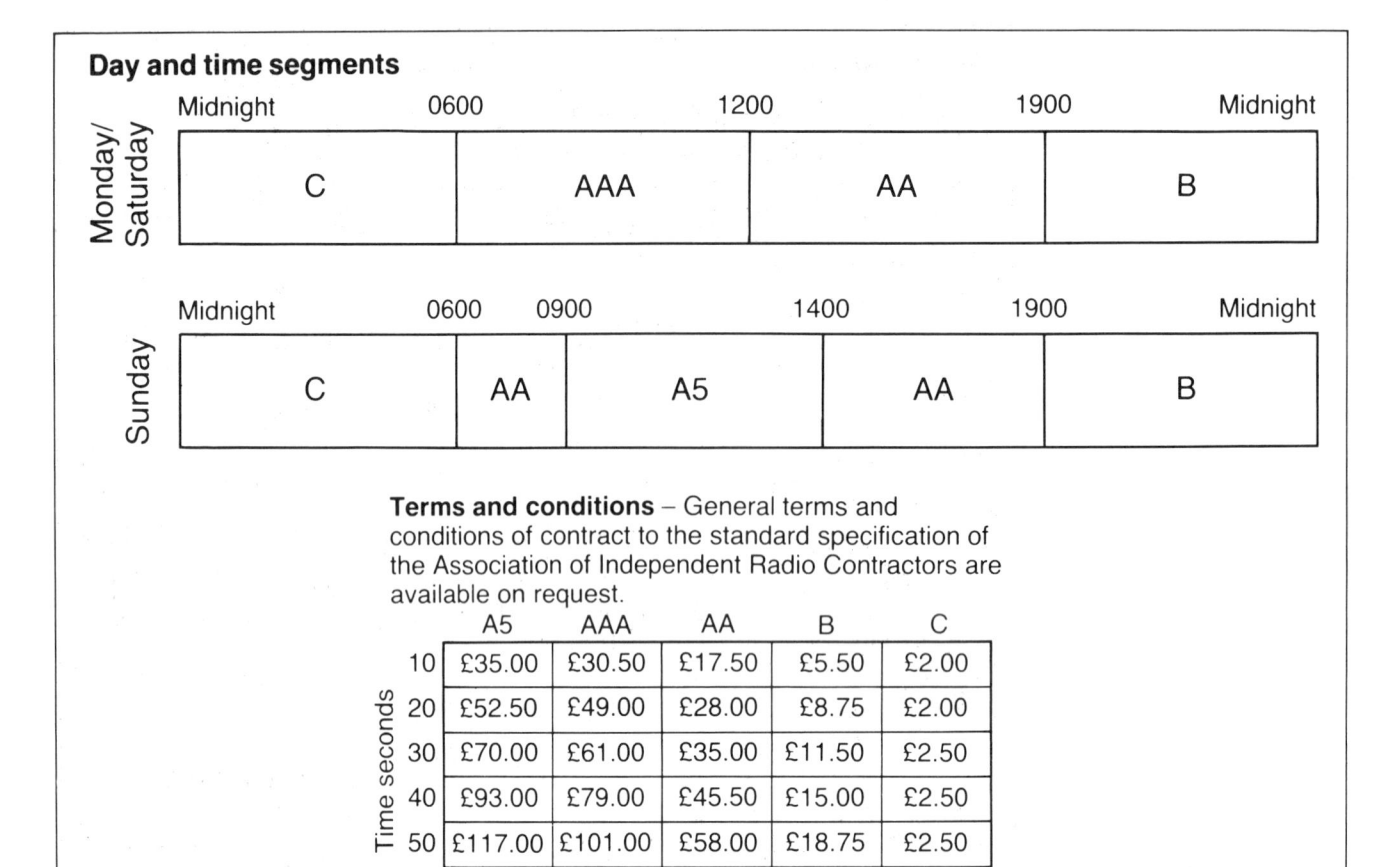

Day and time segments

Fig. 4F Radio Trent rate card

Central East

Regional Rates

A limited amount of airtime may be made available to advertisers whose trading activities are predominantly confined to the Central East area.

– PEAK

18.00 hours – 22.45 hours Monday to Saturday
19.00 hours – 22.45 hours Sunday

30 seconds	£1250
20 seconds	£1040
10 seconds	£625

– OFF PEAK

Up to 18.00 hours and after 22.45 hours Monday to Saturday
Up to 19.00 hours and after 22.45 hours Sunday

30 seconds	£250
20 seconds	£210
10 seconds	£125

Fig. 4G Central TV rate card

2. Write a *justification sheet* to accompany your candidate media list. Give detailed reasons for your choice of media.

Self-assessment

1. List and discuss *four* types of advertising campaign.
2. Define the term 'market segmentation'.
3. What is a 'target audience'?
4. What would an advertising agency be doing if it was 'trafficking' adverts?
5. Explain the role of the media planner in an advertising agency.
6. What is a candidate media list?
7. What is a 'cost per thousand' and why is it of use to advertisers?

PART 3 Assignments and Projects

1 *Producing promotional material*

This assignment contains the following sections:

- **Description of task**
- **Familiarisation with basic terms, techniques and procedures**
- **Group organisation and group decisions**
- **Pre-testing a draft, or sample, of the artefact**
- **Assessment of the artefact**
- **Self-assessment**

Description of task

In this practical assignment you have to design and produce promotional material for a national **pressure group**, which includes the following artefacts:

- A leaflet;
- A poster;
- A design for a badge or a car-sticker.

You should bear in mind the following points when producing your artefacts:

1. The content of the artefacts should accurately represent the social or political viewpoint of the pressure group you have chosen.
2. You should work in a small group of three or four students.

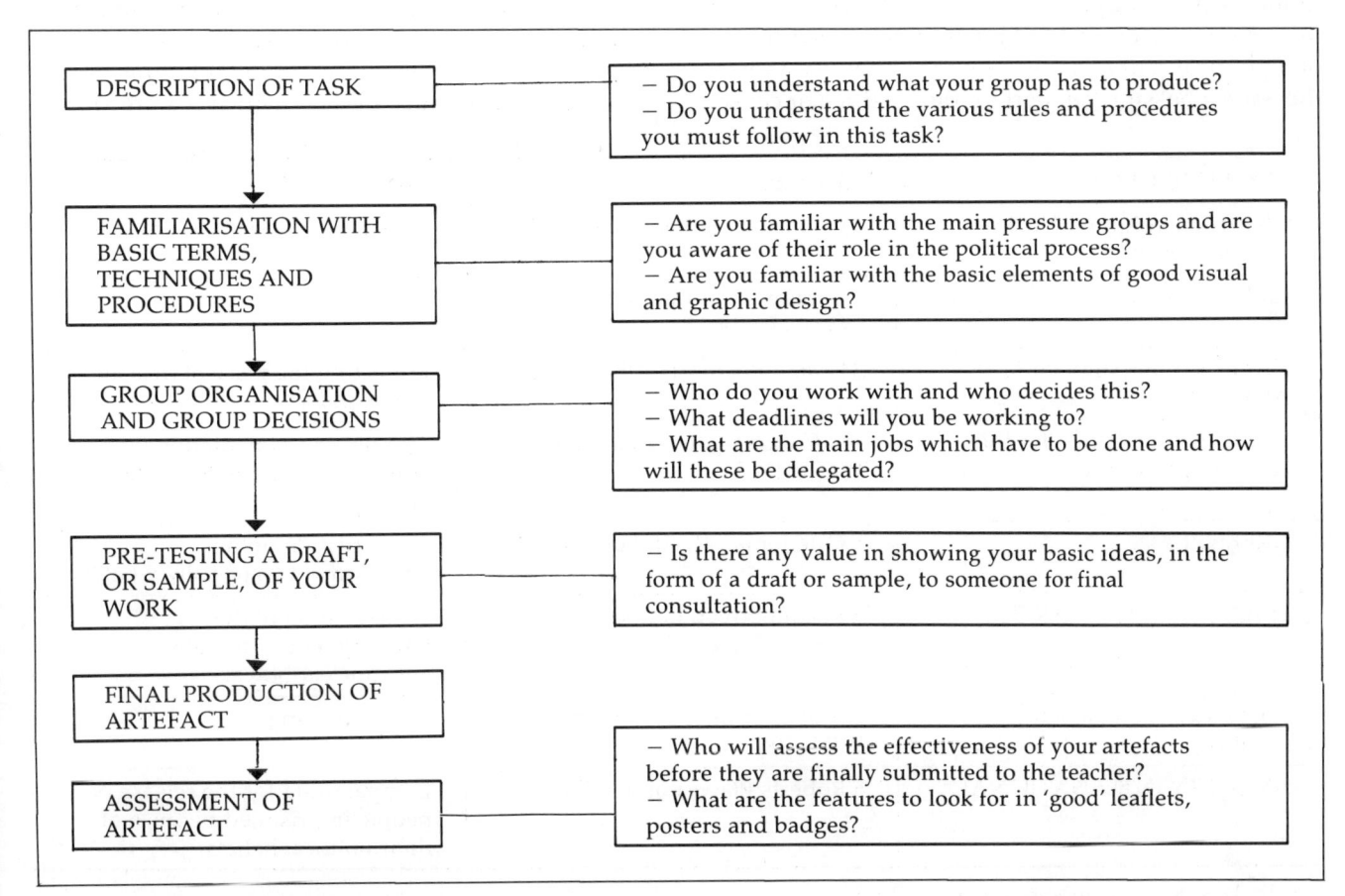

Fig. 1a Producing promotional artefacts

3. The promotional material you produce should reflect the basic elements of visual design explained in the next section of this assignment.
4. At the end of the assignment you will be asked to submit a written assessment of your artefacts.

It's obvious that in order to produce such artefacts you will need to be familiar with some basic guidelines for producing handbills, posters and badges — in short, material which needs **visual impact**. You will also need to be confident about working within a group. Fig. 1a is a flowchart to help to give you a clearer picture of the work ahead. Each major step represented in the flowchart is discussed in more detail throughout the sections in this assignment.

Familiarisation with basic terms, techniques and procedures

What is a pressure group?

A **pressure group** can be defined as a collection of people with a common viewpoint who campaign to influence public opinion and/or government policy on a particular social or political issue. Pressure groups are an essential part of our democratic process, since they give ordinary people the opportunity to get involved in politics without necessarily having to join a political party. Indeed, it is relatively rare for pressure groups to align themselves with any one political party; on the contrary, they try to win the widest possible support for their particular cause.

To use the jargon of the political world, pressure groups are a key part of the extra-parliamentary political process.

Most pressure groups are single-issue campaigns, in that they confine their activities to one particular issue or area of concern only. The Campaign for Nuclear Disarmament is a pressure group in that it has been publicly campaigning for over 25 years for Unilateral Nuclear Disarmament by Britain. Fig. 1b lists some of the more well-known pressure groups in Britain with a brief summary of their policies. You may be able to add to this checklist.

Visual impact

Pressure groups use a wide range of material to disseminate their ideas and publicise their cause. This material may include such media as posters, leaflets, car-stickers, badges, tee-shirts, and so on. Although these media may differ greatly in the detail of their design and content, they should possess an element of **visual impact** i.e. they should feature visual designs, or written captions, which are so immediately eye-catching that they 'grab' the attention of the passer-by (Fig. 1c). Even a leaflet which may contain a great deal of detailed written text should have an eye-catching cover design or title page.

Producing visual designs which are both eye-catching and memorable requires skill and imagination. However, there are some basic rules which are easy enough to follow. An important thing to remember is to produce designs which feature simple

PRESSURE GROUP	ADDRESS	BASIC POLICY
CND (Campaign for Nuclear Disarmament)	11 Goodwin Street, London N4	Unilateral Nuclear Disarmament
LIFE	7 Parade, Leamington Spa, Warwickshire	Anti-abortion
CAMRA (Campaign for Real Ale)	34 Alma Road, ST. Albans. Herts	Protecting the place of 'real ale' in our pubs
BUAV (British Union for the Abolition of Vivisection)	143 Charing Cross Road, London WC2H DEE	Against experimentation on animals (especially for make-up, etc.)
GREENPEACE	5 Caledonian Road, London N11	Conservation of the environment (especially whales)
FRIENDS OF THE EARTH	9 Poland Street, London	Conservation of the environment (especially anti-nuclear power)
ASH (Action on Smoking and Health)	27–35 Mortimer Street, London WIN 7RJ	Anti–smoking
AMNESTY INTERNATIONAL	5 Roberts Place, London EC1	Campaigning for the release of people imprisoned because of their political beliefs

Fig. 1b Well-known pressure groups in Britain

and bold images and avoid an excessive use of written text. For example, when designing a poster, or a leaflet cover, it is all too easy to say too much in words so that the end result looks more like a page of writing taken from a book. Fig. 1d shows a poster which is unlikely to attract the attention of the intended audience for this very reason.

Shape, size, and position of lettering

Of course, words and sentences can themselves be eye-catching when used in an appropriate way. Most printed material, including the words you are now reading, uses a **typeface** which is uniform in size and shape and which is arranged along straight, horizontal lines. This is a natural consequence of using mass-production printing processes and the need to produce large quantities of text which is recognisable and legible. However, the fact that we expect printed text to be arranged neatly in straight lines should not blind us to the possibilities of shaping and arranging words to produce special effects. For example, we can shape letters and phrases in such a way that they reflect the meanings we may wish to convey. Fig. 1e is a simple illustration of some of these possibilities.

Many designs aimed at children and teenagers need to be informal or 'relaxed', and this may be another reason why the graphic designer may deliberately move away from the use of conventional typeface. For example, the CND handbill shown in Fig. 1f uses handwritten lettering with an informal layout in an attempt to convey a youthful, 'streetwise' image.

Fig. 1c 'Grabbing' the attention of the passer-by

Fig. 1d A poster with little visual impact

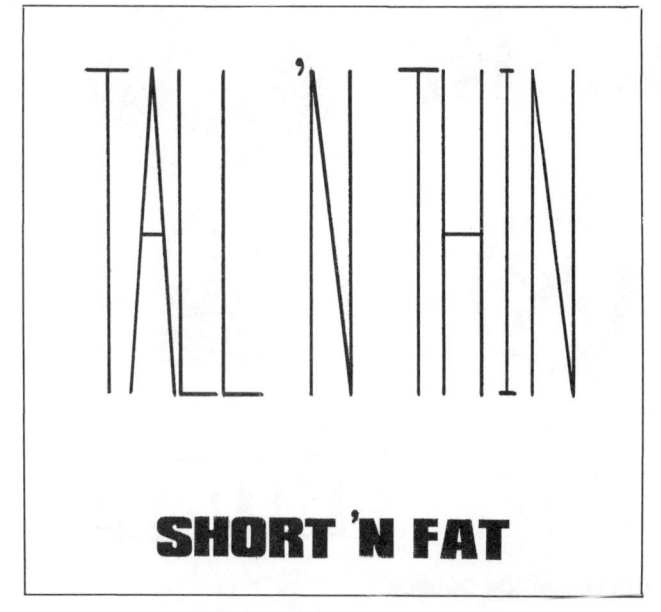

Fig. 1e The shape of a word can sometimes reflect its meaning

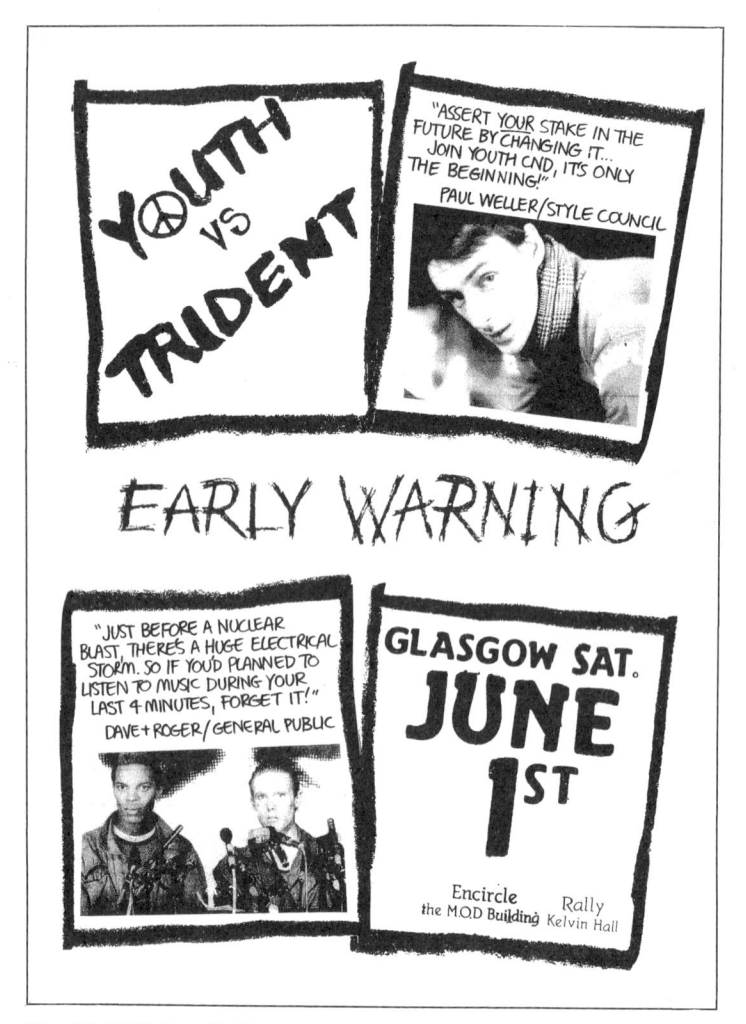

Fig. 1f CND handbill

Fig. 1g Contrasting logos

Not only should you think carefully about the shape and size of the lettering you may use, you should also think carefully about its position within the overall design. Avoid the temptation to begin writing in the top left-hand corner of the design space just out of habit. For example, consider the possibility of centring headings on either side of an invisible line running down the centre of the design.

Logos

Many pressure groups use the letters of their own names to form a familiar and instantly-recognisable symbol of their organisation. Such symbols are called **logos** and they are normally used as a hallmark on all of the publications and publicity material produced by a particular organisation. Although logos often feature the title of the pressure group, they can sometimes be purely visual, as in the case of the logo for the pressure group ASH. Fig. 1g shows several contrasting logos.

Slogans

Another way in which words can be used to have immediate impact is by exploiting their 'musical' potential. For example, the **slogan** 'Beanz Meanz Heinz' not only has a surprising visual effect, but it also possesses a rhythmical, echoing quality. Effective visual and graphic design often incorporates a simple, memorable slogan into a clear and equally simple visual image. The cover from the Health Education Council leaflet shown in Fig. 1h is a good example of this combination.

The media of promotion

The **production** and **distribution** of varied and effective promotional material is one of the most important activities of a pressure group. We have already mentioned how this material will probably include such media as posters, leaflets, car-stickers, badges, tee-shirts, and so on. What follows is a description of the main design characteristics of the many different media used by pressure groups.

Posters
– No smaller than A3 in size
– High in visual impact, low in detailed, written text
– Usually a clear, simple image with a simple, bold slogan
– Usually carries a logo

Handbills
– Handed out on the street, or pushed through letter boxes
– Usually single sheets of A5, unfolded

Measles is misery

and your child needn't have it

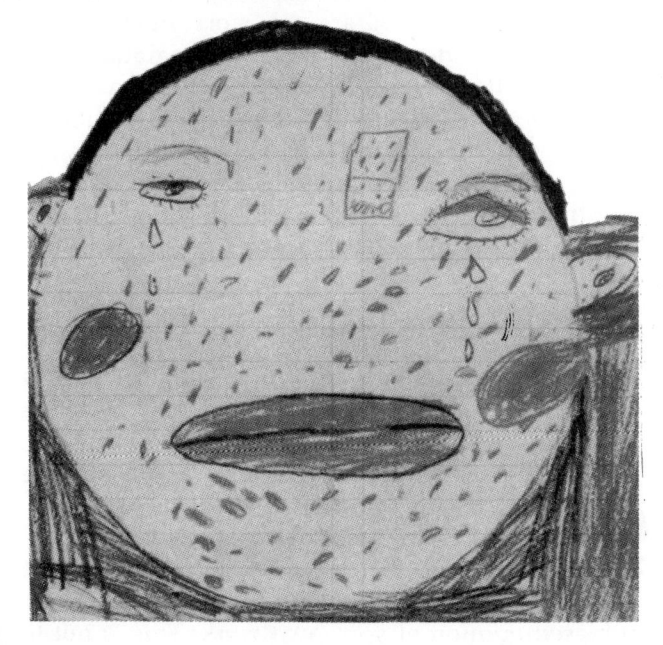

Fig. 1h Combining an effective slogan with a simple image

— High in visual impact on the front, more detailed written information on the reverse side
— Usually includes a 'tear-off' section on the reverse side with an address for requesting further information
— Usually carries a logo

Leaflets

— A single sheet, usually A4, often folded once to produce a front cover of A5 size (alternatively, the sheet could be folded vertically more than once to form several panels of text)
— High in visual impact on the front cover, more detailed written information on the inner panels
— Usually contains a 'tear-off' section with an address for requesting further information
— Usually carries a logo

Factsheets

— Usually a single sheet of A4 or A5, unfolded
— Often low in visual impact with key facts about the aims and issues associated with the pressure group listed on both sides of the sheet
— Usually requested by individuals who are sympathetic to the pressure group and who wish to find out more about the aims and issues involved
— Usually carries a logo

Car stickers

— Usually just a logo, a slogan, or a simple visual image

Labels

— For sticking on things such as brief-cases, satchels, folders, coat lapels, collecting tins, and so on
— Usually just a logo, a slogan, or a simple visual image

Badges

— Usually just a logo, a slogan, or a simple visual image

Tee-shirts

— Usually just a logo, a slogan, or a simple visual image silk-screened onto the fabric

Group organisation and group decisions

You should now be sufficiently familiar with the aims of your chosen pressure group, and with basic elements of visual design, to enable you to produce the necessary promotional material. However, before you can produce your artefacts there are certain key decisions about procedure which your working group should make. Here are some of the points which you should discuss and agree before you start any actual production work.
— Who will decide how your class is to be divided up into the smaller working groups? Should this be decided by the class as a whole, or by your teacher? Would it be better for you to work with a friend, or someone you don't normally sit with? Would it be better to mix different personality types together, or to try and put them in separate groups — for example, introverts in one group and extroverts in another?
— How much time should be given to producing the artefacts? Would it be useful to work to a series of written deadlines? If so, will you have a series of 'mini-deadlines', one for each particular stage of the production process? Who should decide and monitor the deadlines you may use?
— Would it be useful to elect one member of the group as a co-ordinator whose job it would be to regulate and bring together the various activities of the group?
— What approach will you decide to use? Obviously, this may depend upon the kind of issue you have chosen to promote. For example, for some issues a humorous approach might prove effective in capturing the attention of the audience. However, for some issues a more serious approach may be more appropriate. You may even feel that the only appropriate and effective way is to shock the audience by presenting the issues in a very stark and direct manner.

— How many themes will your group decide to use? Will you choose a different theme, and a different approach, for each individual artefact, or will you decide to use the same theme throughout in order to emphasise the fact that your separate artefacts are aspects of a single well thought-out promotion?

— What are the major jobs which have to be done to produce the artefacts, and who will do what? Will you delegate particular jobs to particular individuals, or will you all do a bit of everything?

Pre-testing a draft, or sample, of the artefact

In any design and production process, whether it be for a communication artefact or for a manufactured product, it is essential that a draft or mock-up of the basic idea be tested, or checked, before final production begins. In the communication and media industry there would be two groups of people who should be consulted and shown a draft of your basic idea. Firstly, there is the **audience** at whom the message of the artefact is directed. For example, if you were unsure as to whether the register, or the content, of the artefact was appropriate, you could always ask a sample of the audience for their opinion. In advertising and manufacturing this would be called **market research**. Secondly, the **client** who commissioned the artefact would normally want to see the basic idea to be reassured that he or she was getting broadly what was asked for.

As we shall see in the chapter on projects, **pre-testing** an artefact, and consulting with a client, are key features of good project work. In this particular assignment it would be useful to pre-test artefacts like a poster by showing more than one version of a draft design to other students of your school or college. As we discussed in Chapter 1, You the Receiver, perception is a very individual process and what may strike you as a very original and effective design may appear less appealing to others. In the case of a leaflet your draft should take the form of a mock-up; that is, a sheet of paper folded into the size and shape of your final artefact and containing a rough sketch of your text layout.

Whatever draft designs of your artefacts you choose to make, you should at least make sure that you have submitted them to your teacher for discussion before any real production work begins. In this way you will get a useful second opinion on your basic ideas, and become used to the process of pre-testing and consultation.

Assessment of the artefact

Let us assume that you have now produced the finished designs for your promotional material. However, your work is not yet finished. Your next task is to produce a written assessment of your artefacts. This raises the very important question of what makes a 'good' artefact? What are we looking for when we assess an artefact? Are we looking at the amount of work and effort which has been put into the finished product? Is it the quality of the technical aspects of the production which should impress us most? Or are we more interested in whether the artefact arouses and maintains the interest of the audience? Other key questions to ask are: who assesses, and what methods should be used? Before you begin the final part of the assignment, you should try and answer some of these questions by discussing the following three issues: Who assesses? How should we assess? What questions should be asked?

Who assesses?

One way of assessing your work would be to rely upon your own opinion, or that of your working group, to say how 'good' it is. After all, you may say, we are the ones who best understand what the artefacts are trying to achieve. However, this may not be the most satisfactory way of reaching a conclusion. It may be that there are too many factors which would prevent you from reaching a clear, unbiased opinion of your own work. This is not to suggest that you would cheat, or that you would not make a conscious effort to be fair. The point is that we are likely to be prejudiced in favour of our own work, even though we may not be conscious of this. (Remember the discussion in Chapter 1 of the power of the mind to influence our interpretation of people and events?)

Perhaps a more effective way of assessing your artefacts would be to ask the opinion of other people. An obvious example would be to try out the material on the audience for which it was intended. After all, one test of how 'good' your artefacts are would be to see how effective they are in holding the attention of the audience. Another example might be to show your work to someone who is experienced at producing promotional material; an advertising agency, for example. Such an expert would certainly be able to comment on your basic ideas, and perhaps also on the technical aspects of your production.

Whatever individuals, or group of individuals, you choose to show your artefacts to, it is important that you include some outside opinion in your evaluation. In this particular assignment it may not be practicable to test your work on the intended audience, or to consult the opinions of experts. In this case you may decide upon the compromise of trying out your artefacts on those members of the class not involved in your working group. For the purposes of this assignment, in order to get some feedback fairly easily and quickly, this may be the best option.

How should we assess?

Whichever opinions you decide to base your assessment upon, what will be the method you will use to obtain and record them? Will you ask people to fill out a questionnaire which you can collect and analyse later? Will you show your finished material to a group and then have an informal general discussion afterwards? Would it be better to interview each member of this group separately? Is there a particular method of obtaining and recording feedback which is more effective than others, or doesn't it matter which way you do it?

What questions should be asked?

Whatever method of obtaining feedback you choose, whether you use a questionnaire or an interview technique, you need some idea of the kind of questions you want answering. Here are a few examples, organised under the four headings of: Use of the medium, Quality of presentation, Relevance of content, Appropriateness of approach.

Use of the medium. Have the various possibilities of each medium been developed intelligently and imaginatively within the conventions normally used? Specifically:
— Does each artefact have sufficient visual impact to win the attention of the audience? In the case of the poster and the car sticker the overall design should be effective at a distance of several metres. In the case of the leaflet the front cover should have a clear and attractive design which is distinct from the more detailed text.

Quality of presentation. Have the artefacts been produced to a good technical standard? Specifically:
— Is there an overall impression that the material has been produced with care and thought, or is there evidence of 'sloppiness'?
— If a paste-up technique has been used, are the various elements of the design mounted neatly and cleanly to form a single whole?
— Is the lettering and printed text legible?

Relevance of content. This category only applies to the leaflet in that it is the one artefact in this assignment which is likely to contain any detailed information. Specifically:
— Is the information contained in the leaflet a fair and accurate reflection of the aims of the chosen pressure group?
— Is the information contained in the leaflet sufficiently simple and general to appeal to the wide audience of people unfamiliar with the aims of the chosen pressure group?

Appropriateness of approach. Is the general approach sufficiently bold and direct to win the attention and sympathy of the audience, whilst at the same time showing a sensitive handling of serious and delicate issues? Specifically:
— Is the approach too bland to win the support and sympathy of the audience? For example, in the case of the leaflet is there so much detailed information that it is difficult to discern any clear and convincing points of view?
— Is the approach too flippant or too 'casual' for the seriousness of the chosen issues? Is the approach too shocking and too direct for the handling of sensitive issues?

Self-assessment

1. In planning and making your promotional material your group made a series of decisions and carried out a number of tasks. Produce a flowchart which represents the main decisions and tasks involved in producing your artefacts.
2. What is a 'pressure group' and what do pressure groups do?
3. List the various media of promotion which pressure groups normally use to disseminate their ideas. Write brief notes on the main characteristics of each medium.
4. What is meant by 'visual impact'? Discuss how you would attempt to ensure that a poster design had visual impact.
5. What is a 'logo'?
6. Produce a written guide which communication students might use to assess communication artefacts. Be sure to begin your guide with a brief discussion of what we might mean by a 'good' artefact.

2 *Producing an illustrated booklet*

This assignment contains the following sections:
- Description of the task
- Familiarisation with basic terms, techniques, and procedures
- Group organisation and group decisions
- Pre-testing a draft, or sample, of the artefact
- Assessment of the artefact
- Self-assessment

Description of the task

In this practical assignment you have to produce a brief, illustrated booklet introducing a major topic in communication studies. The points you must bear in mind when producing your artefact are as follows:

1. The booklet should be suitable for use with students who are new to a communication studies course which is similar to the one you have been following.

2. The booklet should be a brief and general introduction to one of the following topics: Non-verbal communication, Purposes of communication, Techniques of persuasion in the media.

3. Booklets will be produced by small working groups with three or four students in each.

4. At the end of the assignment submit sufficient photocopies of the booklet to enable each working group to have a copy. Also submit the original sheets from which you made your copies.

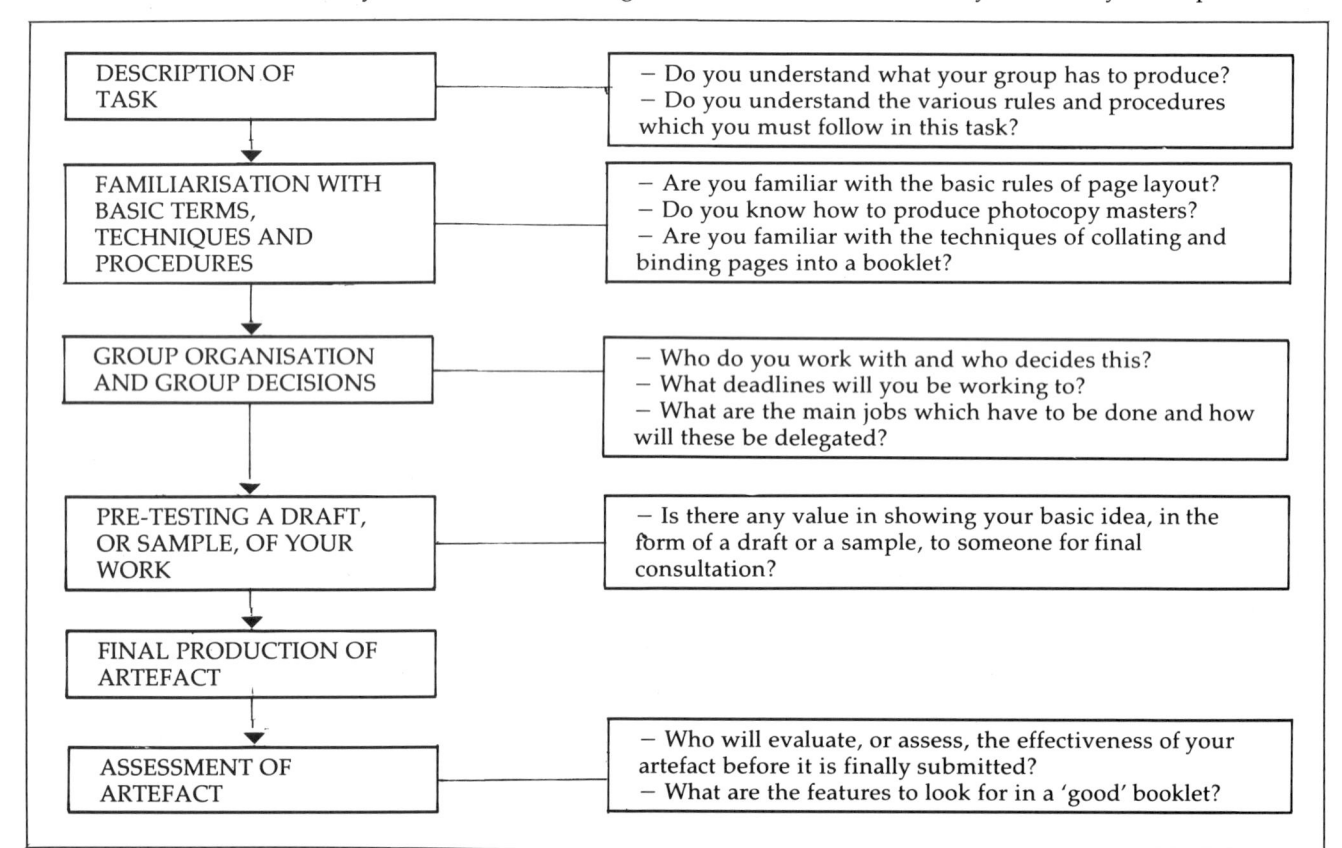

Fig. 2a Producing a booklet

5. At the end of the assignment you will be asked to submit a written assessment of your artefact.

It's obvious that in order to produce such an artefact you will need to be familiar with the basic techniques of making a booklet, and also to be confident about working within a group. Fig. 2a is a flowchart to help to give you a clearer picture of the work ahead. Each major step represented in this flowchart is discussed in more detail throughout the sections of this chapter.

Familiarisation with basic terms, techniques, and procedures

Format and page layout

By **format** we mean the physical size and shape of the booklet. What will be the format of your booklet? A4 or A5 are two common sizes which you may like to consider. A further point is whether your booklet will be **landscape**, or **portrait** A4 or A5. Some possible booklet formats are shown in Fig. 2b. A further possibility would be to consider using A4 sheets folded and stapled down the centre to form an A5 'pocket size' booklet. Equally, you could photocopy onto A3 – double the size of A4 – and fold and staple into A4.

No matter how original and imaginative your artefact turns out to be, there are some basic rules of page layout which all booklets, and books, should follow. What are these basic rules or conventions? You will know from your own experience that most books have the following features:
– A title page, a contents page, an introduction, and the main body of the text divided into sections or chapters.
– Each page numbered; sometimes there are also chapter or section numbers.
– Consistency of major headings. For example, if one chapter or section heading is printed in a certain size and style of lettering, then all chapter or section headings should use this style and size.
– Consistency of page layout. For example, if one page of the text is arranged into several vertical columns, then it's advisable that all pages should be arranged in this way.
– Depending upon its purpose, the book or booklet may simply end with a final chapter, or it may finish with a definite conclusion, or a glossary, or an index.
– An appropriate balance between visual illustration and written text. The 'feel' of a book can be determined by the amount of visual illustration it contains. For example, some instruction manuals can appear 'unfriendly' to the user because they may not contain sufficient visual material. One further point is that whatever visual material is included it should be

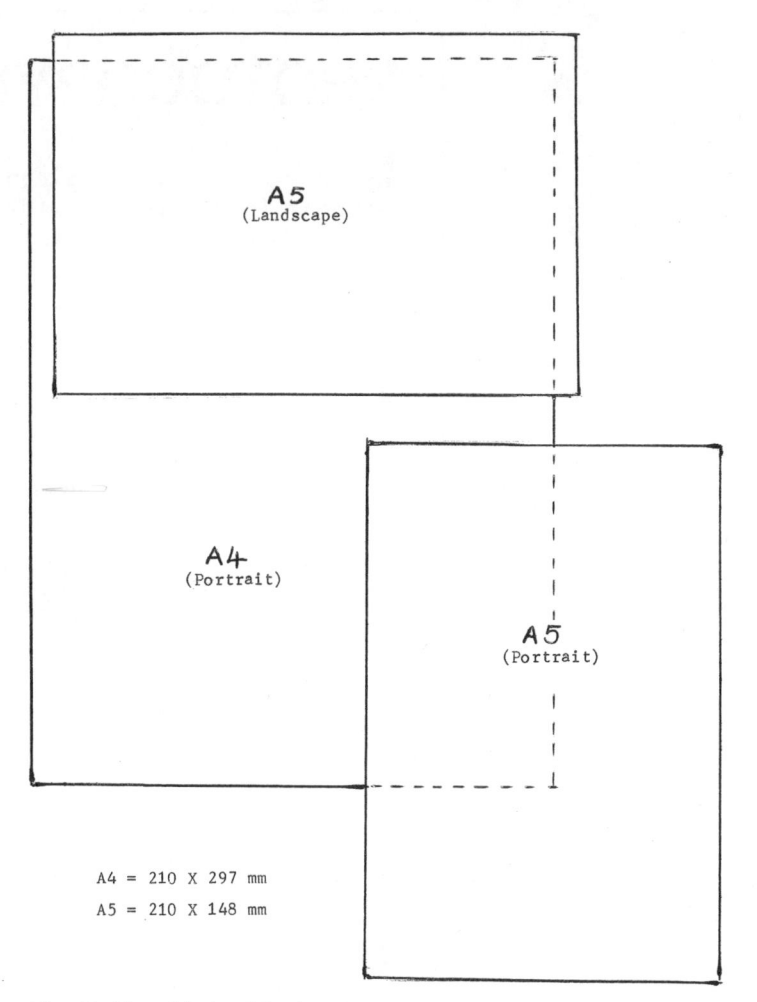

A4 = 210 X 297 mm
A5 = 210 X 148 mm

Fig. 2b Possible booklet formats

positioned sensibly within the written text so as to appear relevant.

In this assignment, your group may decide that only some of the conventions listed above are relevant. However, it is important that you should discuss the overall organisation of the contents of your booklet and agree upon some basic rules. Without these your artefact may appear disorganised and it may be difficult for the reader to follow.

Producing photocopy masters

The object of this assignment is to produce several copies of an illustrated booklet. However, it is worth remembering the simple and obvious point that before this can be achieved, you must first produce a single set of **masters** from which all of your booklets will later be photocopied. Your masters should be kept in a safe place, separate from the photocopied sheets which you will collate and bind together for distribution. There are certain basic rules of producing photocopy masters which you should bear in mind. These are:

PHOTOCOPYING

1. Leave at least a two centimetre margin around an A4 master. Don't forget that a wider margin may be required at the left-hand-side, to allow for stapling, binding etc.

2. don't forget **varied** text can **BE** *"PASTED-UP"* to produce *A. "Master"*

3. Don't forget that poor, "un-contrasty" visuals like this:

Produce poor unclear photocopies like this:

Whereas, clear, "contrasty" visuals like this:

Produce clear photocopies like this:

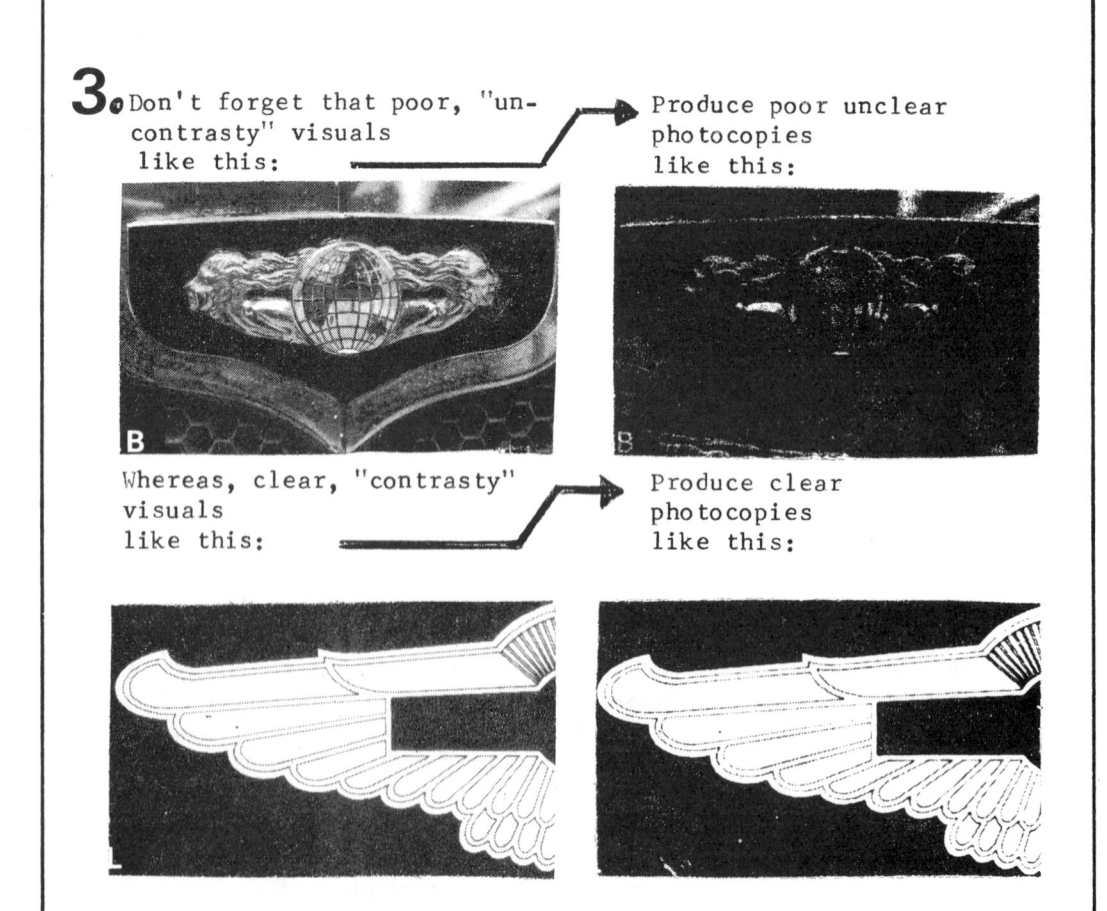

Fig. 2c Points to consider when producing photocopy masters

— Always produce your masters using just one side of a single sheet. There are two main reasons for this. The first is that if you use both sides of a sheet, and then make a major error on one side, you may end up throwing away twice the amount of work. The second reason is that any material which has been arranged on the reverse side of a master may have a tendency to photocopy through onto the finished copies. (If you want your finished copies to be printed on both sides of the page — 'back to back' — then this can easily be done at the photocopy stage.)

— Always leave a clear, unused margin around the edge of each master. It's often useful to agree upon a standard margin (say 2cm on an A4 master) and then draw these lightly in pencil on each master before you begin.

— The left-hand margins may have to be wider than the other margins, depending upon the method you choose to bind your booklet.

— Don't forget that masters can be built up by arranging and sticking a variety of separately-produced pictures, titles and pieces of writing onto a single sheet of paper. The resulting master is called a 'paste-up', and although the original may look like a jigsaw, the resulting photocopies will look 'clean' and 'even'.

— Don't forget that most photocopiers only produce black and white copies. It's important to remember that many of the different shades in a colour photograph will be photocopied as a variety of indistinct greys. For this reason, try and build up masters which use pictures which have clear contrast between areas of light and shade.

Fig. 2c summarises some of the basic points to remember when producing photocopy masters. Fig. 2d shows an example of 'ready-made' illustrations and symbols which are commercially available.

Fig. 2d Examples of 'ready-made' illustrations

Collating and binding

Collating refers to the process of arranging your photocopies in the correct order, and in the correct quantities, ready for binding into the finished artefact. There are mechanical collating machines, and some photocopiers with automatic collators, which will do the job for you. However, the method you are most likely to use is simply to lay out your photocopies on a very long table!

As for binding, there are several different methods which you could use. Here are some possibilities.
— Punch a hole in the top left-hand corner of the photocopies and tie them together using a 'treasury tag'.
— Staple the photocopies along the left-hand margin.
— Staple the photocopies down the centre fold of the folded booklet. For this you will probably need a long-arm stapler to reach to the centre of the booklet.
— Buy a special plastic comb to slide down the left-hand edge of the photocopies.
— Use a commercial spiral binding machine to perforate the left-hand edge of the sheets which are then bound together with a plastic spiral comb.
— Simply perforate the sheets using a hole punch and present them in a ring binder.

Group organisation and group decisions

You should now be aware of most of the basic techniques involved in producing an illustrated booklet. However, before you can go away and produce your artefact there are certain key decisions about procedure which your working group should make. Here are some of the points which you should discuss and agree before you start any actual production work:
— Who will decide how your class is to be divided up into the smaller working groups? Should this be decided by the class as a whole, or by your teacher? Would it be better for you to work with a friend, or someone you don't normally sit with? Would it be better to mix different personality types together, or to try and put them in separate groups — for example, introverts in one group and extroverts in another?
— How much time should be given to producing the artefact? Would it be useful to work to a series of written deadlines? If so, will you have a series of 'mini-deadlines', one for each particular stage of the production process? Who should decide and monitor the deadlines you may use?
— Would it be useful to elect one member of the group as a co-ordinator whose job it would be to regulate and bring together the various activities of the group?
— What approach will you decide might be most appropriate for your audience? Should you use a lighthearted approach, possibly following a cartoon, or comic-strip, style? Or should your booklet be more serious and more formal, more like a proper text-book? Fig. 2e shows two contrasting approaches used by students in this assignment.
— How detailed should your booklet be? Should it be merely an illustration, a 'bringing to life', of the basic points, or should it go beyond this, into greater detail? (At this point you may wish to refer back to the original description of the task.)
— What are the major jobs which have to be done to produce the booklet, and who will do what? Will you delegate particular jobs to particular individuals, or will you all do a bit of everything?

Pre-testing a draft, or sample, of the artefact

In any design and production process, whether it be for a communication artefact or for a manufactured product, it is essential that a draft or mock-up of the basic idea be tested, or checked, before final production begins. In the communication and media industry there would be two groups of people who should be consulted and shown a draft of your basic idea. Firstly, there is the **audience** at whom the message of the artefact is directed. For example, if you were unsure as to whether the register, or the content of the artefact was appropriate, you could always ask a sample of the audience for their opinion. In advertising and manufacturing this would be called **market research**. Secondly, the **client** who commissioned the artefact would normally want to see the basic idea to be reassured that he or she was getting broadly what was asked for.

As we shall see in the chapter on projects, pre-testing an artefact, and consulting with a client, are key features of good project work. In this particular assignment it may be appropriate to pre-test your idea on other students in your class. After all, your class is probably not very different in age from the audience at which the booklet is aimed. Whether or not you pre-test your idea on the audience, you should certainly submit something to your teacher who, in this case, is the client. In this way you will get a useful second opinion on your basic idea, and become used to the process of client consultation.

What is it then that you should submit to a client? There are a number of different possibilities for each different medium. However, in the case of a booklet the following should be sufficient to enable the client to comment usefully on your basic idea:
— A copy of your contents page, showing the overall organisation and contents of the proposed booklet.
— A detailed mock-up of a typical page, or section, to show the type of page layout you intend to use and to illustrate the balance between written text and visuals.

Hi, I'm Butch, the talking doggie hero of this booklet. Bet you didn't know that dogs could talk! But get this, I can communicate in other ways too, and for all sorts of reasons. The aim of this booklet is to explain the various reasons why people (and dogs for that matter) communicate with each other. But anyway, less of the talking and away we go. ....

Very often we communicate with people in order to achieve or obtain something, like a pint of beer in the picture below. We call this the "instrumental function" of communication.

Write two of your own examples below.

Fig. 2e Differing approaches to the subject

Assessment of the artefact

Hopefully, you have now produced several copies of your finished booklet. However, your work is not yet finished. Your next task is to produce a written assessment of your artefact. This raises the very important question of what makes a 'good' artefact? What are we looking for when we assess an artefact? Are we looking at the amount of work and effort which has been put into the finished product? Is it the quality of the technical aspects of the production which should impress us most? Or are we more interested in whether the artefact arouses and maintains the interest of the audience? Other key questions to ask are: Who assesses and what methods should be used? Before you begin the final part of your assignment, you should try and answer some of these questions by discussing the following three issues: Who assesses? How should we assess? What questions should be asked?

Who assesses?

One way of assessing your booklet would be to rely upon your own opinion, or that of your working group, to say how 'good' it is. After all, you may say, we are the ones who best understand what the artefact is trying to achieve. However, this may not be the most satisfactory way of reaching a conclusion. It may be that there are too many factors which would prevent you from reaching a clear, unbiased opinion of your own work. This is not to suggest that you would cheat, or that you would not make a conscious effort to be fair. The point is that we are likely to be prejudiced in favour of our own work, even though we may not be conscious of this. (Remember the discussion in Chapter 1 of the power of the mind to influence our interpretation of people and events?)

Perhaps a more effective way of assessing your artefact would be to ask the opinion of other people. An obvious example would be to try out the booklet on the audience for which it was intended. After all, one test of how 'good' your artefact is would be to see how effective it is in holding the attention of its audience. Another example might be to show your booklet to someone who is experienced at producing books and booklets; a commercial publisher, for example. Such an expert would certainly be able to comment on some aspects of your artefact. However, would they be the best people to say whether your artefact was a good piece of communication on its particular subject for its particular audience?

Whatever individuals, or group of individuals you choose to show your artefact to, it is important that you include some outside opinion in your evaluation. In this particular assignment it may not be practicable to test the artefact on the intended audience, or to consult the opinions of experts. In this case you may decide upon the compromise of trying out your artefact on those members of the class not involved in your working group. For the purposes of this assignment, in order to get some feedback fairly easily and quickly, this may be the best option.

How should we assess?

Whichever opinions you decide to base your assessment upon, what will be the method you will use to obtain and record them? Will you ask people to fill out a questionnaire which you can collect and analyse later? Will you show copies of the booklet to a group and then have an informal general discussion afterwards? Would it be better to interview each member of this group separately? Is there a particular method of obtaining and recording feedback which is more effective than others, or doesn't it matter which way you do it?

What questions should be asked?

Whatever method you choose to obtain feedback, whether you use a questionnaire or an interview technique, you need some idea of the kind of questions you want answering. Here are a few examples, organised under the four headings of: Use of the medium, Quality of presentation, Relevance of content, Appropriateness of approach.

Use of the medium. Have the various possibilities of the medium been developed intelligently and imaginatively within the conventions normally used for producing booklets? Specifically:
- Is the booklet organised in such a way that it is easy to follow and easy to make sense of? Has the booklet been organised into chapters, sections, or units? Is there a contents page which spells out the general organisation?
- Is there sufficient consistency in the layout of the text? For example, are the section, and sub-section, headings consistent in size and style throughout the booklet? Are the margins consistent from one page to another? In general, does the booklet look as though it has been designed by several different people with little thought to its overall 'feel'?
- Is there an appropriate balance between visual material and written text? Are there too many illustrations, or too few? Has the visual material been located intelligently within the text, having regard to its relevance, and with a sensitive awareness of the use of space?

Quality of presentation. Has the booklet been produced to a good technical standard? Specifically:
- Is the writing, or printing, legible?

− Are there ugly lines and shadows across the page, making it obvious where a paste-up technique has been clumsily used?

− Are the diagrams and pictures clear, neat, and reasonably attractive?

− Is the overall impression one of neatness and tidiness?

− Have the pages been correctly collated and adequately bound?

Relevance of content. Is the content of the booklet relevant to the aim of introducing a key topic in communication studies to new students? Specifically:

− Does the booklet accurately cover one of the subject areas asked for in the task?

− Does the booklet cover information which was not asked for in the task?

− Is there too much or too little information for the stated purpose of the booklet?

− Are there any areas which have been covered in too much detail, and are there other areas which have not been covered enough?

Appropriateness of approach. Is the general approach of the booklet, and the register of the text, appropriate to the student audience? Specifically:

− Is the approach too serious and formal?

− Is the approach too informal, too jokey or flippant?

− Are words and terms used which are too complicated or too specialised for new students to understand? Does the text contain jargon which is not explained?

− Is the language used so simple that it seems to 'talk down' to the audience?

Self-assessment

1. As we have seen in earlier chapters, a model is a simple means of structuring and presenting an idea or process. One model which is often used to analyse communication processes (Lasswell's model 1948) poses the following questions:

   > Who
   > says What
   > to Whom
   > How
   > with What effect.

   Use this model to analyse the message communicated by your booklet.

2. In planning and making your booklet, your group made a series of decisions and carried out a number of tasks. Produce a flowchart which represents the main decisions and tasks involved in producing your booklet.

3. Briefly describe the format of your booklet and the overall organisation of its contents. State the main reasons for your group's choice.

4. Produce a list of 'do's' and 'dont's' for making good photocopy masters.

5. Produce a written guide which communication students might use to assess communication artefacts. Be sure to begin your guide with a brief discussion of what we might mean by a 'good' artefact.

3 *Producing a tape/slide sequence*

This assignment contains the following sections:

- Description of the task
- Familiarisation with basic terms, techniques and procedures
- Group organisation and group decisions
- Pre-testing a draft, or sample, of the artefact
- Assessment of the artefact
- Self-assessment

Description of the task

In this practical assignment you are asked to work with a small group of students to help produce a short tape/slide sequence which will be entered for a national media competition. The rules of the competition state that:

1. The sequence should be approximately ten minutes in length and consist of no more than thirty 35mm slides.
2. The subject of the sequence should be your school or college, and the audience should be the parents of prospective pupils and students. The aim of the tape/slide is to present a broad picture of the life of the school or college.
3. Each sequence submitted will be judged in terms of technical presentation, sensitive and imaginative use of the medium and the appropriateness of the artefact to the stated audience.

At the end of this practical assignment, when the tape/slide sequence has been finished, you are asked to produce a written assessment of your artefact.

It's obvious that in order to produce such an artefact you will need to be familiar with basic techniques of tape/slide production, and also to be confident about working within a group. Fig. 3a is a flowchart to help to give you a clearer picture of the work ahead. Each major step represented in this flowchart is discussed in more detail throughout the sections of this chapter.

Familiarisation with basic terms, techniques and procedures

The various audio and visual elements of tape/slide

It is very tempting to look at tape/slide as a kind of 'poor man's video'; that is, as a medium for use when there is no access to video equipment. However, if tape/slide is handled sensitively, and used for the right purpose, it can be a very effective medium. Can you think of any examples where tape/slide might be a more appropriate medium to use than video?

At its worst, tape/slide could be just one monotonous voice linked loosely to a sequence of unimaginative or irrelevant slides. At its best, tape/slide could be a rich association of natural sounds and lively, colourful voices synchronised sensitively and expertly to a sequence of varied and interesting images.

The first stage in learning about tape/slide is to become aware of the various audio and visual possibilities of the medium. Some of these are listed below:

Audio. – Natural sounds; street noises, the wind in trees, a baby crying, etc.
– Music; as an introduction, for dramatic effect, etc.
– Commentary; simple description, open questions, question and answer, etc.
– Dialogue; interviewer and interviewee, characters in slides talking, etc.
– Silence.
– Combinations of the above; commentary over background music, use of special-effect sounds, etc.
– Fading or 'dissolving' sounds one into another.

Visual. – Captions; for introductory titles, for breaking the sequence into sections, etc.
– Copying from books and other material; drawings, diagrams, maps, etc.
– Captions superimposed on pictures.
– Camera angle and camera shot; close-up shots, long shots, low-angle shots, etc.

Combining and overlapping audio and visual elements. – Linking sound with vision; can the spoken commentary be used to link images by a

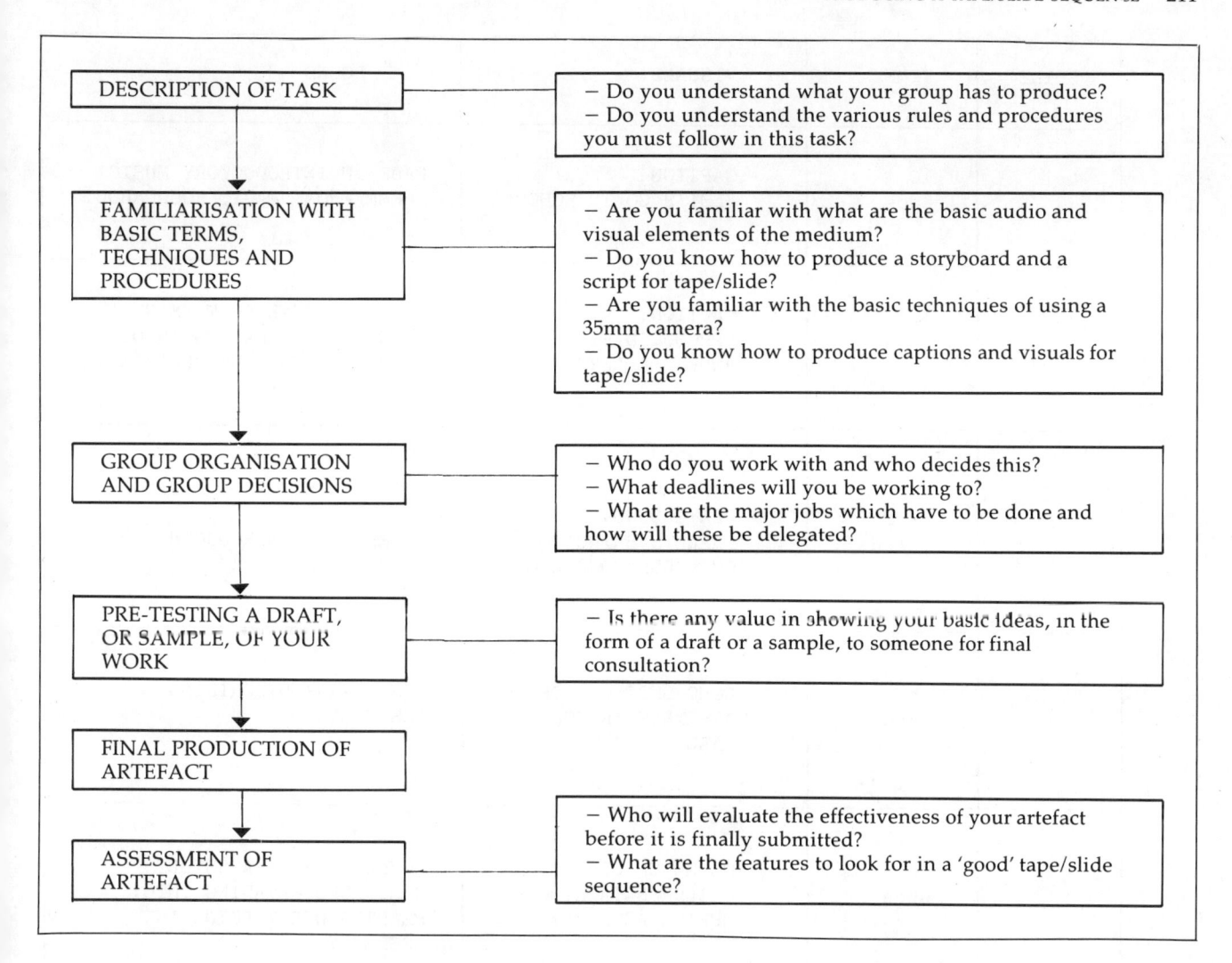

Fig. 3a Producing a short tape/slide sequence

sentence being spoken as one slide ends and the succeeding slide begins?
— Speed or pace of the sequence; should a spoken commentary dictate when the slides change, or should the changing of slides be dictated by other factors?
— If a twin projection system is available — two projectors synchronised together — how should images be faded, one from another, to complement the sound?

Storyboards and scripts

One of the first major jobs you will have to do before you can go out and actually 'shoot' your slides, is to produce a **storyboard**. A storyboard is really just a blueprint of your basic idea. It shows a list of the slides you intend to use, in the correct order with some indication of the corresponding commentary and sounds. Storyboards are used in the planning stages of both tape/slide and video production. In fact, they can be used in the planning

and production of any artefact which involves some sequence of images and words, for example, graphic illustration, cartoon strips, etc.

The storyboard has two main uses:
— It helps the creator to plan and visualise his or her first thoughts on the main sequence of events in the tape/slide, video or cartoon. In this sense the storyboard is a planning and thinking aid.
— It provides the creator with something concrete to show to a second person in order to seek advice, or approval, before any actual production work begins. This is particularly important in the case of an artefact which has been commissioned by a client who will need to be consulted in the early stages to be reassured that his or her money is likely to be well spent. For example, most television commercials produced by advertising agencies begin their life in the form of a storyboard of some kind.

As we can see, a storyboard is a very practical and useful device. For this reason it is not possible to lay down a fixed, agreed framework for the layout of storyboards. The exact layout which is used will

SLIDE	TIME	VISUALS	SOUND
1	10 secs	CAPTION "LET'S GO TO SCHOOL"	FADE IN INTRODUCTORY MUSIC – THEME FROM "MAGIC ROUNDABOUT"
2	15 secs	CAPTION: "PRODUCED BY ANNE SMEDLEY"	MUSIC – THEME FROM "MAGIC ROUNDABOUT", FADING INTO: SOUNDS OF CHILDREN PLAYING
3	15 secs	LONG SHOT OF SCHOOL PLAYGROUND, SHOWING PARENTS BRINGING CHILDREN TO SCHOOL	CHILDREN'S VOICES FADING INTO: COMMENTARY INTRODUCING TAPE/SLIDE
4	15 secs	LONG SHOT OF MORNING ASSEMBLY IN SCHOOL HALL	COMMENTARY DESCRIBING ASSEMBLY
5	10 secs	CLOSE UP OF TWO CHILDREN TALKING DURING ASSEMBLY	COMMENTARY ON ASSEMBLY CONTINUED – FADING INTO: HEADTEACHER TALKING IN ASSEMBLY
6	15 secs	MID SHOT OF CHILDREN IN PAINTING LESSON	BACKGROUND SOUNDS OF PAINTING CLASS FADING INTO: COMMENTARY ON PAINTING
7	10 secs	CLOSE UP OF CHILD "BUBBLE PAINTING"	COMMENTARY EXPLAINING THE DIFFERENT TYPES OF PAINTING TECHNIQUES

Fig. 3b Extract from the storyboard 'Let's go to school'

SLIDE NO.	TIME	SLIDE	RECORDING/COMMENTARY
1	10 secs	TITLE CAPTION	FADE UP MUSIC
2	15 secs	CREDIT CAPTION	MUSIC FADE OUT MUSIC FADE IN CHILDREN'S VOICES
3	15 secs	LS/PLAYGROUND	FADE OUT CHILDREN'S VOICES "ANOTHER DAY BEGINS" PAUSE "LET'S GO TO SCHOOL!" PAUSE "THESE SLIDES WILL SHOW YOUR CHILD'S FIRST EXPERIENCES OF SCHOOL"
4	15 secs	L/S ASSEMBLY	"EACH DAY BEGINS WITH ASSEMBLY — WITH SONGS AND PRAYER, TOGETHER" PAUSE "IT'S PROBABLY VERY SIMILAR TO YOUR OWN EXPERIENCE AS A CHILD — THOUGH OF COURSE........."
5	10 secs	C/U CHILDREN TALKING	"............... IT MAY BE A LITTLE LESS FORMAL NOW!" QUICKLY FADE IN HEADTEACHER TALKING TO CHILDREN SENDING THEM TO THEIR FIRST LESSON
6	15 secs	M/S PAINTING LESSON	FADE UP BACKGROUND NOISES OF PAINTING CLASS. FADE OUT BACKGROUND NOISES. "PAINTING IS USUALLY THE FIRST LESSON OF THE DAY — IT PROVIDES A PARTICULARLY ENJOYABLE START TO SCHOOL."
7	10 secs	C/U CHILD PAINTING	"CHILDREN ARE ENCOURAGED TO EXPERIMENT WITH A VARIETY OF TECHNIQUES — NOT ONLY BRUSH PAINTING BUT, AS IN THIS CASE, BUBBLE PAINTING

Fig. 3c Extract from the script 'Let's go to school'

depend upon the job in hand and upon the style and preferred practice of the creator. However, in video and tape/slide certain key features are usually standard for all storyboards. For example, there are usually separate columns for images, sounds/ commentary, time, and additional notes. The information in the images column may be presented visually in the form of diagrams or sketches, or it may be presented in the form of written notes. The information concerning the commentary should be reasonably detailed, though not a word-for-word record of what is to be said — this is one of the jobs of the **script**. A typical tape/slide storyboard is shown in Fig. 3b. This is taken from a tape/slide sequence which was produced by a communication studies student and which was aimed at parents with young children about to start school.

Whereas a storyboard is a draft outline of the basic idea, the **script** gives the exact details needed for the final production of the tape/slide or video. In the case of tape/slide, the script is little more than a word-for-word record of the spoken commentary with an indication of time, sound effects, and the point at which each slide changes. Tape/slide scripts have three main uses:

— They provide an accurate blueprint of what has to be recorded for the soundtrack. If the tape/slide does not have a recorded sound track, then the script provides the user with a record of the commentary which can be read out with the showing of the slides.

— They provide an accurate guide as to when each slide is to change.

— They provide the potential user with an opportunity to pre-view the sequence before it is actually used.

Fig. 3c shows the script which was developed from the tape/slide storyboard shown earlier.

Scripts for video and film are usually a little more complex than for tape/slide. For example, in television there are several different types of script: scripts for actors, for camera crew, for editors, etc. However, in each case the script gives precise details and instructions, rather than simply the draft ideas included in a storyboard.

Photographic skills and techniques

It is beyond the scope of this book to discuss the specific skills of handling a 35mm camera. Features such as focussing, shutter speed and aperture control tend to be specific to each particular model, and so are best left to the manufacturer's instruction manual.

However, there is one skill which is common to all photography, irrespective of the camera being used. This skill is the way in which the photographer composes the scene he or she is about to photograph

(i)

(ii)

(iii)

Fig. 3d Common faults in picture composition (i), (ii), (iii) through the camera's viewfinder. Perhaps the single most common error made by the amateur photographer is simply to hold the camera up and to press the shutter release with little thought as to how the scene is composed within the picture-frame of the viewfinder. Each of the three photographs shown in Fig. 3d represents a particular failure to compose the scene properly before the shutter release was pressed. Can you say what each of these faults are and how they could have been avoided?

Fig. 3d i) shows the common error of simply standing too far away from a human subject. In a photograph like this one we are not particularly interested in looking at trees and bushes etc; we are really only interested in the human figure. Consequently, a great deal of the available picture space has been wasted by the photographer standing too far away. Perhaps the reason why this error commonly occurs is that the amateur photographer may feel physically close to the subject when the picture is taken even if this is not the case, and consequently there is a failure to appreciate that the camera 'translates' the scene differently. As a general rule when taking pictures, use the viewfinder to tell you how close to get to the subject, rather than relying upon conventions such as how comfortable you feel next to your subject.

In Fig. 3d ii), the photographer is now closer to the subject but appears to be unaware that the camera can be turned through 90 degrees to form a portrait, rather than a landscape effect. The taller and narrower portrait format would frame the standing human body more appropriately than would the landscape format. The general rule here is to be aware that the 35mm camera can be used in these two positions and that a conscious decision should be made to choose the appropriate format each time a picture is taken.

In Fig. 3d iii) the photographer is close to the subject and has chosen the appropriate camera format. However, care has not been taken to ensure that all the relevant aspects of the subject are adequately included within the picture-frame of the viewfinder. As with the two points mentioned above, the general rule is to compose the picture consciously and carefully through the viewfinder before pressing the shutter release.

In addition to the points discussed there are many other elements involved in good picture composition which are too numerous to mention here. The main thing is to ensure that you make a conscious effort to think about picture composition each time you look through the viewfinder. Provided that you do this, you are likely to acquire some of the various skills of good picture composition by experience.

Designing and making captions

Many useful and interesting slides can be made by copying from books, magazines and newspapers, etc. For this a 'flat-copy stand' should be used to secure the camera above the material to be copied. In addition to using images from books, etc. you may wish to design and produce your own material. A common example of this would be to produce title captions using Letraset and images photocopied from the *Instant Art* books (*Instant Art*: Camera Ready Art for Beginners and Printers. Graphic Communication Centre Ltd, 1981).

When producing your own two dimensional images to copy it is important to bear in mind what is known as the **aspect ratio** of the 35mm format. As we discussed above, the 35mm camera has a rectangular picture shape which can be used in portrait or landscape format. The shape of a particular image i.e. the relationship between the vertical and the horizontal dimensions, is known as its **aspect ratio**. The exact aspect ratio of the 35mm camera, as reflected in the negative size and shape, is shown in Fig. 3e. (Notice how all standard television sets have a particular aspect ratio which is somewhat squarer than that of the 35mm camera.)

It is important to be aware of the aspect ratio of the 35mm format when designing your own captions. All too often, students produce caption designs which do not match the appropriate aspect ratio and therefore do not make the best use of the available picture space. Fig. 3f shows one bad, and one good example, of awareness of aspect ratio.

Group organisation and group decisions

You should now be aware of most of the basic techniques involved in producing a tape/slide sequence. However, before you can produce your artefact there are certain key decisions about procedure which your working group should make. Here are some of the points which you should discuss and agree before you start any actual production work.
— Who will decide how your class is to be divided up into the smaller working groups? Should this be decided by the class as a whole, or by your teacher?

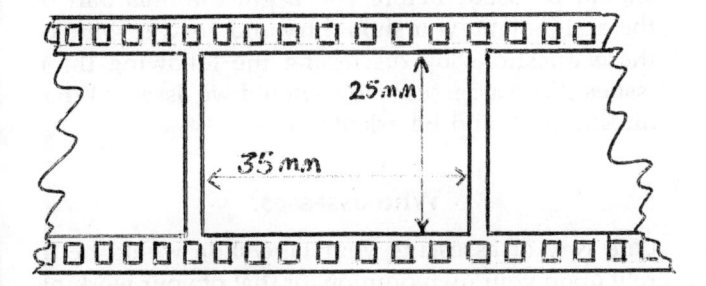

Fig. 3e Aspect ratio of the 35mm camera

Fig. 3f Awareness of aspect ratio in caption design

Would it be better for you to work with a friend, or someone you don't normally sit with? Would it be better to mix different personality types together, or to try and put them in separate groups — for example, introverts in one group and extroverts in another?
— How much time should be given to producing the artefact? Would it be useful to work to a series of written deadlines? If so, will you have a series of 'mini-deadlines', one for each particular stage of the production process? Who should decide and monitor the deadlines you may use?
— Would it be useful to elect one member of the group as a 'co-ordinator' whose job it would be to regulate and bring together the various activities of the group?
— What approach will you decide might be most appropriate for your audience? What register will you choose for your commentary? What areas of your school or college do you think should be included in this tape/slide? What list of slides will you agree upon for your storyboard?
— What are the major jobs which have to be done to produce the tape/slide, and who will do what? Will you delegate particular jobs to particular individuals, or will you all do a bit of everything?

Pre-testing a draft, or sample, of the artefact

In any design and production process, whether it be for a communication artefact or for a manufactured product, it is essential that a draft or mock-up of the basic idea be tested, or checked, before final production begins. In the communication and media industry there would be two groups of people who should be consulted and shown a draft of your basic idea. Firstly, there is the **audience** at whom the message of the artefact is directed. For example, if you were unsure as to whether the register, or the content, of the artefact was appropriate, you could always ask a sample of the audience for their opinion. In advertising and manufacturing this would be called **market research**. Secondly, the **client** who commissioned the artefact would normally want to see the basic idea to be reassured that he or she was getting broadly what was asked for.

As we shall see in the chapter on projects, **pre-testing** an artefact, and consulting with a client, are key features of good project work. In this particular assignment it may not be appropriate to pre-test your idea on your target audience. However, it is important that you submit your storyboard to your teacher for discussion before any real production work begins. In this way you will get a useful second opinion on your basic idea, and become used to the process of pre-testing and consultation.

Assessment of the artefact

Hopefully, you have now produced a finished tape/slide sequence. However, your work is not yet finished. Your next task is to produce a written assessment of your artefact. This raises the very important question of what makes a 'good' artefact? What are we looking for when we assess an artefact? Are we looking at the amount of work and effort which has been put into the finished product? Is it the quality of the technical aspects of the production which should impress us most? Or are we more interested in whether the artefact arouses and maintains the interest of the audience? Other key questions to ask are: Who assesses, and what methods should be used? Before you begin the final part of the assignment, you should try and answer some of these questions by discussing the following three issues: Who assesses? How should we assess? What questions should be asked?

Who assesses?

One way of assessing your tape/slide would be to rely upon your own opinion, or that of your working group, to say how effective it is. After all, you may say, we are the ones who best understand what the artefact is trying to achieve. However, this may not be the most satisfactory way of reaching a conclusion. It may be that there are too many factors which would prevent you from reaching a clear, unbiased opinion of your own work. This is not to suggest that you would cheat, or that you would not make a conscious effort to be fair. The point is that we are likely to be prejudiced in favour of our own work, even though we may not be conscious of this. (Remember the discussion in Chapter 1 of the power of the mind to influence our interpretation of people and events?)

Perhaps a more effective way of assessing your artefact would be to ask the opinion of other people. An obvious example would be to try out the tape/slide on the audience for which it was intended. After all, one test of how 'good' your artefact is would be to see how effective it is in holding the attention of its audience. Another example might be to show your tape/slide to a skilled photographer, or an audio/visual aids technician. Such 'experts' would certainly be able to comment on the technical aspects of your artefact. However, would they be the best people to say whether your artefact was a good piece of communication?

Whatever individuals, or group of individuals you choose to show your artefact to, it is important that you include some outside opinion in your evaluation. In this particular assignment it may not be practicable to test the artefact on the intended audience, or to consult the opinions of experts. In this case you may decide upon the compromise of trying out your artefact on those members of the class not involved in your working group. For the purposes of this assignment, in order to get some feedback fairly easily and quickly, this may be the best option.

How should we assess?

Whoever you choose for your evaluation, what method will you use to obtain and record their opinions of your artefact? Will you ask people to fill out a questionnaire which you can collect and analyse later? Will you show the tape/slide to a group and then have an informal general discussion afterwards? Would it be better to interview each member of this group separately? Is there a particular method of obtaining and recording feedback which is more effective than others, or doesn't it matter which way you do it?

What questions should be asked?

Whatever method you choose to obtain feedback, whether you use a questionnaire or an interview technique, you need some idea of the kind of questions you want answering. Here are a few examples,

organised under the four headings of: Use of the medium, Quality of presentation, Relevance of content, Appropriateness of approach.

Use of the medium. Are the various possibilities of the tape/slide medium developed in an imaginative and intelligent way? Specifically:
– Is a varied and appropriate mixture of sounds, music and voices used for the soundtrack?
– Is the soundtrack used to link one image with another in a smooth sequence, or do the slides follow mechanically one after another?
– Are the images eye catching, i.e. are they clear, varied in subject and interesting?
– Is the relationship between the soundtrack and the slides obvious and clear?

Quality of presentation. Have the slides and the commentary been produced to a good technical standard? Specifically:
– Is the soundtrack clear and audible, free from any interfering outside noises?
– If a number of tapes have been edited together, is the final recording a smooth integration of sounds?
– Are the slides too dark or too light?
– Are any slides obviously out of focus?
– Have the slides been taken using the appropriate picture format and camera angle?
– If an automatic tape/slide synchroniser machine has been used, have the slides been made to change at the appropriate point in the soundtrack?

Relevance of content. Is the content of the tape/slide relevant to the aim of presenting a general picture of your school or college to parents? Specifically:
– Does the sequence cover the main areas of interest?
– Are there any major areas of interest which have been omitted?
– Are there any subjects which have been dealt with in too much detail?
– Are there any subjects which have been depicted in a way which is likely to create an unfavourable impression?

Appropriateness of approach. Is the general approach of the tape/slide, and the register of the commentary, appropriate to the audience? Specifically:
– Is the approach and register too formal or too informal for the audience?
– Are any words or expressions used which are likely to be offensive to the audience?
– Does the commentary appear to 'talk down' to the audience, perhaps by using words and expressions which are too simple, or by using explanations which are too obvious?
– Is the approach likely to stimulate and maintain the interest of an adult audience?

Self-assessment

1. As we have seen in earlier chapters, a model is a simple means of structuring and presenting an idea or a process. One model which is often used to analyse communication processes (Lasswell's model 1948) poses the following questions:

> Who
> says What
> to Whom
> How
> with What effect.

Use this model to analyse the message communicated by your tape/slide sequence.

2. In planning and making your tape/slide sequence, your group made a series of decisions and carried out a number of tasks. Produce a flowchart which represents the main decisions and tasks involved in producing your tape/slide sequence.
3. What is the purpose of a storyboard and how does it differ from that of a script?
4. What is meant by 'aspect ratio'? Why is it important to understand the notion of aspect ratio when designing captions?
5. Produce a written guide which communication students might use to assess communication artefacts. Be sure to begin your guide with a brief discussion of what we might mean by a 'good' artefact.

4 Producing a radio advertisement

This assignment contains the following sections:

- **Description of the task**
- **Familiarisation with basic terms, techniques, and procedures**
- **Group organisation and group decisions**
- **Pre-testing a draft, or sample, of the artefact**
- **Assessment of the artefact**
- **Self-assessment**

Description of the task

In this practical assignment you have been asked by your teacher to write and produce a short radio advertisement. The advert is for the Midland Promotions Company, based in Leicester, who want to publicise their new 'Balloonagram' service. You will be asked to produce a written script for the advert and then make a simple sound recording from that script. You will be given detailed instructions in a later section but you should bear in mind the following points when producing your artefact:

1. The finished artefact should be as near to 30 seconds in duration as possible. In a real commercial radio station a period of, for example, two minutes is allotted for the commercial break. It is much easier to fill this time with adverts timed at 10, 20 or 30 second periods. In addition, these standard times help the advertising department to produce a simple **rate card** which they use to charge the clients.
2. The adverts should be planned, written and produced by small groups with three or four students in each.
3. Since you will be asked to tape-record your finished scripts, you will need to make the necessary arrangements for recording. You will need at least one tape-recorder and a supply of audio-cassette tapes.
4. At the end of the assignment you will be asked to submit a written assessment of your artefact.

It's obvious that in order to produce such an artefact you need to be familiar with the basic guidelines for writing radio advertising **copy** and be confident about working within a group. Fig. 4a is a flowchart to help to give you a clearer picture of the work ahead. Each major step represented in the flowchart is discussed in more detail throughout the sections in this assignment.

Familiarisation with basic terms, techniques and procedures

The nature of your medium

Unlike the printed media (newspapers, magazines etc.) radio is a **transitory** medium. When an advert appears in the *Daily Express*, the reader has the option of studying it for as long as he or she wants, or not, as the case may be. However, radio does not have this kind of permanence. A radio advert only lasts for a specified, pre-arranged time. As soon as it finishes it is replaced by another advert or a return to the main part of the programme. If the listener only has the radio on at certain times of the day he or she might only listen to this particular advert once.

For these reasons, a radio advert has to have **aural impact**, just as a poster has to have **visual impact**. The effect on the listener has to be immediate; remember, the aim of advertising is to persuade consumers to buy goods or use services. The copywriter (the person at the radio station who writes scripts for the adverts) can achieve this kind of aural impact by working to a set of guidelines and techniques which we discuss in detail below.

Remember, at all times, that radio is a *spoken* medium. Unlike television, which can back up words with striking visual images, radio has to rely upon a combination of the spoken word, music, and acoustic sound effects to achieve its impact. Your completed artefact will be a piece of oral communication, although you will also produce a written script.

Language

Because of the transitory nature of the medium, scripts for radio adverts tend to be written in an easy-to-understand register. When you come to write your script you should use a simple voca-

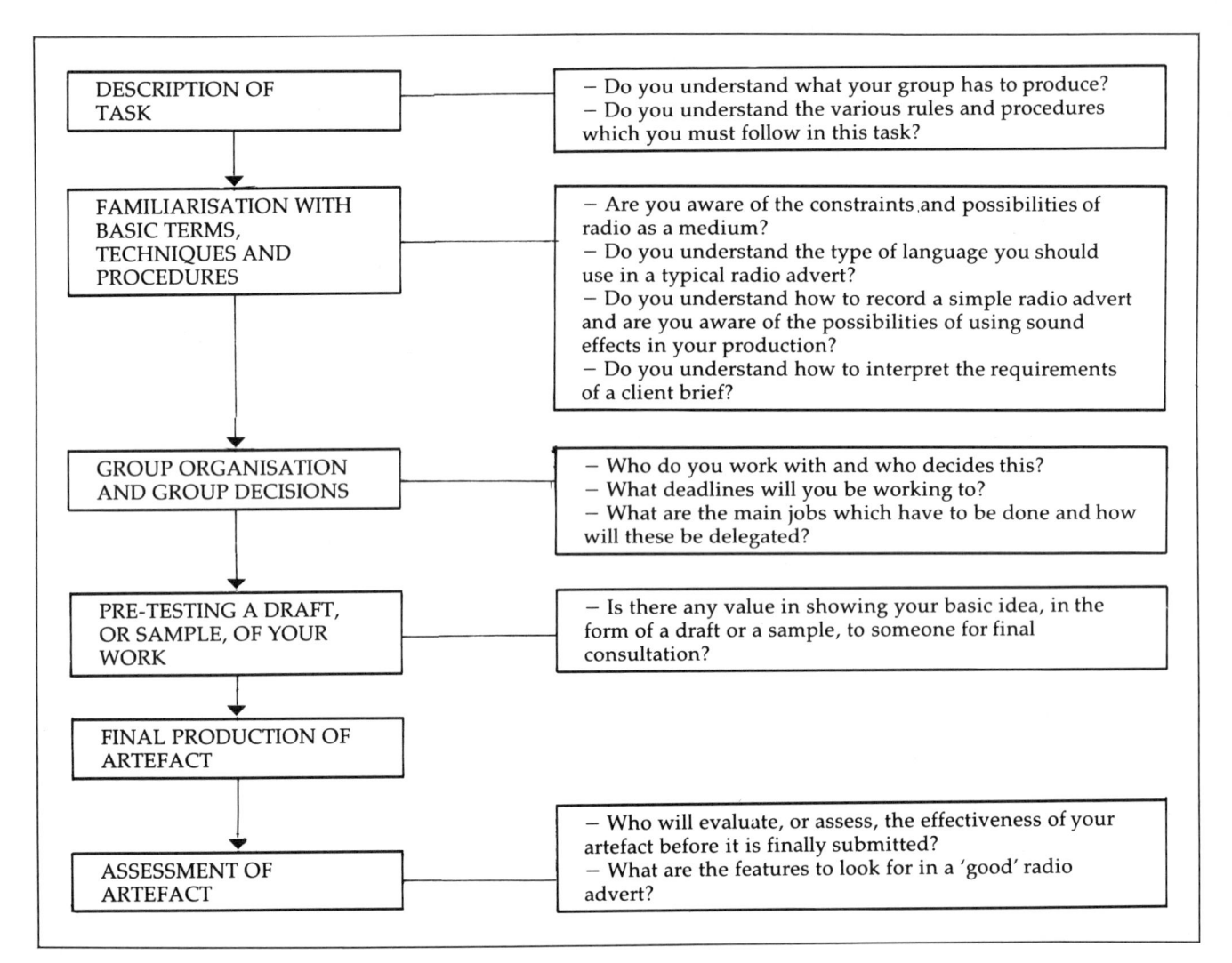

Fig. 4a Producing a radio advertisement

bulary and syntax i.e. uncomplicated words and sentences. If you are opting for the **hard sell** approach, short 'punchy' sentences will be the order of the day, whereas if you want to use the **soft sell** angle, a more 'poetic' style of presentation might be more appropriate.

You should also avoid using jargon and unnecessary abbreviations. For example, if you were advertising new homes you would probably not talk in terms of 'bijoux' houses or a des. res. (desirable residence).

The sound picture

Radio may be an oral/aural medium but it is still possible to do interesting things by creating what is called a **sound picture**. By this term we mean the enhancement of the spoken work by the use of music (for example jingles or background music) or sound effects (SFX). The sound image you are attempting to create should, of course, conjure up positive **connotations** in the minds of the audience. For example, if you were advertising suntan oil you might decide to use calypso-style background music throughout the advert. Appropriate use of music and sound effects by the recording engineer (usually taken from the station's music library) helps the advert to have the aural impact discussed earlier.

Legal constraints

All advertising copywriters must be fully aware of the legal constraints on radio advertising as well as the requirements of the Independent Broadcasting Authority's Code of Advertising Standards and Practice. For example, you would not be allowed to advertise children's toys by including the following line:

'Buy Jellytoys now ... don't let your kids feel left out.'

This would contravene the Code which prohibits adverts which might make people feel inferior to others if they do not make a purchase.

29-31 Castle Gate, Nottingham NG1 7AP   Telephone 0602 581731

PROPOSED SCRIPT

№ 12696

ILKESTON CO-OP TRAVEL   30 SECONDS

MVO   ONE DAY ONLY, TUESDAY THE 18th OF FEBRUARY, ANY
             ADULT BOOKING A COSMOS HOLIDAY IN THE SUMMER SUN
             WILL GET TWENTY POUNDS IN VOUCHERS IMMEDIATELY TO
             SPEND IN OUR STORE, PLUS OUR USUAL GENEROUS OFFER
             OF TEN POUNDS FOR EVERY HUNDRED POUNDS SPENT ON THE
             BASIC COST LATER. COME AND SEE THE COSMOS LUXURY
             COACH AT ILKESTON ON THE 18th OF FEBRUARY AND BOOK
             YOUR HOLIDAY. ILKESTON CO-OP TRAVEL. PHONE 0602 -
             323546. THE PIONEERS OF LOW COST TRAVEL.

Music Title	Composer/Arranger	Licensor	Use	Duration

Music Declaration Yes/No

Accounts Department

Studio

Voices: Name   *Chris Kay*

　　　 —:—

　　　 —:—

COST *£38-00*

Fig. 4b Ilkeston co-op travel

29-31 Castle Gate, Nottingham NG1 7AP   Telephone 0602 581731

PROPOSED SCRIPT   № 12697

THE SWINGING SPORRAN   30 SECONDS

*****   FUN, LIVELY MUSIC

MVO   EVER TRIED DRINKING BEER FROM A SWINGING SPORRAN?
             WELL NOW'S THE TIME TO GIVE IT A WHIRL WITHOUT
             SPILLING A DROP, BECAUSE THE SWINGING SPORRAN IS
             THE PUB OF YOUR DREAMS! GALLONS OF GOOD BEER.......
             MOUNTAINS OF MOUTH-WATERING, HOME-COOKED FOOD.
             DELICIOUS TRADITIONAL AFTERNOON TEAS WITH SCONES,
             JAM AND CREAM...... LUNCHTIME AND EVENING BAR MEALS
             OF GENUINE ENGLISH CHARACTER. FROM SHEPHERD'S PIE
             TO PLOUGHMAN'S LUNCH, YOU'LL THRILL TO A BITE IN
             THE SPORRAN - NEXT TO WOOLCO ON THE A6 LEICESTER
             ROAD, OADBY. IT'S SO.......ENGLISH!

Music Title	Composer/Arranger	Licensor	Use	Duration

BANJO HOEDOWN - SOB6061A/4

Music Declaration Yes/No

Accounts Department   COST ₹38-00

Studio
Voices: Name   LAWRENCE REW   + MUSIC ₹35-00

    —:—
    —:—

Fig. 4c The Swinging Sporran

Advertising also has to work within the laws of the land. The law of libel, for example, states that you cannot make defamatory statements about somebody. So, if you were to include the following sentence in an advert for a local pub, you would be committing libel:

'The White Horse, a great pub — better than the King's Head, where he puts the slops back in the barrel.'

Awareness of your audience

Copywriters attempt to identify a typical potential customer for the product or service they are advertising. If they try to gain a clearer idea, and an understanding, of the type of person they are trying to influence, then we can say they are trying to be aware of the needs of their audience. By putting yourself in the place of your audience, the style you adopt in your advert should be more appropriate to the needs and expectations of that audience.

The product or service you are advertising

Always remember to include the client's name and address/telephone number in the advert!

Length

As we have already noted, your advert must be as near to the client's desired length as possible — 30 seconds in this assignment. When you have written your script, try reading it aloud at the appropriate speed whilst a friend times it with a watch. If you underrun or overrun you will need to amend your script accordingly.

Figs. 4b and 4c show how these guidelines are put into practice at a typical commercial radio station, Radio Trent. Fig. 4b is a script for a simple 30 second 'male voice over' for a local travel firm whilst Fig. 4c is a script for a local pub which has background music throughout. Note how all amounts are stated in words rather than figures i.e. ten pounds rather than £10. This is to guard against mistakes being made when the commercial is being recorded.

Procedure

Like most enterprises, advertising on local radio is a team effort with a number of key people pooling their different expertise. Fig. 4d shows the basic process of creating an advert at a typical radio station.

For this assignment you will need to work from a **client brief** which is Fig. 4e. Your first task, therefore, is to write a script for a 30 second commercial for Midland Promotions according to the instructions contained in your client brief. You will then record your script onto an audio cassette.

Basic recording

The main emphasis in this assignment is on the process of making a radio advert rather than the professionalism of the finished artefact. Even so, you will still want to make as good a job as possible of recording your script. The simplest way to do this is obviously just to use a normal tape recorder with either a built-in or separate microphone. However, if you want to be a bit more ambitious and include jingles or background music you will need two tape recorders, connected together through the appropriate DIN sockets.

Group organisation and group decisions

You should now be aware of most of the basic techniques involved in producing a radio advert. However, before you can produce your artefact there are

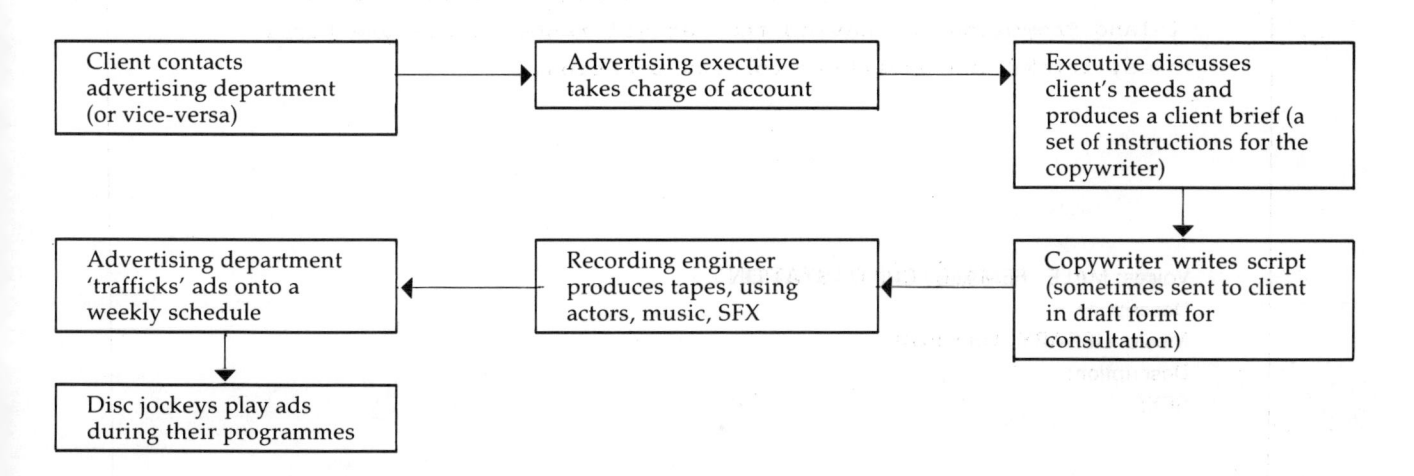

Fig. 4d Creating an advert

Radio Trent

Executive	AS	Order No.:	
Contact:	CHRIS TAYLOR	Date:	5.2.86.
		Tel:	558358
Client:	MIDLAND PROMOTIONS		
Address:	41a BELVOIR STREET,	Account No.:	
	LEICESTER		

Demo Script: YES / NO   Required By:

Campaign commence: 6.2.86.   Script sent/approved: Production Date:

Duration: 30 seconds   6.2.86.

Suggested no. of commercials: TWO

Main copy points:

To promote balloonagrams for every occasion - ie. Birthday,
Anniversary, Birth, Retirement, Get-well, Party. Personalised
balloon with own message - can be picked up and delivered
personally, can be sent by post, or delivered by a character
of your imagination - ie. Gorilla, Kissagram girl or man, Donald
Duck, grottygram, a tasteful stripagram. Delivered anywhere in the
country. Also specialised service - STUNTAGRAM. Can be delivered
by parachute - we will try and meet all requirements. Also push
Midland Promotions as having the largest range of costume hire,
jokes, tricks and novelties for any occasion.

Voices: MALE / FEMALE / CHILD / STATION
Description:
Music: LIBRARY / ORIGINAL
Description:
SFX:

Fig. 4e   A client brief

certain key decisions about procedure which your working group should make. Here are some of the points which you should discuss and agree before you start any actual production work.

— Who will decide how your class is to be divided up into smaller working groups? Should this be decided by the class as a whole, or by your teacher? Would it be better for you to work with a friend, or someone you don't normally sit with? Would it be better to mix different personality types together, or to try and put them in separate groups — for example, introverts in one group and extroverts in another?

— How much time should be given to producing the artefact? Would it be useful to work to a series of written deadlines? If so, will you have a series of 'mini-deadlines', one for each particular stage of the production process? Who should decide and monitor the deadlines you may use?

— Would it be useful to elect one member of the group as 'co-ordinator' whose job it would be to regulate and bring together the various activities of the group?

— What approach will you decide might be most appropriate for your audience? Should you opt for a light-hearted approach, or should your advert be more sober in style?

— What are the major jobs which have to be done to produce the advert, and who will do what? Will you delegate particular jobs to particular individuals, or will you all do a bit of everything?

Pre-testing a draft, or sample, of the artefact

In any design and production process, whether it be for a communication artefact or for a manufactured product, it is essential that a draft or mock-up of the basic idea be tested, or checked, before final production begins. In the world of radio advertising the person you would pre-test your script on is the **client** (the person who has asked you to advertise the goods or services). A copywriter might show the client a draft of the proposed script which would outline:

— The general approach being taken (humorous, mock-serious etc.);

— A rough sketch of the kind of text or dialogue to be used.

The draft script will then be developed into the finished artefact, taking into account the views of the client.

As we shall see in the following chapter on projects, pre-testing an artefact and consulting with a client are key features of good project work. In this particular assignment it may be appropriate to pre-test

your ideas on other students in the class, since you will be unable to liaise with either a client or the audience for the advert (the radio listeners). It may also be a good idea to submit a draft of your script to your teacher before proceeding with the recording of your advert. In this way you will get a useful second opinion on your basic idea, and become used to the process of client consultation.

Assessment of the artefact

Hopefully, you have now written your script and recorded your advert. However, your work is not yet finished. Your next task is to produce a written assessment of your artefact. This raises the very important question of what makes a 'good' artefact? What are we looking for when we assess an artefact? Are we looking at the amount of work and effort which has been put into the finished product? Is it the quality of the technical aspects of the production which should impress us most? Or are we more interested in whether the artefact arouses and maintains the interest of the audience? Other key questions to ask are: Who assesses, and what methods should be used? Before you begin this final part of the assignment, you should try and answer some of these questions by discussing the following three issues: Who assesses? How should we assess? What questions should be asked?

Who assesses?

One way of assessing your advert would be to rely on your own opinion, or that of the working group, to say how 'good' it is. After all, you may say, we are the ones who best understand what the artefact is trying to achieve. However, this may not be the most satisfactory way of reaching a conclusion. It may be that there are too many factors which could prevent you from reaching a clear, unbiased opinion of your own work. This is not to suggest that you would cheat, or that you would not make a conscious effort to be fair. The point is that we are likely to be prejudiced in favour of our own work even though we may not be conscious of this. (Remember the discussion in Chapter 1 of the power of the mind to influence our interpretation of people and events?)

Perhaps a more effective way of assessing your artefact would be to ask the opinion of other people. An obvious example would be to try out the advert on the audience for whom it was intended, commercial radio listeners in this case. Another idea might be to show your advert to a copywriter at your local independent radio station. He or she would certainly be able to comment on its originality, professionalism and suitability for its audience.

Whatever individuals, or groups of individuals,

you choose to show your artefact to, it is important that you include some outside opinion in your evaluation. In this particular assignment it may not be practicable to test the artefact on the intended audience, or to consult the opinions of experts. In this case you may decide upon the compromise of trying out your artefact on those members of the class not involved in your working group. For the purposes of this assignment, and in order to get some feedback fairly quickly, this may be the best option.

How should we assess?

Whichever opinions you decide to base your assessment upon, what will be the method you will use to obtain and record them? Will you ask people to fill out a questionnaire which you can collect and analyse later? Will you present the advert to a group and have an informed, general discussion afterwards? Would it be better to interview each member of the audience separately? Is there a particular method of obtaining and recording feedback which is more effective than others, or doesn't it matter which way you do it?

What questions should be asked?

Whatever method you choose to obtain feedback, whether you use a questionnaire or an interview technique, you need some idea of the kind of questions you want answering. Here are a few examples, organised under the four headings of: Use of the medium, Quality of presentation, Relevance of content and Appropriateness of approach.

Use of the medium. Have the various possibilities of the medium of radio been developed intelligently and imaginatively within the conventions normally used for producing radio adverts? For example:
– Have you made use of relevant musical and sound effects?
– Does the combination of commentary, sound effects and music create a 'sound picture' with aural impact?

Quality of presentation. – Is the script written or typed clearly and legibly?
– Has the advert been recorded to an acceptable standard? Is the soundtrack clear and audible, free from any interfering outside noises?

Relevance of content. – Is the content of the script relevant to the instructions in the client brief? Have you mentioned all the services listed in it?
– Is your style of language appropriate to the requirements of your client brief, the nature of a 30 second commercial and the needs of your audience?
– Have you avoided using complicated words and phrases unsuitable for your audience and the nature of the medium?
– Have you mentioned the name and address/ telephone number of the client?

Appropriateness of approach. – Is the 'angle' you have chosen appropriate to your intended audience?
– Is your approach too formal, or too informal, for the audience?
– Is the approach likely to stimulate and maintain the interest of the audience?

Self-assessment

1. What do the following abbreviations stand for: MVO and SFX?
2. Define the term 'awareness of your audience'.
3. Discuss how you might create a 'sound picture'.
4. What is the role of the client brief in radio advertising?
5. In planning and producing your advert, your group made a series of decisions and carried out a number of tasks. Produce a flowchart which represents the main decisions and tasks involved in producing your radio advert.
6. Discuss and justify the 'angle' you used in the presentation of your advert.

PROJECTS

This chapter contains the following sections:
- Introduction
- The project process
- Oral presentation of project work
- Self-assessment

Introduction

What is a project?

Any process which involves planning, designing and then making something substantial could be termed a **project**. You will probably hear the word 'project' used in a variety of different ways: it might refer to a long practical task which you are required to complete during a course in Communication Studies or some other subject; it might be used to describe an assessed component in a course, one which you would need to carry out successfully in order to achieve a good overall grade; it might be a full-scale enterprise taking several months of work which needs to be very carefully prepared and executed, with every stage being recorded and explained in a systematic way.

This chapter should be read in conjunction with the sections on Practical Assignments and Case Studies. The Practical Assignments used in this book can be thought of as miniature projects in their own right. Here we will look at the process of planning and completing a full-scale project in the field of Communication Studies — one which will take at least several weeks' work from start to finish. You can use this chapter to help you prepare for any such project including, for example, the assessed project work required by an 'A' Level Communication Studies syllabus.

This chapter assumes that you will be working alone but if you are planning a project with a group of people, you can make modifications to suit your own particular needs.

A full-scale project of the sort we are now considering consists of two major components:

— The **artefact**. This is the word used to describe the thing you have made; it might be a booklet, a teaching pack, a tape/slide sequence, a video film, a radio programme, a report, or anything else which is acceptable within the brief you are given.

— The **record of progress**. You will need to keep a careful record of your progress as time goes by. Your ideas, your plans, your actions, your successes and failures — they all need to be recorded in an organised and clear way. You might write a diary of some kind; you might keep a task-by-task series of record sheets; you might compile a log book.

Product and process

When you think about a project — your own or somebody else's — it is very tempting to focus all your attention upon the completed artefact. You may be very impressed by a video film someone has made, or decide that a project in the form of a game for children was well-designed and extremely useful in teaching youngsters a series of skills. Here you would be spending your time considering the **product** — the final tangible outcome of several weeks or months of work. But it is equally important to consider the **process** involved in the production of any final artefact. If you think back over a project of your own, two things should give you satisfaction: there is the artefact itself, which is something you have created by the sweat of your brow — but there is also the learning process you have gone through in bringing the artefact to completion. One of the main reasons for doing project work at all is so that you may learn from your mistakes, find out about your own strengths and weaknesses, and generally learn to be a more effective communicator.

In other words, process is as important as product.

Examples of projects

Before thinking about the process involved in project work you might find it useful first of all to look at two completed projects, each using a different **medium**. The medium you are to use may be specified for you in advance; if you have an open choice, however, you might choose a medium from among the following:

- leaflet;
- booklet;
- magazine;
- report;
- manual;
- guide;
- teaching pack;
- game;
- radio programme;
- tape/slide sequence;
- video film.

The two projects illustrated were completed by college students as part of the assessment procedure for an 'A' Level in Communication Studies; for each we have indicated essential details concerning the project. One or two terms used may require a word or two of explanation:

– **Audience.** This refers to the person or group of people who will make use of your final artefact.

– **Client.** If you produce an artefact which you will present to a person for him or her to use with an *audience*, then that person is your *client*.

If you were to design a project on guitar-playing for a specific group of musicians, then they would be your *audience*. But if you were to make a teaching pack for a school teacher to use with children, then the teacher would be your *client*, and the children would be the *audience*.

– **Evaluation.** We know how important *feedback* can be in the communication process. Once you have finished producing your artefact, you can present it to your client and/or your audience in order to test it out and get an honest and detailed assessment of its strengths and weaknesses. Once your artefact has been assessed for you in this way, you should be in a position to make an overall *evaluation* not just of the *product*, but also of the project *process* in total.

A student project: Let's learn together: It's fun!

Name of student: Beverley Hodgkinson

The artefact: A package for teachers to help them when teaching numeracy to junior school children, consisting of a board with stick-on numbers and discs, a series of work cards, and a teacher's handbook.

The client: A junior school teacher.

The audience: Junior school children aged five to seven.

Aim: To help the children understand numbers; to help them add and subtract numbers.

Evaluation: Beverley conducted a **pre-test** using a sample of the finished artefact. She then carried out a final testing stage by asking the client to fill in a questionnaire, while she watched and photographed a group of children using the artefact.

Comments: Beverley was able to have regular meetings with her client, a local junior school teacher, to discuss progress step-by-step as the project proceeded. She was able to use the feedback she obtained in this way to produce exactly the kind of artefact which would be of most use to her client.

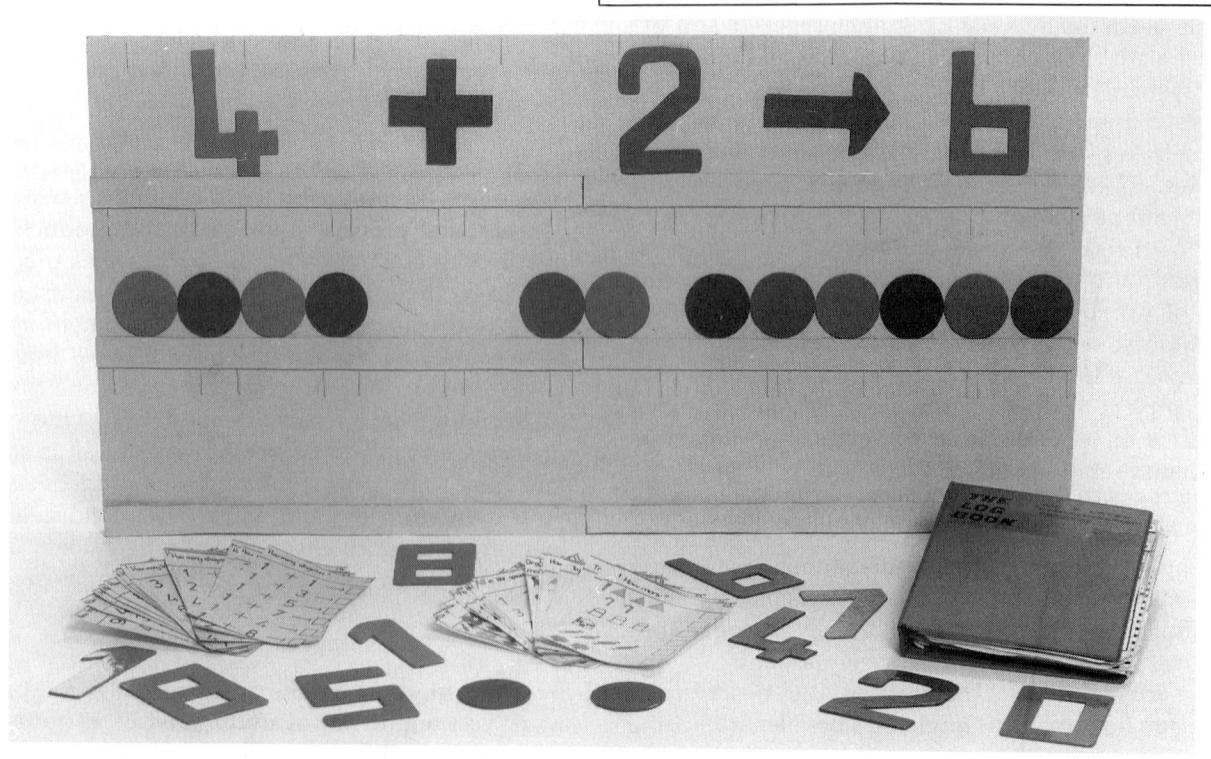

Fig. A Student project: Let's learn together: It's fun!

A student project:
An award scheme for young gymnasts

Name of student: Nicola Fossey

The artefact: Three wall charts showing gymnastics routines stage-by-stage; certificates to be awarded to young gymnasts who successfully complete specified gymnastics routines; a teacher's handbook.

The client: A number of local gymnastics teachers.

The audience: Young junior school children from local schools.

Aim: To devise an attractive and relevant award scheme for young gymnasts which will improve their understanding of the subject and encourage them to progress to higher standards of performance.

Evaluation: Nicola showed her clients a draft design for her wall charts and a draft teacher's handbook in order to obtain feedback before finally completing her artefact. Once she had finished the project she had a meeting with her clients to discuss its strengths and weaknesses, and she observed and recorded the progress made by one group of young gymnasts who followed her scheme over a period of six weeks.

Comments: Nicola had a number of teachers acting as clients for her; she sought their views on her intended project very early on, and in consultation with them she was able to produce an artefact that would be of real use to the children for whom it was designed.

From the descriptions given of these two projects, you should be aware of the kind of process you have to go through in order to produce an effective final artefact. Note especially that:
- The needs of a specific audience and/or client had to be researched and then kept in mind;
- The chosen medium had to be suited to its task;
- The project had to be tested and evaluated.

Fig. B Student project: An award scheme for young gymnasts

Good and bad projects

Bearing these two projects in mind, then, we are in a position to say that a 'good' project is one which:
— Is designed for a specific **audience**;
— Sets out to meet the established **need** of that audience;
— Is planned in consultation with a **client** if appropriate;
— Has a clear and specific **message**;
— Is communicated by the most appropriate **medium**.
A 'bad' project, by contrast, would be one which:
— Has no real sense of audience;
— Is unaware of, or ignores, audience need;
— Has a vaguely-defined message;
— Uses an inappropriate medium.

A project of the sort we are describing here is not meant to be an exercise in self-indulgence. You are not saying: 'I've always been interested in ponies, so I'll do a project on ponies', but rather: 'My researches have made it clear that a particular person or group is in need of a specific communications artefact; I will produce that artefact for them.'

Notice that neither of the examples we have shown you is aimed at a vague audience like the 'general public'; your audience has to be very specific — it needn't be a large audience, but it must consist of people you can communicate with as your project develops.

TASK

A project will only be fully effective if it covers an appropriate subject area for an appropriate audience and uses an appropriate medium or format.

This task is designed to help you think clearly about these three factors; it should also be of use to you when planning a project of your own.

Below are three lists under the headings:
— Titles
— Audiences
— Media

Pick a number of project *titles* from the first list and write down clearly what each one means to you. Some of the titles are self-explanatory; others can be interpreted in a number of different imaginative ways.

Select the most appropriate *audience* or *audiences* for each of your chosen titles.

Now pick the most appropriate *medium* for each from the third list.

This is not an exercise which has *right* and *wrong* answers; you must decide whether you have matched a title, an audience and a medium in the most appropriate and relevant way.

TITLES
1 My car's making a funny noise.
2 Basic football skills
3 The local music scene
4 Nightlife
5 This is our local community project
6 Young and unemployed
7 Alternative clothing for teenagers
8 Horse care
9 Going to school
10 Fun with numbers
11 Single parent problems
12 Horses on the main road
13 First aid with Janet and John
14 CND
15 Buying a car
16 Selling yourself

AUDIENCES
a First-time horse owners
b School children 11—14 yrs
c Single people, late teens
d School leavers
e Girls, 14—18
f Boys, 14—18
g School children, 8—11 yrs
h Car drivers
i Drivers with no mechanical knowledge
j Teenagers
k Young parents
l Single parents
m Rotary Club and Women's Institutes
n Youth club leaders and head teachers
o Teenagers on the dole
p The general public

MEDIA
1 Video
2 'Comic strip' booklet
3 Tape/slide sequence
4 Badges, tee-shirts, etc.
5 Board game
6 Radio programme/audio tape
7 Illustrated work cards
8 Fact sheets
9 Information leaflet

The project process

Getting an idea

Now that we have some idea about project artefacts and appropriate media, and have thought about the relationship between an artefact and its audience, we can focus upon the process necessary to start a project and to bring it to a successful conclusion.

We assume here that you can choose your own project title, your own audience and/or client and your own medium. Freedom of choice is in many ways a luxury to be enjoyed, but if you are not sure exactly what you want to do, the initial choice of project can pose all sorts of problems.

You will need to have more than one initial idea for a project which will work; things can go wrong,

and if you are forced to abandon one idea after working on it for only a short period of time, it's comforting to know that another realistic choice is there as a safety net. You may decide:
— That you want to put across a certain **message** ('Wildlife must be protected from human interference').
— That you would like to fulfil the needs of a particular **audience** ('I would like to help would-be photographers who are intimidated by difficult manuals on photography').
— That you wish to explore the possibilities of a particular **medium** ('I would like to see what can be done to make a tape/slide sequence a really effective medium of communication').
— That you can straightaway think of an initial idea which includes a message, an audience and a medium or format all at once. ('I would like to produce a tape/slide sequence which will help would-be photographers to stop feeling uneasy about using a camera for the first time').

If you do think of a message or a medium first of all when you are planning your project, that does not alter the fact that your principal aim is to satisfy the needs of your chosen audience. You must be prepared to abandon or modify your ideas about a message or a medium in the light of audience need.

In order to come up with two or three firm ideas for your project, you are best to begin by writing down any and every idea you can think of, good or bad, ambitious or modest, complicated or simple. From this list you can slowly and carefully narrow down your possibilities to a core of really practicable project ideas.

Consider the following questions, which are designed to help you think about compiling your original list:
— What subjects are you studying at school, at college or at home? Could you produce a simple aid to beginners in this subject? Could you help publicise the subject?
— What particular interests do you have? Could you produce an artefact connected with this area of interest?
— Do you belong to, or do you have access to, any group of people who share a common interest? Do they have needs which your project could meet?
— Do you know any individuals or groups in your locality who need some help with publicity or marketing? Can you produce something for them?
— Which project media do you feel happy about using? Which do you have access to? Which could you learn about in the time available to you?

Confirming the idea

We will now assume that you have two or three initial ideas for your project — we can think of them

as 'hunches' which may or may not prove to be practicable as time goes by.

The next stage is called **confirming the idea** — when you test the viability of your choices.

There is one very simple and obvious way to test any idea at the outset and that is, to try and establish whether there is a 'gap in the market'. If you decided to produce a beginners' guide to playing snooker, and then found out by talking to people or by visiting your local library that there were already a dozen or so guides of the type you were envisaging already available, you would need to shelve this idea and start thinking again. If you use a client, he or she can probably let you know straightaway whether the project you have in mind has already been done many times before.

If your early researches suggest that there probably is a 'gap in the market' which you could fill, it is time to contact your audience and/or client. You must decide exactly who this is to be. Ideally you would choose a person or group of people whom you can visit and discuss things with face-to-face. Failing that, you will need to use some form of written communication such as a letter or a questionnaire, supplemented if necessary by the use of the telephone.

You must approach your audience and/or client in any way that seems appropriate and get a response to your initial idea. Courtesy and good sense would suggest that you ought to have written or typed out a summary of this idea for the client or audience to examine; if you are to have a face-to-face meeting with your chosen person, think about sending him or her a copy of your written idea in advance. At this stage the exact nature of the message you wish to get across in your final artefact, and the precise choice of medium, must be a matter for consultation between you and your client or audience. You must pay close attention to the responses you get, and be prepared to modify your plans accordingly. To obtain a full response from a large group of people you might choose to use a questionnaire; if you are to have a face-to-face meeting, prepare a series of questions you wish to have answered.

By the time you finish this first consultative stage you should either have rejected, confirmed or modified your initial idea. You should now be able to answer the following questions:
— Who exactly are my audience and/or client?
— Have I established the need or needs of my audience and/or client?
— Have I decided upon an appropriate medium?

You are now in a position to define your project formally, under the following headings:
— Audience;
— Client (where appropriate);
— Purpose;
— Medium/media.

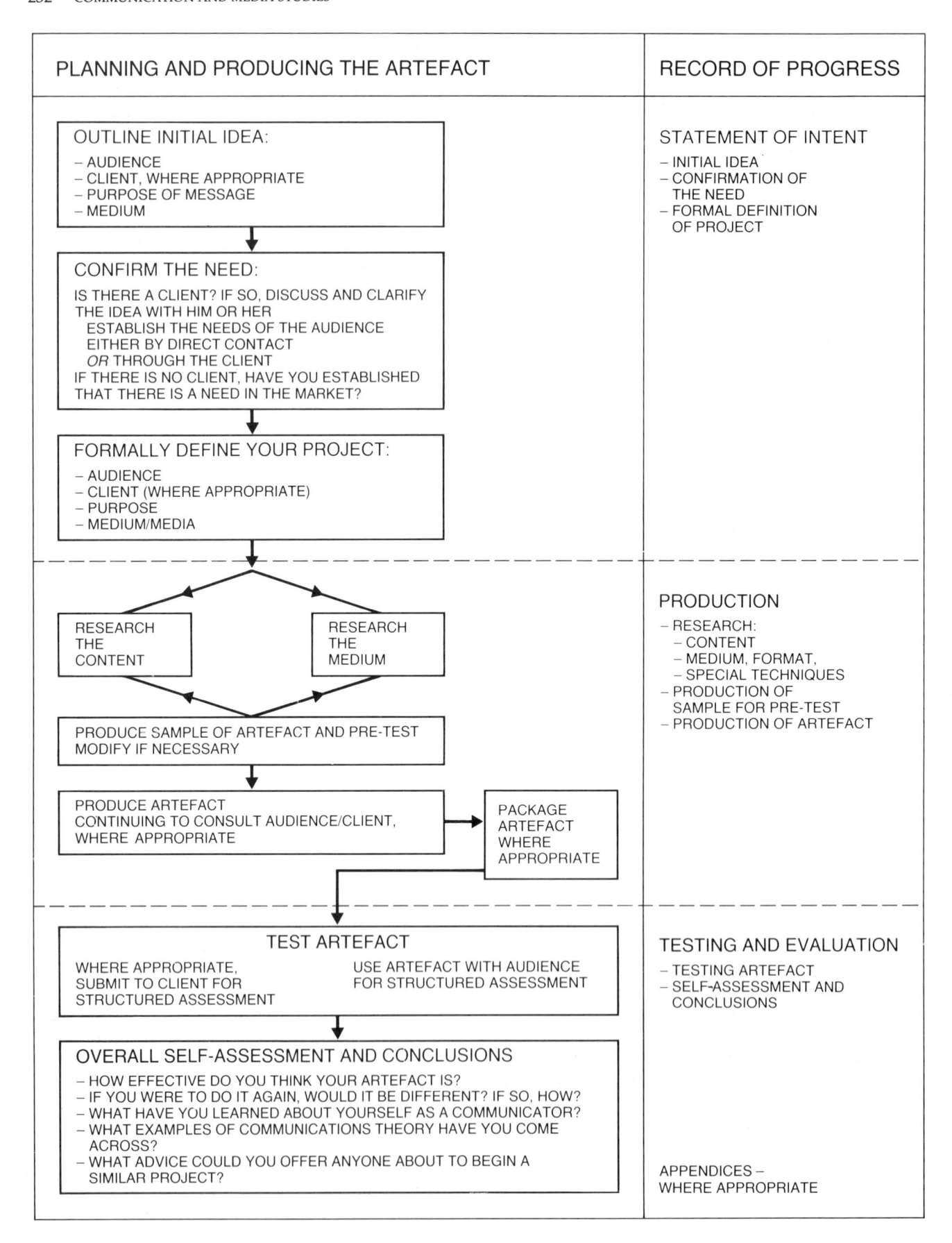

Fig. C Project procedure and organisation

Research; production; testing

Look at the flow diagram, Fig. C, which shows project procedure and organisation. As you proceed with your project follow the process outlined in the column headed 'Planning and Producing the Artefact'. The right-hand column indicates how your record of progress reflects each stage you have reached in your planning and production.

So far you have reached the first dotted line; you have defined your project formally and should be ready to start on the research stage of the process. You may notice that this flow diagram is very similar to the diagrams we have used to help you complete the tasks which appear in the 'Practical Assignments' section of this book. The process of completing a project is in some ways just a sophisticated and expanded version of the process needed for a practical assignment. A full-scale project may contain a number of practical assignments within it, and your need to plan carefully and to think ahead is even more crucial in a project than it is in a simpler assignment. If you cannot organise your energies and your time effectively, your project will suffer as a result.

We now concentrate on the lower section of the flow diagram from the point we have already reached, giving a brief explanation of the stages which remain:

— **Research the content.** The **content** of your project — that is, the information and the material that goes into it — may already be familiar to you in broad outline if you are dealing with a subject you know well. But you will almost certainly have to research the subject further — writing off for information, asking experts and using libraries may all be necessary. You will probably need illustrations as well as printed facts, and you will need to feel that your final artefact is accurate and comprehensive. You may have to wait for some information to arrive; time spent waiting will need to be used in a constructive way if you are to avoid a last-minute rush to get your project finished.

— **Research the medium.** The medium you choose may be one you already feel happy with, or it may be fairly new to you. Working through the 'Practical Assignments' in this book should help you feel confident about handling certain media and planning related tasks. Whatever medium you use, you will probably want to experiment and conduct one or two trials. There will be questions you need to ask yourself according to the medium you have chosen:
— What page size should my booklet be? How should each page be laid out?
— What sort of titles should I use for my tape/slide sequence?
— What kind of music will be most appropriate? How many pages will my manual contain? How will it be bound?

— What material should I use to make the parts of my children's game? How should I colour the various parts?
— How long will my video film be? Whose voice shall I use for the narrative?

A number of experimental drafts produced early on will save you valuable time and effort later as your project nears completion.

— **Produce a sample of the artefact and pre-test.** You should not have forgotten your client or audience as soon as you began research on your project — the more contact you have with the people for whom the artefact is produced, the better. Fairly soon after you have begun planning the actual project — just how soon will depend upon overall time-scale — you should produce a sample of your finished project to give to your client and/or audience by way of what we will call a **pre-test**. This may take the form of a **draft** of some description, like a storyboard for a tape/slide sequence — or it may be a sample page in preparation for your booklet or part of a game you are preparing. You will want your client or audience to give you some structured feedback on this sample, so prepare questions to be answered or points you need clarifying. The pre-test is the first stage in the **evaluation** process for your project; if it is successful, you can proceed with confidence, and if reservations are expressed you can make modifications in good time before having committed yourself completely to the design of the final artefact.

— **Produce the artefact.** With appropriate research and the pre-test behind you, you can now proceed with the production of your final artefact. The more thought you have put into its design in advance, and the more feedback you have received in the early stages, the better it will be. The temptation at the beginning of the project process may have been to get on with the making of the artefact as soon as possible; now you can do just that, and with luck you should thoroughly enjoy yourself as you do so. Package your final artefact if you need to: put your game in a colourful box, get a folder or ring binder for your tape/slide sequence, liven up the appearance of your video-tape sleeve.

— **Test your artefact.** Once you have finished your project and made as good an artefact as you can in the time allowed, it is time for the final **testing** and subsequent **evaluation**. You must have a final consultation with your client and/or audience and obtain full and structured feedback. It isn't enough to hand your artefact to your client or audience and say: 'What do you think of this?' Hand it over formally and let the person or people see and use it; if the artefact is to be used in an active way — such as a game to be played by children — then photograph people as they use it and put the photographs in your record of progress. Produce a series of questions or a questionnaire if appropriate, and do everything you can to get honest and even critical comments on what you have done. People will normally praise your work and congratulate you upon it; make it clear to them that you would also like them to find fault if they can — that will help you assess the project more fully and evaluate your own skill as a communicator.

— **Assess yourself and your overall performance.** Use the questions given in the flowchart to compile a balanced and frank evaluation of both product and process, including an analysis of your own abilities and shortcomings. You should feel that you could do better if you had the project to do all over again; this should have been a learning experience for you.

Record of progress

Precisely because the process of producing an artefact is as vital as the finished artefact itself, it is very important that you keep a detailed **record of progress** as you proceed.

Look back at Fig. C. The right-hand column, 'Record of Progress', shows how such a record should cover every stage of the project process from the initial idea through to the final self-assessment. You should always keep such a record up-to-date and in step with whatever you are doing by way of planning and producing your artefact.

Why is it important to keep a record of progress? — It allows you to maintain a record of what you have done, why, and with what success. It will allow you — or anyone else who reads it — to gain an overall picture of the project process in a way that would be impossible by just looking at the finished artefact alone.

— It should force you to plan ahead, and also to think more clearly about your project by committing your thoughts to paper as you proceed.

— It allows you to reflect upon what you have learned about communication as a process and yourself as a communicator.

What should a record of progress look like? There are no hard and fast rules, but you would normally wish to choose one of three possible formats: a **diary,** a **task record** or a **log book.**

— A **diary** is the simplest method of keeping a record of progress. An extract from such a diary follows. It was written by a student by the name of Iain Boyd at the stage when he wanted to discuss his proposed 'A' Level project — a brochure for anglers — with his client:

> *Date*: 5th June 1987
> *Activity*: I spent the afternoon at the offices of the Erewash Borough Council discussing a draft outline of my proposed project, a brochure called 'Angling in Erewash'.
>
> I had a long talk with the Chief Executive of the Council, who had kindly agreed to meet me and help me out, and he suggested that I add one or two things to my draft brochure — like a list of telephone numbers of Angling Club Secretaries and a simple map of the area. I also decided that an A5 format would be the most appropriate for my brochure.
> *Result*: I was glad to have had the chance to discuss my proposed project in this way — it put me on the right track from the start, and I could now carry on confidently.
>
> I shall produce an A5 brochure with a list of Angling Club Secretaries and their telephone numbers, together with a map of the area.

A diary has several advantages as a record of progress: it is simple and straightforward, it keeps the project process in chronological order and it is easy to refer back to.

— A **task record** is rather like a diary, in that you keep a chronological account of what you have done, together with your thoughts about it. It consists of a number of sheets of paper, preferably arranged in a ring binder, each sheet giving a structured report on an important task in the project process. Not every single task would merit such a treatment — you would normally limit yourself to writing up the vital tasks only in this detailed fashion.

A task record sheet or sheets would look something like the one shown opposite. A task record has several advantages: each task can be written up in the same structured way giving an overall consistency to your record; the structure itself forces you to think every task through, and you can begin filling in each task sheet in advance of carrying out the task itself.

— A **log book** is the most complete and systematic method of keeping a record of progress. You will probably find that an A4 loose-leaf ring binder with subject divider cards would make an ideal log book. Into it you can put anything and everything relative to the process of completing your project:

— A dated calendar of progress;

— Task record sheets of the kind already described;

— Examples of materials obtained during your researches;

— Examples of designs or test-pieces;

— Questionnaires;

— Records — written or visual — of the validation process;

— Your self-assessment.

TASK SHEET NUMBER ONE: MEETING WITH CLIENT 5TH JUNE, 1987

1. DESCRIPTION OF TASK

To produce a rough draft outline of my project and to discuss its suitability with the intended client, Erewash Borough Council.

2. RATIONALE FOR TASK

To get as much feedback on my project as early as possible to help me tailor it to the client's needs and expectations.

3. PREPARATION FOR TASK

I prepared a rough draft of my project — just an outline of the main sections it would contain, one or two examples of illustrations I have planned to use and a full contents list. I have called it 'Information for anglers in Severn-Trent fishing waters.'

4. METHOD

I thought of phoning my client — the Chief Executive of Erewash Borough Council — to discuss my draft proposal, but I decided that it would be better if he could see the material I had prepared and if we could have a conversation together with this material in front of us. I only used the phone to make an appointment to see the Chief Executive; I met him in his office on 5th June.

5. RESULTS

The client liked my list of contents, but suggested that I add one or two things to it — like a list of telephone numbers of Angling Club Secretaries and a simple map of the Severn-Trent Area.

  We also decided in discussion that an A5 format — pocket size — would be more suitable than the A4 format I was considering at first.

6. REFLECTION

The task was of great value to me — it gave me a kind of 'early warning', allowing me to change the intended size of my brochure before I had done too much detailed work on it. Generally it gave me confidence to think that the client was happy with what I was planning and the way it was going. I was rather nervous at the meeting we had — I hadn't written down my questions in a sensible order, and hadn't numbered them, so when I got home I found I had forgotten to ask one or two key questions. Next time I shall list my questions first, then put them in sequence and number them.

7. IMPLICATIONS FOR FUTURE WORK.

I shall now:
— Plan my brochure as an A5 publication.
— Obtain a list of Angling Club Secretaries and their telephone numbers.
— Proceed with research and the writing of the brochure.

Its greatest single advantage is its flexibility: within reason you can put anything into it; you can keep the chronological flow of a diary and include the task sheet of a task record.

Look more closely at the 'Record of Progress' column in Fig. C p. 232. A diary or a task record would cover the headings listed in this column, starting with the **initial idea** and continuing through to **self-assessment and conclusions**, even if you wouldn't use these actual headings as you progressed. But if you keep a log book, you can divide it up into the three major sections listed — **statement of intent, production** and **testing and evaluation** — and let various page-headings cover each item within the major sections. In other words, the structure of your log book can reflect the process of completing the project. You can add extra material at the end under the heading of **appendices** — that is, a series of items which don't really belong anywhere else, each one called an appendix.

If you use the flowchart we have been examining, by referring to the right-hand column you can decide *what* needs to go into your log book and *when*.

The style of language you use when writing up a log book is up to you. You will probably find that brief notes would look rather too informal, but that you want to keep parts of the log book fairly 'chatty' as you outline your thoughts, hopes and fears and your achievements and disappointments. You could write up some parts of the log book in an informal way, but use the structured approach suggested in the task record section for every major task.

A log book is the ideal method of recording your progress if you have the time to complete it. An effective artefact and a comprehensive log book together make up a package of which you can be really proud.

Oral presentation of project work

Some examinations in Communication Studies require students to make a brief oral presentation of their project work in front of a small audience.

You should use your general skills in communication when planning and delivering your 'oral'. First look carefully at the 'Language' section of this book (Chapters 4 and 5) and then read the following brief summary of points to remember when delivering a short talk.

Giving a talk is a skilful business; people who appear to speak easily and naturally in public have usually done a great deal of preparation which may be hidden beneath their apparent ease of delivery.

— **Preparation.** You need to prepare a talk carefully in advance; write down what you might wish to say, then give the talk a structure which the listeners can follow. You might like to bear in mind a structure

which was said to be the favourite of a sergeant-major instructor in the army:

> 'First I tells 'em what I'm gonna tell 'em;
> Then I tells 'em;
> Then I tells 'em what I've told 'em . . .'

Give the talk a clear beginning and a firm ending; make brief notes (on small cards, if you like . . .) which will remind you where you are going; prepare any audio or visual aids carefully in advance. Think about the timing of a talk — rehearse it out loud if you can, and see how long it lasts.

Have empathy with your audience — choose a register they will be able to understand, explain any jargon you use, and consider whether a touch of humour here and there will help to liven up the proceedings and loosen up the atmosphere.

— **Presentation and delivery.** Be bold and convincing, not self-apologetic in your approach.

Use your voice to best effect. Don't mumble, but don't shout. Try to adjust your volume to the room. Avoid 'um' and 'er' — and don't be afraid to pause occasionally in order to vary the pace. Be clear — this is a talk, not a conversation, and you must project your voice and speak steadily and distinctly. Don't forget to use the 'paralinguistic' features of language — volume, stress, tone, pace and pause — to give variety to your delivery.

Use body language intelligently. Stand or sit upright, don't slouch. Decide where to put your hands so that they don't worry you as you talk, use them to emphasise what you say, but try to avoid mannerisms like scratching your head or stroking your hair. Don't stare into space as you talk — try and let your eyes take in every member of the audience at some stage. Don't be afraid of eye contact — it can make you more dominant, less nervous than your audience.

Try to relax — and try to convey to your audience your sense of pride in the successful aspects of your project.

Self-assessment

1. What do we mean by saying that 'Process is as important as product'?
2. Give *four* examples of different project media.
3. Distinguish between a client and an audience.
4. How would you set about confirming an initial idea for a project?
5. What is meant by a 'pre-test'? Why is it important?
6. Give *three* reasons why it is important to keep a record of progress.
7. Outline *three* hints on the use of the voice and *three* hints on the use of body language which you might give to a person who was about to give an oral presentation on a completed project.

Index

STOKE-ON-TRENT TECHNICAL COLLEGE
DEPARTMENT OF GENERAL EDUCATION
AND ADULT STUDIES
MOORLAND ROAD, BURSLEM
STOKE-ON-TRENT, ST6 1JJ
TELEPHONE: STOKE-ON-TRENT 85258